Ecclesiology and the Scriptural Narrative of 1 Peter

Ecclesiology and the Scriptural Narrative of 1 Peter

Patrick T. Egan

◥PICKWICK *Publications* • Eugene, Oregon

ECCLESIOLOGY AND THE SCRIPTURAL NARRATIVE OF 1 PETER

Copyright © 2016 Patrick T. Egan. All rights reserved. Except for brief quotations in critical publications or reviews, no part of this book may be reproduced in any manner without prior written permission from the publisher. Write: Permissions, Wipf and Stock Publishers, 199 W. 8th Ave., Suite 3, Eugene, OR 97401.

Pickwick Publications
An Imprint of Wipf and Stock Publishers
199 W. 8th Ave., Suite 3
Eugene, OR 97401

www.wipfandstock.com

PAPERBACK ISBN: 978-1-4982-2467-3
HARDCOVER ISBN: 978-1-4982-2469-7

Cataloguing-in-Publication Data

Egan, Patrick T.

    Ecclesiology and the scriptural narrative of 1 Peter / Patrick T. Egan

    xxii + 274 p. ; 23 cm. Includes bibliographical references and index.

    ISBN 978-1-4982-2467-3 (paperback) | ISBN 978-1-4982-2469-7 (hardback)

    1. Bible. Peter, 1st—Criticism, interpretation, etc. 2. Bible. New Testament—Relation to the Old Testament. 3. Bible. Old Testament—Quotations in the New Testament. I. Title.

BS2795.52 E41 2016

Manufactured in the U.S.A.   03/23/2016

For my wife, Kristin, who has encouraged and supported me through each stage of this adventure. Her hope has shone most brightly when we were beset with seemingly insurmountable obstacles.

Contents

Preface | ix
Abbreviations | xiii

1. 1 Peter and the Modern Discourse on the Use of Scripture | 1
2. The Hermeneutical Picture of 1 Peter | 44
3. The Use of Scripture in 1 Peter 1:13—2:10 | 76
4. The Use of Scripture in 1 Peter 2:11–25 | 120
5. The Use of Scripture in 1 Peter 3:1—4:11 | 153
6. The Use of Scripture in 1 Peter 4:12—5:11 | 194
7. Conclusion | 213

Bibliography | 227
Subject Index | 247
Author Index | 251
Scripture Index | 257

Preface

THIS WORK BEGAN IN 2006 as a PhD thesis under the supervision of Professor Richard Bauckham. I am grateful that he would take me on as his last student before retirement. Dr. Grant MacAskill took over supervising duties midway through my studies. These gentlemen provided direction, insight and wisdom that have made an indelible mark on my life and scholarship. I also want to thank Alan Torrance, Markus Bockmuehl, Kristen De Troyer, Bruce Longenecker, Mark Elliott, Stephen Holmes, and Nathan MacDonald for many formative discussions surrounding biblical studies and theology. Finally, I would like to thank my examination readers, Drs. Kelly Iverson and Todd Still. Their constructive feedback has benefited me greatly.

My research began as the result of repeated readings of 1 Peter, during which it became evident that the use of scripture was central to the content and message of the letter. It seemed to me that an investigation of 1 Peter's use of scripture would elucidate the interpretive practices of the early church. I had read Richard Hays' *Echoes of Scripture in the Letters of Paul* with great admiration, feeling that he had set out many stimulating avenues to pursue. My master's work had been carried out under the supervision of David Pao, who likewise stimulated my interests through his work on the Lukan corpus. The discussion regarding the use of scripture in the early church was a burgeoning area of study, yet it seemed very much centered on Paul and the Gospel. Thus, a study in the Petrine corpus would add value to the work that had brought great insights into the hermeneutics of the early church.

It so happened that my research coincided with a flowering of work on the use of scripture in 1 Peter, with works by Andrew Mbuvi, Abson Joseph, and Kelly Liebengood appearing within the last few years. To this was added the publication of *The Commentary on the New Testament Use of the Old Testament*, edited by D. A. Carson, and the ongoing work of Steve Moyise, which have both also provided further insights into Petrine hermeneutics. It would seem, then, that warrant for another volume on the use of scripture in 1 Peter requires some justification. Several points can be made in support of the current project.

The present monograph seeks to account for all uses of scripture in 1 Peter in a comprehensive manner. Many studies have sought to focus around a few key passages, which provide a great depth of analysis in specific areas. The time is ripe now for a study to draw together the many loose strands into a picture of the overall epistle.

I have sought in this study to range from text critical considerations to theological implications. On the one hand, it is necessary in a study of one author's use of other texts to establish the text used before evaluating how it was used. On the other hand, much of the value of a study of this kind centers on what one makes of the author's use of other texts.

Ultimately, the result of this study is a clarification of a major theological insight into the use of scripture in 1 Peter. The central theological consideration brought forward in the Petrine hermeneutic is ecclesiological in nature. In a relatively short piece of writing, 1 Peter provides a rationale for understanding the scriptures of Israel as communications to the church, models the church on a scripturally-informed understanding of the messianic role of Christ, and projects a vision of the restoration of divine presence among his people as occurring within the church.

These points give some warrant for the production of a new book on this project. Yet the ultimate warrant rests in the contribution this volume makes to the ongoing discussion concerning Petrine hermeneutics, not to mention the general study of the early church's use of scripture.

This publication comes only a few years after completing the original PhD thesis and remains largely unchanged from its previous form. Work on this topic is, of course, ongoing and it is with regret that I have not been able to consult Benjamin Sargent's recently published monograph, *Written to Serve* (London: T. & T. Clark, 2015).

I owe a tremendous debt of gratitude to a great many people who have supported me and helped me during my years of study and writing. I am grateful to the team at Wipf and Stock for their willingness to publish this book.

The postgraduate community of St Mary's College in St Andrews offered a supportive and lively intellectual environment that challenged and delighted my family and me. Thanks also go to the staff and scholars at Tyndale House, Cambridge. Our summer in Cambridge was a highlight and greatly rounded out areas pertaining to my thesis. I also benefited from insights gained from the resident and visiting scholars at the Hochschule at Wuppertal, Germany, when I was invited to present some of my work there.

My family and I have grown through involvement with several church communities. I am thankful for the spiritual support we received from College Church in Wheaton, the Parish Church of the Holy Trinity in St Andrews, the St Andrews Free Church, and All Souls Anglican Church in Wheaton.

Funding for my PhD studies was provided through a grant from the Ministry and Education Foundation. Our family is grateful for the vision of MEF and feels honored to have been recipients of their generosity.

Our families have encouraged and upheld us at every stage of this adventure, even when their own adventures contained unforeseen trials. To my parents, I owe a debt that can never be repaid. To my wife's parents and our siblings, a special note of thanks is offered for their support and enthusiasm for our overseas adventure. Our children, Laura, Shannon, Joanna and Cameron, have been a joy and a source of unremitting love throughout the course of this project. My wife, Kristin, has been a constant source of encouragement and support, and to her this book is dedicated.

Abbreviations

AB	Anchor Bible
ABD	*Anchor Bible Dictionary*, edited by D. N. Freeman. 6 vols. New York: Doubleday, 1992
AnBib	Analecta biblica
ANRW	*Aufstieg und Niedergang der romischen Welt*, edited by Hildegard Temporini and Wolfgang Haase. Berlin: De Gruyter, 1972–2015
ANTC	Abingdon New Testament Commentaries
ASNU	Acta seminarii neotestamentici upsliensis
AUSS	*Andrews University Seminary Studies*
BDAG	Danker, F. W., W. Bauer, W. F. Arndt, and F. W. Gingrich. *Greek-English Lexicon of the New Testament and Other Early Christian Literature*. 3rd Ed. Chicago: University of Chicago Press, 2000
BDF	Blass, F., A. Debrunner, and R. W. Funk. *A Greek Grammar of the New Testament and Other Early Christian Literature*. Chicago: University of Chicago Press, 1961
BeO	*Bibbia e eriente*
BHT	Beiträge zur historischen Theologie
BL	*Bibel und Liturgie*
BSac	*Bibliotheca Sacra*
BECNT	Baker Exegetical Commentary on the New Testament
BETL	Bibliotheca ephemeridum theologicarum Lovaniensium
BIOSCS	Bulletin of the International Organization of Septuagint and Cognate Studies
BZAW	*Beihefte zur Zeitschrift für die alttestamentliche Wissenschaft*
CBET	Contributions to Biblical Exegesis and Theology

CBQ	Catholic Biblical Quarterly
CTM	Concordia Theological Monthly
DJD	Discoveries in the Judaean Desert
DSS	Dead Sea Scrolls
DSSHU	Sukenik, E. L. *The Dead Sea Scrolls of the Hebrew Univeristy*. Jerusalem: Magnes, 1955.
DSSSMM	Burrows, M., ed. *The Dead Sea Scrolls of St. Mark's Monastery*. 2 vols. New Haven: American Schools of Oriental Research, 1951.
ECM	Editio Critica Maior
EDSS	*Encyclopedia of the Dead Sea Scrolls*. Edited by L. H. Schiffman & J. Vanderkam. Oxford: Oxford University Press, 2000.
EKKNT	Evangelisch-katholischer Kommentar zum Neuen Testament
ESV	English Standard Version
ETR	Etudes théologiques et religieuses
FOTL	Forms of the Old Testament Literature
FRLANT	Forschungen zur Religion und Literatur des Alten und Neuen Testaments
HeyJ	Heythrop Journal
HNT	Handbuch zum Neuen Testament
HNTC	Harper's New Testament Commentaries
HTR	Harvard Theological Review
IBC	Interpretation: A Bible Commentary for Teaching and Preaching
ICC	International Critical Commentary
JBL	Journal of Biblical Literature
JETS	Journal of the Evangelical Theological Society
JSJSup	Supplements to the Journal for the Study of Judaism
JSNT	Journal for the Study of the New Testament
JSNTSup	Journal for the Study of the New Testament, Supplement Series
JSOT	Journal for the Study of the Old Testament
JSOTSup	Journal for the Study of the Old Testament, Supplement Series
JSS	Journal of Semitic Studies
JTS	Journal of Theological Studies
LHBOTS	Library of Hebrew Bible/Old Testament Studies
LD	Lectio devina

LEH	Lust, J., E. Eynikel, & K. Hauspie, *A Greek-English Lexicon of the Septuagint*. 2 Vols. Stuttgart: Deutsche Bibelgesellschaft, 1992–1996.
LSJ	Liddell, H. G., R. Scott, & H. S. Jones, *A Greek-English Lexicon*. 9th ed. Oxford: Clarendon, 1996
LXX	Septuagint
MNTS	McMaster New Testament Studies
MS	Manuscript
MT	Masoretic Text
NA27	*Novum Testamentum Graece*, Nestle-Aland, 27th ed.
NAC	New American Commentary
NASB	New American Standard Bible
NIV	New International Version
NovT	Novum Testamentum
NovTSup	Supplements to Novum Testamentum
NCB	New Century Bible
NICNT	New International Commentary on the New Testament
NICOT	New International Commentary on the Old Testament
NIDNTT	*New International Dictionary of New Testament Theology*. Edited by C. Brown. 4 Vols. Grand Rapids: Zondervan, 1975–1985.
NRSV	New Revised Standard Version
NRTh	La nouvelle revue théologique
NSBT	New Studies in Biblical Theology
NTAbh	Neutestamentliche Abhandlungen
NTD	Das Neue Testament Deutsch
NTG	New Testament Guides
NTM	New Testament Monographs
NTOA	Novum Testamentum et Orbis Antiquus
NTS	New Testament Studies
OG	Old Greek
OTL	Old Testament Library
OTS	Old Testament Studies
PG	*Patrologia graeca*. Edited by J.-P. Migne.
RAC	Reallexikon für Antike und Christentum
RB	Revue biblique
RVV	Religionsgeschichtliche Versuche und Vorarbeiten

SBEC	Studies in Bible and Early Christianity
SBL	Studies in Biblical Literature
SBLDS	Society of Biblical Literature, Dissertation Series
SBLMS	Society of Biblical Literature, Monograph Series
SBLSBS	Society of Biblical Literature, Sources for Biblical Study
SBLSCS	Society of Biblical Literature, Septuagint and Cognate Studies
SBLSymS	Society of Biblical Literature, Symposium Series
SDDSRL	Studies in the Dead Sea Scrolls and Related Literature
SJT	Scottish Journal of Theology
SNTSMS	Society of the New Testament, Monograph Series
SSEJC	Studies in Scripture in Early Judaism and Christianity
STDJ	Studies on the Texts of the Desert of Judah
SUNT	Studien zur Umwelt des Neuen Testaments
TDNT	*Theological Dictionary of the New Testament*. Edited by G. Kittel and G. Friedrich. Translated by G. W. Bromiley. 10 vols. Grand Rapids: Eerdmans, 1964–76.
TDOT	*Theological Dictionary of the Old Testament*. Edited by J. G. Botterweck, H. Ringgren & H.-J. Fabry. Translated by J. T. Willis, G. W. Bromiley, D. E. Green & D. W. Stott. 15 Vols. Grand Rapids: Eerdmans, 1974–2006.
THAT	*Theologisches Handwörterbuch zum Alten Testament*. Edited by E. Jenni & C. Westermann. 2 Vols. Munich: Chr. Kaiser, 1971–1976.
THNTC	Two Horizons New Testament Commentary
TNTC	Tyndale New Testament Commentaries
TS	Theological Studies
TWOT	*Theological Wordbook of the Old Testament*. Edited by R. L. Harris, G. L. Archer & B. K. Waltke. Chicago: Moody, 1980.
TynBul	Tyndale Bulletin
VTSup	Supplements to Vetus Testamentum
WBC	Word Biblical Commentary
WBComp	Westminster Bible Companion
WTJ	Westminster Theological Journal
WUNT	Wissenschaftliche Untersuchungen zum Neuen Testament
ZAW	Zeitschrift für die alttestamentliche Wissenschaft
ZNW	Zeitschrift für die neutestamentliche Wissenschaft und die Kunde der älteren Kirche

Biblical Texts

Old Testament

Gen	Genesis
Exod	Exodus
Lev	Leviticus
Num	Numbers
Deut	Deuteronomy
Josh	Joshua
Judg	Judges
Ruth	Ruth
1–2 Sam	1–2 Samuel
1–2 Kgs	1–2 Kings
1–2 Chr	1–2 Chronicles
Ezra	Ezra
Neh	Nehemiah
Esth	Esther
Job	Job
Ps/Pss	Psalms
Prov	Proverbs
Eccl	Ecclesiastes
Song	Song of Solomon
Isa	Isaiah
Jer	Jeremiah
Lam	Lamentation
Ezek	Ezekiel
Dan	Daniel
Hos	Hosea
Joel	Joel
Amos	Amos
Obad	Obadiah
Jonah	Jonah
Mic	Micah
Nah	Nahum
Hab	Habakkuk
Zeph	Zephaniah

Hag	Haggiai
Zech	Zechariah
Mal	Malachi

New Testament

Matt	Matthew
Mark	Mark
Luke	Luke
John	John
Acts	Acts
Rom	Romans
1–2 Cor	1–2 Corinthians
Gal	Galatians
Eph	Ephesians
Phil	Philippians
Col	Colossians
1–2 Thess	1–2 Thessalonians
1–2 Tim	1–2 Timothy
Titus	Titus
Phlm	Philemon
Heb	Hebrews
Jas	James
1–2 Pet	1–2 Peter
1–2–3 John	1–2–3 John
Jude	Jude
Rev	Revelation

Apocrypha and Pseudepigrapha

1–4 Macc	1–4 Maccabees
Sir	Sirach/Ecclesiasticus
Wis	Wisdom of Solomon
2 Bar.	2 Baruch
1–2 En.	*1–2 Enoch*
4 Ezra	4 Ezra

Pss. Sol.	Psalms of Solomon
Sib. Or.	Sib
T.Naph	Testamentof Naphtali
T. Ab.	Testament of Abraham

Dead Sea Scrolls

CD	Cairo Genizah copy of the *Damascus Document*
1QIsa^a	Isaiaha
1QIsa^b	Isaiahb
1QpHab	*Pesher Habakkuk*
1Q19	*Book of Noah*
1QapGen	*Genesis Apocryphon*
1QMyst	*Book of Mysteries*
1QS	*Rule of the Community*
1Q28b	*Rule of Blessings* (Appendix b to 1QS)
1QM	*War Scroll*
1QH	*Thanksgiving Hymns*
4Q161–165(pIsa^{a-e})	*Pesher Isaiah*$^{a-e}$
4Q166–167(pHos^{a-b})	*Pesher Hosea*$^{a-b}$
4Q169(pNah)	*Pesher Nahum*
4Q170(pZeph)	*Pesher Zephaniah*
4Q171, 173 (pPs^{a-b})	*Pesher Psalms*$^{a-b}$
4Q174(Flor)	*Florilegium*
4Q177(Catena)	*Catenaa*
4Q186	*Horoscope*
4Q285	*Sefer Hamilḥamah*
4Q435–436	*Barkhi Nafshi*$^{b-c}$
4Q534–536	*Book of Noah*$^{a-c}$
6Q8	*papyrus Enoch, Giants*
11Q13(Melch)	*Melchizedek*

Philo

| Agr. | De agricultura |
| Det. | Quod deterius potiori insidari soleat |

Deus	Quod Deus sit immutabilis
Gig.	De gigantibus
Leg.	Legum allegoriae
Mos.	De vita Mosis
Plant.	De plantatione
QG	Quaestiones et solutions in Genesin

Josephus

A.J.	*Antiquitates judaicae*
B.J.	*Bellum judaicum*

Apostolic Fathers and Other Greek and Latin Works

Barn.	Barnabus
1–2 Clem.	*1–2 Clement*
Bib. Hist.	Diodorus Siculus, *Bibliotheca historica*
Ant. Rom.	Dionysius of Halicarnassus, *Antiquitates romanae*
Adv. Haer.	Irenaeus, *Adversus haereses*
1 Apol.	Justin, *First Apology*
Dial.	Justin, *Dialogue with Trypho*

New Testament Manuscripts

P^{72}	Bodmer Papyrus VII
P^{125}	Oxyrhynchus Papyrus 4934
B	mss
01	Sinaiticus
02/A	Alexandrinus
03/B	Vaticanus
04	Ephraemi
018	Mosquensis
025	Porphyrianus
044	Athous Lavrensis
049	Great Lavra, A' 88
5	Bibliothèque nationale de France, Gr. 106

33	Bibliothèque nationale de France, Gr. 14c
81	British Library, Add. 20003
93	Bibliothèque nationale de France, Coislin Gr. 205
301	Bibliothèque nationale de France, Gr. 187
307	Bibliothèque nationale de France, Coislin Gr. 25
1241	Saint Catherine's Monastery, Gr. 260
1243	Saint Catherine's Monastery, Gr. 262
1739	Great Lavra, B' 184

Septuagint Manuscripts

26	Vatican Library, Vat. gr. 556
239	Bologna Bibl. Univ., 2603
449	Milan Biblioteca Ambrosiana, D. 96

1

1 Peter and the Modern Discourse on the Use of Scripture

Introduction

THE GROWING LITERATURE ON the use of scripture in the New Testament points to an ongoing struggle to come to grips with how the early church drew upon the Hebrew scriptures.¹ This volume contributes to this literature by considering the role of Isaiah in 1 Peter. This brief epistle contains numerous uses of scripture both explicit and subtle in their deployment. Isaiah stands out as the most prominent source in terms of proportion (well over half the quotations in 1 Peter are from Isaiah) and distribution (each chapter in 1 Peter draws upon Isaiah). First Peter is not alone in its appropriation of Isaiah. A brief perusal of the index "*Loci citati vel allegati*" in NA27 provides evidence that, apart from the Psalter, Isaiah has been drawn upon more than any other source by the authors of the NT. This strongly suggests that Isaiah was formative in the thought of the early church. The extent to which this was true in general, we may expect the same to be true for 1 Peter in particular. For all its brevity, 1 Peter gives voice to some of the issues theologians have raised throughout the ages regarding the relationship of the two testaments in the Christian canon.

Many have focused on the way scripture has influenced the christology of 1 Peter, and rightfully so.² One need only look at the way Isaiah 53

---

1. The work of Childs (*Struggle to Understand Isaiah*, 5–21) immediately comes to mind. After a brief review of the Septuagint, he locates the impetus of the Christian struggle with Isaiah in the NT.

2. Achtemeier ("Christology of 1 Peter," 147) makes the point that Isaiah "plays a key role in this important passage for understanding the Christology of 1 Peter." He sees more of a general "appropriation of the language of Israel for the Christian communities" in 1 Peter ("Suffering Servant," 187; "Christology of 1 Peter," 142–43) rather

is put to use in 1 Pet 2:21–25 to identify the important dynamic between scripture and christology. However, 1 Peter issues bold statements regarding the relationship between the church and the scriptures emanating from Israel's history. For instance, the claim is made that the church is the intended audience of the prophets of old (1 Pet 1:10–12). Throughout 1 Peter, issues concerning the nature and purpose of the church (2:6–10) or concerning the conduct of believers (2:12—3:16) draw directly upon Isaiah, insisting that scripture speaks to the concerns of the church. In many instances, christological claims built on scripture—such as the use of Isaiah 53 in 1 Pet 2:21–25—reveal themselves to be ecclesiological appropriations of scripture on closer inspection. In this particular case, 1 Pet 2:21 establishes that the christology built on Isaiah 53 serves as an example (ὑπογραμμός) for the church to follow. There has not yet been a study devoted to the correlation of Isaianic texts and the ecclesiology 1 Peter.

I propose that the ecclesiology of 1 Peter draws upon the narrative of the restoration of divine presence among his people presently experiencing suffering, which is informed largely by the themes and images of the Isaianic corpus, so that the church is identified as participants in this scriptural narrative through its participation in Christ, who is understood to be the messiah of the scriptures. The narrative of Isaiah, and most prominently Isaiah 40–66, depicts a suffering people who receive the good news of God's restored presence. First Peter takes up this narrative in order to address the churches of Asia Minor with a story that meaningfully situates their suffering within an unfolding drama. The gospel message of the Christ event provides the means by which the scriptures of Israel are able to address the Anatolian churches and by which the churches are enabled to participate in the scriptural story.

In order to fully attend to this Petrine construction of ecclesiology with Isaianic texts, several factors must be addressed.[3] The hermeneutics employed in 1 Peter, to the extent that they are made explicit, must be considered in connection with observations about what texts are used, how they are used, interrelationships between texts and their ultimate deployment in specific rhetorical settings. The cumulative picture from such observations

---

than a more direct connection between Isaiah and ecclesiology. Affirmations of the connection between Isaiah and Petrine christology have most often occurred within the confines of hymnic theories (e.g., Schlosser, "Ancien Testament et christologie," 65–96; Osborne, "Guide Lines," 381–408; Richard, "Functional Christology," 121–40; Pearson, *Christological and Rhetorical Properties*).

3. Important works on the ecclesiology of 1 Peter generally approach the question from the vantage point of socio-rhetorical methods without connecting Peter's theology of the church to scripture. Representative works are Elliott, *Home for the Homeless*; Feldmeier, *Die Christen*; Schlosser, "Aimez la fraternité."

reveals for us some of the interpretive techniques by which scripture was brought to bear upon questions centering on the church. Of course, to consider *how* a text was read requires a knowledge of *what* the text said. A recent flowering of scholarship on the Septuagint has brought to our attention key questions about the state of the text in the first century. Comparisons must be made between the text as quoted in 1 Peter and the evidence available for the text of scripture. Differences between Petrine quotations and their *Vorlagen* may reveal interpretive strategies. Yet, not every use of scripture provides enough material for text-critical evaluations. Cases such as these complicate the attempt to analyze thoroughly all the uses of scripture. But the overall effect of the uses of scripture in the letter allows us to arrive at positive conclusions about Petrine hermeneutics.[4]

The present thesis considers how Isaiah is drawn upon to address the concerns of the various churches in Asia Minor. Inasmuch as 1 Peter is a pastoral address to the far-flung communities of ancient Anatolia, it is necessary to consider the situation of the audience and the strategies employed to minister to that audience. Thus, another factor to be addressed in this thesis is a consideration of how Peter *applied* scripture to his audience. It is the pastoral role taken up by Peter that reveals much about what texts are selected and how they are employed within the context of the letter. In short, the individual uses of scripture point to a larger scriptural narrative in which the addressees are depicted as participants. Through this narrative, Peter is able to account for present suffering by showing that suffering is integral to the scriptural narrative, but so too is future glory, which is presented as the hope of believers.

A thorough study of Petrine hermeneutics is overdue in light of advances in research on 1 Peter as well as continuing conversations about the interpretive practices in the first century. Well over thirty years have elapsed

---

4. The term "scripture" is preferred to "Old Testament." "Scripture" is used when discussing texts that would have been authoritative at the time 1 Peter was written. To use the phrase "Old Testament" in this instance would be anachronistic on two levels. "Old Testament" implies a set of canonical texts, which are now considered to be unstable at the time of 1 Peter. The idea of an "old" testament implies a "new" testament, a distinction that does not pertain in 1 Peter. In chapter 2 the term "prophets" will be argued as Old Testament prophets who are contrasted with contemporary gospel preachers. This is done largely because the scholarly discussion has maintained use of this terminology. The phrase "Old Testament" will be used in rare cases to signify the 39 books contained in the Old Testament. The phrase "Hebrew Bible/Scriptures" is not helpful here because it is most likely that Greek was the language of the scriptures read and cited by Peter as well as what was available in Asia Minor. The phrase "scriptural discourse" is used throughout to denote the presence of formative scriptural subtexts revealed in Petrine contexts through quotation, allusion or echo. See Greene, *Light in Troy*, 50–51.

since Elliott's famously titled review of research on 1 Peter, "The Rehabilitation of an Exegetical Step-child."[5] Most studies on 1 Peter since then reflect a certain obligation to interact with the image of 1 Peter as in need of rehabilitation because it often receives less attention than other family members such as the Gospels or the writings of Paul. Indeed, since 1976, when Elliott wrote his review of research, a considerable amount of attention has been given to 1 Peter. It is not the place of the present study to assess the state of well-being of this brief but important epistle. There may still be a certain amount of neglect and ill-usage even to this day. Perhaps the present work will go some way toward a greater sense of the critical role 1 Peter ought to play within NT studies.

In this chapter, the backdrop of this study will be erected. It begins by surveying the field of scholarly discussion centered on the use of scripture in 1 Peter. The present study adds to this discussion by pointing to the distinctive contribution scripture makes to the ecclesiology of 1 Peter. Pauline hermeneutics has seen a wellspring of focused attention in ways that have not been present in the Petrine discussion. By listening in on the Pauline discussion concerning the use of scripture, strategies are opened that will better enable us to explore the role scripture plays in the ecclesiology of 1 Peter, and to explain how the scriptural narrative informs the identity of the church. Following on this, sections will be devoted to studying the audience and the author. Understanding the original audience allows us to picture more clearly the first people addressed by 1 Peter. At the same time, there exists a tension between the general nature of the address—highlighted by the circulatory nature of the epistle—and the ever-growing knowledge of ancient Anatolia. So, inasmuch as it is possible to do so, a sketch of the recipients in Asia Minor is offered to clarify who is being pictured as participants in the narrative of scripture. If the ecclesiology of 1 Peter is informed by a scriptural narrative, it is therefore necessary to consider how the author has interacted with the texts of scripture. Here, recent discussions surrounding Paul may be leveraged to provide insights for how Peter has accessed scriptural texts.

Scholarly Background to the Present Study

This is not the first study to consider the role of scripture in 1 Peter. The scholarly discussion has generally treated the subject of scripture in 1 Peter in an atomistic fashion. The present thesis seeks to articulate a more comprehensive and holistic study of scripture than heretofore achieved. To

---

5. Elliott, "Rehabilitation," 243–54.

situate better the current study in this discussion, I begin with an overview of this scholarly background. Numerous topics are tied up in any scholarly discussion regarding the use of scripture in the NT. The following are the most important issues in the conversation specifically surrounding 1 Peter. Not all of the studies of scripture in 1 Peter have dealt with each of these issues, but they resurface consistently in the literature.

The Text of Scripture

A foundational question centers on the textual version(s) used in 1 Peter. It is insufficient simply to adduce a scriptural passage employed at a particular point in an author's argument. The fact that multiple versions of scripture existed imposes the burden of determining the Petrine *Vorlage*.

Few now argue for a Hebrew text directly underlying the quotations and allusions in 1 Peter. Voorwinde articulates a strong opinion regarding a Petrine preference for the Hebrew based largely on the faulty assumption that Paul went to the Gentiles and Peter shared the gospel with the circumcised exclusively (Gal 2:7).[6] More common is the view that 1 Peter exhibits an underlying Greek text. Glenny considers Petrine citations to be "closer to the LXX than the Masoretic Text with the exception of the quotation of Proverbs 10:12 in 1 Peter 4:8 and Isaiah 8:14 in 1 Peter 2:8."[7] The majority of scholars are confident that the Septuagint is the source used in 1 Peter.[8]

Determining whether there is a Greek or Hebrew *Vorlage* only scratches the surface of textual issues. Recensional activity in the textual history of the "Septuagint" has ramifications for the study of scripture in 1 Peter.[9] This has been greatly overlooked in studies on the role of scripture in 1 Peter. For instance, Schutter seeks to identify text-types as a significant component of his methodological procedure.[10] However, he never clarifies what text-types

---

6. Voorwinde, "Old Testament Quotations," 6.

7. Glenny, "Hermeneutics," 292.

8. Osborne, "Guide Lines," 73; McCartney, "Use of the Old Testament," 56; Elliott, *1 Peter*, 12.

9. For an overview of recensions of the Greek text, see Jobes and Silva, *Invitation to the Septuagint*, 46–56. The term "Septuagint" is itself a scholarly construct. Use of the term often adds confusion to an already complex textual history. The translation of the Greek version of the Bible occurred over a length of time, with individual books having distinct textual histories. On the definition of the Septuagint, see ibid., 30–33. In this thesis OG (Old Greek) will be used to refer to the critical editions of each book. The abbreviation of Septuagint, LXX, will be used only to differentiate from the Hebrew version, for instance with the Psalter. More will be said later about the complexities of the textual transmission.

10. Schutter, *Hermeneutic*, 170.

were available to Peter. It is quite common among scholarship to identify ways in which scripture has been adapted by the author.[11] But without considering recensional activity prior to and within the first century, the ability to speak confidently of the adaptation of scriptures has no firm basis. Beaton's overview of Jewish exegetical practices and the textual environment of the Second Temple period is instructive. His location of Matthew during a period of textual fluidity with texts incorporating exegetical alterations would hold true for 1 Peter as well.[12]

These issues demonstrate that care must be taken to consider the textual history of the Greek text and draw upon other versions where the text of 1 Peter differs from any of the extant Greek versions.[13] It is generally acknowledged that revision of the Greek text was already underway in the pre-Christian era.[14] Thus, we cannot assume that the text of scripture in the NT has as its *Vorlage* the OG. Furthermore, allowances must be made for differences in the transmission history of the individual books of the Septuagint.[15] If the transmission history of a Septuagint book is unclear, it becomes problematic placing an occurrence of scripture in 1 Peter within that transmission history. These new advances in Septuagint studies make it necessary to bring the study of scripture in 1 Peter up to date.[16]

---

11. E.g., Glenny, "Hermeneutics," 292.

12. Beaton, *Isaiah's Christ*, 60–61.

13. The "steps for determining the textual basis for a citation in the NT" provided by McLay, *Use of the Septuagint*, 133–34 are helpful in this regard.

14. See, for instance, Wilk, *Die Bedeutung des Jesajabuches*, 19–42.

15. Also, our access to the transmission history differs from book to book.

16. See Tov, *Text-critical Use of the Septuagint*, 10–15 for a history of research on the Septuagint. One of the recent discussions that confounds the study of scripture in the NT centers on a more serious consideration of the Septuagint as "translation literature." Krause ("Contemporary Translations," 64–67) expresses how the LXX was intended to exist alongside the Hebrew in a relationship of dependence upon it, but it also carved out its own autonomous existence. Thus to posit either a Hebrew or Greek *Vorlage* for NT quotations and allusions requires greater sensitivity to the interrelationship of these two versions, on which see also Pietersma, "New Paradigm." Adding to this interrelationship is a growing interest in the relationship of LXX to DSS (Tov, *Greek and Hebrew Bible*, 285–300; Ziegler, "Vorlage der Isaias-Septuaginta"). There is a growing interest in evaluating the use of Greek scriptures in the NT as textual evidence in the study of LXX (e.g., Jobes, "Septuagint Textual Tradition," 311–33). Hengel (*Septuagint as Christian Scripture*, 26) finds the onset of fervor for the Septuagint as the authoritative text about the time of Justin with subsequent debate being engaged by Origen, Jerome and Augustine (ibid., 47–56). See Childs, *Struggle to Understand Isaiah*, 19–20. It seems that debate surrounding the Septuagint and Hebrew text existed during the apostolic era. While the Septuagint served as the basis for missionary proclamation and teaching in the Greek speaking world, there was significant recourse to the Hebrew as evidenced by consistent divergence from the Septuagint text in the NT.

Defining Scriptural Occurrences

Different kinds of uses of scripture have not been uniformly defined by scholars.[17] Many questions bear upon this matter of definition. Are introductory formulae a defining characteristic? How many words must correspond with the source text? Does authorial modification or alteration bear upon how these textual occurrences are defined?[18] One of Schutter's contributions was a move toward classification that distinguishes between quotations, allusions and biblicisms.[19]

Observed in aggregate, a continuum from lengthy, explicit citations to discrete, implicit echoes. The terms "citation" and "quotation" are often used synonymously. In this study, I define *citation* as any use of scripture which is cited as such—e.g., "David says . . ." (Rom 11:9), "As written in the book of the words of Isaiah the prophet" (Luke 3:4), or the more general, "For it is contained in scripture" (1 Pet 2:6). A *quotation* is a more explicit use of scripture and an *allusion* is a less explicit use of scripture.[20] The overlap between the two is intentionally left opaque, reflecting the fact that the NT authors appear to have no clear distinction in their various uses of scripture. The use of introductory formulae is an unnecessary characteristic of a quotation, since explicit uses of scripture often occur without any introductory formula. Instead, introductory formulae sometimes mark out a use of scripture as more explicit. Furthermore, establishing a number of words to distinguish between quotation and allusion cannot be anything but arbitrary.

The term "echo" has been successfully employed in biblical studies by Hays. In his study of Pauline hermeneutics, he drew upon the work of Hollander's intertextual readings of Milton.[21] On the continuum between more and less explicit uses of scripture, there is a "vanishing point" at which "intertextual relations become less determinate."[22] Thus, *echo* will refer here

---

17. See the ongoing criticism Porter levels on the discipline (e.g., "Use of the Old Testament," "Further Comments," and "Allusions and Echoes").

18. Gréaux, "Elect Exiles," 30–32; Voorwinde, "Old Testament Quotations," 4; McCartney, "Use of the Old Testament," 46; Osborne, "Guide Lines," 65; Aitken, *Jesus' Death*, 18.

19. Schutter, *Hermeneutic*, 35–36.

20. See Hays, *Echoes*, 23; but see his elaboration in Hays, *Conversion of the Imagination*, 34–37. Porter's insistence on carefully defined categories—formulaic quotation, direct quotation, paraphrase, allusion and echo—is too precise and introduces concepts foreign to ancient authors ("Allusions and Echoes," 29).

21. Hays, *Echoes*, 18–21.

22. Ibid., 23. Along these lines, Ciampa ("Scriptural Language and Ideas," 42–43) correctly points out that every text is part of "an ongoing discourse" pertaining to an infinite number of issues. This discourse influences the author, often times without the

to the most subtle of intertextual resonances.[23] We will return to Hays's work on echoes in due course.

Emphasis on Quotations

A propensity to emphasize the most explicit uses of scripture has dominated studies of 1 Peter. Several studies intentionally exclude allusions.[24] Other studies account for allusions, but neglect to factor them into their work in meaningful ways.[25] This is one of the shortcomings of Schutter's project. Having provided a taxonomy of uses of scripture in 1 Peter, the body of his analysis is limited to five passages featuring the most explicit quotations in 1 Peter.[26] Two studies making greater use of allusions are the dissertations by McCartney and Gréaux. McCartney's approach accounts for allusive material by way of themes and motifs.[27] Gréaux produces several lists of passages that are echoed throughout 1 Peter. However, the structure of his

---

author consciously knowing it. What is helpful about working with an ancient set of texts within a cultic sub-culture is that the parameters of this discourse are "more narrowly defined" (ibid., 45). Thus, it is not impossible to describe a set of prominent issues pertaining to the first century *milieu*. For this thesis, it is less important to demonstrate the influence Isaiah has on the early church; this is already a given. Instead, it is to spell out with some specificity how Isaiah has made its presence known in 1 Peter.

23. This least explicit or less determinate use of scripture does not imply less significant. Hays (*The Conversion of the Imagination*, 36–37) argues that depending on "the distinctiveness, prominence, or popular familiarity of the precursor text" in concert with the rhetorical prominence the author gives the echoed text, one may talk about the "relative weightiness of the material cited." The concept of "intertextuality" is used throughout this thesis to denote the incorporation of one text or source into a new composition. Challenges to this use have been raised by Porter ("The Use of the Old Testament," 79–96), and rightfully so since the term originally had more to do with the plurality of meanings brought to a text by readers (see also Kristeva, "Word, Dialogue and Novel," 34–61). Moyise ("Intertextuality" 17–18) has helpfully spelled out how the term has been employed in particular ways in biblical studies . This thesis usually uses the term in the sense of "intertextual echo," but at points "dialogical intertextuality" comes into play, particularly as scripture is shown to impact the thought of the author.

24. E.g., Moyise, "Isaiah in 1 Peter," 175; Köstenberger "The Use of Scripture," 230; Voorwinde, "Old Testament Quotations," 4. The reasons for limitation are rarely expressed.

25. E.g., Glenny ("The Hermeneutics," 71) lists allusions to the OT, but none of these are addressed in the remainder of his study. The same holds true for Osborne, "L'utilisation des citations," 64–77.

26. These are 1:22–23 (Schutter, *Hermeneutic*, 124–30), 2:4–10 (ibid., 130–38), 2:21–25 (ibid., 138–44), 3:7–17 (ibid., 144–53) and 4:14–19/5:1–10 (ibid., 153–66).

27. McCartney, "Use of the Old Testament," 104. The three motifs he lists are election, the cult and judgement.

1 Peter and the Modern Discourse on the Use of Scripture 9

argument is such that allusions and echoes are only considered after explicit quotations are addressed. This bifurcation interrupts the flow of the argument of 1 Peter and tacitly indicates that the more explicit material is more important than the less explicit material.[28]

This study will follow a sequential format placing quotations and allusions within the flow of the Petrine argument. This has the advantage of assessing the role of a quotation or allusion based not on its explicitness but on the basis of its role within the author's argument. Furthermore, each use of scripture, whether it functions at an explicit or implicit level, will be examined to the fullest possible extent in order to arrive at a more comprehensive picture of the use of scripture in 1 Peter than has previously been given.

Conceptual Frameworks

To this point, the scholarly discussion has been considered as it relates to the data of scriptural texts occurring in 1 Peter: what texts are used and how do we define these occurrences? Here we turn to another discussion pertaining to how this data coheres. What are the organizing principles scholars have provided for understanding the role of scripture in 1 Peter?

There have been two major views on how the variety of scriptural texts come together in a conceptual framework. The first centers on the theme of suffering. Osborne deduces that scripture was used "in order to understand what happens in the life of the community and to console it."[29] References to scripture are drawn from contexts that develop the theme of suffering, which is then applied to a particular "Christian attitude towards suffering."[30] Schutter finds this focus on suffering resident in the suffering/glory motif, expressed in the first instance at 1 Pet 1:11. He sees 1:10–12—and this motif in particular—as the hermeneutical key of 1 Peter.[31] This idea is taken further by Pearson who infers that the suffering/glory motif is "derived from the humiliation/vindication theme of the Servant Songs of Deutero-Isaiah, especially Isaiah 53."[32] So, the suffering/glory motif is not only a means of

---

28. The work of Bacq (*De l'ancienne*, 19) on Irenaeus calls for a more even-handed approach. He finds that the distinction between explicit citations and simple allusions and subsequent emphasis on explicit citations are made for heuristic reasons. He counters, however, that "simples allusions scripturaires peuvent très bien jouer le rôle de citations clés."

29. Osborne, "L'utilisation des citations," 70: "Il se réfère à l'AT pour comprendre ce qui se passe dans la vie de sa communauté et pour la consoler."

30. Ibid., 75.

31. McCartney, "Use of the Old Testament," 123.

32. Pearson, *Christological and Rhetorical Properties*, 43.

organizing the scriptural texts in 1 Peter, but is also derived from scripture. Pearson's study, however, is hampered by an atomistic approach stemming from her form-critical methodology. She begins by identifying several hymns in 1 Peter in order to develop the christological underpinning to the letter.[33] These hymns—located at 1:3–12, 1:18–21, 2:21–25, 3:18–22[34]—provide a christological pattern of death and resurrection drawn together by the suffering/glory motif.[35] Despite the valuable insights she provides in her study, the isolation of hymnic elements needlessly hinders a fuller exploration of how christology relates to ecclesiology and the broader development of a scriptural narrative within 1 Peter.[36] The motif of suffering and glory to which these studies point and the critical role of 1 Pet 1:10–12 will be considered in chapter 2 in order to assess the special issues that have surrounded this passage in previous scholarship.

The second major conceptual framework centers on the idea of exile or diaspora.[37] The imagery of diaspora or exile frames the letter in 1 Pet 1:1; 2:11 and 5:13. Martin expounds this in a study unrelated to the role of scripture in 1 Peter. He contends that "the controlling metaphor of 1 Peter is the Diaspora."[38] The concept of the diaspora is a metaphor borrowed from early Judaism and applied to the Christian community.[39] He recognizes that Isaiah is important among the literary sources that inform this metaphor.[40] This means that many of the metaphors he analyzes have their background in the scriptures.[41] Dubis, reading 1 Peter alongside early Jewish apocalyptic

---

33. The criteria used to identify these hymns may be found in Stauffer *New Testament Theology*, 338–39; see also Pearson, *Christological and Rhetorical Properties*, 8.

34. Pearson, *Christological and Rhetorical Properties*, 5.

35. Ibid., 8–9.

36. For a recent critique of form-criticism, focused particularly on the criteria for identifying hymnic material in the NT, see Peppard, "'Poetry,'" 322–29.

37. The most influential voice on the concept of continuing exile and the hope of restoration is Wright, *The New Testament*, 268–72.

38. Martin, *Metaphor and Composition*, 144.

39. Ibid., 148.

40. Ibid., 149. He also lists Jeremiah, Ezekiel, Daniel, Esther, *4 Ezra*, *2 Baruch*, *1 Enoch*, *Sibylline Oracles*, *1–4 Maccabees*, Josephus, *Testament of the Twelve Patriarchs* and Philo as literary sources for the concept of diaspora (ibid., 149–50).

41. Martin is less concerned with the source of the metaphors than the role these metaphors play in the structure of 1 Peter. Thus, one of the benefits of the present study is to bolster some of Martin's claims by making more explicit the connections between some of these metaphors and their scriptural sources. The same can be said with regard to the work of Bechtler (*Following in His Steps*, 208) where he analyzes the role of metaphors which are used to depict the liminality of the community. He emphasizes that these metaphors are "mostly drawn from the LXX."

literature,⁴² asserts that 1 Peter is "shaped by the apocalyptic notion of messianic woes."⁴³ He substantiates this by looking at general apocalyptic features of 1 Peter and then particularly for 1 Pet 4:12–19. An important conclusion he reaches is that "the messianic woes pattern of 1 Peter fits well into 1 Peter's overarching motif of exile and restoration (1:1, 17; 2:11–12; 5:9–10, 13)." As was the case for Martin's overarching diaspora motif, Dubis finds that Isaiah 40–55 informs the motif of exile and restoration and significantly overlaps the suffering/glory motif.⁴⁴ This is an important and suggestive synthesis of two conceptual frameworks.

Gréaux, drawing upon the method developed by Hays, further extends this line of thought by seeing the use of scripture as contributing to "a continuing diaspora metaphor."⁴⁵ Similar to previous studies, he finds that Isaiah plays a key role in developing this metaphor by way of second exodus language.⁴⁶ The result is that "references to the Old Testament in 1 Peter are drawn from sections of the Old Testament that contain exodus, second-exodus or diaspora themes in their context."⁴⁷ He has taken as his starting point a particular metaphor (diaspora) and used this to "listen" for echoes of scripture. This metaphor, though, does not always fit individual passages employed in 1 Peter. Mbuvi likewise sees "lingering exile" as the background to 1 Peter.⁴⁸ He, however, pursues the temple as the framework for 1 Peter, incorporating "the concepts of exile, judgment and restoration providing the cultic language by which 1 Peter addresses the concerns of identity and alienation with which his audience was struggling."⁴⁹

The application of categories drawn from Second Temple literature for NT epistles is not altogether straight-forward if the work of Christ inaugurated the end of exile and the restoration of the people of God. For 1 Peter, there is no explicit reflection on the inclusion of Gentiles or the persistent rejection of Christ by the majority of Jews in the first century, as is the case in Romans or Galatians.⁵⁰ Instead, the ideas of Israel and Gentile

---

42. Dubis (*Messianic Woes*, 6) includes rabbinic literature along with texts from Qumran, *Syriac Apocalypse of Baruch*, *Apocalypse of Abraham*, *Jubilees*, *Testament of Moses* and Revelation. He is aware of the fact that 1 Peter is not an apocalypse but argues that it "shares in the worldview of the apocalypses" (ibid., 39).

43. Ibid., 45.

44. Ibid., 187.

45. Gréaux, "'To the Elect Exiles,'" 25.

46. Ibid., 76.

47. Ibid., 88.

48. Mbuvi, *Temple*, 8, 31.

49. Ibid., 125.

50. On which, see Hafemann, "Paul and the Exile of Israel."

are metaphors for insiders and outsiders without any apparent reference to the ethnic problems such metaphors raise. Continuing exile is not the best framework for 1 Peter, since redemption is already assumed for the audience (esp. 1:14–19). Elliott has argued for the prominence of the terms πάριοκος and παρεπίδημος in 1 Peter, even though few have accepted his argument that these depict the audience's literal status in Asia Minor.[51] Taken as metaphors depicting the audience, the passages that frame the letter (1:1, 17; 2:11; 5:13) show no evidence of any connection with the scriptural texts of the letter. This does not mean there is no relationship between these metaphors and scripture, but the use of exile/diaspora as a unifying theme for the scriptural discourse of 1 Peter is dubious.

Thus, it is necessary to reconsider how scripture in 1 Peter coheres. Like previous studies, I find the motif of suffering and glory as integral to understanding the relationship between the letter and the scripture it uses. But I see it as constituting a scriptural narrative of God's redemptive work among his people, which presupposes at the outset the work of Christ and the proclamation of the gospel (1:12, 25; 4:17). The restoration of divine presence—God's glory—among his people presently experiencing suffering is the story Peter finds in scripture concerning the people of God, which he then portrays as a narrative in which the church now participates through Christ. To be sure, this story as drawn from Isaiah recaptures much of the Exodus narrative in the context of an exilic experience. However, Peter's use of the narrative does not depict the church as in exile, but as the locus of the restoration of God's glorious presence among his people.

Mbuvi, I believe, comes closest to articulating this when he identifies the spiritual house in 1 Peter "as the anticipated Jewish eschatological temple, now fulfilled in the community of believers, based on their relations with Jesus Christ the Messiah."[52] However, his reading of the temple as a unifying concept drawing upon images of exile, judgment and restoration needs to be reversed. Instead, the temple ought to be viewed as one of the images that populates the scriptural narrative of divine restoration. The narrative is not expressed through the symbol of the temple, but the temple is one of many images that are used to retell the story of Israel anew. More promising is the direction taken by Joseph who draws upon a narratological analysis of 1 Peter using a methodology developed by Mieke Bal.[53] He proposes a four-part *fabula* patterned after the scriptures of Israel, namely election, suffering, faithful response and vindication. This fabula "gives

---

51. Elliott, *A Home for the Homeless*, 48–49. See also Horrell, *1 Peter*, 50–52.
52. Mbuvi, *Temple*, 109.
53. Joseph, *A Narratological Reading*, 40–44.

theological significance to the suffering of his audience and sketches for them the nature of faithful response."[54] These four elements create a framework for the message of 1 Peter, and the bulk of Joseph's work is devoted to tracing the themes of election, suffering, faithful response and vindication throughout 1 Peter. Joseph's use of narrative and his sensitivity to theological hermeneutics provides a promising avenue for studying 1 Peter, an avenue that will be further developed at the end of the next chapter. However, the four elements are perhaps too abstract. It might be possible to construe all biblical and extra-biblical texts in this way. The works of Mbuvi and Joseph present two ends of a spectrum, one which presents a conceptual framework (the temple) which is too narrowly focused and one which presents a conceptual framework which is too broad. By considering an Isaianic narrative structure, a passage through these two extremes might be forged. God's redemption as put forward in 1 Peter presents a story in language consistent with Isaiah's understanding of the restoration of the divine presence among God's people.

Listening in on the Pauline Discussion

The epistolary genre shared between the Pauline and Petrine letters affords an opportunity to listen in on the issues discussed by scholars working in this area. It is hoped that listening to the Pauline conversation will inform study of the Petrine text. Petrine studies have lagged behind Pauline studies, and the application of methodological advances will bring the study of Peter's use of scripture up to date.[55] In other words, we may borrow from Paul with payoff for Peter. At the same time, broadening this discussion beyond the Pauline corpus should go some way toward deepening our understanding of early Christian hermeneutics as it occurs within the epistolary literature of the NT.[56]

54. Ibid., 30.

55. This discussion begins with the work of Hays's 1989 monograph, *Echoes in the Letters of Paul*. For a survey of literature and issues arising in the generation of scholarship from the discovery of the Dead Sea Scroll to the late 1980s, see Marshall, "An Assessment of Recent Developments." For a literature survey of pre-Qumran scholarship on the use of scripture in NT, see Tasker, *The Old Testament in the New Testament*. Hays's evaluation of the work of Ellis and Hanson and his response to previous work on Pauline hermeneutics occurs in *Echoes*, 11–14.

56. Indeed, such a conversation ought also to deepen our understanding of the entire NT. However, it does seem that there are differences between the appropriation of scripture in the gospels and what we find in the epistles. To support this broad assertion, I appeal to the differences in genre as well as the focus on the life of Jesus in contrast to the more didactic nature of the epistles occasioned by the needs of the church.

Allusive Echo

A landmark study in Pauline use of scripture is *Echoes of Scripture in the Letters of Paul* (1989) by Hays. The title of the book alludes to Hollander's *The Figure of Echo*[57] and draws upon it, among other literary studies, to develop a method of hearing the "rhetorical and semantic effects" that reverberate when a text alludes to another text.[58] This method pushes the discussion of the use of scripture in Paul away from the most explicit quotations. opening up vistas in which less explicit scriptural resonances may be heard. Hays writes, "Allusive echo functions to suggest to the reader that text B should be understood in light of a broad interplay with text A, encompassing aspects of A beyond those explicitly echoed."[59] This interplay, termed "metalepsis" by Hollander, allows scholars "(a) to call attention to them so that others might be enabled to hear; and (b) to give an account of the distortions and new figuration that they generate."[60]

Is a modern literary approach an imposition on the text, though? Would the application of a literary theory developed in the past fifty years not bear marks of anachronism? A subtle answer to this question comes in a brief citation of what Fishbane calls "inner-biblical exegesis."[61] Subtle forms of interpretive resonances are already apparent throughout the Hebrew Bible.[62] Thus, what modern literary criticism has provided is the language with which to speak about textual phenomena that occur not only in the use of scripture by NT authors, but within that scripture itself.

Hays developed seven tests by which intertextual echoes may be identified.[63] He cautions that these cannot be used as a scientific method "because exegesis is a modest imaginative craft."[64] The first test is *availability* which refers to whether an author has access to a source.[65] *Volume* refers to

---

57. Hollander, *The Figure of Echo*.

58. Hays, *Echoes*, 19.

59. Ibid., 20.

60. Ibid., 19.

61. Ibid., 21. See also 27, where Hays discloses his intent "to produce late twentieth-century readings of Paul informed by intelligent historical understanding."

62. Fishbane, *Biblical Interpretation*, 5–10; "Inner-Biblical Exegesis," 34–35.

63. Wagner (*Heralds of The Good News*, 11–12) narrows the seven criteria to five "particularly important" for his purposes: *volume, recurrence, historical plausibility, thematic coherence* and *satisfaction*. Compare this with the discussion of allusions (*Anspielungen*) in Paul in relation specifically to Isaiah in Wilk, *Die Bedeutung*, 266–68.

64. Hays, *Echoes*, 29.

65. Ibid., 29–30; *The Conversion of the Imagination*, 34. This later essay updates several of the tests significantly.

"how insistently the echo presses itself upon the reader."[66] This has three interconnected factors. The first factor pertains to "the degree of verbatim repetition of words and syntactical patterns."[67] Beyond simply identifying what text is in use, this factor raises questions about the author's *Vorlage*—whether the text was Greek, Hebrew or Aramaic, whether there are changes to the text, and whether these occur as a variant in the manuscript tradition or are intentionally altered by the author. The second factor has to do with "the distinctiveness, prominence, or popular familiarity of the precursor text," which differs from the availability of a text.[68] It is one thing to say that Isaiah was available for the author and readers, but it is another to discern the prominence of the suffering servant as compared to, say, a woe oracle against Cush. The third factor relates to the rhetorical emphasis placed on the text in the flow of the epistolary discourse.[69]

Recurrence takes into consideration the use of a particular passage elsewhere by the same author. He writes, "When we find repeated Pauline quotations of a particular OT passage, additional possible allusions to the same passage become more compelling."[70] Hays allows for a range of meaning with regard to the term "passage" which may include larger units of scripture (e.g., Isa 40–55). *Thematic coherence* coordinates two sources of meaning. The source text must be understood to contribute meaning to the discourse in which it is quoted. Does this meaning match the context of the discourse and how does the use of the source text inform that discourse? This does not simply occur on an instance-by-instance basis, but accounts for the overall argument. So, if Isaiah (or portions thereof) may be shown to be instrumental to the development of the overall argument, then "we may assume that other possible echoes of that same text elsewhere in the same letter are likely to be theologically significant rather than merely the product of our own interpretive fantasy."[71]

Historical Plausibility considers both the interpretive *milieu* of the Second Temple period as well as the ability of the original audience to understand the meaning of what is being interpreted. One of the difficulties with this test is the fact that early Christian interpretation—although indebted to a Jewish interpretive tradition—significantly breaks with the Jewish

---

66. Hays, *The Conversion of the Imagination*, 35.
67. Ibid., 35. Original emphasis removed.
68. Ibid., 36. Original emphasis removed.
69. Ibid., 37.
70. Ibid. Original emphasis removed.
71. Ibid., 40.

interpretation of its time.⁷² Things are further complicated when we attempt to account for the audience. Would a predominantly Gentile audience pick up on intra-Jewish interpretive debates? Hays suggests, "If, however, it can be shown that Paul's allusions to Scripture do have analogies and parallels in other contemporary writings, then we are on firmer ground in placing interpretive weight upon them."⁷³ *History of Interpretation* considers whether others throughout the centuries have likewise discerned an allusion or echo. Finally, *satisfaction* attempts to answer the questions, "Does the proposed intertextual reading illuminate the surrounding discourse and make some larger sense of Paul's argument as a whole?"⁷⁴

These tests provide a road map for confirming the use of intertextual echoes. However, they are not a scientific manual that may be used to identify and classify various species of textual phenomena. Therefore, these tests inform the present study, enabling us to be sensitive to the presence of themes and images populating 1 Peter which contribute to the scriptural narrative.

Ecclessiocentricity

One of the surprising results of Hays's work is his insistence that Paul's reading of scripture is not governed by christological interpretations, but produces readings that are ecclesiocentric.⁷⁵ Thus, Paul expresses a "conviction that Scripture is rightly read as a word addressed to the eschatological community."⁷⁶ The church is founded upon the scriptures of Israel, and Paul proves this more by demonstration rather than by treatise.⁷⁷ Paul grapples explicitly with issues surrounding the inclusion of Gentiles and how the Law is to be read in light of Christ. Hays produces a reading that, perhaps, overly differentiates christological and ecclesiological interpretation; but even if he has overreached, he has brought to our attention the profound importance ecclesiology holds in understanding Paul's hermeneutics.

Wagner's study of Romans 9–11 augments this to some extent by focusing on how Paul reads his own ministry in the scriptures. He contends

---

72. The Christ event has significant ramifications for differentiating the interpretive activity of the early church from that of early Judaism. This will be explored further in the next chapter.

73. Hays, *The Conversion of the Imagination*, 41.

74. Ibid., 44.

75. Hays, *Echoes*, 86.

76. Ibid., 123. He cites Rom 15:4 and 1 Cor 10:11.

77. Ibid., 160.

that Paul finds himself at a momentous stage in history in which God's work among the Gentiles requires a reconsideration of the covenant with Israel.[78] Paul argues, based on his reading of Isaiah, for a "two-stage process" in which "Paul finds himself playing a pivotal role in this drama of cosmic redemption: he is not only a herald bearing the message of redemption to the Gentiles, but also a chosen instrument through whom God will provoke his own people to jealousy and so effect their salvation."[79]

The present study finds many correlations between the ecclesiological readings of scripture by Paul and Peter. These will be spelled out in the chapters to follow. Unlike Paul, though, Peter seems less preoccupied with justifying his mission.[80] Only in 1 Pet 5:1 does he mention his own ministry. But when he does, he draws upon the language of scripture developed over the course of his letter and casts himself in the role of witness to suffering and partaker in glory. Also unlike Paul, Peter does little to deal with issues centering on the Gentile inclusion.[81] The reasons for this are unclear. Ever present is the temptation to read 1 Peter in light of tensions within the community, and perhaps the letter served to address some of these tensions. But these are never made explicit. What is made clear, though, is that the scriptures of Israel address ecclesiological concerns, particularly as the church in Asia Minor has experienced suffering.

Narrative Substructure

A suggestive line of argument put forward by Hays contends against the accusation that Paul's use of scripture is highly eclectic and self-referential.[82] Instead, Paul's hermeneutic shows a commitment to an underlying narrative based on "fundamental themes of the biblical story."[83] Therefore, the seemingly scattered scriptural quotations "derive coherence from their common relation to the scriptural story of God's righteousness."[84] On the

78. Wagner, *Heralds of The Good News*, 41.
79. Ibid., 359.
80. E.g., ibid., 32–33.
81. Goppelt, *A Commentary on I Peter*, 6–7.
82. And to this point Marks ("Pauline Typology," 80) comes under fire, since he finds Paul "affirming the priority of his own conceptions by imposing them on the earlier tradition." Hays (*Echoes*, 159) contends that such a perspective is beholden to generations of "misreadings" of Paul "that ignore his roots in Scripture or highlight antithetical aspects of his relation to it."
83. Hays, *Echoes*, 157.
84. Ibid., 157. For Paul, then, the phrase δικαιοσύνη θεοῦ is key to understanding his hermeneutic. Such phraseology is not entirely absent in 1 Peter (see 2:23), but it

basis of this narrative, Paul can envision the gospel as a continuation of the narrative.[85] Furthermore, scripture can be read as addressing the needs of the community primarily because the community participates within the narrative.[86] These ideas are important for the present thesis, particularly for demonstrating the key role scripture plays in the ecclesiological hermeneutic of 1 Peter. The link between scripture and the churches of Asia Minor lies not in a patchwork of passages deemed suitable by Peter, but in a narrative that unifies all of scripture and enables Peter to locate the church within an overarching drama.

Wagner, a student of Hays, further focuses these ideas in his work on the use of Isaiah in Romans. Building upon the recognition of linking terms (*gĕzērâ šāwâ*) between scriptural quotations in Paul, he finds that texts have been selected by Paul "for reasons beyond simple catchword associations." Paul shows an "awareness of significant thematic as well as verbal connections between the texts."[87] Such connections are not unique to Paul, but are apparent in the interpretive tradition inherited by Paul.[88] These connected texts become "in some sense mutually interpreting for Paul," whether the connection occurs between Isaianic texts or with texts drawn from outside Isaiah.[89] The net effect is that "Isaiah does make significant and distinctive contributions to Paul's particular retelling of the story of God, Israel, and the Gentiles in Romans," even if it is not the only voice within Paul's scriptural discourse.[90] Wagner identifies a narrative constituent of Isaiah. He writes:

> In terms of Isaiah's larger three-act 'plot line' of rebellion, punishment, and restoration, Paul locates himself and his fellow believers (Jew and Gentile) in the final act of the story, where heralds go forth with the good news that God has redeemed his people.[91]

This is in many ways similar to the overarching narrative articulated by Hays, but confines such a narrative within a single book. The difference between an overarching narrative uniting all of scripture and a particularly

---

would be a stretch to claim it as Peter's understanding of "the ground of the narrative unity between Law and gospel."

85. Ibid., 160.
86. Ibid., 160–64.
87. Wagner, *Heralds of The Good News*, 347.
88. Ibid., 148. He cites in particular the inter-Isaianic linkages apparent in the Greek translation (n. 19).
89. Ibid., 351.
90. Ibid., 352.
91. Ibid., 354.

Isaianic narrative is subtle. The overarching narrative provides bridges between different individual narratives contained within the disparate books of scripture. Isaiah appears to have provided for the early church a self-contained articulation of the more-or-less complete narrative (albeit with other passages orbiting around it and even competing with it) as evidenced by its high frequency of quotation in the NT and its prominence in the manuscript tradition.

Both Hays and Wagner have recognized that Paul has not played fast and loose with the text of scripture, but rather has pursued interpretive strategies consistent with the narrative that extends from scripture to the gospel and ultimately to God's work in and through the church as the eschatological community. Inasmuch as Paul has "used" scripture to argue his case, it remains true that scripture itself exerts pressure upon Paul as an interpreter. Hays's turn of phrase—"Gospel interprets scripture; Scripture interprets gospel"[92]—expresses this idea. In the consideration of the hermeneutics involved in 1 Peter, it is reasonable to expect the same kind of dual pressure to be apparent. The text of scripture supplies metaphors, structures and phrases that are determinative for the shape of Peter's argument just as much as Peter's concerns for the church shape his reading of scripture.

In line with this scholarly trajectory, Gignilliat suggests that the narrative substructure of Paul's use of the OT is more theologically oriented than accounted for in previous scholarship.[93] He argues that Paul's reading of scripture is "a genuine extension of the text in light of its true subject matter in Jesus Christ."[94] The scriptures provide "warrant for Paul's role in this redemptive drama" depicted most prominently in Isaiah 40–66.[95] Gignilliat proposes that Paul's thought is influenced by "Isaiah's canonical message of redemption and its attendant key figures (the Servant and the servants of the Servant)."[96] In expounding the key role this Isaianic figuration plays in Paul's second letter to the Corinthians, he writes:

> These servant followers of the Servant, the offspring promised in Isa 52.10, carry on the task of the Servant as light to the nations, and restorers of Zion. They, like the Servant, suffer in righteousness (Isa 57.1); however, they do not take on the unique role

---

92. Hays, *Echoes*, 160.
93. Gignilliat, *Paul and Isaiah's Servants*, 16.
94. Ibid., 22.
95. Ibid., 38.
96. Ibid., 2.

of the Servant, who is the incarnation of Israel and vicarious sin-bearer.[97]

Like Paul, Peter appears to be sensitive to the unique role of the singular servant (1 Pet 2:22–25), yet develops the imitative potential of the servant's righteous suffering (2:21). In the next chapter, it will be demonstrated how the plural servants are key to understanding how Isaiah depicts the narrative of divine restoration. Unlike Paul, Peter does not go to lengths to identify his own mission in the categories raised in Isaiah 40–66 (although he does show himself to be a participant in them in 1 Pet 5:1). Instead, he pictures how the church participates in the drama of restoration in the role of the plural servants.

Comparison with the Interpretive Practices of the Second Temple Period

There is a significant line of scholarship devoted to the study of Paul's reading of scripture in comparison with other contemporaneous literature.[98] Since the discovery of manuscripts at Qumran in 1947, there has been a wealth of materials with which to compare Paul's use of scripture.[99] Lim compares textual modification in the commentaries of Qumran and the letters of Paul.[100] In the post-Qumran scholarly discussion, the stability of the Greek or Hebrew texts in the first century can no longer be assumed. He writes, "The Qumran pesharim and Pauline letters are dated to a period when the textual situation is fluid and more than the three textual traditions of the MT, LXX, and SP should be posited."[101] From this he argues that work on the Pauline text form "should be carried out not only with extant witnesses written in Greek, but also with Hebrew sources."[102] Most prominently among these Hebrew sources are the biblical scrolls and the pesharim of Qumran. Lim's study challenges previous work on the use of scripture in 1 Peter. For one, Lim dismantles the phrase "Midrash pesher." He suggests that the hybridization of genres "should, in our opinion, be left

---

97. Ibid., 53.
98. An important example is Ellis, *Paul's Use of the Old Testament*.
99. See Brooke, "Biblical Interpretation at Qumran," 289–300 for a history of research on biblical interpretation in the scrolls.
100. Lim, *Holy Scripture*, 95.
101. Ibid., 22. See also Brooke, "Biblical Interpretation at Qumran," 317.
102. Lim, *Holy Scripture*, 142.

out of a discussion of pesherite or Pauline exegeses."[103] This matches in many ways Hays's critique of Midrash.[104] He correctly points out how the rabbinic writings of later centuries represent different historical backgrounds than was true for Paul in the first century.[105]

Yet, the discontinuity between the exegetical practices before and after the fall of Jerusalem is not as stark as might be supposed. Brooke suggests that many of the exegetical practices codified in the rabbinic writings were in fact used by Philo and in the Targums as well as in the Dead Sea Scrolls.[106] An example is the use of key term links, or gĕzērâ šāwâ. The use of this interpretive technique is important in the present study. What the current debate demonstrates is that this technique is less a characteristic of Midrashic interpretation than it is a common practice throughout the history of interpretation of scripture.[107] Another important technique for the present study is ʾal tiqrēʾ, or intentional "misreadings" of the text. With regard to the interpretive tradition surrounding the Hebrew version, the use of ʾal tiqrēʾ involves the interpreter taking advantage of textual peculiarities, variants or exchanging similar letters.[108] What is unclear is whether this interpretive technique is drawn into the interpretive tradition surrounding the Greek version. If so, some of the differences between quotation and *Vorlage* may stem from this technique.[109]

These insights drawn from comparisons with Qumran point to text critical issues overlooked in most studies of scripture in 1 Peter. The instability of the text in the first century complicates our understanding of Peter's *Vorlage*. A simple comparison of critical editions of the Greek text can no longer be the basis of a serious study of the NT appropriation of scripture. Lim pushes further by broadening the problem to Hebrew texts, and Brooke draws considerations of Jewish interpretive techniques into the study of NT interpretive techniques. Wagner's study exemplifies an approach that is sensitive to these issues by comparing the wording of Pauline quotations with OG Isaiah while consulting variant manuscripts before proceeding to "the

---

103. Ibid., 139.

104. Hays, *Echoes*, 10–14.

105. Ibid., 11. Contra Ellis, *Prophecy and Hermeneutic*, 151–99 and Hanson, *Studies in Paul's Technique*, 209–24. For a succinct introduction into the use of Midrash and pesher in NT interpretation, see Snodgrass, "The Use of the Old Testament," 420–22.

106. Brooke, *Exegesis at Qumran*, 16–17, 355.

107. Brooke ("Biblical Interpretation at Qumran," 299) suggests that for midrash "in its strict sense the term is both inappropriate and anachronistic."

108. Brooke (*Exegesis at Qumran*, 284) shows how this was practiced at Qumran.

109. See Bauckham, "James and the Jerusalem Church," 456–57 for an application of this technique at the Jerusalem council.

later Greek versions, the church fathers, and quotations in other NT writings" and to "Hebrew forms of the text, including MT, the Dead Sea Scrolls, the Isaiah Targum, and the Peshitta."[110]

Such work is necessary to identify the *Vorlage(n)* behind the quotations and allusions found in the NT. However, it must also be recognized that problems associated with the textual situation in the first century are manifold. McLay presents a number of difficulties including the fact that there was no canon for the early church along with the pluriformity of scripture in the Second Temple period.[111] By this he means that scripture existed in different languages, sometimes in multiple literary editions (i.e., Daniel), each with variant readings and undergoing a process of interpretation incorporated into the textual transmission. Alongside this situation also exists the possibility that revision has occurred.[112] This diversity of texts complicates an assessment of Peter's *Vorlage*, so that statements about authorial change or variants in the manuscript tradition must be made tentatively at best. This is true even where the extant manuscript tradition shows no evidence for differences occurring in 1 Peter.[113]

The discussion in Pauline circles allows us to briefly assess difficulties that have arisen in the Petrine discussion, particularly as it relates to the hermeneutics of 1 Peter and its relationship with midrash. The work of Schutter is the seminal study of Petrine hermeneutics. He finds that a pesher-like hermeneutic, similar to that found in Qumran, was employed in 1 Peter.[114] He begins by investigating 1 Pet 1:13—2:10 to determine its genre and considers homiletic midrash the most likely candidate in terms of "form, hermeneutical presuppositions, methods, and practices."[115] He then looks at 1:10–12 "where explicit information exists concerning the author's hermeneutic,"[116] and corroborates the correspondence between 1 Peter and Jewish hermeneutical conventions.[117] Several texts from Qumran are placed

---

110. Wagner, *Heralds of The Good News*, 16–17.

111. On matters bearing on canon, see McLay, "Biblical Texts," 38–42; Ulrich "The Canonical Process," 267–91; McDonald and Sanders, *The Canon Debate*.

112. McLay, "Biblical Texts," 55–58.

113. Moyise, "Quotations," 16–17.

114. However, see Brooke, "Biblical Interpretation at Qumran," 299–300. He correctly points out that the pesharim have dominated the discussion of biblical interpretation at Qumran, but that scholarship must "allow for several kinds [of texts] than that of the pesharim alone."

115. McCartney, "Use of the Old Testament," 99. More recently on genre, see Dryden, *Theology and Ethics*, 37–53.

116. McCartney, "Use of the Old Testament," 100.

117. Ibid., 109.

next to 1:10–12 to demonstrate the pesher-like hermeneutic employed.[118] The suffering/glory motif first expressed in 1:11 is then explored as the basis for identifying Petrine hermeneutics. He concludes, "Each passage was seen also to have correlations with the S/G of 1.11, establishing its antithesis as an important organizing principle in the author's understanding of Christian doctrine."[119]

Glenny's thesis comes to contradictory conclusions regarding midrash. He finds that "the evidence in 1 Peter supports the theory that midrash is a genre of literature rather than a hermeneutical methology [sic]."[120] This stems partly from the fact that Glenny finds the hermeneutical centerpiece not to be 1 Pet 1:10–12 but rather 2:6–10 which establishes "a pattern which Peter demonstrates between Israel, the Old Testament People of God and the church, the New Testament People of God."[121] So, despite techniques that exhibit pesher-like qualities (e.g., 1:24–25; 2:6–10), the use of different hermeneutical methodologies in 1 Peter "argues against classifying the hermeneutics as midrash."[122]

McCartney stands between these studies regarding Petrine hermeneutics. Whereas Glenny saw 1 Pet 2:6–10 as centrally important, McCartney finds in 1:10–12 a means by which the OT is applied to the church. He writes, "In accordance with the principle of 1:10–12, the Scripture is about Christ, but through Christ the Scripture also describes believers."[123] Instead of a direct appropriation of scripture between the OT people of God and the church, McCartney identifies how Christ is an indispensable step between the OT and the church.

Pearson contends that Isaiah 53 not only stands behind the suffering/glory motif in 1 Peter,[124] but plays an important role in drawing together the various sources in 1 Peter.[125] Although she discerns a pesher-like exegesis, she thinks Isaiah 53 is at the center of the various texts on display in 1 Peter. For her, christology is the fundamental category standing behind the Petrine use of scripture.

---

118. Ibid., "Use of the Old Testament," 109–23; see also Bauckham, "James, 1 and 2 Peter, Jude."
119. McCartney, "Use of the Old Testament," 168.
120. Glenny, "The Hermeneutics," 292.
121. Ibid., 289.
122. Ibid., 292
123. McCartney, "Use of the Old Testament," 102.
124. Pearson, *Christological and Rhetorical Properties*, 9.
125. Ibid., 43.

Clearly confusion has arisen in the Petrine discussion concerning midrash and pesher. This is not surprising in light of the difficulty associated with these terms.[126] For one, the two terms do not appear to be synonymous.[127] Midrash has been defined by Porton as "a type of literature, oral or written, which has its starting point in a fixed canonical text, considered the revealed word of God by the midrashist and his audience, and in which this original verse is explicitly cited or clearly alluded to."[128] Porton, though, is careful to differentiate midrash as activity from later rabbinic midrash. Teugels, along these lines, discourages "use of the term 'midrash' outside the rabbinic corpus," but does admit that there is something comparable to the literature of early Judaism and early Christianity.[129] The essential element for rabbinic midrash, according to Teugels, is the "Oral Torah" which transmits a "chain of tradition" from which authority is derived.[130] To be sure, such oral traditions existed in the Second Temple era, but were not self-consciously collected in literature aimed at preserving authoritative interpretations.[131] Such being the case, scholars still tend to speak of midrash as an interpretive activity in distinction from the genre and aims associated with later rabbinical literature.[132] Even so, the association of the term with later rabbinic practices cautions us against using the term even to describe the underlying interpretive practices shared between Second Temple Judaism, the early Church and Tannaitic Judaism.

Pesher, on the other hand, more often refers to a particular exegetical method or to the genre of literature that employs this kind of method.[133] Schutter's identification of a pesher-like technique in 1 Peter is sound, but this does not entail that the genre is midrashic. Lim, for instance, demonstrates how the evidence from Qumran does not support the designation of a Midrash genre.[134] Carmignac clarified our understanding of pesher as a genre by distinguishing "un *pèshèr* «continu»" and "un *pèshèr* «discontinu» ou «thématique»."[135] The characteristics of the former exhibit

---

126. Alexander, "Midrash and the Gospels," 1.

127. See Lim, *Holy Scripture*, 48–51; Brooke, *EDSS* 1:298.

128. Porton, "Midrash," *ABD* 4:819.

129. Teugels, *Bible and Midrash*, 169. See also Campbell, *The Exegetical Texts*, 37.

130. Teugels, *Bible and Midrash*, 167.

131. Here Teugels (*Bible and Midrash*, 166–69) draws upon the work of Jaffee, *Torah in the Mouth*, esp. 67–68.

132. Porton, "Midrash," *ABD* 4:819. See also Neusner, *What is Midrash?*, 31–33; Brooke, *The Dead Sea Scrolls*, 69.

133. See Dimant, "Pesharim, Qumran," *ABD* 5:244.

134. Lim, *Holy Scripture*, 50–51.

135. Carmignac, "Le document de Qumrân," 361.

continuous quotations of biblical text, with the technical use of the term 'pesher,' followed by an interpretation.[136] Lim is careful to define the continuous pesharim as a genre, but the exegetical practices displayed in the thematic pesharim do not, per se, constitute a genre.[137] Dunn, comparing the exegetical practices of the Qumran pesharim with NT use of quotations, notes that NT quotations differ from the continuous pesharim inasmuch as they does not provide a quotation and then produce an interpretation; "the actual quotation of the text embodies its interpretation within the quotation itself."[138] This distinction is important because it moves our understanding of the interpretive practices of the early church away from the generic features of the pesharim and enables us to focus on the principles in use.[139] In the course of this study, it will be assumed that such pesher-like interpretive techniques contribute to the creative, narratival reading of scripture found in 1 Peter. As was the case in Qumran, where texts were creatively brought together, Peter also brings texts together to draw out themes and images that are integral to the narrative of God's restoration. However, the decisive work of Christ and the proclamation of the gospel press us to look beyond the issues raised by the diverse and thorny issues contained within recent debates on the interpretive techniques of ancient Judaism. At many points, these issues inform the present study, but only insofar as they illuminate the way in which the Isaianic narrative is drawn into 1 Peter.

Unambiguous Quotations

The study of Pauline hermeneutics has generated studies focused on determining Paul's *Vorlagen*. Koch developed a set of criteria to identify explicit uses of scripture which helps establish Paul's citation technique.[140] He distinguishes a quotation—a formulation that is from an external source and is recognizable as such[141]—from allusion and paraphrase which are more fully integrated into the context of the letter.[142] This distinction considers whether the reader is able to recognize (*erkennen*) that the author is using an external source. In contemplating how an author indicates to an audience

---

136. Lim, *Holy Scripture*, 40.
137. Ibid., 52–53.
138. Dunn, *Unity and Diversity*, 91.
139. See ibid., 93–102.
140. Koch, *Die Schrift*, 11–23.
141. Ibid., 11.
142. Ibid., 17.

that he is quoting an external source, Koch provides seven categories based on textual indicators. These are:[143]

1. Quotations with unambiguous (*eindeutig*) introductory formula
2. Quotations already specifically cited in the context
3. Quotations emphasized by subsequent interpretation (*nachträgliche Interpretation*)
4. Quotations incongruous with the context
5. Quotations that differ stylistically in their context
6. Quotations that are indirectly marked with simple conjunctions
7. Totally unlabeled quotations (*ungekennzeichnete Zitate*)[144]

It is only when these unambiguous quotations are identified that scholars may proceed to reckon with Paul's use of scripture from the standpoint of a stable set of data.[145]

Stanley builds upon the work of Koch by both refining the distinguishing characteristics of citations but also expanding considerably upon the characteristics of the first-century readers of Paul. The definition of quotation or citation is limited to "places where the author's appeal to an outside source is so blatant that any attentive reader would recognize the secondary character of the materials in question."[146] Stanley streamlines the criteria by limiting blatant citations to three: "(1) those introduced by an explicit quotation formula . . . (2) those accompanied by a clear interpretive gloss . . . and (3) those that stand in demonstrable syntactical tension with their present Pauline surroundings."[147] This tightened set of criteria provides for him a set of "assured citations" that allows him to identify, isolate and catalogue the "author's normal citation technique."[148] This supports the aim of his study of finding places where Paul has adapted the text of scripture.

---

143. Koch (*Die Schrift*, 21–23), with his list of verses, provided for each category from the undisputed Pauline corpus.

144. This last category is more fully explained earlier as something belonging to a tradition or common knowledge shared between the author and reader: "wenn es sich um einen Satz, Ausspruch o. dgl. handelt, der zum gemeinsamen Bildungs- und Überlieferungsgut von Verfasser und Lesern gehörte" (Koch, *Die Schrift*, 15).

145. Ibid., 12–13.
146. Stanley, *Paul*, 4.
147. Ibid., 37.
148. Ibid., 32.

One of the strengths of both studies is that they work from more recent advances made in Septuagint research.[149] The present state of research in 1 Peter has lagged in this respect. The main weakness of the approach, though, is the insistence upon a criteria of explicitness. By isolating the most explicit citations, one is not able to assess the overall picture of normal usage. Instead, the result is a picture of normal usage in explicit cases. However, if an author "normally" works at a less explicit level, the criteria established by Koch and Stanley have already weeded out what amounts to the author's "normal" practice. The reasons for insisting on a criteria of explicitness are understandable. For one, the data are easier to process in this case and allow one to work from more certain cases to less certain cases. But another reason for insisting on this criteria has to do with the ability of the audience to perceive the use of scripture. To this concept we now turn.

Audience Competence

Stanley questions "whether Paul's Gentile readers would have understood even some of his more explicit quotations."[150] His full investigation of Paul's readers is carried out in a study entitled *Arguing with Scripture*. Assuming a literacy rate of 10–20 percent, the problem of illiteracy among Paul's original audience is significant.[151] This situation is further compounded by the limited availability of scrolls.[152] If Paul's congregations were mostly composed of illiterate Gentiles, what hope did they have of following his skilled use of scripture when employed subtly?[153] There is a discrepancy, then, between Paul's use of scripture and the ability of his audience to perceive his use of scripture.[154] Stanley suggests four possible explanations for this discrepancy. It is possible that (1) there was an established program whereby Gentile audiences were taught to study and memorize the Jewish scriptures. Or (2), Paul assumes a shared scriptural background between him and his audience where there, in fact, was none. Or perhaps (3), Paul addressed his letters to the literate elite and expected these to explain to illiterate members of the audience the scriptural nuances in his letters. Or

149. See n. 16 above.
150. Ibid., 35.
151. Ibid., 44, 55. He bases this on Harris, *Ancient Literacy*.
152. Ibid., 42, 44, 55.
153. Stanley, *Arguing with Scripture*, 45–46.
154. The ability of present scholarship to identify allusions highlights the problem of where "meaning" is to be located: in the author, reader or text. See Moyise, "Quotations," 24–25.

(4), Paul understood that his use of scripture would go largely unrecognized except for some key scriptural passages but would be appreciated and accepted all the same.[155] Elements of these four explanations lead him, then, to spell out four generalizations. First, "illiteracy did not prevent the Gentiles in Paul's congregations from knowing something about the Jewish Scriptures."[156] Stanley suggests that the Decalogue and important biblical figures such as Abraham, Moses, Elijah and David would have been well known.[157] Second, "Paul's letters leave no doubt that his patterns of thought and expression were heavily molded by the Jewish Scriptures."[158] This suggests that not all allusions to scripture are rhetorically significant.[159] Third, concerning Paul writing primarily for the literate members of his audience, Stanley writes, "Paul may have been directing his argument primarily to the literate members of his churches (or more precisely, to those who were familiar with the Jewish Scriptures) when he penned his biblical quotations."[160] Finally, "when Paul quotes from the Jewish Scriptures in his letters, he invariably has a rhetorical purpose."[161]

Wagner responds to the reader-centered approach by setting forth his understanding of the first recipients of Paul's letter in Rome. He recognizes that, with limited evidence, it is nearly impossible to arrive at an accurate reconstruction of Paul's audience regarding their ability to perceive quotations and allusions.[162] Rather than limit oneself to an historical reconstruction of the first audience, he suggests that our understanding of the historical evidence work in tandem with a consideration of the ideal reader "encoded in the letter itself."[163] He further proposes that it was likely that multiple encounters with Paul's letter would have occurred.[164] These proposals go

---

155. Stanley, *Arguing with Scripture*, 49.

156. Ibid., 50.

157. We must ask how they would know these things. Was there a textual/oral means of appropriating this knowledge? The Decalogue and the four figures he suggests cover a wide range of scriptural material from different genres. Either they had far more access to scripture than Stanley allows, or even this knowledge is inconsistent with his reconstruction.

158. Ibid., 51.

159. On the rhetorical significance of quotations, see Stanley, "The Rhetoric of Quotations," 44–58.

160. Stanley, *Arguing with Scripture*, 51.

161. Ibid., 52.

162. Wagner, *Heralds of the Good News*, 34.

163. Ibid., 35.

164. Ibid., 36–37. See also Watson, *Paul and the Hermeneutics of Faith*, 127–28.

a long way toward answering the claim that there was a low level of reader competence among the first recipients of Romans.[165]

Furthermore, Wagner considers Paul's relationship to Isaiah not simply as someone reading the written text, but also as someone committing large portions of Isaiah to memory.[166] He proposes that "we should imagine Paul interacting with scripture in a *variety* of modes, including meditation on memorized passages, hearing of spoken texts, personal reading of written texts, and collection of and reflection on excerpts from larger texts."[167] The role of memory is also important for our understanding of the audience. It cannot be suggested that the audience was composed uniformly of people as competent as Paul, but many of the traits that mark him as a competent reader of scripture would carry over to the upper end of an audience of mixed capabilities.

What has emerged in such discussion is that Paul was an exceptionally competent reader of scripture. But the gap between him and "ordinary" readers and hearers of scriptures is not always easy to discern. In the case of someone like Peter, it can be difficult to accurately rate his reader competence against that of Paul's. At the same time, there do appear to be certain presuppositions (Jewish exegetical practices, christological kerygma, gospel mission, etc.) that are shared within the early church, making the comparison between Paul and Peter valid.

Picturing the Original Audience

Stanley's contribution to the study of Paul's use of scripture challenges previous studies by questioning the assumption that one can simply study Paul in abstraction from the communicative process his letters represent.[168] The same holds true for Peter and the study of his use of scripture. In the thesis I propose for 1 Peter, then, it is necessary to remain sensitive to the rhetorical context in which scriptural texts are used in 1 Peter. However, there are some features of Stanley's work that must be refined before taking them fully on board.

---

165. See Moyise, *Evoking Scripture*, 44–48 for a competent assessment of the author-centered and reader-centered approaches. In the end, he advises readers of Paul to take both approaches into account.
166. Wagner, *Heralds of the Good News*, 20–28.
167. Ibid., 26.
168. Stanley, *Arguing with Scripture*, 59–60.

Literacy and Orality

First, the issue of illiteracy among the majority of the original audience of early Christian epistles must be further nuanced. One fault of Stanley's portrayal of ancient illiteracy is the equating of literacy with social elites. The result of this equation is a dismissal of the significance of orality.[169] To take an example, he writes, "It seems improbable that the illiterate members of Paul's churches would have been motivated to raise questions about Paul's use of scripture, and it is even more unlikely that they would have been able to understand and critique the answers if they were offered."[170] It seems that the stigmas associated with modern illiteracy have been retrojected onto the ancient world, even though no evidence exists indicating that illiteracy was stigmatized. There is an assumption expressed here that illiteracy entails an inability to understand the written word read aloud and an inability to engage in critical thought.[171] However, in a culture where oral modes of communication dominated, this assumption is unfounded.[172]

Stanley works with the assumption that most, if not all, of Paul's audience were Gentiles (a concept that matches the current scholarly opinion regarding the Petrine audience in Asia Minor).[173] However, there was likely a higher level of Jewish presence than Stanley assumes.[174] If Paul's audience were composed of a greater number of Jewish listeners, then the competency of the audience would be raised significantly with regard to familiarity with the Jewish scriptures. Furthermore, if the leadership of the early church was composed of people who were familiar with scripture (even if illiterate), a great deal more may be expected of the audience than Stanley allows. We may expect that the leadership of the early church worked to educate those less familiar with the scriptural heritage that belonged to the early church. This is a point Wagner raises in his critique of Stanley's thesis, to which he adds the likelihood of "multiple public readings."[175] All of these areas of

---

169. Stanley addresses this more fully in "The Social Environment," 20–26.

170. Stanley, *Arguing with Scripture*, 57 n. 50.

171. Stanley, though, finds that part of this inability stems from the imposition of interpretive renderings upon the text by the literati, making it virtually impossible for the listener to differentiate written text from oral tradition ("The Social Environment," 21–22).

172. Several assumptions regarding literacy, orality and memory in the ancient world are addressed in Thomas, *Literacy and Orality*, 5–28.

173. Stanley *Paul*, 35–36, 338; *Arguing with Scripture*, x, 1–3.

174. Wagner, *Heralds of the Good News*, 34–36.

175. Ibid., 37.

consideration contribute to a picture of the early church as more competent hearers of scripture than has been granted by Stanley.

This means that the authors of NT epistles did not have to work only at the most explicit level to indicate the use of scripture to their audience. Should we assume that everyone would have heard more subtle uses of scripture? By no means! But we can assume that there were members of the audience who caught a great deal more than the reader-centered approach has allowed. In all likelihood, the members who caught more were usually those in a position to explain what they learned to others.

Second, the scarcity of biblical scrolls intersects significantly with the first test Hays proposed: *availability*. Scholars are in agreement that Paul accessed scripture in written form. It is likely that Paul used written excerpts from previous study of scrolls as the source of (most of) his quotations.[176] We must also ask, however, the extent to which the audience was familiar with scriptural texts. How do we go about quantifying what was available? A simple perusal of Fraenkel's *Verzeichnis* of Greek manuscripts provides us a picture of our extant manuscripts for the different books of the Bible. The index of manuscripts for individual books indicates that the most popular books were the Psalter (with the most manuscripts by far), Genesis, Isaiah, the Odes of Solomon, Exodus and Proverbs.[177] At Qumran, the books of Isaiah, Genesis, Psalms, Deuteronomy, Exodus and Leviticus, along with *Jubilees*, the *Hodayot*, and *Rule of the Community* rounds out the picture of availability.[178] This profile corresponds significantly with the books most used by NT authors. This correspondence suggests that authors were aware that the availability of biblical scrolls was a significant issue.

Ultimately the proposition that 1 Peter draws upon a scriptural narrative, which is informed by the themes and images of discrete scriptural texts, makes it so that the force of Peter's argument resides less in the recognition of each individual text that is quoted or alluded to and more in the recognition of the dramatic narrative in which Peter depicts his audience as participants. In other words, stories were able to communicate effectively to widespread audiences.[179]

---

176. Lim (*Holy Scripture*, 150–52) has an extended discussion in which Hatch's *excerpta* theory is preferred to Harris's *testimonia* theory. See also Stanley, *Paul*, 79. Wagner (*Heralds of the Good News*, 24–27) wants to include memory as a significant factor behind Paul's use of scripture. He thinks it incredible "that once Paul expended the labor to find and excerpt a passage, he promptly forgot all about its original setting" (ibid., 25).

177. Fraenkel, *Verzeichnis der griechischen Handschriften*, 472–97.

178. Brooke, "Biblical Interpretation at Qumran," 301.

179. This is consistent with the findings of Barrier (*The Acts of Paul and Thecla*,

Ethnic Composition[180]

It must also be recollected that early church expansion ran along the rails of the synagogues.[181] Trebilco's book *Jewish Communities in Asia Minor* makes a compelling case for the presence of Jewish communities in several of the cities included in the original circuit of 1 Peter.[182] This establishes that the original audience of 1 Peter consisted of some mix of Jewish and Gentile Christians who would vary in their ability to hear the use of scripture in the discourse of 1 Peter.

According to the prescript of 1 Peter, the audience is located across a rather large amount of territory in Asia Minor. The geographical names listed in 1 Pet 1:1 refer to the provinces of Pontus, Galatia and Cappadocia, located in the Eastern half of the Anatolian peninsula, along with Asia and Bithynia, located in the Western half. At a minimum, the circuitous route by which the letter was carried followed the coasts of the Black Sea to the North, the Marmara sea to the Northwest and the Aegean Sea to the West. However, it is more likely that the circuit was much larger, encompassing even as much as three-quarters of Asia Minor and extending as far south as the Taurus Mountains.

In all likelihood, the route the letter-carrier followed would have passed through major urban centers in these provinces. A possible route would begin in Tyana in Cappadocia heading north through Ankara to the cities along the Black Sea—such as Sinope—then West to Nicomedia and Nicea, then Southward into any number of population centers such as Acmonia and Sardis in the interior and Pergamum and Smyrna along the Aegean coast.[183]

The listing of the geographical centers in 1 Pet 1:1 can be coordinated with other such listings in Acts 2:9–10 and Revelation 2–3. The passage in

---

14–15) with regard to early Christian novels, particularly as it relates to the issue of literacy in the provinces of Asia Minor.

180. The following section summarizes a paper presented at the Society of Biblical Literature Annual Meeting—Letters of James, Peter, and Jude Section, 21 November 2010. My thanks go to the participants for their interaction and encouragement.

181. See Schnabel, *Early Christian Mission*, 2:1300–1301.

182. The most likely places 1 Peter would have traveled were the most populated places in Asia Minor in the provinces he names: Pontus, Galatia, Cappadocia, Asia and Bithynia. Thus, Trebilco's work on Sardis in the province of Asia is quite relevant to our picture of the original audience of 1 Peter (*Jewish Communities*, 37–54). See also Rajak, "The Jewish Diaspora," 53–68.

183. See the extensive treatment of missionary routes in Asia Minor in Schnabel, *Early Christian Mission*, 1:819–48. See also his treatment of the geographical regions listed in 1 Pet 1:1 (ibid., 724–28).

1 Peter and the Modern Discourse on the Use of Scripture

Acts describes a convocation in Jerusalem of diaspora Jews who traveled from far reaches of the world. From Asia Minor are listed delegates from Cappadocia, Pontus, Asia, Phrygia and Pamphylia. The listing of these regions early in Acts may indicate how Peter has come to know the people addressed in the epistle. Particularly relevant to the present concerns of this thesis is the identification of peoples from these regions as ethnically Jewish. The cities named in Revelation also overlap with the regions listed in 1 Pet 1:1. Ephesus, Smyrna, Pergamum, Thyatira, Sardis, Philadelphia and Laodicea are all within the province of Asia, the region most likely to be the end of the circuit for 1 Peter.

From these considerations, it seems that the regions addressed by Peter are broadly familiar within the sphere of early Christianity and that the areas are not isolated from the missionary activity more often associated with southern Asia Minor. Additionally, the Aegean area—both the interior and the coastal regions—appear to have been the residence of several prominent Jewish communities. Paul Trebilco's work on Jewish communities in this area goes a long way toward helping us understand the ethnic diversity of the people residing in this region.[184]

Bechtler has recently argued that the situation addressed in 1 Peter centers on "*intragentile* conflict."[185] This turn away from the more standard identification of the audience as mixed with Jewish and Gentile Christians demands some further consideration. First, he contends that "the presence of Jewish Christians and gentile God-fearers among 1 Peter's intended audience cannot be deduced from the letter itself." Instead, one must look to sources outside the letter, such as evidence of Jewish presence in Asia Minor or other literary sources. He then argues, "A distinction must be made between the actual, historical communities, which almost certainly did include some Jewish Christians and former God-fearers, and the addressees of the letter, who are gentiles."[186] The key piece of evidence provided for this claim is the adjective πατροπαραδότος in 1:18 describing an inheritance from one's ancestors. He writes, "The adjective πατροπαραδότος derives from Hellenistic Greek rhetoric, where it was used positively to indicate that which was traditional and, as such, venerable and trustworthy."[187] The problem with this assertion is the weakness of the evidence. This term shows up only five times prior to the NT, and then in only two authors dated merely a century

---

184. Trebilco, *Jewish Communities*.
185. Bechtler, *Following in His Steps*, 63.
186. Ibid., 62.
187. Ibid., 63.

prior to the NT.¹⁸⁸ It is difficult to substantiate a literary influence here; particularly since in 1 Peter the adjective is used in such a negative way.

While it is certainly true that one cannot deduce an ethnically Jewish audience from the scant evidence in 1 Peter, it is equally true that this scant evidence is also elusive when it comes to *eliminating* any Jewish presence from among the audience.¹⁸⁹ Equating πατροπαραδότος with "Hellentistic Greek rhetoric" only identifies the source from which the term derives but says nothing about how it is applied in 1 Peter. We simply cannot determine from this one adjective whether it is being applied to an exclusively Jewish or Gentile audience. Because it is possible to interpret the key passages pertaining to the identity of the audience (1:14, 18; 4:3–5) as relevant to either a Jewish or Gentile background, it does not appear responsible to decisively eliminate one or the other from consideration based merely on a "mirror-reading" technique.¹⁹⁰ As a mixed audience, it is valuable to see how recipients of the letter may have felt ostracism not merely from a Gentile context but the Jewish adherents to the gospel may also have been alienated from their Jewish communities.

Audience Suffering

In order to better understand the way Peter develops the scriptural narrative in his letter, it is necessary to consider the kind of suffering the audience has experienced that motivates Peter to produce such a scripturally nuanced pastoral response. The language used in 1 Peter to describe the situation of the audience draws together a number of different ideas. First, the audience is depicted variously as in exile (παρεπίδημος; 1:1; 2:11), in the dispersion (διασπορά; 1:1), as experiencing a time of sojourn (παροικία; 1:17) and as sojourners (πάροικος; 2:11). These designations highlight the experience of alienation experienced by the audience. Second, Peter suggests that the audience has experienced a time of testing (πειρασμός; 1:6; 4:12 and δοκίμιον; 1:7) that results in a purification of the believers (see 1:22; 4:1–2). Third, and most prominent among the ideas, the language of suffering captures the essence of the concerns held by the churches of Asia Minor. The terms πάσχω

188. The references belong to the historians Diodorus Siculus, *Bib. Hist.* 4.8.5; 15.74.5; 17.2.3; 17.4.1 and Dionysius Halicarnassus, *Ant. Rom.* 5.48.2.

189. It must be added that a determination of the ethnicity of the audience in one way or the other does not negate the rest of Bechtler's illuminating work. One may apply the concept of liminality to the social context of either Jewish of Gentile Christians in Asia Minor without difficulty (*Following in His Steps*, 118–56).

190. On the pitfalls of mirror-reading, see Barclay, "Mirror-Reading a Polemical Letter."

1 Peter and the Modern Discourse on the Use of Scripture 35

(2:19, 20, 21, 23; 3:14, 17, 18; 4:1, 15, 19; 5:10) and πάθημα (1:11; 4:13; 5:1, 9) are joined with a host of other terms that amplify the experience of the addressees.[191] The variety and frequency of the language used in 1 Peter points to the importance of the audience's situation for understanding both why and how Peter's scriptural discourse works within the letter. In short, Peter draws upon scripture to address the concerns the church has in light of its experience of suffering. In order to better understand the connection of the Petrine scriptural discourse to the situation of the audience, it is necessary to briefly consider recent discussion concerning the kind of suffering experienced by the church.

Views have changed over time regarding the nature of the suffering experienced by the Christians addressed in 1 Peter. Early in the previous century, there were many who connected the situation of the audience with official persecutions.[192] Particularly relevant to their view was the letter by Pliny to Trajan which requested guidance regarding how to deal with Christians brought before him. Efforts to closely link the two letters—and thereby establish a basis for the theory of official persecution—were hampered by the conciliatory tone of 1 Peter toward the government,[193] making it unlikely that the Christians were experiencing the same kind of persecution depicted in Pliny's letter.

Reacting to this and building upon newly developed social-scientific methods, scholars articulated that the audience experienced suffering in the form of verbal abuse and social ostracism.[194] Elliott, for instance, finds that "all the pertinent terms refer to verbal rather than physical abuse or legal action."[195] Bechtler, who correctly challenges the major assumption underlying Elliott's work—namely that the terms παρεπίδημος along with παροικία and πάροικος refer to a literal foreign residence on the part of the addressees of 1 Peter,[196] agrees with Elliott that the audience experiences

---

191. Λυπέο (1:6), λύπη (2:19), καταλαλέω (2:12; 3:16), λοιδορία (3:9), ἐπηρεάζω (3:16), βλασφημέω (4:4), and ὀνειδίζω (4:14) are all verbal in nature. See also Elliott, *1 Peter*, 100–101.

192. Windisch, *Die katholischen Briefe*, 80; Beare, *First Epistle of Peter*, 30–34, 188.

193. This may be contrasted with the perspective taken in Revelation regarding the Roman empire. See, e.g., Green, *1 Peter*, 8–9.

194. Kelly, *Epistles of Peter and of Jude*, 5–10; Best, *I Peter*, 36–42; Achtmeier, "Newborn Babes," 211; Michaels, *1 Peter*, lxiii–lxvi; Davids, *First Epistle of Peter*, 10; Goppelt, *Commentary on I Peter*, 36–45; Elliott, *1 Peter*, 100; Schreiner, *1, 2 Peter, Jude*, 30; Green, *1 Peter*, 8.

195. Elliott, *Home for the Homeless*, 80.

196. Bechtler, *Following in His Steps*, 81. See also BDAG, 775.

"sustained verbal abuse and slanderous accusation."[197] Feldmeier locates the situation in the foreignness (*Fremdheit*) experienced by the recipients who were formerly part of the social community in which they reside. The source of social ostracism is not government officials, but "former fellow-citizens."[198] The addressees were once natives within the dominant community, but are now considered as foreigners because of their participation in the Christian community and rejection of the "sacral institutions" of the Roman Empire.[199] It was only in the third century that a global persecution of Christians occurred that was sanctioned by official policy.[200]

More recently, Horrell has suggested that the course of scholarship has tended to recommend a false alternative. He writes, "To pose as alternatives informal public hostility and official Roman persecution, as Elliott and others do, is to misconstrue the situation that pertained, broadly speaking, from the time of Nero until the third-century persecution under Decius (c. 250 c.e.)."[201] Horrell would rather see both options as viable causes of hostility towards the Christians of Asia Minor.[202]

This scholarly discussion, as it continues to probe into the form of suffering experienced in Asia Minor, presents a field of study that would take us far from the present concerns of this thesis. Instead of reading for the details of the audience's suffering in 1 Peter, the goal here is to identify how suffering is addressed in 1 Peter. Feldmeier has correctly shown that Peter's interpretation of the situation is highly theological. He writes, "the foreignness of the Christians is not in its essence derived from protests against society, but from correspondence to God and belonging to his new society."[203] Yet, it is important to understand further the societal constraints within which the audience experiences its foreignness.

Elliott and Bechtler have shown convincingly how the categories of honor and shame are an integral part of Peter's admonition to his audience. In light of the evidence supporting the view that the recipients of 1 Peter have had their honor challenged,[204] Elliott observes that "the patent aim of the letter is to propose a specific course of action" in response to public

---

197. Ibid., 94.
198. Feldmeier, *Christen als Fremde*, 109; *First Letter of Peter*, 2.
199. Feldmeier, *First Letter of Peter*, 5.
200. Feldmeier, *Christen als Fremde*, 106; *First Letter of Peter*, 4.
201. Horrell, *1 Peter*, 56.
202. Ibid., 53–59.
203. Feldmeier, *First Letter of Peter*, 14.
204. Elliott, "Disgraced yet Graced," 169–71.

challenges of honor.[205] The specific strategy is to bless and show honorable conduct when faced with insult and slander.[206] It is shown how the strategy is theologically oriented inasmuch as 1) the "criterion of honorable conduct is not simply public opinion but the 'will of God,'" 2) Christ "is held up as the paramount exemplar and enabler of such honorable conduct," 3) others are led to the faith, and 4) "suffering itself is cast in a positive light."[207] In Bechtler's view, the challenges to honor arise from the discord that occurs between fellow citizens that arises from a "fundamental clash of symbolic universes." Therefore, the strategy of 1 Peter "is a legitimation of the addressees' symbolic universe that would render life within a hostile society intelligible and tolerable" to their unbelieving neighbors.[208] A thorough investigation of all the factors related to the social-scientific enterprise to which these discussions are indebted stands outside the present thesis. But the symbolic universe Bechtler points to has in many ways been constructed upon the foundation of a scriptural discourse. Therefore, it is necessary throughout to demonstrate how the scriptural narrative in 1 Peter contributes to an address that provides a strategic response to suffering.

In light of this, it is important to consider how Bechtler challenges Schutter's consideration of "the possibility of routine criminal prosecution"[209] as the supposed situation addressed in 1 Peter. Schutter finds in 1 Pet 2:13–17; 3:13–17 and 4:15 details "that render an application to a forensic setting especially cogent."[210] This situation is not foundational for most of Schutter's work, but does bear upon his understanding of how Peter's use of scripture contributes to the letter's response to suffering. In his consideration of the allusion to Ezek 9:6, Schutter finds that the original context of Ezekiel 9 matches 1 Peter's concerns regarding capital punishment.[211] By using Ezek 9:6, then, "the author discloses that the collective assault against Christians represents nothing less than the start of the Last Judgment itselt [sic]."[212] Has Schutter identified properly the situation and the response to suffering that extends from his construal?

Bechtler admits that 1 Peter may "envision sporadic charges being brought against Christians by their detractors" but that the letter more

---

205. Ibid., 170.
206. Ibid., 171.
207. Ibid., 172.
208. Bechtler, *Following in His Steps*, 106–7.
209. McCartney, "Use of the Old Testament," 14.
210. Ibid., 15.
211. Ibid., 162. He calls this "the main issue in I Pet. 4.14f."
212. Ibid., 163.

clearly reflects "a situation of sustained verbal abuse and slanderous accusation of Christians by their nonbelieving neighbors."[213] In support of his critique of Schutter's view, he shows that key terms on 1 Pet 2:13–17; 3:13–17 and 4:15 can be understood apart from *cognitio extra ordinem* proceedings.[214] Instead, Bechtler offers the language of honor and dishonor as "the key to understanding the problem of suffering in 1 Peter."[215] In light of this language, he suggests the strategy outlined above. Bechtler's critique shows that Schutter's view of the addressees' situation was too narrow and proposes a more general statement of the conflict experienced by Christians in Asia Minor. Such a general articulation of the situation allows us to reconsider how scripture has figured into Peter's response to suffering.

In the final analysis, suffering is presented in 1 Peter as one of the narratival motifs that unites the scriptural narrative of ancient Israel with the work of Christ, and in which the church is identified as participants inasmuch as they share in the sufferings of Christ. Peter also spells out, though, that the narrative of God's restoration is not negated by present suffering.

Conclusion

Based on these issues, a picture emerges of the audience addressed by 1 Peter.[216] It is assumed that somewhere between 10–20 percent of the original audience was literate.[217] This corresponds with the percentage provided by Stanley, and there is no reason why the literacy rate should be lower in Asia Minor than in Rome.[218] Although the majority, then, were illiterate, this does not entail that

---

213. Bechtler, *Following in His Steps*, 93–94.

214. Ibid., 88–92. The term ἐκδίκησις (2:14), Bechtler agrees, does reflect the legal function assigned by Schutter. Instead, ἔπαινος (2:14), καταλαλέω (2:12), ἀπολογία (3:15) and the terms in the vice list (4:15) can be read in a more general sense outside such a juridical setting.

215. Ibid., 94.

216. The relationship between the implied audience and the real audience need not be as stark as indicated by Stanley (*Arguing with Scripture*, 62–65).

217. It is also the case that literate does not entail elite. It is quite possible that servants were trained in the skill of writing. The address to οἰκέται in 2:18ff. might imply that these are household servants whose education has included this skill. The scriptural allusions to Isaiah 53 contained there indicate an expectation that the οἰκέται (as well as the broader audience) would comprehend less explicit allusions to scripture.

218. Harris (*Ancient Literacy*, 141) sees a decline in literacy from a high-point in the Hellenistic period based on the decline in educational philanthropy. But see Pleket (Review of *Ancient Literacy*, 421–23) who questions this, seeing instead a continuation of the Hellenistic schools sponsored by benefactors in later periods. This places the eastern Roman empire on equal footing with the western half.

they were unable to hear subtle allusions to scripture. In an oral culture, literacy cannot be the litmus test for the perceptive abilities of the original audience. It seems better to categorize many in the audience as "aurally competent." As the letter is read aloud, they would be able to interact with an argument featuring scriptural quotation and allusion in much the same way as their literate counterparts. There certainly would be many that would not comprehend the subtle incorporation of scripture into the epistolary discourse. However, this lack of comprehension may have been the impetus for the leadership of the church to teach about the more subtle elements of the epistle. The presence of the letter carrier at the original reading stands as another source to clarify and expand on points that remained unclear.[219]

Across the continuum of listener competence we may apply our knowledge of the ethnic mixture of the regions of Asia Minor. We cannot assume that every Jewish member of the audience was also a literate or aurally competent audience member. However, it can be expected that the early leadership of the church was well versed in the Jewish scriptures. In some cases, these might be Gentiles who had attached themselves to the synagogue prior to joining the church. We cannot know what scriptures were available at the numerous synagogues sprinkled throughout the diaspora. But we can assume the presence of enough scriptures to support weekly synagogue meetings.[220] So, for those who had a background in the synagogue, there was arguably a greater ability to comprehend more subtle scriptural articulation. It also seems that the synagogue practice of reading scripture and teaching carried over into the church, which quickly came to include a sizeable Gentile population. Even if there was no "rigorous program of Scripture study and memorization"[221] in the early church, we can assume that it was reasonably expected that those newly initiated into the practices inherited from the synagogue would grow in their knowledge of scripture.

From these considerations, the picture of the original audience of Peter's epistle takes shape. The letter was carried to a number of different communities each with a unique set of members in the audience. The audience was ethnically mixed with varying proportions of Jewish and Gentile listeners. The literacy rate of the audience, the factor highlighted by Stanley, has been considered less significant in this study since the culture was more orally oriented. The public reading of the letter did not require literary competence but aural competence. The major factor bearing upon listener competence, then, is the availability of local scripture texts. It was argued

---

219. See Head, "Named Letter-Carriers," 296–98.
220. See Safrai,"Education and the Study of the Torah," 966–67.
221. Stanley, *Arguing with Scripture*, 49.

above that NT authors appear to draw prominently from the most widely available sources, encouraging the greatest possible listener competence. And finally, the presence of church leaders (as well as the letter carrier) who had a higher level of competency were able to assist those with lower levels of competence in hearing more subtle uses of scriptural texts.

The Christians to whom 1 Peter is addressed have faced suffering, largely from the conflict arising from their faith in Christ. The verbal abuse and social challenge that is felt by the audience demands a response, and 1 Peter was crafted to supply the beleaguered elect in Asia Minor with a defense. One of the most significant aspects of the argument contained in 1 Peter is the way in which scripture supplies key concepts to Peter's response to suffering.

Peter and His Bible

There are several factors that now must be dealt with in light of the scholarly discourse on the use of scripture in Paul's letters. The epistolary prescript proposes that the author of this letter is Peter, whose historical connection to Jesus and the early church is chronicled elsewhere in the NT.[222] Modern scholarship has contested this proposition, raising doubts about Petrine authorship. The evidence put forward by those accepting Peter as the author of the letter and by those suggesting pseudonymity is far too extensive to address in this thesis and holds little bearing for the present project.[223] It is assumed that the author of 1 Peter wrote the epistle within the latter half of the first century.[224] The letter presents itinerant ministry (1:12), concern

---

222. Most prominently in the four Gospels and Acts, but see also 1 Cor 1:12; 9:5; 15:5; Gal 1:18; 2:7–14.

223. Scholars upholding Petrine authorship include Hort, *First Epistle of St Peter*, 1–7; Selwyn, *First Epistle of St Peter*, 32; van Unnik, "Teaching of Good Words," 92–93; "Christianity," 80; Reicke, *Epistles of James, Peter, and Jude*, 69–72; Grudem, *1 Peter*, 21–33; Michaels, *1 Peter*, lv–lxvii; Dalton, *Christ's Proclamation*, 77–91; Guthrie, *New Testament Introduction*, 762–81; Marshall, *1 Peter*, 21–24; Schreiner, *1, 2 Peter, Jude*, 26–36; Jobes, *1 Peter*, 18–19; Green, *1 Peter*, 6–8. Scholars assuming that 1 Peter is pseudepigraphical are Beare, *First Epistle of Peter*, 43–50; Best, *I Peter*, 49–51; Brox, *Der erste Petrusbrief*, 43–51; McCartney, "Use of the Old Testament," 4–7; Goppelt, *Commentary on I Peter*, 48–50; Feldmeier, *Christen als Fremde*, 193–98; *First Letter of Peter*, 32–39; Achtemeier, *1 Peter*, 42–43; Elliott, *1 Peter*, 118–30; Richard, *Reading 1 Peter, Jude, and 2 Peter*, 9–11; Horrell, *1 Peter*, 20–23.

224. Elliott (*1 Peter*, 136–38) lists eight factors leading him to date 1 Peter after 72 c.e. See Best, *I Peter*, 63–64; Brox, *Der erste Petrusbrief*, 38–41; Michaels, *1 Peter*, lxii–lxvi; McCartney, "Use of the Old Testament," 4–7; Davids, *First Epistle of Peter*, 9–11; Thurén, *Rhetorical Strategy*, 30–31; Goppelt, *Commentary on I Peter*, 46–47; Achtemeier, *1 Peter*, 49–50; Senior, *1 Peter*, 7–8; Feldmeier, *Christen als Fremde*, 39–40;

1 Peter and the Modern Discourse on the Use of Scripture 41

for the well-being of believers in Christ (esp. 3:13–17; 4:12–16; 5:9) and the proclamation of the gospel (1:12, 25; 3:1) as aspects of the early church that are consistent with a picture of Peter.[225] At the same time, these aspects might also be the hallmarks of any number of people in the early church, making it less important for the purposes of this thesis to settle on the exact identity of the author. As discussed above, the letter assumes that the audience has experienced suffering, but does little to describe the situation with any specificity.[226] For the sake of brevity and consistency, the author of 1 Peter will be referred to in this thesis as Peter.[227]

Drawing upon the similarities between Peter and Paul as developed above, it is possible to recover to some extent Peter's relationship with the scriptural texts used in 1 Peter.[228] One of the recurring themes in recent scholarship on Paul's use of scripture is the recognition of how difficult it would be for the apostle to carry with him a set of biblical scrolls. So how would Peter have appropriated the scripture used throughout 1 Peter? Lim's championing of Hatch's *excerpta* theory is quite compelling. With this in mind, we can picture Peter studying biblical scrolls at a synagogue or library and taking notes that would have been handy in his preaching ministry.[229] Many of the passages cited in 1 Peter are drawn together by key terms. It is possible that Peter came to the text searching out particular concepts and that his notebook would be organized around these terms. The overwhelming majority of passages come from Isaiah. It is reasonable to expect that Peter had access to Isaiah and studied it extensively.

Stanley fills out the picture of Paul's study of scripture significantly. He writes, "Paul copied his excerpts from a variety of manuscripts housed at

---

Horrell, *1 Peter*, 22–23. Kelly (*Epistles of Peter and of Jude*, 26–30) does not consider a date as early as 64 unreasonable. See Selwyn, *First Epistle of St Peter*, 62; Schreiner, *1, 2 Peter, Jude*, 36–37; Jobes, *1 Peter*, 18. Beare (*First Epistle of Peter*, 28–43) argues for a second century date.

225. On the life of Peter, see Cullmann, *Peter*; Perkins, *Peter*; Lapham, *Peter*; Hengel, *Saint Peter*; Bockmuehl, *Remembered Peter* and *Simon Peter*.

226. One of the more sophisticated arguments supporting the authenticity of 1 Peter (among some other NT epistles) is Bauckham, "Pseudo-Apostolic Letters," 123–49.

227. This differs slightly from the stance taken by Schutter in his assessment of the hermeutics in 1 Peter. He finds that the arguments for and against authenticity have stalemated, but adopts as his "working-hypothesis" that "I Peter is a pseudepigraph, because that remains the dominant scholarly opinion, but it must be admitted that the matter is far from resolution" (*Hermeneutic*, 7).

228. Again, the picture developed here could pertain to any number of individuals who engaged in an itinerant ministry, and no connection is made here with the historical Peter of the gospels.

229. See Sperber, "Rabbinic Knowledge," 629–30.

sites all around the eastern Mediterranean world, where he was a constant traveler."[230] If Peter was likewise engaged in missionary work in the same region, it would not be surprising to find him using a variety of manuscripts housed locally. Variants in the Peter's *Vorlage*, then, may derive from manuscripts copied by different scribes throughout the region. Variants might otherwise enter at the point where the text is copied into Peter's notebook. It is also possible that a variant might occur at the point where the text is copied from the notebook into the letter. In the case of Peter, there is also the possibility that some kind of Semitic interference comes into play. If his first exposure to scripture was in Aramaic or Hebrew, his memory might "interfere" at any stage of his study of the Greek text. The possibility that Peter had recourse to manuscripts in multiple languages and made comparative studies of the text cannot be ruled out entirely, but this is highly unlikely.

Regarding memory, Wagner challenges Stanley's assumption that Paul primarily used written texts.[231] If Peter accessed scripture in the same way Paul did, we would expect that memory plays a significant role in his use of scripture.[232] Having read through Isaiah to excerpt pertinent passages, he likely would have remembered the larger context from which he pulled these passages.

Finally, it is likely that Peter came to the written text not simply to write a discrete letter. Acts 6:9 indicates that Peter's study of scripture served the purpose of proclaiming the gospel. Peter's scripture study probably was first intended to support his itinerant missionary endeavors. First Peter may be the culmination of work carried out over many years in which the concepts of the epistle were delivered orally to several audiences. This being the case, we can see how the study of written texts, the meditation and memorization of passages of scripture, and the preaching of the gospel all contribute to the use of scripture in 1 Peter.

The Approach of the Present Study

Having perused the relevant scholarly work on the use of scripture in 1 Peter and then drawing upon recent work on Paul's use of scripture, we are now in a position to articulate how this study will be carried out.

---

230. Stanely, *Paul*, 78.
231. Wagner, *Heralds of the Good News*, 24–27.
232. Bockmuehl (*Simon Peter*, 31) considers there to be "a more harmonious relationship between Peter and Paul than some ancient and many modern interpreters suspect based on Gal. 2:11–14."

In the next chapter, I will consider the role of 1 Pet 1:10–12 as the hermeneutical key of 1 Peter. This passage will be explored to determine if the expressed hermeneutic supports the proposition that the ecclesiology of 1 Peter is informed by a scriptural narrative. Inasmuch as this is the case, a further section teases out how the motif of suffering and glory, initiated in this passage, functions as the terminology of conflict and resolution in the scriptural narrative. Understanding how this motif functions in 1 Peter allows us to appreciate the role Isaiah plays in the formation of the scriptural narrative in 1 Peter.

Chapters 3–6 are the heart of this study and cover the three main sections of 1 Peter: 1:13—2:10; 2:11—4:11; 4:12—5:11. For each use of scripture, the text is examined to determine how Peter has worked with the text. Caution is urged concerning the nature of authorial alteration of the text, since the transmission history of scripture remains obscure in spite of the many manuscripts available to us.[233] The wider context for each passage is then explored. This is not to imply that the wider context is necessarily determinative for the meaning of the quoted text. Rather, it allows us to see how meaning has either remained consistent or been altered as it is placed inside a new rhetorical setting. Often scriptural texts are brought together, and such intertextual readings provide insights into the Petrine reading strategy. The rhetorical setting in which these scriptural texts are set is also considered since the scriptural narrative depicted in the letter serves as an act of communication between author and audience.

The last chapter will summarize the results of chapters 3–6 and spell out more fully the implications of this study. It is proposed that the ecclesiology of 1 Peter portrays the church as participants in the scriptural narrative of the restoration of divine presence among the people of God presently experiencing suffering by means of their participation in Christ, who is assumed to be the messiah of the scriptures. This scriptural narrative depends in large part upon Isaianic themes and images.

---

233. See Lim, *Holy Scripture*, 69–94 with regard to the Hebrew text, and Stanley, *Paul*, 38–50 with regard to the Greek text.

2

The Hermeneutical Picture of 1 Peter

Introduction

THIS THESIS CONTENDS THAT Peter's ecclesiology draws upon the narrative of God's restoration by identifying the church as participating in a grand scriptural narrative. An important passage in developing this thesis is 1 Pet 1:10–12. Here Peter provides the most explicit articulation of his hermeneutical perspective. In order to understand how this passage works within the scope of Peter's use of scripture it is necessary to enter into the dialogue centering on how this passage functions as the hermeneutical key of the letter. From there, it will be necessary to develop the two key terms "suffering" and "glory" to demonstrate the pivotal role they play in portraying the scriptural narrative of 1 Peter. Then, the terms will be explored within the book of Isaiah to see how this voice within the chorus of scriptures gives expression to suffering and glory.

1 Peter 1:10–12 as Hermeneutical Key[1]

The extensive use of scripture in 1 Peter raises questions regarding how these texts cohere. The sequence of scriptures in 1 Peter has the appearance of haphazardness. While Isaiah 40, 53 and Psalm 34 achieve prominence, they are intermingled with such passages as Lev 19:2; Ps 117[118]:22 and Prov 11:3. By devoting some attention to 1 Pet 1:10–12 it is suggested that

---

1. This section of the chapter was presented as a paper at the Tyndale Fellowship New Testament Study Group, Tyndale House, Cambridge on 8 July 2008. I would like to thank Howard Marshall, Steve Walton, Mike Thompson and Richard Bauckham for their kind and helpful responses to my paper.

the coherence of scriptural quotations in 1 Peter may be located in the key terms "suffering" and "glory."

The struggle to understand 1 Pet 1:10–12 as a hermeneutical key that unlocks the organizing principle at work in 1 Peter has been longstanding.[2] The strategy taken to date draws attention to a few key words deemed to be technical terms for the exegetical method used by Peter when compared with similar language used in the Dead Sea Scrolls. While this approach correctly highlights the importance of this passage, it has muted the true significance this passage holds for understanding the use of scripture in 1 Peter.

The aim of this chapter is to spell out how this passage governs the construal of the quotations and allusions that follow it in the letter.[3] Any investigation of Petrine hermeneutics must deal with this passage in order to appreciate the scriptural narrative that undergirds the letter. A close reading of the passage reveals less about a technical theory of interpretive methods, but discloses much about the broad contours the author's reading of scripture. In this passage certain theological concerns are brought forward in a panoply of statements that reflect upon how the scriptural voice of the past bears upon the realities of the audience. It is in this theologization that the interpretive lens is revealed. The key to unlock the use of scripture in 1 Peter is found through considering the theological framework established in this passage. Moving through the passage sequentially, it will be shown that a theological hermeneutic is the distinguishing feature that moves 1 Peter beyond the Jewish hermeneutical tradition identified by Schutter.[4] It is important to keep in mind, though, that the following does not argue against the hermeneutical traditions inherited from Second Temple practices. Instead, it points out that 1 Pet 1:10–12 is not bent on articulating a Jewish

---

2. This passage has also been central to debates surrounding whether NT authors respected the intended meaning of the original authors of scripture. See Kaiser, "Eschatological Hermeneutics," 94–96; "Single Intent," 56–57; Payne, "Fallacy of Equating Meaning," 77–78. This debate raises numerous problems that are tangential to the current project.

3. My use of "construal" here relies upon the thought of Vanhoozer (*First Theology*, 28–30, 141–43) who develops a concept by Kelsey (*Uses of Scripture*, 2–3) whereby theologians make decisions "about how to *construe* the scripture they actually use to help authorize theological proposals" (2, italics original). The difference between the work of Kelsey and Vanhoozer and the present project is that the author in question is not a modern theologian but an ancient author using scripture to authenticate a theological argument. Full consideration of the many issues this concept raises for Petrine hermeneutics cannot be raised at this point.

4. Similarly, Gignilliat (*Paul and Isaiah's Servants*, 24–25) points to Paul's theological distantiation from the Jewish presuppositions that generated the interpretive context contemporaneous with the NT.

interpretive practices reveals the Christian theological categories that are assumed in the letter's use of scripture.[5]

The Role of the Prophets

The opening section of 1 Peter hails the blessing of God for the work of salvation accomplished on behalf of the elect. Here is the initial statement that the message of scripture is for the church. The ecclesiological reading of scripture in 1 Peter begins by connecting the prophets to the message of salvation for the elect. The salvation provided by God for his elect looks forward to the revelation of Jesus Christ (1:7, 13) as well as backward to the resurrection of Jesus Christ (1:3). This salvation is further traced back in redemptive history to the prophetic testimony of scripture. Two main issues surround Peter's concern for the prophets. First, what does the term "prophets" mean? Second, what activity is being indicated on the part of these prophets? Clarifying these two issues will assist us in developing an understanding of one component of the ecclesiological hermeneutic in the letter: that the church draws upon the received traditions of an authoritative prophetic voice.[6]

Who Were the Prophets?

Selwyn proposes that the prophets of 1 Pet 1:10 were not OT prophets but those with the gift of prophecy in the early church. They carried the gospel to Asia Minor prior to the dissemination of Peter's letter. His argument is based on several points. First, Selwyn connects prophecy in the OT to early Christian prophets, largely based on "tradition of religion" assumptions.[7] This includes an identification of prophecy as a holdover "of the institutional life of the Jewish Church of that period" that is drawn into early Christianity.[8] There are differences, though, between the prophets of old and prophecy in early Christianity. Commenting on 1:10, he considers that "the term ἐξηραύνησαν suggests that it was the Christian prophets who were especially

---

5. The distinction between Jewish and Christian exegetical practices would be almost impossible for the first century. The question centers not on the mechanics of how they read texts, but to what end did they read their texts.

6. This parallels the observations made by Brooke ("Place of Prophecy," 541) to the effect that the Qumran community saw themselves as justified in appealing to the prophets inasmuch as they saw themselves as living out the return from exile.

7. Selwyn, *First Epistle of St Peter*, 134, 260–61.

8. Ibid., 261.

in our author's mind, since this activity does not correspond to what we are told in O.T. of the prophets nor to what Jewish thought ascribed to them."[9] The distinguishing feature of early Christian prophets is a "preoccupation with the fact and faith of the Messiah" which provides "a powerful impulse to the study of the ancient Scriptures."[10]

Second, Selwyn finds problems with the identification of the prophets of 1:10 with the OT prophets. The terms "seeking" and "searching" are unknown in the scriptures as "activities of the O.T. prophets."[11] Instead, he finds parallels in Ephesians 2:20; 3:5; 4:11 and John 5:39.[12] Furthermore, the phrase "the spirit of Christ" cannot be found "if applied to the O.T. prophets."

Finally, as support for the view that the prophets of 1:10 are early Christian prophets, he turns to 1:11. There are no "indications of interest in the time of fulfillment" in OT prophecy. This may be contrasted with such figures as Zechariah and Simeon depicted in Luke 1–2 or the Revelation of John.[13] The concerns of the early Christian community predominate in 1:11. The phrase τὰ εἰς Χριστὸν παθήματα means "christward" sufferings rather than sufferings "destined for" Christ; an interpretation which is more in keeping with early Christian prophets than those in the OT. The plural "glories" likewise refers not to Christ but to Christians.[14] For Selwyn, the referent of the term "prophets" cannot be the OT prophets, but must be the early Christian prophets who played a vital role bringing the gospel to Asia Minor. It was these early Christian prophets who searched the scriptures to answer questions about Christian suffering.

Schutter accepts Selwyn's proposal, qualifiedly so, but finds this to have little bearing on "the question of the relationship which the author of I Peter

---

9. Ibid., 134.

10. Ibid., 261.

11. Ibid., 262.

12. The passages he adduces as parallels are not as compelling as he suggests. He makes the point that Ephesians exhibits an equivalence between apostles and prophets. Yet, in Eph 3:5 we read of things not known in other generations, but that have "now (νῦν) been revealed to his holy apostles and prophets." Unlike Eph 3:5, the prophets mentioned in 1 Peter are working prior to the present (νῦν) activity of the revelation of the gospel (1:12). See G. Stählin, "νῦν," TNDT 4:1106–23. John 5:39 mentions a searching of scriptures, but this is not the activity of prophets from either era. It is part of Jesus' critique of the Jews in opposition to his ministry.

13. Selwyn, First Epistle of St Peter, 263. Zechariah and Simeon present problems that Selwyn leaves unaddressed. Luke depicts them not as early Christian prophets, but as "holdovers" from an older era in which expectation of the messiah still exists.

14. Ibid., 264

had with the Scriptures."[15] This is because the main concern of Schutter's project is to discern the connection between 1 Peter and the hermeneutics of the Qumran community. Schutter identifies a Jewish hermeneutic at work in 1 Peter that may be termed "pesher-like."[16] The hermeneutic Schutter discerns is characterized by, among other things, a "radical eschatological viewpoint" and "elaborate pneumatology."[17] The view that the prophets of 1:10 were early Christian prophets lends itself to Schutter's study. The nameless, itinerant prophets become the locus of the interpretive activity standing behind 1 Peter through which the pesher-like hermeneutic has been transmitted. It may be affirmed that 1 Peter shares affinities with Jewish hermeneutics, but it cannot be assumed that the prophets here can so easily be connected with the interpretive practices of Qumran and Peter.

Best challenges Selwyn's arguments by contesting several main points. He puts forward a simple argument against Selwyn's proposal. The νῦν of verse 12 "suggests a considerable time-interval between the work of the prophets and that of the missionaries and is more suitable if they are taken to be OT prophets."[18] If early Christian prophecy is the referent of the term "prophets," would Peter make such an epochal distinction between the prophets and the missionaries? Selwyn's denial of any seeking or searching activity among the OT prophets is met with "evidence of prophets seeking truth."[19] Best lists among his examples Isa 6:11 where Isaiah shows an interest in temporal fulfillment by asking, "How long, O Lord?" Concerning the phrase τὰ εἰς Χριστὸν παθήματα, he follows Hort's interpretation that these are sufferings "destined for" Christ, but he can also see that in 1 Peter "sufferings are also destined for the Christian (3:17; 4:12–19)."[20] Best allows some room for Selwyn's interpretation of the phrase, but does not find a strict reference to Christian suffering but "a double reference" to the historic sufferings of Christ as well as those "destined for the Christian."[21]

Achtemeier perceives two principal points to Selwyn's proposal. The first concerns the term ἐξηραύνησαν. This verb can refer either to the task of "searching Scripture" or to "seeking the testimonies of the Lord or even seeking out the Lord himself," and it is this latter sense that he finds most

15. Schutter, *Hermeneutic*, 103.

16. Ibid., 123.

17. Ibid., 109. Both of these characterizations are overstated. Though eschatology does play an important role, it is hardly radical, and though pneumatology appears at points, it is hardly elaborate (contrast 1 Peter with Acts or Revelation on these points).

18. Best, *I Peter*, 84.

19. Ibid., 83.

20. Ibid., 81.

21. Ibid., 83–84.

fitting to this context.²² Thus, for Achtemeier, Selwyn over-emphasized the use of this term for a specific early Christian or early Jewish practice. The second point concerns the phrase τὰ εἰς Χριστὸν παθήματα. Achtemeier finds a parallel in the phrase εἰς ὑμᾶς in 1:10 where the sense is "the grace that is yours." It follows, then, that τὰ εἰς Χριστὸν παθήματα be understood in the same sense as "the sufferings that are Christ's."²³ The supposition that early Christian prophets who focused attention on sufferings on behalf of Christ is rendered unnecessary.

These scholars have done much to clarify what is meant by prophets. There are sufficient reasons to doubt Selwyn's, and therefore Schutter's, claim that these are early Christians with the gift of prophecy. It is reasonable to consider that as the OT prophets, not only for the reasons posited by Best and Achtemeier, but also because of the conspicuous way in which scriptural quotations and allusions appear quite frequently after this section. There is no indication of a shared hermeneutical outlook with contemporary early Christian prophets in 1 Pet 1:10. Instead, Peter informs his audience that the OT prophets engaged in an activity that marked their age. He will emphasize that the revelation of Christ compels him to connect the OT prophecies with the gospel that has now been preached. To anticipate the conclusion, the mention of prophets here points to the source of the scriptural narrative Peter draws upon for his ecclesiology.

What Were the Prophets Doing?

The work of the prophets constitutes a second issue in 1 Pet 1:10. According to Schutter—who follows Selwyn regarding the identity of the prophets as early Jewish Christians—the activity of these prophets informs us about Petrine hermeneutics inasmuch as the author of 1 Peter saw himself as part of that prophetic community. In this view, early Christian exegesis involved seeking and searching scripture for the meaning of present events. However, the argument above contends that the prophets in 1 Pet 1:10 were the prophets of the OT. Therefore, it is necessary to reconsider what Peter depicts as the activity of the prophets.

The depiction of the prophets' activity centers on two verbs, ἐκζητέω and ἐξεραυνάω. Goppelt finds a formulaic understanding of the verbs "search" and "inquire" in the writings found at Qumran.²⁴ The Community Rule (1QS 5.11) contrasts the people of the covenant with those outside

22. Achtemeier, "Suffering Servant," 185; idem., *1 Peter*, 108.
23. Achtemeier, *1 Peter*, 110.
24. Goppelt, *Commentary on I Peter*, 99–100; see also Schutter, *Hermeneutic*, 101.

the covenant. The latter "have neither inquired (לוא בקשו) nor sought after (ולוא דרשהו) Him concerning His laws that they might know the hidden things in which they have sinfully erred; and matters revealed (והנגלות) they have treated with insolence."[25] Drawing upon the language used in Zephaniah 1:6, those outside the covenant will stand under judgement because of their refusal to learn from divine revelation.

The use of בקש and דרש in Zeph 1:6 are not technical terms for interpretive activity.[26] The passage describes "those who turned aside from the Lord, who do not seek the Lord or inquire of him." Here, the Lord is the object of search and inquiry.[27] In both 1QS 5.11 and Zeph 1:6, the terms identify those who are apart from the Lord and express what is desired by the Lord. These contexts do not formulate an approach to scriptural interpretation nor are they examples of applied scriptural interpretation. As such, they do not offer a fitting comparison for understanding the role of prophets as depicted by Peter.

The pressing question is to determine what the prophets in 1 Peter 1:10 were doing. An example similar to 1 Pet 1:10–12 occurs in 1QpHab 7.1–8 with regard to temporal fulfillment. Interpreting Hab 2:1–2, the commentator clarifies that "God told Habakkuk to write down that which would happen to the final generation, but He did not make known to him when time would come to an end."[28] Similarly, the commentator writes regarding 2:3b, "Interpreted, this means that the final age shall be prolonged, and shall exceed all that the Prophets have said."[29] The subsequent generation has an advantage over the prophets because the temporal question that plagued the prophets is made known to the later generation. The elements of temporal distance, limitation of prophetic knowledge and subsequent interpretation by later generations provide better grounds for comparison.

The point being made in 1 Peter 1:10–12 is that the grace revealed already in the prophetic literature lacked but one thing, its temporal manifestation. The churches in Asia Minor have experienced this grace in the present (νῦν) and are no longer vexed by questions that confounded the prophets. The activity of the prophets is less concerned with interpreting the

---

25. Vermes, *Complete Dead Sea Scrolls*, 104.

26. The LXX has ζητέω and ἀντέχω. If technical interpretive jargon was as prominent as supposed by Goppelt and others, the translator appears to have overlooked this. See for בָּקַשׁ *TWOT* 126; *TDOT* 2:229-41; *THAT* 1:333-35 and for דֶּרֶשׁ *TWOT* 198-99; *THAT* 1:460-66; *TDOT* 3:293-307.

27. This lends support to Achtemeier's indication that (ἐξ-)ἐραυνάω, rather than being a technical term, more generally points toward the search for the Lord or his will.

28. Vermes, *Complete Dead Sea Scrolls*, 481.

29. Ibid., 482.

scriptures and more interested in discerning the will of the Lord. Their role in prophesying grace does not mitigate their limitations and leaves them to look forward to what remains to be revealed. The question posed in Isa 6:11 epitomizes the inquiry of the prophets, "How long, O Lord?"

The temporal nature of the prophetic inquiry is emphasized in 1:11. The prophets attempt to "search into the time" (καιρός) which "the spirit of Christ was indicating within them."[30] Schreiner points out that "the prophets did not know when the prophecies would be fulfilled, whereas Petrine believers live in the days of fulfillment."[31] For Peter, the advent of Jesus as the Christ marks the beginning of a new epoch in which the scriptures must be reinterpreted. The questions of the prophets are taken up by Peter so that he may point out the position his audience holds. They are beneficiaries of the prophetic activity of previous generations but have an advantage over them by having seen the fulfillment of those prophecies.

Reference to the prophets, then, connects the author's hermeneutic to the message of scripture. The prophets express the salvation of God that was disclosed to them, despite their own inability to discern important aspects of what was revealed through them. As Peter takes up the narrative strands of scripture, he will offer a reading that places the churches in Asia Minor within the drama of that message of divine salvation. As shall be developed further below, Peter summarizes the contours of the scriptural narrative with the two concepts "suffering" and "glory." This basic schema enables him to draw connections between Israel's story, the story of Christ and the story of the church. For now, let us turn to how Christology informs the hermeneutics of 1 Peter.

A Christological Kerygma

One of the most remarkable phrases of this passage is "the spirit of Christ." To what does this refer? What does this contribute to our understanding of Petrine hermeneutics? Two issues stem from this phrase, each dealing with the activities attributed to "the spirit of Christ."[32] Having determined who the prophets are in 1 Pet 1:10, the next item to consider concerns who was

---

30. The difficulties encountered by scholars when interpreting εἰς τίνα ἢ ποῖον καιρόν need not be rehearsed here. The interrogative τίνα can be understood either as a substantival pronoun meaning "what person" or as an adjective modifying καιρόν along with ποῖον meaning "what time or what kind of time." On either reading, the temporal nature of the prophetic activity is present.

31. Schreiner, *1, 2 Peter, Jude*, 74.

32. This phrase occurs outside our passage only in Rom 8:9.

speaking through them. By determining the meaning of the phrase πνεῦμα Χριστοῦ, a clearer picture of Peter's view of scripture will emerge.

The mention of the Holy Spirit in 1:12 provides a clue about the phrase πνεῦμα Χριστοῦ. The adverb νῦν in 1:12 makes a distinction between the time of the prophets and the time of the missionary preachers, but it also accounts for a distinction between the work of the πνεῦμα Χριστοῦ and the πνεῦμα ἅγιον.[33] One possibility is that the distinction concerns the role of the Holy Spirit in the different eras. A different possibility is that a distinction is made between two persons.

Another clue is found immediately following the phrase πνεῦμα Χριστοῦ, where the sufferings of Christ are mentioned. The repeated use of the term Χριστός is significant for clarifying the phrase πνεῦμα Χριστοῦ. The manner in which one phrase is interpreted will have a bearing on how the corresponding phrase ought to be interpreted. If the sufferings are Christ's, then the spirit must also be Christ's. However, many have called for the translation "the sufferings for Christ." In this case, we could speak of the "messianic spirit" and the "messianic sufferings."[34] So, it is necessary first to take a closer look at the phrase τὰ εἰς Χριστὸν παθήματα.

The phrase τὰ εἰς Χριστὸν παθήματα contains an awkward grammatical construction. It is fairly rare to have the prepositional phrase εἰς + noun embedded in an articular construction.[35] In each instance outside our passage the meaning is such that the action of the head noun is directed toward the object of the preposition. In this case, the phrase in 1 Peter 1:11 would be "the sufferings for Christ," which would be understood as the sufferings endured by the elect on behalf of Christ. Within the same passage, however, an equally rare construction occurs which sheds light on this phrase. In 1:10, the same construction occurs but this time governed by the preposition περί.[36] The phrase περὶ τῆς εἰς ὑμᾶς χάριτος can be translated as "concerning the grace that was to be yours" (NRSV; ESV) or "concerning the grace that is coming to you" (NIV; NASB). These parallel constructions—rare in biblical literature—occurring in neighboring verses signify that the best translation of τὰ εἰς Χριστὸν παθήματα is "the sufferings coming to Christ" or "the sufferings that were to be Christ's."[37] Based on these gram-

---

33. Note also that the spirit and Christ are distinct from one another in the epistolary prescript (1:2).

34. At the lexical level, it would be difficult to propose two different meanings for the same term occurring in such close proximity.

35. In the NT, apart from this passage, are Acts 20:21; 26:6; Col 2:5; cf. 2 Macc 11:19; 4 Macc 4:4; 11:12; 12:14.

36. The only other passage in the NT is Acts 24:24; cf. 3 Macc 4:7.

37. Achtemeier (*1 Peter*, 110) comes to the same conclusion based on this parallel.

matical considerations, the best interpretation of πνεῦμα Χριστοῦ is that the pre-incarnate Christ is speaking through the prophets. Further insight into Peter's thoughts about the pre-existent Christ can be found in 1 Pet 1:20. It reads, "He was foreknown before the foundation of the world but was made manifest in the last times for your sake."[38]

Peter's identification of the preexistent Christ as the means of revelation to the prophets is unique. The dominant scriptural viewpoint is that the spirit of the Lord speaks through the prophets.[39] Compared with the rest of the NT, the theological claim made here is unparalleled.[40] In 1 Peter there is now a christological assertion concerning the idea of inspiration.[41] Peter describes the pre-existent spirit of Christ partaking in two interrelated activities. First, the Spirit of Christ manifests the prophetic message of salvation and grace proclaimed by the prophets. Literally, the pre-existent Christ "pre-witnesses" (προμαρτύρομαι) the work of Christ.[42] While the prophets were mediators of divine messages regarding the Christ, it was Christ himself who spoke through them. Second, the Spirit of Christ "pre-witnessed" the two-fold nature of the work of Christ. Peter initiates in 1:11 the motif of the sufferings of Christ and the subsequent glories that percolates throughout the epistle. The coupling of suffering and glory occurs again in 4:13 where the elect rejoice in sharing Christ's suffering and rejoice when his glory is revealed. First Peter ends with this same pattern, "And after you have suffered a little while, the God of all grace, who has called you to his eternal glory in Christ, will himself restore, confirm, strengthen and establish you" (5:10).

The work of Christ establishes a pattern the elect themselves will follow.[43] Schutter thinks it is mistaken "to assume that the personal and col-

---

The translations here have a possessive sense which is foreign to the normal use of the preposition εἰς. It is possible to render these two phrases as expressing advantage ("the grace that is for you") and disadvantage ("the sufferings against Christ" or "the sufferings to be inflicted against Christ").

38. Green (*1 Peter*, 214) also connects 1:11 with 1:20 regarding the pre-existence of Christ.

39. E.g., 1 Sam 10:6; 2 Sam 23:2; Isa 61:1; Ezek 11:5.

40. Esp. Goppelt, *Commentary on I Peter*, 98; Elliott, *1 Peter*, 346.

41. Dietrich Bonhoeffer's statement that "Christus war realiter, nach Fleisch und Verheißung—und David war sein Zeuge" offers an attractive comparison by a modern theologian struggling with the identity of the church in the lead-up to WWII ("König David," 879). When this address to the Finkenwalde students was published, Bonhoeffer revised "realiter" to "wirklich," perhaps to strengthen the sense of actualization (*Junge Kirche* 4 [1936]: 64–69).

42. See Strathmann, "μαρτύρομαι, διαμαρτύρομαι, προμαρτύρομαι," *TDNT* 4:511.

43. This look toward the glory to be revealed raises another significant aspect of Petrine hermeneutics—an eschatological hermeneutic. Although implicit in the

lective frames of reference are somehow fundamentally incompatible with each other."[44] However, the question remains whether in 1:11 the frames of reference are indistinguishable. The exegesis provided here suggests that the motif in 1:11 refers to Christ personally. Christ is both the proclaimer and the proclaimed.[45] Peter sees in Christ the original proclaimer of the gospel message as well as the subject of the gospel message. Christ is the heart of the kerygma of the early church and stands as the hermeneutical assumption in Peter's use of scripture.

The importance of christology within the Petrine hermeneutic cannot be overemphasized. The christological nature of 1 Peter has attracted the attention of numerous scholars.[46] Thus, we may add to the picture of Petrine hermeneutics the texture of christological reflection which bears on how scripture was read. It must be remembered, however, that this cuts in two directions. On the one hand, the advent of Christ reshapes the understanding of scripture for the early church; on the other hand, scripture remains immensely influential with regard to how the early church understood that advent, the events of the cross and the expected revelation of Christ.

The work of Christ is of fundamental importance throughout the epistle. What must be kept in mind, though, is that the author's christology operates most often at a background level. This does not mean that there are not episodes of profound christological reflection. Most importantly, the application of the words "suffering" and "glory" to Christ initiates a narratival sequence in which Christ stands as a centerpiece between the stories of Israel and of the church.

An Ecclesiological Hermeneutic

The church is integral to Peter's reading of scripture. This may be observed in the repeated address to the audience in 1 Pet 1:10–12. There are two statements that deserve closer treatment to draw out the ecclesiological nature of the Petrine hermeneutic. The first statement concerns the role the prophets

---

present section, it is spelled out more clearly in 1:5, 7, 13; 2:12; 3:16; 4:7, 13; 5:4, 10.

44. Schutter, *Hermeneutic*, 107.

45. Here I am consciously evoking Rudolf Bultmann's famous dictum, "Aus dem Verkündiger ist der Verkündigte geworden" (*Theologie des Neuen Testaments*, 35). However, Peter's thesis clearly runs counter to Bultmann's in claiming that Jesus' messianic consciousness was pre-incarnate.

46. Achtemeier, *1 Peter*; "Christology of 1 Peter"; Bechtler, *Following in His Steps*; Davies, "Primitive Christology," 1972; Howe, "Christ, the Building Stone;" "Cross of Christ;" Pearson, *Christological and Rhetorical Properties*; Richard, "Functional Christology;" Tuñi, "Jesus of Nazareth."

play on behalf of the church (1:12a). The prophets received messages from the spirit of Christ and in turn prophesied (προφητεύω) messages of grace (χάρις) and salvation (σωτηρία). Peter claims that they were aware of the fact that their message awaited a time of fuller understanding.[47] The second statement concerns the work of early Christian gospel preachers (1:12b). Whereas the prophets of old were important in providing a message of grace to the church, the contemporary scene is marked by gospel preaching. The importance of this preaching may be seen in the repetition of the ἀγγελ- root in the verbs ἀναγγέλω and εὐαγγελίζω.

This focus on the church and its present situation is part of the Petrine hermeneutic. The address of this gospel proclamation to those in the "diaspora" of Asia Minor highlights the ecclesiological nature of Peter's reading of scripture. Scripture is interpreted not only through a christological lens, but also in such a way that the contemporary church may be addressed by the message of old as told through the preaching of evangelists.

A particular feature of 1 Peter that stands out in light of the ecclesiological nature of the Petrine hermeneutic is the application of scriptural texts to the church. Ecclesiology is frequently an extension of christological reflection. Christology and ecclesiology are interpenetrating categories throughout 1 Peter, as may be seen in several prominent passages.[48] The stone passages of 1 Peter 2:6–8 are anticipated in verses 4 and 5. The unique "living stone" is related to the corporate "living stones." Then, when the stone passages are cited in verses 6–8 relating Christ to the stone laid in Zion (Isa 28:16), the rejected stone (Ps 117[118]:22) and the stone of stumbling (Isa 8:14), they lead to allusions to the church as chosen (Isa 48:20), a royal priesthood and a holy nation (Exod 19:6), a people for possession (Isa 43:21) who proclaim the excellencies (Isa 42:12) of God. The architectural language portrays Christ as the focal point of a new building. The scriptural allusions then describe the people who inhabit that new building. Thus, the same terminology flows back and forth between christology and ecclesiology.

Another passage involving the melding of christology and ecclesiology is found in 1 Pet 2:21. This verse leads into several references to Isaiah 53 in the following verses. Many have commented on the christological reading of the Isaiah 53 passages in 1 Peter 2:22–25, but few devote much attention to the ecclesiological implications of 2:21.[49] The example left by Christ which

47. Achtemeier (1 Peter, 111) notes how the OT prophets were aware of this, listing Num 24:17; Deut 18:15; Hab 2:1–3.

48. The two passages identified here are not the only places where christology and ecclesiology stand together. See also 1 Pet 3:14–15; 3:17 and 4:1.

49. Elliott, to take one example, provides no comment regarding the ecclesiological

the church must follow is one of suffering. The details of these passages will be worked out at a later point.[50]

The ecclesiological nature of 1 Peter provides an added dimension to the Petrine hermeneutical picture. The extent to which the church saw itself as the community of Christ (Χριστιανός; 4:16), the scriptures bearing testimony to Christ also speak to the community surrounding him. As Hays suggests regarding Paul, the primary role of scripture in 1 Peter is to elucidate the church as the community of God's people.[51] Christology is not absent, but it most often functions as the basis of faith—the kerygma—assumed by Peter and his audience. The community does not require an argument that convinces them that the scriptures speak of Christ. They need an argument that scripture speaks to *them* and addresses their situation. Peter addresses their situation by informing his ecclesiology with a scriptural narrative of divine restoration, identifying the church as participants in the drama of redemption through their participation in Christ.

A Theological Interpretation

The theological nature of the letter is already apparent in the prescript where God the Father foreknows the elect, the Spirit sanctifies the elect and Jesus Christ obeys and sprinkles his blood for the elect (1:2).[52] The introductory section of the letter begins with an explication of the relationship between God the Father and Jesus Christ as it bears upon the salvation of the elect (1:3). It is not surprising, then, to find at the closing of the introductory section reference to the work of the Holy Spirit.[53] Whereas Christ inspires the prophets of old with the message of the work of Christ (1:11), the Holy Spirit is active in the promulgation of the gospel message through preachers (1:12).

Peter communicates the advantage the elect have over the prophets of old in light of the advent of Christ and the revelation of the gospel. The elect also have an advantage over the angels. A word play occurs in which several ἀγγελ- cognates appear in 1:12, which has led to this musing about the angels. The upshot is that the work of salvation that has been

---

implications of Peter's reading of Isaiah 53 in this section (*1 Peter*, 522–39, 541). It is likely that the connection between 2:21 and Isaiah 53 has been overlooked due to the hymnic theories that overshadowed this section in the early twentieth century.

50. See chapter 5.
51. Hays, *Echoes*, 86.
52. See Agnew, "1 Peter 1:2," 68–73.
53. See also the further mention of "the Spirit of glory and of God" in 4:14.

communicated to the elect by several means; something in which the angels share no participation. Instead, the elect are shown the advantage they have over the heavenly host in that God has revealed his salvation to humanity. The discussion of angels serves a purpose in the Petrine hermeneutic. Played against the backdrop of Jewish apocalyptic interpretation wherein angels play a more prominent role in divine revelation, Peter's description of revelation involves God directly in the process of revelation.

The picture that 1 Peter 1:10–12 conveys regarding Petrine hermeneutics is multifaceted. The process by which Peter interprets scripture is highly theological. This may be observed throughout the letter in a variety of theological assertions (1:3, 12, 15, 17, 20; 2:3, 15, 21; 3:15, 17, 18, 20, 22; 4:6, 9, 19; 5:2, 10), which reveal all the more the extent to which there is a theological backdrop to 1 Peter. The scriptures stand as the authority by which theological assertions are made and yet the scriptures have already been read by means of theological concepts. The authority of scripture established in 1 Pet 1:10–12 moves forward into the main body of 1 Peter, a letter teeming with scriptural quotations, allusions and echoes.

The hermeneutics of 1 Peter may be described as a complex picture. The appeal to the prophets indicates an appropriation of scripture's authority as the basis for the argument to follow in the epistle. Peter inherits Jewish interpretive practices, but these are extended dynamically to a realization of God's work in Jesus Christ. This christology is largely assumed in 1 Peter and serves in many ways to develop ecclesiology. Scripture is read in such a way that it bears upon the theology and praxis of the church. Because the christological element is in place, the church benefits from its situation in time due to the fact that the promise of scripture has now been announced through the preaching of the gospel of salvation. Rather than explicating his indebtedness to Jewish interpretive practices, 1 Pet 1:10–12 announces the theological categories that will inform the readings of scripture to follow in the letter. Green writes in reference to 1 Pet 1:10–12:

> Peter recognizes the past testimony of the Spirit of Christ in providing a theological pattern by which to construe the meaning of Scripture. This pattern consisted of the *fabula*, or story behind the story, of the *Vindication of the Suffering Righteous*.[54]

The *fabula* to which Green points is the subject of this thesis. The story of restoration is not merely a story that addresses the church, it is a story in which the church participates. It is theologically oriented inasmuch as it

---

54. Green, *1 Peter*, 256. Emphasis original.

recognizes in scripture the outworking of God's redemptive plan through Christ among the people of God.

Returning for the moment to Schutter's consideration of 1 Pet 1:10–12 as the hermeneutical key of 1 Peter, he based his conclusion on three factors: 1) the placement of the passage just prior to the main body of the letter, 2) the use of technical language concerning interpretive activity, and 3) the repeated use of the suffering/glory motif which first appears in this passage. The first of his points remains valid and is one of the primary factors that contributes to the importance of the passage. The second of his points, however, must be questioned. Designating a few terms as technical jargon must be demonstrated from a wider array of literature. Schutter has only drawn attention to a parallel between a few passages. I do not contest that parallels exists between the exegetical strategies employed at Qumran and in the early church. However, the parallels do not sufficiently account for the full picture of Petrine hermeneutics.[55]

What I spell out in this chapter demonstrates that important theological categories must be factored into Petrine hermeneutics. The appeal to scripture in support of theology is the singular contribution made in 1 Pet 1:10–12 and therefore distinguishes it in important ways from the Second Temple interpretive practices it so clearly draws upon. This theologization serves as the hermeneutical key of 1 Peter and is manifested in the scriptural narrative that supports the ecclesiology of the letter.

The suffering/glory motif now deserves special attention. The next section will look more closely at this. Two aspects of this motif will be considered: 1) the role the motif plays in 1 Peter, and 2) the derivation of this motif from scripture. In both, the motif will be shown to be instrumental in the depiction of the scriptural narrative of divine restoration.

---

55. Schutter (*Hermeneutic*, 171) eventually announces "the close connexion between Christology and ecclesiology in the letter" as "an integral part of the way he read the Scriptures." However, he never articulates how Peter is able to find in the scriptures an address to the church. I believe this stems largely from his understanding of Peter's use of scripture as a proof-text (172). Hays (*Conversion of the Imagination*, 38–40) contends that "it is possible to mount a strong argument that Paul is not just randomly proof-texting in his allusions to Isaiah but that Isa 40–55 is fundamentally formative for his understanding of what God is doing in the world through the proclamation of the gospel: God is revealing his eschatological righteousness, ending the exile of his people, and bringing the Gentiles to see and understand." Thus, by identifying the scriptural narrative that informs Peter's ecclesiology, we are able to address this lacuna.

The Suffering/Glories Motif and 1 Peter

Schutter develops three significant points in support of his assessment of 1 Pet 1:10-12 as the hermeneutical key of 1 Peter. First, this passage is situated at the end of the introductory section (1:3-12) and at the beginning of the main body of the letter.[56] Second, he identifies several groups of terms "relating to interpretative activities and mechanisms."[57] Prominent among these terms is the technical language paralleled at Qumran (he sees ἐκζητέω, and [ἐξ]εραυνάω as equivalent to בקש and דרש in 1QS 5.11 which is drawn from Zeph 1:6).[58] Third, he points out the significance of the motif of sufferings and glories repeated throughout the letter which is first expressed in this passage.[59]

From these points and a thorough exegesis of the passage, Schutter concludes that 1 Peter evinces "a peculiarly Jewish hermeneutical tradition which became a major force in the early Church." Beyond this, he points to the suffering/glory motif as "a means for examining OT references outside of the body-opening for points of contact with the author's hermeneutic."[60] This, then, forms the basis of one of the two parts of his methodology. He begins by looking for "a modified text-type."[61] Variants are brought alongside "numerous additional features which were documented for a pesher-like approach to scriptural exposition."[62] The second move of his procedure is the correlation of scriptural references with the suffering/glory motif.[63] These methodological steps confirm, for Schutter, the presence of a pesher-like interpretation of scripture in 1 Peter. However, if 1:10-12 does not utilize technical terminology for interpretive activity, can the suffering/glory motif be used to identify instances of pesher-like interpretation as Schutter sets forth. To be sure, the hermeneutical traditions inherited from Second Temple practices (such as *gĕzērâ šāwâ* and *'al tiqrē'*) are active in 1 Peter. However, 1 Pet 1:10-12 is not bent on articulating a Jewish hermeneutic but a Christian hermeneutic. Furthermore, Moyise counters Schutter's claims about the suffering/glory motif, stating that "none of the cited passages ar-

---

56. Schutter, *Hermeneutic*, 100.

57. Ibid., 101.

58. But see H. Greeven, "ἐκζητέω," *TDNT* 2:894-95; M. Seitz, "ἐραυνάω," *NIDNTT* 3:532-33.

59. Schutter, *Hermeneutic*, 107-8.

60. Ibid., 109.

61. Ibid., 123, 170.

62. Ibid., 170. By this (as well as at 114) he means the thirteen principles outlined in Brownlee, "Biblical Interpretation," 54-76.

63. Ibid., 123.

ticulate a 'suffering followed by glory' theme, either for a future figure or for God's people."[64] Such a claim is not only fatal to Schutter's larger project, it forces us to reconsider the function of the motif and its relationship to the uses of scripture in 1 Peter.

What role, then, does this motif play? Moyise suggests, "It would thus appear that 'sufferings' followed by 'glories' is a general indication of what the author of 1 Peter thought the prophets spoke about, but not a hermeneutical key for interpreting each and every verse."[65] Because this motif recurs in the letter, it is necessary to consider the function of suffering/glory in the thought of 1 Peter. Including 1:11, the combined motif occurs four times (4:13; 5:1, 10). However, there are other significant passages in which one of the terms or cognates (δόξα/δοξάζω and πάθημα/πάθημα) appear. These also must be considered in order to understand how the motif is transformed in 1 Peter.

The motif in 1:11 received some attention above. Two points must be reiterated. The motif represents the content of the prophetic preaching found in scripture concerning the work of Christ. According to Peter, the prophets predicted that Christ would suffer and after that would be glorified. Secondly, this prophetic message concerns Christ at this point in the letter. Several scholars want to place a corporate understanding of the motif here, making the phrase less about the individual sufferings of Christ and his subsequent glories and more about the sufferings experienced by the church on behalf of Christ and their subsequent glories. However, this corporate understanding is not expressed in the context. As will be shown, this motif is transformed from the individual iteration in 1:11 to a corporate iteration in the last half of the letter. This transformation depends upon the participatory ecclesiology to be developed in Peter's argument. The church participates in and through Christ, so that what begins as simple christology is shown to be multivalent; incorporating profound ecclesiological aspects.

The next occurrence of the combined motif is 1 Pet 4:13—"But rejoice insofar as you share Christ's sufferings (παθήμασιν), that you may also rejoice and be glad when his glory (τῆς δόξης αὐτοῦ) is revealed." Here, as in the previous occurrence of the combined motif, the sufferings belong to Christ. Yet, the audience is said to share (κοινωνέω) these sufferings. Unlike in 1:11, it is clear that a corporate aspect has been incorporated into Christ's sufferings. It should be noted, however, that glory is not a shared aspect but belongs to Christ at his revelation. One half of the combined motif has been

---

64. Moyise, *Evoking Scripture*, 93.
65. Ibid., 94.

transformed from a solely christological understanding to a corporate or ecclesiological understanding.

Between these two occurrences of the combined motif, the terminology of suffering and glory has undergone development. The cognate term πάσχω pervades the servant section of the household code (2:18-25) in which Isaiah 53 is drawn upon through several allusions. In this section, household servants are commended for enduring while suffering unjustly while doing good (2:19, 20). The morally righteous suffering servants are recipients of divine grace (χάρις). The example of Christ is presented in 2:21-25 in terms of the suffering servant of Isaiah 53. Christ also suffered (ἔπαθεν, 2:21), and he was a sufferer who was likewise morally righteous (2:22-23) even while suffering (2:23).[66]

The relationship between righteous sufferers and the suffering Christ is expanded in 1 Pet 3:13—4:1. In 3:14, Peter more directly addresses his audience when he writes, "But even if you should suffer (πάσχοιτε) for righteousness' sake, you will be blessed." A requirement that Peter expresses for those who would be followers of Christ is that they uphold a standard of moral righteousness.[67] This idea is reiterated at 3:17, "For it is better to suffer (πάσχειν) for doing good, if that should be God's will, than for doing evil." The suffering of righteous followers of Christ is once again related to the suffering of Christ in 3:18: "For Christ also suffered (ἔπαθεν) once for sins, the righteous for the unrighteous."[68] The connection between the suffering of Christ and the suffering of Christ's followers is again developed in 4:1, "Since therefore Christ suffered in the flesh (παθόντος σαρκί), arm yourselves with the same way of thinking, for whoever has suffered in the flesh (ὁ παθὼν σαρκί) has ceased from sin." The followers of Christ who suffer for doing what is good are united with Christ in thought and deed (they have suffered "in the flesh"—σαρκί) so that they share in holiness with him.

---

66. Note how the same form of the participle (πάσων) is used for the servants in 2:19 and for Christ in 2:23 which emphasizes the connection shared between Christ and the household servants.

67. The phrase doing good (ἀγαθοποιέω and cognates) is one of the unifying themes in the body middle (2:11—4:11) and closing (4:12—5:11).

68. The manuscript tradition for 3:18 is fairly unstable. Most of the best manuscripts for 1 Peter read ἀπέθανεν (P[72], 02, 04, *passim*) here rather than ἔπαθεν (03, 025, 81, *passim*). The UBS committee argued for the reading ἔπαθεν based on internal evidence and the editors of ECM have retained this reading. This issue has a few implications. The lack of clarity regarding the original text entails a measure of caution when interpreting this text. Furthermore, since several of the major uncials carries the reading ἀπέθανεν, many readers of 1 Peter throughout the history of interpretation have not read the text here in the way I propose. These issues, however, do not undermine my reading of this passage since similar ideas are presented at 4:1.

The term glory (δόξα) receives less attention in the span between 1:11 and 4:13. In 1:21, God raises Christ from the dead and gives him glory. This may be contrasted with the term glory appearing in the quotation of Isa 40:6–8 in 1 Pet 1:24–25. Here, all humanity has glory "like the flower of grass" which withers and falls off. So, Christ is shown to be given glory superior to the fleeting glory of humanity. Two additional occurrences of the cognate verb are found at 2:12 and 4:11. In 2:12 the "Gentiles" speak against the elect. However, because of the good conduct of the elect, these revilers "may see your good deeds and glorify God (δοξάσωσιν τὸν θεόν) on the day of visitation." In 4:10–12, the elect are to carry on their work—whether in speech or service—with the result that "in everything God may be glorified (δοξάζηται ὁ θεός) through Jesus Christ." Both of these passages envision God being glorified universally in the eschaton. Here, the "glories" are not shared with followers of Christ but belong to God alone. God is glorified by humanity through Jesus Christ, but at this stage of the letter believers are not included in the concept of glory.

Suffering and glory receive their most intense articulation in the letter in 4:12–19.[69] The combined motif in 4:13 is followed in 4:14 with a repetition of the term δόξα. Drawing from the language of Isa 11:2, where the spirit of God rests upon the branch of Jesse, Peter adds the term δόξα to this allusion to indicate now for the first time in the letter that the elect participate in divine glory. The inclusion of the term δόξα in the Isaianic quotation points to Peter's understanding of the narrative of restoration of divine presence. God's glory now rests upon his people. The ideal of suffering as a morally righteous follower of Christ is again expressed in 4:15–16. Instead of suffering as evildoers, they should suffer as Christians in order that God may be glorified (δοξάζω) in the name of Christ.

The final two instances of the combined motif occur in 1 Peter 5. Peter designates himself in 5:1, "a witness of the sufferings of Christ (τῶν τοῦ Χριστοῦ παθημάτων), as well as a partaker in the glory (δόξα) about to be revealed." Taking up the language of 4:13, where the elect are designated as sharers (κοινωνεῖτε) in Christ's sufferings, Peter designates himself using the imagery applied both to Christ and his audience; linking Peter with his audience in significant ways.[70] Peter applies the combined motif of sufferings and glory to himself. Having demonstrated to his audience that they participate in Christ through the combined motif, he now reveals his own participation in the motif. In 5:9–10, the combined motif appears for the last time in the letter. The sufferings experienced by the addressees are globalized.

---

69. See chapter 6 for more detailed argumentation.
70. See chapter 6.

Followers of Christ experience similar sufferings elsewhere in the world. The motif not only connects the sufferings of the elect with those of Christ, but also to the author of this epistle (5:1) and to the brotherhood of Christians worldwide (5:9). Peter concludes by drawing a distinction between the elements of sufferings and glory. By means of their identity in Christ, the elect are called to eternal glory (ἡ αἰώνια δόξα). This expansive glory is contrasted with sufferings, which last a little while (ὀλίγον). Suffering has been the element of the motif most emphasized throughout the letter and has received the most development in the letter. It is only at the end of the letter that glory is applied directly to the audience (4:14; 5:4, 10). Glory is emphasized as the ultimate inheritance of the suffering servants of Christ.

The language of suffering and glory spans the letter and unites a variety of sections. From this it can be concluded that the suffering/glory motif bears significance for our understanding of the letter. However, the significance assigned to it in our overview of the letter differs from that which Schutter assigned to it. Although scripture is incorporated into the motif at points (e.g., 2:18–25; 4:12–19), this is not the controlling metaphor that unifies the quotations and allusions used in 1 Peter. Instead, the motif of suffering and glory—both as individual concepts and as a combined motif—serves to link the church to a scriptural narrative of the restoration of divine presence through participation in Christ. This brings us back to 1 Pet 1:10–12. The prophetic witness is capsulized in the two concepts of Christ's sufferings and his subsequent glories. This is the narrative of Christ to which the scriptures attest, according to Peter. The church, too, participates in this narrative—suffering followed by glory—through participation in Christ. The next section of this chapter will explore ways in which Isaiah contributes to this scriptural background.

The Suffering/Glories Motif and Isaiah

Having looked at the role of the suffering/glory motif in 1 Peter, the motif was examined in connection with key developments within the argument of 1 Peter. In this section these terms will now be shown to conform to patterns established in the Isaianic program of restoration.

From the opening of Isaiah, the Lord inflicts judgment on Israel and Judah because of sin and rebellion (1:4).[71] The Lord calls his people to cease doing evil and learn to do good (1:16–17). The rebellion of the people is described as injustice or unrighteousness and most often is presented in

---

71. Watts, *Isaiah 1–33*, 10, 17–19; Sweeney, *Isaiah 1–4*, 104–8; idem., *Isaiah 1–39*, 63–65; Childs, *Isaiah*, 12–23; Friesen, *Isaiah*, 29–31.

terms of injustice done to orphans, widows and the poor (e.g., 1:17; 3:14–15; 10:2). The injustice of the leaders contrasts the promised figure who rules "with justice and with righteousness" (9:7).[72] Isaiah's commission in chapter 6 is a focal point of the early portion of the book where he is established as the ideal follower of the Lord.[73] In 8:11–15, the Lord addresses him, telling him "not to walk in the way of this people" (8:11) but to turn his focus on the disciples designated as his children (8:16, 18).[74] So, from the beginning of the Isaianic corpus, we see that the concepts of sin, judgment and restoration are active in ways that correspond with Isaiah 40–66.

One of the major divisions of the book of Isaiah occurs at Isaiah 40.[75] In contrast to the commission at Isaiah 6 where the prophet is told to preach a message that will fall on deaf ears, blind eyes and hearts that will not understand (6:10), a new commission occurs in Isaiah 40 in which a proclamation of comfort is given from the mountaintops with the good news, "Behold your God" (40:9).[76] Thus, Isaiah 40–66 opens with a kerygma concerning the restoration of divine presence.

In Isaiah 40–53 the character of the servant of the Lord is developed.[77] Among the most perplexing issues in Isaianic studies is the identity of the servant. The ability to interpret the servant as Israel is evident as early as Isa 41:8–9.[78] Identification of the singular servant of Isaiah 40–53 with a singular messianic figure has led to the prominent Christian interpretation of the servant as a prediction of Jesus.[79] The clarity with which theologians such as Calvin and Barth saw a direct link between Isaiah 53 and Jesus Christ has recently been explored by Gignilliat. Barth was particularly aware of the historical and hermeneutical questions that make the linkage difficult, but, considered as a matter of revelation, the link is fairly straight forward.[80]

72. Oswalt, *Book of Isaiah*, 1:43; Childs, *Isaiah*, 84–85.

73. Uhlig, *Theme of Hardening*, 71. Bauckham (*God Crucified*, 50–51) identifies an intertextual link between Isa 6:1 and 52:13. The Hebrew version is linked by the verbs רוּם and נָשָׂא whereas the Greek is linked by the verb ὑψόω and δόξα/δοξάζω.

74. Watts, *Isaiah 1–33*, 119–20, 122; Childs, *Isaiah*, 75–76.

75. On the relationship between Isaiah 1–39 and 40–55(66), see the reviews of scholarship in Williamson, *Book Called Isaiah*, 1–18 and "Recent Issues," 21–39. This study will not be able to interact with the important questions relating to the composition history of Isaiah.

76. Brueggemann, *Isaiah 40–66*, 5.

77. On the general background of Isaiah 40–55 on early Christian thought, see Bauckham, *God Crucified*, 47.

78. Smith, *Isaiah 40–66*, 153.

79. Brueggemann, *Introduction to the Old Testament*, 168. See also Childs, *Isaiah*, 422; Hermisson, "Fourth Servant Song," 46.

80. Gignilliat, "Who is Isaiah's Servant?," 125.

Four separate servant songs were identified by Duhm.[81] The four songs—Isa 42:1–9; 49:1–13; 50:4–9; and 52:13—53:12—have generated a significant amount of research which need not be reviewed here.[82] More recently, the unity of Isaiah has been articulated not on the basis of single authorship,[83] but as a result of redaction-critical studies.[84] Within this body of growing literature, thematic links have been explored that resituate the once isolated songs within Isaiah.

Seitz distinguishes two servants in the final form of Isaiah, "The first is Israel and the second is an individual."[85] For him, Isaiah 40–48 presents Israel as the servant and an individual servant emerges in Isaiah 49. Decisive for Seitz is the presentation of a first-person voice in Isaiah 49, which first emerges in Isa 48:16.[86] This anonymous individual will serve the Lord through righteous suffering and death.[87]

Wilcox and Paton-Williams concur that a shift occurs at Isaiah 49. They characterize the message of Isaiah 40–48 as placed upon Cyrus, who overthrows Babylon; but then the message shifts in Isaiah 49 to the returning exiles.[88] They propose that the characterization of the servant shifts at the same time the message of the text shifts. Like Seitz, the servant in Isaiah 40–48 is identified as Israel.[89] However, they identify the servant after Isaiah 49 as the prophet whose oracles stand behind Deutero-Isaiah.[90]

More recently, Berges has similarly argued that the servant songs be read within the broader context of Isaiah 40–55.[91] But unlike Seitz and

---

81. Duhm, *Das Buch Jesaja*.

82. See North, *Isaiah 40–55*; Wilcox and Paton-Williams, "Servant Songs"; Melugin, *Formation of Isaiah 40–55*; Reventlow, "Basic Issues," among others.

83. In support of single authorship, see Young, *Book of Isaiah*, 1:8; Oswalt, *Book of Isaiah*, 1:25.

84. For instance, Clements, "Unity of the Book of Isaiah;" Vermeylen, ed., *Book of Isaiah*; Williamson, *Book Called Isaiah*. To these may be added canon-critical studies, who largely accept the compositional history adduced by redaction critics, but find the unity of Isaiah as something "the received tradition designated as the prophecy of Isaiah" (Childs, *Isaiah*, 3; see also Seitz, *Isaiah 1–39*, 4).

85. Seitz, "'You are my Servant,'" 123.

86. Ibid., 127; see also Seitz, "Prophet Isaiah Present," 233; Berges, "Literary Construction," 34.

87. Ibid., 130–31.

88. Wilcox and Paton-Williams, "Servant Songs i," 81. Compare this with the observation by Gignilliat (*Paul and Isaiah's Servants*, 132–33) that the servant passes "from active agent (42:1–4; 49:1–6) to passive agent (50:4–6; 52:13—53:12)."

89. Ibid., 98–99.

90. Ibid., 99. See also Childs, *Isaiah*, 385.

91. Berges, "Literary Construction," 32.

Wilcox & Paton Williams, the servant is actually "the group of authors and composers of the second half of the book."[92] By placing the composition of Deutero-Isaiah in the post-exilic era, Berges is able to posit that the "theological problems of post-exilic times are encapsulated in a concrete literary figure."[93] Thus, the singular servant stands neither for collective Israel, nor for an anonymous individual, but for a small group that "saw themselves in line with the disciples of Isaiah ben Amoz."[94]

To summarize, Isaiah 40–48 presents the servant as Israel. The chosen servant of the Lord (41:8–9) will bring justice to the nations (42:1). However, this servant is said to be blind in 42:19, with language reminiscent of Isaiah's commission in 6:10.[95] The salvation of Israel and the nations is portrayed as a reversal of this blindness (43:1–13).[96] The redemption of Israel is reiterated in the following chapters with frequent repetitions of Israel's designation as "my servant" (44:1–2, 21; 45:4; 48:20).[97] Something new happens in Isaiah 49 in a conversation between the Lord and the servant.[98] An autobiographical tone can be heard in the servant's reply to the Lord, "But I said, 'I have labored in vain; I have spent my strength for nothing and vanity; yet surely my right is with the Lord, and my recompense with my God." Because this servant brings back Jacob and gathers Israel (49:5), the servant here differs from earlier uses of "my servant" as a designation for Israel.[99] This servant takes on the name of Israel in order that he may fulfill the work Israel was called to do but failed to do.[100] Now Israel must obey the voice of the servant (50:10).[101] In Isaiah 53 the severity of the action taken by the servant is fully

---

92. Ibid., 35.

93. Ibid., 36.

94. Ibid., 34.

95. Watts, *Isaiah 34–66*, 131; see also Brueggemann, *Isaiah 40–66*, 49–50.

96. Ibid., 133.

97. Brueggemann (*Isaiah 40–66*, 76) points to larger purposes beyond merely the redemption of Israel. Regarding Isa 45:4, he writes that one of the purposes is "that all the world, beyond Persia and beyond Israel, may acknowledge Yahweh as the creator and only ruler of the world." Another purpose is drawn out of Isa 48:20. "The ground of affirmation for the exiles is not found in Yahweh's love for Israel. It is found, rather, in Yahweh's self-regard" (108).

98. Watts, *Isaiah 1–33*, l–li; Goldingay, *Message of Isaiah 40–55*, 365; Smith, *Isaiah 40–66*, 336–39; Friesen, *Isaiah*, 304, among others.

99. Gignilliat, *Paul and Isaiah's Servants*, 73–74.

100. Goldingay, *Message of Isaiah 40–55*, 369: "Yhwh now declares that the prophet is the one who will fulfill Israel's vocation." Alternatively, Melugin (*Formation of Isaiah 40–55*, 71) considers the change in tone to stem from a contrast between Israel's past failures and the future plan for Israel promised by the Lord.

101. The identity of the servant as individual and as Israel cannot be easily

disclosed.[102] In his afflictions he bears humiliation, affliction and perhaps even death (53:12). Through the righteousness of the servant, the many will be accounted righteous (53:11). Here, Gignilliat's insight is foundational for understanding the key role the servant plays in the redemptive narrative of Isaiah 40–66, "For in Isaiah the crucial aspect of the Servant's work was not in his bringing Israel back from exile per se but in his atoning work on behalf of a people steeped in sin and rebellion."[103] This is the last we hear of the servant and the last time the term is used in the singular through the remainder of the book. Yet, already in Isa 53:10 there is a hint of things to come when it says that "he shall see his offspring."

One thing made clear by these recent studies is that there is no consensus regarding the identity of the servant, particularly in Isaiah 49–53. Yet, the recent shift toward reading Isaiah in a unified way has provided a means of listening again to the voices of those who read Isaiah prior to the Enlightenment.[104] For someone like Peter, the identity of the servant was easily equated with Jesus.[105] But in Peter's reading of Isaiah, evidenced through his use of Isaianic texts, the identity of Jesus as the servant (e.g., 1 Pet 2:22–25) is not something proved, but something assumed. The language of imitation in 2:21 demands a deeper exploration into the ways Peter found Isaiah addressing the concerns of the church.

In Isaiah 54–66 the language turns to the plural "servants."[106] The redemption of God's people is presented in the song of the barren one who will bear offspring that "will possess the nations" (54:3). The covenant of peace is likened to the covenant with Noah (54:9).[107] Those afflicted in exile are promised righteous children who will experience peace. Isaiah 54 ends by declaring, "This is the heritage of the servants of the Lord and their vin-

---

reconciled, though. See Childs, *Isaiah*, 385.

102. The literature on Isaiah 53 is immense and it would be impossible to do justice to the many lines of inquiry that have been generated. More will be explored later in the thesis as it bears upon the use of Isaiah 53 in 1 Peter 2:22–25. Helpfully, a classified bibliography on Isaiah 53 has been produced by Hüllstrung, Feine and Bailey in Janowski and Stuhlmacher, *Suffering Servant*, 462–92.

103. Gignilliat, *Paul and Isaiah's Servants*, 102.

104. Seitz, "Prophet Isaiah Present," 219–20. This is not to say that questions of authenticity and compositional history are unimportant. Rather, these are not the questions that were being asked in the first century.

105. Hofius, "Fourth Servant Song," 185–88.

106. This is not to argue for a division here; merely an observation regarding a shift in language. Seitz is one of the few who suggest a division here ("Isaiah 40–66," 471–74). More common is a division at Isaiah 56; see also Williamson, *Book Called Isaiah*, 19–21; Brueggemann, *Isaiah 40–66*, 164–67; Smith, *Isaiah 40–66*, 516.

107. See Childs, *Isaiah*, 429, 434; Goldingay, *Message of Isaiah 40–55*, 533–35.

dication from me, declares the Lord" (54:17b).¹⁰⁸ Like the suffering servant of Isaiah 53, the servants share in afflictions (54:11). At a later point, the servants appeal to God for compassion and deliverance from adversaries (63:15–19). In the closing chapter of Isaiah, the servants receive their inheritance and vindication from their enemies (65:8–9, 13–16; 66:12–14).¹⁰⁹

At the conclusion of Isaiah the word "glory" (כָּבוֹד; δόξα) is repeated several times (66:11, 12, 18, 19).¹¹⁰ This term occurs frequently in Isaiah.¹¹¹ It is part of the song of the seraphim who call out, "Holy, holy, holy is the Lord of hosts; the whole earth is full of his glory!" (6:3). It is also part of the new commission of Isaiah 40 where it is promised that "the glory of the Lord shall be revealed, and all flesh shall see it together" (40:5). With regard to the servant, the Lord tells him, "You are my servant, Israel, in whom I will be glorified" (49:3).¹¹² Melugin states that it is an important part of "the servant's mission to glorify Yahweh."¹¹³ At 53:3, it is said of the suffering servant that he has no glory or majesty.¹¹⁴ When the servant takes upon himself the judgment of the people, he is also separated from the promised glory. The plural servants appeal to the Lord's glory (63:15) when they ask for mercy and vindication from their enemies (63:15–19). And in the final chapter the Lord reveals his hand to his servants (66:14) and fulfills the

---

108. The Hebrew text uses עֶבֶד consistently in Isaiah 40–66 for both the individual servant of 40–53 and the plural servants of 54–66. The Greek version uses παῖς almost exclusively (with the exception of 42:19; 48:20; 49:3, 5, 7 and 53:11 which use δοῦλος) for the singular servant and δοῦλοι almost exclusively for the plural servants (54:17 and 66:14 being the only exceptions). This could potentially undermine the ability of readers in Greek to pick up on the lexical relationship between the servant and the servants. Revisors of the Greek text tend to replace παῖς with δοῦλος, although not systematically (see 41:8–9; 42:1, 19; 49:6). The rendering of servants as θεραπεύοντες in 54:17 is altered to δοῦλοι by Aquila, Symmachus and Theodotion. It seems that the revisers were aware of the connection between the singular servant and the plural servants by translating עבד more consistently with δοῦλος.

109. Beuken ("Main Theme," 67) states that Deutero-Isaiah speaks only of a singular servant and Trito-Isaiah speaks only of plural servants. Yet he qualifies this with two further observations. First, the initial mention of plural servants comes in 54:17, "precisely *before* the end of DI" (emphasis original). And second, Isa 53:10 promises that the servant will "see offspring." These facts lead him to postulate that Trito-Isaiah is centrally concerned with questions

110. The Hebrew also has frequently תִּפְאֶרֶת, הָדָר, and צְבִי, each of which may be rendered "glory" and are usually translated with δόξα. Note the absence of כָּבוֹד from Isaiah 49–57. See Kittel, "δόξα," *TDNT* 2:242–44; S. Aalen, "δόξα," *NIDNTT* 2:44–52.

111. Brockington, "Greek Translator of Isaiah," 23–32.

112. The Hebrew has the verb אֶתְפָּאָר, meaning "to glorify oneself," and is translated in the Greek version with δοξάζω.

113. Melugin, *Formation of Isaiah 40–55*, 146.

114. Here δόξα translates הָדָר.

promise to make his glory known (66:18-19). Thus, Isaiah 54–66 clearly presents a corporate picture of righteous sufferers who are caught up in the narrative of divine restoration.

From this overview two salient points may be drawn out. First, although the terms used for suffering in 1 Peter (πάσχω, πάθημα) are not used in Greek Isaiah, it sufficiently summarizes the work of the servant in Isaiah 53.[115] Where the concept of suffering is most developed in 1 Peter, several allusions to Isaiah 53 appear within the servant section of the household code. The concept of suffering encompasses more than simply the individual servant in Isaiah. Because the servants of Isaiah 54 are addressed as those afflicted, they are linked to the suffering servant who was afflicted (53:4, 7).[116] Cast in the role of disciples of the suffering servant, the servants of Isaiah 54–66 are the offspring of the singular servant.[117] This indicates that the concept of suffering extends beyond Isaiah 53 to include the sufferings of the community formed around the singular servant; something emphasized in Isaiah 54 and 63. As those who carry out the singular servant's ministry, the plural servants suffer in righteousness as they hope for the realization of God's final act of vindication and restoration.[118] These roles (singular servant and plural servants) are newly assigned within 1 Peter. Christ is depicted as the singular servant who bears the sins of his people (1 Pet 2:22–25), while the church is cast as his disciple servants who participate in the sufferings of Christ in the midst of the inauguration of the restoration of divine presence among the people of God.

Second, the concept of glory is promised in Isa 40:5. The singular servant, although experiencing suffering, is also called exalted (52:13).[119] The plural servants, as disciples of the singular servant, experience the promise of the Lord's revealed glory in Isaiah 66.[120] The culmination of God's

---

115. See Michaelis, "πάσχω," *TDNT* 5:907-8.

116. Childs, *Isaiah*, 430-31; Gignilliat, *Paul and Isaiah's Servants*, 130-31.

117. Blenkinsopp ("Servant and the Servants," 172) concludes that the relationship between the servant and the servants is one of master teacher and disciples. Oswalt suggests that the singular servant of 49–55 purchases righteousness for his people, whereas the plural servants in 54:17 "are the beneficiaries of what he has done" (*Book of Isaiah*, 432). Uhlig (*Theme of Hardening*, 82-83) argues that hardening and reversal for the audience comes "when they listen to the voice of the servant" and "enacts their restoration as the 'servants of the Lord.'" Childs (*Isaiah*, 430) says of the servants that "they are the bearers of the true faith in the next generation."

118. Gignilliat, *Paul and Isaiah's Servants*, 131.

119. See Bauckham, *God Crucified*, 51.

120. Watts, *Isaiah 34–66*, 364.

dramatic restoration results in the vindication and the reward of the servants who have suffered faithfully in righteousness.[121]

While there are other concepts and motifs used in Isaiah, the motif of suffering and glory serves as a sufficient summarization of significant literary elements in Isaiah 40–66. Beyond simply quoting material from Isaiah which uses the suffering/glory motif, it appears that Peter has adopted a strategy that draws upon a narrative of restoration at work among a people who experience righteous suffering as they faithfully hope in the Lord. The suffering/glory motif is first applied to Christ as a singular figure in 1 Pet 1:11 and is transformed over the course of four chapters so that church is also shown to participate in the suffering/glory motif.

In light of these things, I propose that the suffering/glory motif as used in 1 Peter is consistent with usage in Isaiah and captures certain features of the book that support the ecclesiological argumentation of 1 Peter in which frequent recourse is made to scripture. Rather than quoting passages that employ the terms suffering and/or glory, Isaianic passages are drawn from key portions of Isaiah that anchor Peter's argument to an Isaianic narrative of divine restoration. The good news of new birth through the living and abiding word of God (1 Pet 1:22–25) is supported with a passage from Isa 40:6–8. In 1 Pet 2:4–10, the relationship between the singular living stone and the plural living stones is constructed upon passages from Isa 8:14; 28:16 and 43:20–21. In 1 Pet 2:21, the example of the suffering Christ is given "so that you might follow in his steps" and is supported with passages from Isaiah 53. In 1 Pet 4:12–19 where the combined motif receives its fullest development, the phrase "the spirit of glory and of God rests upon you" echoes Isa 11:2. These Isaianic texts point to a unifying narrative that identifies the church as participating in God's eschatological act of restoration.

Isaianic Narrative in 1 Peter

This chapter has focused on whether 1 Pet 1:10–12 is the hermeneutical key to the epistle, and, if so, how it functions as a hermeneutical key. The way 1 Pet 1:10–12 functions as a hermeneutical key is to establish the theological orientation of how Peter reads scripture. His theology assumes that Christ is central in the thought of prophetic scripture and in the work of the gospel. Yet, the focus is not solely on Christ as the fulfillment of scripture since Peter finds in scripture a means to express the nature and purpose of the church. Since the church is in Christ, a pattern is established whereby what is true of Christ is also true of the church.

---

121. Gignilliat, *Paul and Isaiah's Servants*, 125.

Previous scholarship has argued that this passage uses technical language to express a particularly Jewish hermeneutic similar to that found at Qumran. I contend that the language employed is not technical language since a limited number of other sources contain this language and do not appear to employ it in any technical sense. All the same, there are affinities with the exegetical practice used at Qumran. The use of key-word connections between scriptural texts exemplifies this.[122] But this is not the point of 1 Pet 1:10–12, it is something that functions in the background of the letter. Instead, Peter argues for his particularly Christian exegesis of scripture.

The role of the suffering/glory motif first expressed in 1 Pet 1:11 received extended consideration in light of previous scholarly assumptions that it unifies the scriptural texts employed in 1 Peter. The motif articulated in 1 Pet 1:10–12 centers on the work of Christ, and later the church is identified as participating in the motif as well (4:14; 5:10). To be sure, the terms suffering and glory carry great importance within 1 Peter. Moyise's critique centers on identifying these terms with a theme that connects each individual use of scripture.[123] He is correct insofar as he articulates his understanding of the term "theme." If suffering follow by glory is a theme that must be located within each use of scripture, then there are a good many passages that do not touch upon this theme. But it seems that the terms suffering and glory are not a theme that resides at the level of individual passages, but that they express something of an overarching narrative. As a story, the ideas of conflict (suffering) and resolution (glory) can be a powerful consolation. When the people of God suffer in their particular circumstances, such a story points to a divine plan that redeems suffering and culminates in future blessing. Our review of Isaiah points to how a particular voice within scripture develops the story. The term suffering summarizes the work of the servant in Isaiah 49:1–7 and 53 and the plight of the servants in Isaiah 54:11–17 and 63:15–19. The term glory is used frequently throughout Isaiah and at key points in the structure of Isaiah (i.e., 6:3; 40:5; 66:11, 12, 18, 19). The plight of the servants who follow the singular suffering servant find themselves recipients of the promised revelation of divine glory (Isa 40:5; 66:18–19). As will be seen in the following chapters, Isaiah is not the only voice that contributes to this narrative. And in the context of 1 Peter, this scriptural narrative provides a key for understanding how scripture may directly address the needs of the church.

To this point, I have indicated how the ecclesiology of 1 Peter draws upon an Isaianic narrative. It is therefore necessary to develop here what is

---

122. On the use of key terms in Jewish exegetical practice, see chapter 1.
123. Moyise, *Evoking Scripture*, 93–94.

meant by a narrative and what bearing this has on the present thesis. As has been the case at many points of introduction thus far, it is important to draw upon Pauline discussions to open up resources for the study of Peter.

In his retrospective of narrative approaches to Paul, Longenecker states that "his letters do not simply offer independent snippets of 'truth' or isolated gems of logic, but are discursive exercises that explicate a narrative about God's saving involvement in the world."[124] Thus, narrative approaches to the Pauline epistles have sought to identify the constituent stories that undergird his writing. The term "stories" itself indicates how the task of narrative studies of Paul can produce varied results, since different stories might inform Paul's exposition at different points, or even within a singular point.[125] Consistently, though, scholars have identified a number of dominant stories underlying Paul's theology. Dunn, summarizing the work of Hays, Wright and Witherington, lists four such stories: "(1) the story of the world gone wrong, (2) the story of Israel, (3) the story of Christ, and (4) the story of Christians, including Paul himself."[126] It is not necessary to expound on these stories at this point in order for us to gain an appreciation for how this line of inquiry can benefit the present project.[127]

First, the way in which these stories build on one another points in the direction of formative narratives that generate meaning for subsequent generations. This is true in the sense that beliefs are grounded in foundational narratives.[128] For instance, the belief that the blameless Christ suffered for the sins of others is clearly grounded in the Isaianic narrative of the suffering servant in 1 Pet 2:22–25. But the significance of these stories as generative of meaning is also carried in the sense that they have an organic quality, enabling later generations to interpret their own experiences in light of previous stories. In Longenecker's analysis of the story of Israel in Romans, he notes that "the relationship [of gentile Christians to Israel's ongoing history] is occasionally depicted as organic, with the stories of Christ and of

---

124. Longenecker, "Narrative Interest," 4.

125. Ibid., 10. Longenecker uses the term "internarrational" to describe this "variety of distinct stories."

126. Dunn, *Theology of Paul*, 18 n. 52. See also Hays, *Faith of Jesus Christ*, 5–6; Wright, *New Testament and the People of God*, 407; Witherington, *Paul's Narrative*, 5; Longenecker, "Narrative Interest," 11–13.

127. A helpful summary of narratological studies may be found in Joseph, *Narratological Reading*, 30–40. His study is particularly helpful in that it draws the discussion of narratological analysis of epistolary literature, mainly focused on Pauline epistles, into the study of 1 Peter.

128. Wright, *New Testament*, 38.

Christians as emerging naturally from within the ongoing story of Israel."[129] This organic participation of gentile Christians in the story of God's salvation of Israel is integral to the contours of Paul's theology. In much the same way, 1 Peter will be explored in light of narrival elements that are important within its theology.

In order to better appreciate the potential of a narrative approach for 1 Peter, it is necessary now to consider the issue of methodology. The basic approach has been outlined by Hays in his *The Faith of Jesus Christ* (1983). There he proposes a line of inquiry involving two phases: "we may first identify within the discourse allusions to the story and seek to discern its general outlines; then, in a second phase of inquiry we may ask how this story shapes the logic of argumentation in the discourse."[130] This method is based primarily on three premises:

1. There can be an organic relationship between stories and reflective discourse because stories have an inherent configurational dimension (*dianoia*) which not only permits but also demands restatement and interpretation in non-narrative language.

2. The reflective restatement does not simply repeat the plot (*mythos*) of the story; nonetheless, the story shapes and constrains the reflective process because the *dianoia* can never be entirely abstracted from the story in which it is manifested and apprehended.

3. Hence, when we encounter this type of reflective discourse, it is legitimate and possible to inquire about the story in which it is rooted.[131]

In a similar vein, Joseph recently drew upon the methodology of Mieke Bal in his investigation of the use of scripture in 1 Peter. Bal's theory takes a three-layered approach that differentiates between text, story and *fabula*.[132] In Bal's categorization, *fabula* consists in a set of elements or events that become arranged within a story.[133] The text—in our case a non-narrative epistle—is shaped by a narrator who embeds particular events which draw upon an underlying story.[134] Joseph applies Bal's theory by enumerating four elements of the *fabula* present in 1 Peter: election, suffering, steadfast-

---

129. Longenecker, "Spiritual Blessings," 74.
130. Hays, *Faith of Jesus Christ*, 29.
131. Ibid., 28.
132. Bal, *Narratology*, 5.
133. Ibid., 78–79.
134. Joseph, *Narratological Reading*, 44–47.

ness and vindication.[135] Although Joseph gains new methodological sophistication in his narratological analysis, the elements he identifies are in some ways too generic, which means that the base story underlying 1 Peter becomes an all-encompassing narrative about Israel. What remains to be seen is whether a narrower focus on an Isaianic narrative can clarify further the reflective discourse contained in 1 Peter and the stories underlying it.

Already we have noted how elements of 1 Peter assume a narrative that aligns well with Isaiah. The preponderance of quotations and allusions to Isaiah points in this direction. But the thematic links, particularly with the servant-servants motif and the suffering/glory motif, provide sufficient warrant to engage in an inquiry of how the Isaianic narrative of restoration shapes the logic of 1 Peter.

The story of Israel in 1 Peter has a distinctively Isaianic quality. The proclamation of good news (Isa 40), the suffering servant (Isa 49, 53) and the disciples of the suffering servant (Isa 54, 63, 66), and the ultimate vindication of God's people in a decisive act of diving deliverance (Isa 65–66) outlines the general contours of the Isaianic narrative. It is important to note, though, that passages from outside Isaiah resonate with this Isaianic narrative, particularly Psalms 33[34] and 117[118].

This outline of an Isaianic story of restoration can be mapped out within 1 Peter. There are three movements corresponding to the three major divisions of the body of the letter. First, the proclamation of God's renewed presence among his people occurs in the body opening (1 Pet 1:13—2:10). The contours of this proclamation draw upon the resources of Isaiah 40, whereby the word of God is equated with the gospel (1 Pet 1:25), and a tapestry of quotations and allusions in 1 Pet 2:4–10 which depict a renewed temple service. Second, the call of the churches in Asia Minor to a high moral standard based on the pattern of Christ even in the face of suffering extends across the body middle (2:11—4:11) and into the body closing (4:12—5:10). Prominent in this section of 1 Peter are quotations of Isaiah 53 and Psalm 33[34], among other quotations and allusions. Finally, the body closing extends into the ultimate vindication of God's people in the final judgment. Central to this part of the letter is an allusion to Isa 11:2, placing the churches of Asia Minor in the midst of God's final plan for his people. There it is asked, "What will the end be for those who disbelieve the gospel of God?" This reiteration of the gospel of God correlates with the connection between Isaiah 40 and the proclamation of the gospel in 1 Pet 1:25, creating an arc to the three-movement structure. It is noteworthy that

---

135. Ibid., 50.

the first mention of gospel proclamation (εὐαγγελίζω) occurs in 1:10–12, thus rounding out our understanding of this passage as a hermeneutical key.

This connection between scriptural narrative and the good news of the gospel speaks to the role 1:10–12 plays within an understanding of Petrine hermeneutics.[136] The expression in 1:10–12 emphasizes "the immediacy of the text's word to the community rather than providing specific rules for reading."[137] Therefore the great lengths Schutter goes to demonstrate the pesher-like method produces results that are in actuality ancillary to the primary concerns of Peter's hermeneutics.[138] The story of restoration that undergirds Peter's gospel proclamation makes it natural to view Isaiah as a "hermeneutical center of gravity" within the letter, corresponding significantly with Hays' findings for Paul.[139] In this way, the good news of the gospel is really an extension of the scriptural narrative and addresses directly the people who have believed that gospel proclamation.

Having now established the hermeneutical principles at work in 1 Peter, it is now time to turn to the detailed analysis of each quotation as they occur in 1 Peter.

---

136. Here, I follow the reasoning of Hays, *Echoes*, 160–64, which I think augments his more strident position in Hays *Faith of Jesus Christ*, 63–64.

137. Hays, *Echoes*, 160.

138. See ibid., 161.

139. Ibid., 162–64.

3

The Use of Scripture in 1 Peter 1:13—2:10

Introduction

THE BODY OPENING OF 1 Peter contains a verbal *inclusio* centered on the term ἅγιος. There are numerous other verbal connections with 1:13—2:10, but this linkage is particularly relevant to the study of scripture in 1 Peter because the term ἅγιος is derived in each instance from passages quoted or alluded to from the Pentateuch. In 1 Pet 1:15–16, the term ἅγιος is employed four times to compel the audience to holy conduct based on the holiness formula of Leviticus. The holiness of the Lord demands the holiness of his people. There are two additional uses of ἅγιος in 2:5 and 9. Both of these occurrences describe the church in terms of their nature as a holy people with language drawn from Exod 19:6. This *inclusio*, then, is not simply based on the repetition of a key term, but is based in scriptural texts that undergird the first main section of the epistle. Together, these scriptural texts not only frame this section of the letter, but develop the theme of God's covenant with his people.

Several iterations of Isaianic material with varying levels of explicitness are contained in 1 Pet 1:13—2:10. The Isaianic voice intersects with the traditions drawn from other scriptural texts, such as the Pentateuch, which play off of each other throughout the section. How has the Pentateuch shaped Peter's understanding of Isaiah and *vice versa*? And how does the reading of texts intertextually generate meaning when it is employed in the new rhetorical context of 1 Peter? These questions must be answered, however, after other work has been accomplished. Scriptural quotations and allusions must be set within their rhetorical context and the text of each will be considered with a view to determining the *Vorlage* used by Peter,

The Use of Scripture in 1 Peter 1:13—2:10 77

providing insights into how the text is handled. Along with this, a consideration of the wider context from which the scriptural passages are drawn will help us understand what the fuller passage brings to the argument of 1 Peter.

Levitical Holiness and Isaianic Lamb: 1 Peter 1:13–21

The body opening of the letter (1:13—2:10) contains an exhortation to hope (ἐλπίσατε, 1:13). The initial passage of the first section (1:13–21) uses the familial language of "children" and "Father" to describe the relationship between the elect and God. The argument here centers on the conduct of the elect (1:15, 17, 18). While they remain in their former familial context (1:18), they must now conform to a conduct that corresponds to their new familial context—they now relate to God as Father on the basis of Christ Jesus.[1] The phrase "through him" (δι' αὐτοῦ) initiates a reflection on the participation of the church in Christ that flowers in the body middle of the epistle.

Intermingled in this argument are quotations and allusions from Leviticus and Isaiah. Peter constructs an argument using scripture that connects the work of God in Christ to the conduct of the elect who dwell in the midst of those who do not believe. In 1:13, Peter calls on the elect to place their hope in the revelation of Christ using language reminiscent of the opening blessing section. But this hope does not entail that they neglect their responsibility to live honorably in the present. As children obedient to a holy God, their lives are to be marked by holy conduct in every way (1:15). The concept of conduct (ἀναστροφῇ) is grounded in the scriptures, as we shall see.

Imitation of Divine Holiness (1:16)

The quotation in 1 Pet 1:16 is peculiar because no single verse can be identified as the source. Instead, the phrase occurs five times throughout the book of Leviticus making this a programmatic summarization of the holiness required by God for his people.[2] The selection of this phrase is an apt condensation of Leviticus. However, it complicates our ability to identify

---

1. This does not require an understanding of the audience as either particularly Jewish or pagan. See chapter 1.

2. Gerstenberger (*Leviticus*, 282) demonstrates how the sanctification formula directly connects to the holiness theme that governs the book of Leviticus. See Elliott, *1 Peter*, 361.

a precise context from which Peter has drawn his scriptural phraseology.³ While there are elements of Leviticus that might be more easily related to 1 Peter (for instance, the care for strangers because of their sojourn in Egypt in Lev 19:34 might be compelling) it seems that the use of this stock phrase gives a sense of the Levitical holiness code and is not beholden to any specific context.⁴

Table 3.1: **1 Peter 1:16 and the Levitical Holiness Formula**

1 Peter 1:16	Leviticus 11:44, 45; 19:2; 20:7, 26
διότι γέγραπται ἅγιοι ἔσεσθε ὅτι ἐγὼ ἅγιος	ἅγιοι ἔσεσθε ὅτι ἅγιός εἰμι ἐγὼ κύριος ὁ θεὸς ὑμῖν ἔσεσθε ἅγιοι ὅτι ἅγιός εἰμι ἐγὼ κύριος ἅγιοι ἔσεσθε ὅτι ἐγὼ ἅγιος κύριος ὁ θεὸς ὑμῖν ἔσεσθε ἅγιοι ὅτι ἅγιος ἐγὼ κύριος ὁ θεὸς ὑμῖν ἔσεσθέ μοι ἅγιοι ὅτι ἐγὼ ἅγιος κύριος ὁ θεὸς ὑμῖν

Two ideas swarm around the Levitical holiness formula, which become further developed later in 1 Peter. First, the relationship between the elect and God capitalizes on the alternating of singular and plural forms of

---

3. It is surprising, therefore, to find Schutter (*Hermeneutic*, 36–37 n. 63) insist on a correspondence with Lev 19:2 against other passages. This becomes problematic when he suggests the literary influence of Lev 19:2 in the body opening of 1 Peter (ibid., 95–98). Jobes (*1 Peter*, 113–15) recognizes the more general contribution made by Leviticus. She writes, "By quoting from Leviticus, Peter establishes the principle that the holiness to which the Christian is called in Christ is consistent with God's character as revealed in the ancient covenant with Israel" (ibid., 113). On this, see also Schreiner, *1, 2 Peter, Jude*, 80; Feldmeier, *First Letter of Peter*, 106–7.

4. The command to holiness unifies at least Lev 17–27 (Milgrom, *Leviticus*, 121; Gerstenberger, *Leviticus*, 18). The repetition of the holiness formula argues for unity at the redactional level regardless of the compositional history. More narrowly, the holiness formula connects most directly to the moral laws. Balentine (*Leviticus*, 8–9) states that the command to holiness makes it so that no one "may leave any aspect of life unexamined." See Wenham *Leviticus*, 22–23.

the term ἅγιος.⁵ Milgrom describes the formula in terms of *imitatio Dei*.⁶ The imitative dimension of the formula fits well with the imitative language of 1 Pet 2:21, where Christ—depicted in the language of Isaiah 53—is established as an example for the church. Second, the formulaic language that anticipates the quotation in 1 Pet 1:15 and its application in 1:17 focuses on the conduct of the elect.⁷ They are to conduct themselves (ἀναστράφητε) with reverence (ἐν φόβῳ) toward God. The language of fear or respect, using the φόβος word group, returns later drawing together several scriptural texts in 1 Peter 3.

This being the first explicit quotation of scripture in the letter, a number of observations may be raised here. The introductory formula (διότι γέγραπται), though unique to this passage, is not unexpected and is consistent with Second Temple interpretive practices.⁸ Such formulaic expressions draw attention to the quotation of scripture. Observe, though, that such formulae are limited to the first few quotations (1:16, 24; 2:6). After this, Peter all but abandons introductory formulae.

Additionally, the quotation is preceded (1:15) by an explanatory gloss.⁹ The vocabulary of Peter's gloss matches that of his scriptural quotation, particularly the repetition of the singular ἅγιος and the plural ἅγιοι. Here, Peter explains how his audience has been called by a holy God and, therefore, their conduct must also be holy. Green writes of "the essential human vocation to imitate God" which in this passage correlates the holiness of God with the conduct of believers in Asia Minor.¹⁰

Furthermore, the context utilizes the imagery of the family, picturing God as father and the elect as children.¹¹ As such, the direct relationship between God and the church is brought forward. This does not mitigate the

---

5. Feldmeier (*First Letter of Peter*, 106) points out that holiness describes God himself, but also "can be communicated to place (for example the temple), but also to people who belong to God." The plural ἅγιοι, in its correspondence with the singular ἅγιος, indicates the communicability of this attribute. In 1 Pet 2:4–5, the singular λίθος and plural λίθοι will develop the relationship between Christ and the elect along similar lines.

6. Milgrom, *Leviticus*, 107.

7. Davids, *First Epistle of Peter*, 69.

8. See CD 5.1; 9.5; 11.20; Matt 4:4, 6, 10; 26:31; Mark 14:27; Luke 4:10; 24:46; Acts 1:20; 15:15; 23:5; Rom 1:17; 3:4; 10:15; 12:19; 14:11; 1 Cor 1:19; 3:19; 10:7; 15:45; Gal 3:10, 13; 4:27; Metzger, "Formulas," 300; Fitzmyer, "Explicit Old Testament Quotations," 301; Horton, "Formulas of Introduction," 505–14; Bernstein, "Introductory Formulas," 30–70; Elledge, "Graphic Index," 367–77.

9. Michaels, *1 Peter*, 59.

10. Green, *1 Peter*, 44, 277.

11. See Feldmeier, *First Letter of Peter*, 106–7.

role of Christ in establishing this relationship, which is indicated in 1:13 and then developed further in 1:18–21. However, the use of the *imitatio Dei* concept implies a direct relationship between God and the church, with the mediatorial role of Christ forestalled until 1:18. In this way, the first explicit quotation of scripture inaugurates an ecclesiologically charged reading of scripture whereby the church is held to the same standard of conduct expected of the people of Israel. This call to holiness contributes to the narrative of divine restoration through the notion that divine presence requires the holiness of his people.[12]

The Sacrifice of the Isaianic Servant (1:18–21)

Peter turns now to a new element in support of his argument about the conduct of the elect. In 1:18, the elect are to conduct themselves reverently based on their knowledge of the work of God in Christ. This christological basis brings with it a set of allusions to scripture drawing upon the Isaianic suffering servant in ways that foreshadow 2:21–25. In both passages the quest for hymnic fragments has minimized the Isaianic voice.[13] More recently, scholars have expressed scepticism regarding our ability to identify underlying material.[14] The participle εἰδότες introduces elementary teaching shared by both the author and audience.[15] This basic teaching about Christ is based foremost in an Isaianic narrative of the suffering servant.

The first allusion to Isaiah occurs in 1 Pet 1:18, drawing upon the context immediately prior to the fourth Isaianic servant song. Isa 52:3 promises a ransom (λυτρόω translating גָּאַל) without money (ἀργύριον translating כֶּסֶף) provided by the Lord for those in exile.[16] Peter plays with the phraseol-

---

12. See Joosten, *People and Land*, 201.

13. Bultmann, "Bekenntnis- und Liedfragmente," 10, 14; Deichgräber, *Gotteshymnus*, 169–70; Wengst, *Christologische Formeln*, 161–65. Michaels (*1 Peter*, 53) is skeptical regarding the ability to recover an early Christian hymn, although he takes seriously the possibility of composition from earlier traditions.

14. Goppelt (*I Peter*, 114–21) argues that, of the two points in favor of a christological hymnic fragment, the argument in favor of poetic language is dismissed because much in 1 Peter could be considered poetic and nothing is mentioned that exceeds what would be a necessary ground for paraenesis. See also Michaels, *1 Peter*, 53; Achtemeier, *1 Peter*, 126; Elliott, *1 Peter*, 377–78.

15. Hort, *First Epistle of St Peter*, 75; Kelly, *Epistles of Peter and of Jude*, 72; Goppelt, *I Peter*, 114; Michaels, *1 Peter*, 63; Achtemeier, *1 Peter*, 126; Elliott, *1 Peter*, 369; BDAG 693.

16. The rescue of Israel from Egypt provides a backdrop to the use of λυτρόω in Isaiah 52. In Exodus 6:6 the Lord promises to redeem (λυτρόω translating גָּאַל) his people with a "high arm" and "great judgment." The redemption from slavery in Egypt,

ogy of Isa 52:3 in 1 Pet 1:18-19.[17] The elect are told that they were redeemed not with gold or silver. Thus far, the sense of Isa 52:2 is rendered accurately, even though the term ἀργύριον is embellished by adding χρυσίον and calling both perishable (φθαρτός). These perishable riches are contrasted with the value (τίμιος) of Christ's blood in 1:19.

Table 3.2: **1 Peter 1:18 and Isaiah 52:3**

1 Peter 1:18	Isaiah 52:3
	δωρεὰν ἐπράθητε
εἰδότες ὅτι <u>οὐ</u> φθαρτοῖς,	καὶ <u>οὐ</u> μετὰ
<u>ἀργυρίῳ</u> ἢ χρυσίῳ,	<u>ἀργυρίου</u>
<u>ἐλυτρώθητε</u>	<u>λυτρωθήσεσθε</u>

Further consideration of the broader context of Isaiah 52 helps establish the pivotal role this text plays, particularly in relationship to other Isaianic texts used in 1 Peter.[18] Isaiah 52 depicts the returning exiles as loosening the bonds of slavery (52:2), drawing upon the backstory of Israel's slavery in Egypt (52:4).[19] This passage reiterates important motifs. The proclamation of good news on the mountains in Isa 52:7 echoes Isa 40:1-11.[20] The arm of the Lord in Isa 52:10 further draws upon Isa 40:10,[21] but also anticipates the servant song in 53:1.[22] The relation of Isaiah 52 to the following chapter

---

then, forms a solemn remembrance for Israel (Deut 7:8; 9:26; 13:5; 15:15; 24:18; cf. 2 Sam 7:23; 1 Chron 17:21).

17. Elliott, *1 Peter*, 369.

18. Such an exploration of the context does not imply that Peter had this wider context in view. Instead, it allows us to take into account the setting of the alluded material in order to attend to correspondences and differences between the Isaianic and Petrine contexts. See Hays, *Echoes*, 155; idem., *Conversion of the Imagination*, 25-26; Moyise, *Old Testament in the New*, 4-5.

19. Goldingay, *Message of Isaiah 40-55*, 449. Mettinger ("Israelite Aniconism," 148-51) connects the deliverance from Babylon and the Exodus tradition to the idea of the Divine Warrior.

20. Watts, *Isaiah 34-66*, 216; Mettinger, "Israelite Aniconism," 144; Brueggemann, *Isaiah 40-66*, 139; Wagner, "Psalm 118 in Luke-Acts," 183.

21. Isa 48:14; 51:9; 53:1; 62:8. See Oswalt, *Book of Isaiah*, 2:371.

22. Peter's reading is not sensitive to the compositional history of Isaiah. The present passage is a case in point, with material from Isaiah 52 and 53 juxtaposed. Wagner ("Psalm 118," 184) sees a "web of *intra*textual connections" (emphasis original) between Isaiah 40, 52:7 and 53:1 related to the failure of Israel to believe the message of God's deliverance. See Rom 10:15-16, which brings together Isa 52:7 and 53:1.

is reinforced through key terms and concepts.²³ Therefore, it is not surprising to have both passages provide allusions in 1 Pet 1:18–19. If the exiles are redeemed without money, the question arises on what basis are they redeemed. Isaiah 52:3 issues a proclamation regarding a non-monetary redemption that is patterned upon the exodus from Egypt.

The use of Isa 52:3 connects easily with the diaspora theme that frames 1 Peter.²⁴ The audience of 1 Peter is referred to as "elect exiles of the diaspora" in 1:1. Then in 2:11 they are again called "sojourners and exiles." The use of "Babylon" in 5:13 connects to this theme by referring to a place outside the land of Israel. Leading into the allusion to Isa 52:3 is a reference to "the time of your exile" (τὸν τῆς παροικίας ὑμῶν χρόνον) which links to this framing theme. In 1:18–19, the language of ransom strikes at the heart of believers' emergence from a social setting in which the death of Christ is meaningless. This setting remains, however, the sphere in which the elect carry out their daily lives. The exilic language of 1 Peter does not evoke a sense of punishment for the sins of God's people. Rather, it constructs a view of the world in which one is either in the land of promise or outside the land. Peter places his audience outside the land—in the land of exile—but demonstrates that God is at work outside the land. Peter draws upon Isaiah 52 to express an inaugurated eschatological view of the diaspora existence of the church. Divine grace is experienced in the present by the fact that redemption has happened without money but with something far more precious in the gift of Christ.²⁵ The transformation of believers assumes the purifying work of Christ has dealt with the problem of sin. The hope of resurrection through Christ is placed before believers as the endpoint of their time of exile. This eschatological outlook draws upon the Isaianic promise of return from exile refracted through the accomplished work of Christ.²⁶ The elect are therefore called upon to conduct themselves in their present situation in imitation of divine holiness (1:16) through their participation in Christ (1:21).

The second allusion to Isaiah in 1:19 includes only two words—ὡς ἀμνοῦ—from Isa 53:7.²⁷ The allusion and a tradition about the unblem-

---

23. See Melugin, *Formation of Isaiah 40–55*, 168.

24. But see Richard, *Reading 1 Peter, Jude, and 2 Peter*, 16. He correctly questions the validity of the concept "controlling metaphor."

25. Green (*1 Peter*, 40–41) explores how "the past events in the life of the believer" build toward "present and future realities."

26. Feldmeier, *First Letter of Peter*, 115–17.

27. Hosea 4:16 is another possible source since the words ὡς ἀμνόν appear. However, Hos 4:16 refers to feeding Israel like a lamb whereas Isa 53:7 implies a sacrificial lamb. Despite his scepticism about echoes of Isaiah 53 in 1 Pet 18–19 (*1 Peter*, 63–64), Michaels (ibid., 65) concedes that "ὡς ἀμνόν is the only phrase in this passage that

ished lamb to be sacrificed on the altar (Exo 29:38; Lev 12:6; 14:10; 23:18; Num 6:14; 28–29; Ezek 46:4, 6, 13) are juxtaposed. In each of these verses the noun ἀμνός is modified with ἄμωμος.[28] The use of a catchword linking (gĕzērâ šāwâ) Isaiah 53 and the sacrificial language of the Pentateuch is consistent with usage elsewhere.[29]

Table 3.3: 1 Peter 1:19, Isaiah 53:7 and the Pentateuchal Sacrificial Formula

1 Peter 1:19	Isaiah 53:7	Exo 29:38; Lev 12:6; 14:10; 23:18; Num 6:14; 28–29
ὡς ἀμνοῦ <u>ἀμώμου</u> καὶ ἀσπίλου	ὡς ἀμνὸς ἐναντίον τοῦ κείροντος αὐτὸν ἄφωνος	<u>ἀμνοὺς</u> ἐνιαυσίους <u>ἀμώμους</u>

The combination of texts here is cross interpretive. On the one hand, the holiness of the suffering servant is highlighted, drawing out a prominent theme in Isaiah.[30] While purity of speech and action are highlighted in the song (Isa 53:8–9) the term for holiness—קדש—never occurs. Thus, this interpretive combination makes explicit the holiness of the suffering servant by way of comparison with the sacrifice of the unblemished lamb connected to the holiness code in Leviticus (14:13; 23:20). The theme of holiness has already been launched in 1 Pet 1:16 with the citation of the Levitical formu-

---

might have been drawn from Isa 53 LXX." But see Goppelt, *1 Peter*, 116; Achtemeier, *1 Peter* 129.

28. The OG is necessary for this combined allusion to work. The MT uses two different terms in the sacrificial language of the Pentateuch and in Isa 53:7. The Hebrew term כבש is use for the animal of sacrifice translated as ἀμνός in Greek. In Isa 53:7, רחל is the animal brought before its shearers. The Greek translates both of these terms with ἀμνός making it possible for these passages to be brought together by the key-word association.

29. This is consistent with the findings of Schutter, *Hermeneutic*, 38–39, 43 and Bauckham, "James, 1 and 2 Peter, Jude," 311. Michaels (*1 Peter*, 66) sees several traditions resident here: suffering servant, sacrificial system, and the ram substituted for Isaac (Gen 22).

30. Wells, *God's Holy People*, 135; Beuken, "Theme," 67–87. I am indebted to Steven D. Mason for sharing insights about the Isaianic theme of holiness and its application to 1 Peter.

la. On the other hand, the tradition about the unblemished lamb is extended to Isaiah 53. The sacrificial language of the tradition has resonances with the language of the servant song. The verbs נזה ("sprinkle") in Isa 52:15 and נשא ("bear") in Isa 53:4 occur frequently in the sacrificial language of Leviticus.[31] Although the language of crushing, offering (Isa 53:10), pouring out and interceding (Isa 53:12) do not occur within the sacrificial language, the connection to the iniquities and sins of the people (פשע 53:5, 8; עון 53:6, 11) for which the servant suffers does resonate with the sacrificial language of Leviticus (פשע Lev 16:16, 21; עון Lev 16:21–22). Furthermore, the term אשם in Isa 53:10 is conspicuous in its connection to the sin offering of Lev 5:6–7. These connections between the sacrificial language of the Pentateuch and Isaiah 53 show the extent to which the suffering servant may be interpreted in sacrificial terms. And the combination of allusions in 1 Pet 1:19 implies such an interpretation.

Peter reads Isaiah and Leviticus together, with the suffering servant representing a unique "lamb" for the offering. Peter connects the sin offering of Leviticus to Christ by means of the suffering servant of Isaiah 53.[32] Together—sin offering, suffering servant, Christ event—the salvation of believers is explained so that Peter may call his audience to the high standard of conduct required of his Levitical quotation. Furthermore, through Christ, the believers of Asia Minor are able to participate in the restoration of divine presence because the sacrifice of Christ for sins enables reconciliation between God and humanity.[33]

Further echoes of Isaiah 53 are found in 1 Pet 1:21. Schutter remarks, in light of allusions in 1:18, 19, that "a block of Isaiah comes into view, helping the prospects for another allusion at 1.21."[34] An echo of Isa 52:13 can be heard in the description of Christ's glorification. The exalted status of the servant is depicted in Isa 52:13 so that the servant is lifted up (ὑψόω translat-

---

31. For נזה, see Lev 4:6, 17; 5:9; 6:20; 8:11, 30; 14:7, 16, 27, 51; 16:14–15, 19; cf. Exod 29:21; Num 8:7; 19:4, 18–19, 21. For נשא, see Lev 5:1, 17; 7:18; 10:17; 16:22; 17:16; 19:8; 20:17, 19–20; 22:9, 16; 24:15.

32. This is congruent with the argument by Hengel (*Atonement*, 57–65) in which he highlights the priority of Isaiah 53 over other scriptural influences on the early church's concept of the Christ event as an atonement for many. Hengel has been criticized for overlooking Hooker's work, which considers dubious any allusions to Isaiah 53 behind concepts of the atonement (see the review by Sam K. Willis in *JBL* 102 [1983] 491–93). Yet, concerning this passage, Hooker (*Jesus and the Servant*, 125) admits that, due to the use of Isaiah 53 in 1 Pet 2:21–25, "there may well be a very subsidiary reference to Isa. 53.7"

33. See Gignilliat, *Paul*, 101–6 on the relationship between Christ as the suffering servant and the redemption of sins in Paul's reading of scripture in 2 Cor 5:15—6:10.

34. Schutter, *Hermeneutic*, 38.

ing נשא) and exalted (δοξάζω translating גבה). The use of the term δόξα in 1 Pet 1:21 captures this feature with regard to the exalted status of Christ who is risen (ἐγείρω) and given glory (δόντα δόξαν).[35] Another echo centers on the resurrection of Christ, drawing this time on Isa 53:10. This passage has already been considered with regard to its sacrificial language but also features a resurrection of sorts.[36] The Lord crushes the servant, causing him to suffer,[37] and makes him a sin offering. But after all this the servant sees offspring and has prolonged years.[38] It therefore stands as a possibility that the phrase τὸν ἐγείραντα αὐτὸν ἐκ νεκρῶν ("who raised him from the dead") is interpreting Isa 53:10. Such echoes of Isaiah 53 are consistent with other uses in 1 Pet 1:19 and 2:22–25.

Conclusion

The reading strategy exemplified in this passage places Leviticus and Isaiah together. Peter quotes a passage that is programmatic in Leviticus in order to establish a high standard of conduct: holiness that imitates divine holiness. The combined allusion in 1:19 focuses on the offering for sin using a lamb without blemish, linking Isaiah 53 to the sacrificial system in the Law. Mbuvi interprets this passage in light of his thesis that temple imagery provides the framework for 1 Peter.[39] While it is true the sacrifices instructed for the tabernacle and temple serve as a background for the sacrificial language drawn into 1 Peter, the locus of sacrifice is abstracted in the language of Isaiah 53.[40] Moreover, there is no explicit connection to the temple sacrifice here in 1 Pet 1:19. Instead, the important Isaianic concept centers on

---

35. Aquinas, Symmachus and Theodotion unanimously revise δοξασθήσεται to μετεωρισθήσεται. This seems to be somewhat characteristic of Aquinas who preferred μετεωρίζομαι (see Isa 7:11; 10:33 and 55:9). Interestingly though, at Isa 57:7, the three revisors change μετέωρον to ἐπηρμένον. Justin (*Apol* 50.3), however, retains δοξασθήσεται in his use of Isa 52:13. The raising and glorifying of Christ in 1 Peter (ἐγείρω and δόξα) echoes the Isaianic servant in 53:12 who was raised (ὑψόω) and glorified (δοχάζω).

36. Brueggemann (*Isaiah 40–66*, 148–49) and Oswalt (*Isaiah*, 2:402–3) express concern about using "resurrection" for the servant. Brueggeman suggests "exaltation" as a more descriptive outcome.

37. So NIV, but NRSV has "crush him with pain" and most others have "bring to grief."

38. The Greek version combines these clauses into ὄψεται σπέρμα μακρόβιον, "He will see long-lived offspring."

39. Mbuvi, *Temple*, 125.

40. Ibid., 72.

the servant of the Lord, providing a clear background for the ransom and purification of the elect from their exilic existence.

Isaiah 52 and 53 offer phrases that shape the argument of 1 Pet 1:18–21. These allusions work at a subtle level but indicate how Peter has read the Pentateuch through the lens of Isaiah. The ramification of this strategy is seen in the relative lack of references to the Pentateuch in the rest of the letter.[41] The close proximity of the two Isaianic passages suggests that Peter has read throughout this section. This implies that Peter had direct contact with the written text of Isaiah whereby such allusions could be interpreted alongside one another. A fuller outworking of his reading in this section of Isaiah is revealed later in 2:22–25.

It cannot be assumed that all first-time listeners would pick up on these subtle turns of phrase. However, the explicit quotation from Leviticus, marked as it is by an introductory formula, prepares the audience for an ongoing scriptural discourse. This means that first-time listeners are given an indication about Peter's use of scripture. An audience of mixed perceptive ability and mixed competence with scripture would be able to pick up on much of what Peter was doing with Isaiah, considering that Isaiah was one of the most familiar parts of scripture and Isaiah 53 one of the most familiar parts of Isaiah.

Christology plays an important role in the argument of 1 Pet 1:13–21. Some of the christological items contained in this section are the pre-existence and the advent (φανερόω) of Christ (1:20), the shedding of Christ's blood (1:19), the resurrection and glorification of Christ (1:21) and the hope of Christ's return (1:13).[42] Peter has read scripture in light of Christ, drawing connections from the sacrificial system through the suffering servant of Isaiah 53 to Christ. Yet, his christological reflection serves a further purpose in developing an argument centered on the conduct of the church. It is worth noting that the christology of this section is headed by the participle εἰδότες. The christology is not the part of the argument being developed. It is, rather, being assumed as a shared basis of common belief. The argument builds upon this christological foundation in order to compel the audience to conduct that is holy in light of the scriptural narrative of God's divine presence being restored among his people. The ability of the elect to exhibit the holiness of God is tied to the sacrifice of "the lamb without blemish or spot." The

---

41. The use of Exod 19:5–6 in 1 Pet 2:9 is combined with Isa 43:20–21, further indicating the priority of Isaiah over Peter's reading of the Pentateuch. Characters from Genesis appear in 1 Peter 3: Sarah (3:6) and Noah (3:20–21).

42. Davids, *First Epistle of Peter*, 73–74; Achtemeier, *1 Peter*, 131–32; Hofius, "Fourth Servant Song," 185; Green, *1 Peter*, 210–11. But see Goppelt, *I Peter*, 118–19; Elliott, *1 Peter*, 376–77.

elect are no longer constrained by their former familial associations, they are now children of God through Christ, and their conduct must reflect this reality. The reason they are children of God is because of the ransom Christ paid "without money" in the sacrifice of his blood.

This paraenetic section shows how Peter, the missionary preacher, utilizes scripture in his aim to minister to the church experiencing suffering in Asia Minor. He begins with the belief that the scriptures of Israel address the needs of the church. In keeping with the theological nexus described in the previous chapter, Peter reads scripture through the lens of the Christ event as prophetic words meant to serve the church (1 Pet 1:12). They are part of the family of God. Therefore, their conduct should be of the same essence as their heavenly father who is holy. Furthermore, they are reminded of the purity of the sacrifice made on their behalf when Christ's sacrificial blood was shed.

The Eternal Word and the New Birth: 1 Peter 1:22—2:3

The next two sections (1:22–25 and 2:1–3) go together and further the argument about the conduct of the church. Most scholars see a strong break at 2:1 due to the conjunction οὖν.[43] However, this inferential conjunction draws a conclusion to the argument begun in 1:13.[44] Thematic links binding the units together.[45] The phrase "obedient children" in 1:14 corresponds to "newborn infants" (ἀρτιγέννητα βρέφη) in 2:2, which also connect to the phrase "having been born again" (ἀναγεγεννημένοι) in 1:23.[46] This concentration on new birth features quotations from Isaiah 40 and Psalm 33[34], each contributing significantly to the unfolding argument centered on the conduct of the church.[47]

---

43. Thurén, *Argument*, 105 n. 59.

44. BDAG, 736; LSJ, 1272; BDF, 234–35; see also Ellul, "Un exemple," 20, but see Campbell, *Honor*, 19.

45. Green (*1 Peter*, 48) lists several.

46. Martin (*Metaphor*, 177–78, 187) organizes 1:14—2:10 differently by connecting 1:22–25 with 1:14–21 and 2:1–3 with 2:4–10. For him, the first two sections feature familial relations whereas the second two sections feature the concept of growth. For this to work the concept of building in 2:4–10 must be understood as spiritual growth. However, 2:4–10 emphasizes the building of a community of believers rather than spiritual, moral growth. Instead, the metaphors should be reconfigured so that the first three of his sections are organized around the childhood metaphor with a break occurring between 2:3 and 2:4.

47. Schutter (*Hermeneutic*, 124–30) is correct to consider these two passages together.

Isaianic Gospel and the New Birth (1:22–25)

The church is exhorted to "love one another earnestly" in 1:22, providing a positive ethic that informs the holy conduct required of the elect (1:15–16).[48] In keeping with the previous sections, many key terms are repeated such as "obedience" (ὑπακοή, 1:22; cf. 1:2, 14), "born anew" (ἀναγεννάω, 1:23; cf. 1:3) and "imperishable" (ἄφθαρτος, 1:23; cf. 1:4).[49] The term φθαρτός connects 1 Pet 1:22–25 with the previous passage, significantly drawing together two different Isaianic passages.[50] In 1:18 it is interjected into the Isa 52:3 allusion while in 1:23 it establishes the contrast developed in the quotation of Isa 40:6–8. The use of ἄφθαρτος/φθαρτός not only connects these two passages of 1 Peter but also links two passages from Isaiah.[51] This suggests the presence of a catchword technique (*gĕzērâ šāwâ*) Peter might have used to link these passages.

The exhortation to "love one another earnestly" is based upon the new birth (ἀναγεννάω, 1:23) of the elect.[52] At an earlier stage of the letter, new birth leads to a living hope through the resurrection of Jesus Christ from the dead (1:3). Now Peter further develops the idea of the new birth. The elect are born anew not from a corruptible seed but an incorruptible seed which is equated with the living and abiding word of God (διὰ λόγου ζῶντος θεοῦ καὶ μένοντος, 1:23). The use of σπορά in 1:23 anticipates the agricultural language of Isa 40:6–8 about to be quoted.[53] Peter's anticipatory use of key terms is a noteworthy feature of his use of scripture. This was seen in 1:15 prior to the quotation of the Levitical formula and will occur again in 2:4–5 in anticipation of the quotations of 2:6–10.

The quotation of Isa 40:6–8 emphasizes the abiding nature of the word in contrast to the fleeting nature of humanity.[54] In 1 Pet 1:24–25, the text of

---

48. The command to "love one another earnestly" is picked up later in 4:8 and further developed.

49. Elliott, *1 Peter*, 382.

50. The term φθαρτός is fairly rare in biblical literature. It is noteworthy that this term occurs in Isa 54:17, a passage that will be investigated at a later stage. Other occurrences are 2 Macc 7:16; Wis 9:15; 14:8; Rom 1:23; 1 Cor 9:25; 15:53, 54.

51. There are many connections between Isa 40:1–11 and 52:1–12. These include several verbal (e.g., "comfort," "desert places") and conceptual links (e.g., proclamation on mountains, the Lord's arm).

52. The use of ἀναγεννάω in 1:3 and 23 are the only uses of this term in the NT.

53. Schutter (*Hermeneutic*, 40, cf. 36, 93) calls this an iterative allusion. Such allusions feature "key-word repetitions" (55) which are integral to the pesher-like technique observed by Schutter (127).

54. Elliott (*1 Peter*, 382) sees the quotation as providing "substantiation concerning the permanence of the word of God by which the believers have been born; and v 25b

Isa 40:6–8 is largely the same as OG Isaiah with some minor differences. The inclusion of ὡς before χόρτος is a minor point and appears to be influenced by the use of ὡς before ἄνθος in the parallel clause.[55] The term ἀνθρώπου in Isa 40:6 is rendered αὐτῆς in 1 Pet 1:24. The use of αὐτῆς agrees with the MT against the OG.[56] While this is a clear change from the OG, it should be noted that the revisors Aquila, Symmachus and Theodotian all changed the phrase from πᾶσα δόξα ἀνθρώπου to πᾶν τὸ ἔλεος αὐτῆς. This makes it difficult to assert that Peter has changed the text here and indicates that there was a consistent effort in the textual transmission to alter this term in light of the Hebrew text. Although we cannot argue for a relationship between the text in 1 Peter and any of the revisors, this evidence suggests that Peter likely had a revised Greek text of Isaiah. Similarly, the clauses—"for the spirit/breath of the Lord blew upon it, surely the people are grass"—found in the MT are omitted in both the OG and 1 Peter.[57] Lastly, there is a change from τοῦ θεοῦ ἡμῶν (Isa 40:8) to κυρίου (1 Pet 1:25) leading some to conclude theological reshaping of the text has occurred.[58]

---

clarifies this word of God as that which has been proclaimed to the believers as 'good news.'" See also Goppelt, *I Peter*, 127–28; Davids, *1 Peter*, 78–79; Achtemeier, *1 Peter*, 142; Green, *1 Peter*, 54; Feldmeier, *First Letter of Peter*, 124; Moyise, *Evoking Scripture*, 82–83. James 1:9–11 draws upon the language of Isa 40:6–7 in similar fashion. However, because 40:8 is not incorporated, the argument centers more upon the fickleness of human means with no reference to the word. Yet, Jam 1:18 may echo Isa 40:8 with language mirroring 1 Pet 1:23. See Sundberg, "On Testimonies," 276.

55. Several important mss including Alexandrinus (02) and the corrector of Sinaiticus (01) along with several important minuscules (33, 206, 254, 307, 453, 468, 945, 1735, 1739, 2492) do not include ὡς here.

56. See Jobes, "Septuagint," 318.

57. Aquila, Symmachus and Theodotian each add these clauses in their revisions. This means that whatever Greek text was used by Peter has gone thru some revision, but these clauses had not yet been included.

58. See Schutter, *Hermeneutic*, 128; Elliott, *1 Peter*, 390–91; Moyise, *Evoking Scripture*, 83–84.

Table 3.4: 1 **Peter 1:24–25 and Isaiah 40:6–9**

1 Peter 1:24–25	Isaiah 40:6–9

Διότι
 πᾶσα σάρχ ὡς χόρτος καὶ πᾶσα
  δόξα αὐτῆς ὡς ἄνθος χόρτου·
 ἐξηράνθη ὁ χόρτος καὶ τὸ ἄνθος
  ἐξέπεσεν· τὸ δὲ ῥῆμα κυρίου
  μένει εἰς τὸν αἰῶνα.
 τοῦτο δέ ἐστιν τὸ ῥῆμα
 τὸ εὐαγγελισθὲν εἰς ὑμᾶς.
	πᾶσα σάρξ χόρτος καὶ πᾶσα δόξα
	  ἀνθρώπου ὡς ἄνθος χόρτου
	 ἐξηράνθη ὁ χόρτος καὶ τὸ ἄνθος
	  ἐξέπεσεν τὸ δὲ ῥῆμα τοῦ θεοῦ
	  ἡμῶν μένει εἰς τὸν αἰῶνα
	 ἐπ' ὄρος ὑψηλὸν ἀνάβηθι
	 ὁ εὐαγγελιζόμενος Σιων ὕψωσον τῇ
	  ἰσχύι τὴν φωνήν σου
	 ὁ εὐαγγελιζόμενος Ιερουσαλημ
	 ὑψώσατε μὴ φοβεῖσθε εἰπὸν
	 ταῖς πόλεσιν Ιουδα ἰδοὺ ὁ θεὸς
	 ὑμῶν

Has Peter reshaped this text or has he encountered a text that offers this reading? The term κύριος is established early (1:3) as a reference to Jesus as Lord rather than as a synonym for God the Father. However, there are insufficient repetitions of this relationship leading up to 1:25 to establish κύριος as synonymous with Christ. It is not until 3:15 that a clear reference to Christ as κύριος occurs, thus making the term ambiguous for our passage.[59] Closer to the quotation of Isa 40:6–8, Peter reminds his audience of the new birth "through the living and abiding word of God" (διὰ λόγου ζῶντος θεοῦ καὶ μένοντος, 1:23). Had Peter wanted to make a christological claim in Isa 40:8, one would expect it here at the introduction to the quotation. In the first chapter of 1 Peter each christological claim uses the term Χριστός instead of κύριος (1:7, 11, 13, 19). By way of comparison, the quotation of Prov 3:31 in 1 Pet 5:5 provides a counterexample whereby θεός is used instead of κύριος. Thus, the evidence points away from an intentional theological reshaping of the text, particularly since no theological points are derived from the use of κύριος.

Schutter considers the use of κύριος in 1:25 to be highly suggestive in his understanding of Peter's use of pesher-like practices. He sees Peter

---

59. Contra Schutter, *Hermeneutic*, 126, who sees 2:3 as the next reference to Christ. This requires, however, a highly interpreted understanding of 2:3. On 3:15, see chapter 6.

"exploiting a double-meaning" inherent in the genitival relationship between ῥῆμα and κύριος. The message is both "from the Lord" and "about the Lord."[60] This exploitation, though, is dependent upon the identification of κύριος with Jesus. Such an identification is not as clear as Schutter makes it out to be. Not all have been convinced by the insistence that κύριος = Jesus.[61] As I suggest above, it is necessary to look in the surrounding context for evidence of a christological claim. Schutter finds this in the use of LXX Ps 33:8 in 1 Pet 2:3.[62] He writes, "The allusion's paranomasia (χρηστὸς=Χριστὸς) does in fact serve to identify the κύριος of the psalms with Jesus, such that a Scriptural foundation is given for associating Jesus with that title in addition to God."[63] Such a reading relies upon the assonance of χρηστὸς and Χριστὸς, and support exists for the confusion of these two terms in the manuscript tradition.[64] Although some are hesitant to make much of this assonance,[65] the more fundamental problem with Schutter's reading lies in the layers of "concealed meaning" espoused therein. He recognizes that the christological point is not the primary purpose of Ps 33:8 in 1 Pet 2:3 and that such a reading "depends upon the recognition of a concealed meaning in the form of the paranomasia, 'kindness'='Christ.'"[66] The evidence for Schutter's "Christo-centric frame of reference" is not altogether convincing in light of the more prominent themes surrounding the quotation of Isa 40:6–8.[67] The framing of the quotation with the phrase διὰ λόγου ζῶντος θεοῦ καὶ μένοντος in 1:23 and τοῦτο δέ ἐστιν τὸ ῥῆμα τὸ εὐαγγελισθὲν εἰς ὑμᾶς in 1:25 suggests that the most important term in the text was ῥῆμα.[68]

The theological claim being made centers on the relation of the church to the narrative of scripture. This is made clear in the explanation at the end

---

60. Schutter, *Hermeneutic*, 126.

61. See Richard, *Reading 1 Peter*, 73–74; Feldmeier, *First Letter of Peter*, 131 n. 108.

62. But observe how Moyise (*Evoking Scripture*, 84) critiques this move.

63. Schutter, *Hermeneutic*, 128. See Caragounis, *Development*, 533–37 regarding the substitution of eta for iota.

64. P[72], P[125], 018, 049, 33, 1241, 1243, 1852, 2298 *inter alia*. See Quinn, "Notes," 243–44; Elliott, *1 Peter*, 404; Caulley, "Chrestos/Christos Pun," 376–87.

65. Such as Schreiner, *1, 2 Peter, Jude*, 102.

66. Schutter, *Hermeneutic*, 128.

67. Schutter (*Hermeneutic* 129) observes ways in which the passage relates to the situation of the audience, but finds that the relationship of scripture to the audience comes not through direct relationship but through 1) a christological reading of scripture which connects to 2) the suffering/glory motif by which the message of the passage relates, in light of 1:10–12, to the audience. Moyise (*Evoking Scripture* 83) points out, "The quoted words do not appear to say anything about the 'sufferings' and 'glories' of Christ or his people."

68. Green, *1 Peter*, 53.

of 1:25. Peter expounds that the word (ῥῆμα) is "the good news preached to you" (τὸ εὐαγγελισθὲν εἰς ὑμᾶς). The word of the Lord is the seed bed from which springs the new birth of the elect. Thus, the church is able to make a direct appropriation of the narrative of scripture for its theology and ethics. Consideration of the Isaianic quotation in the context of the Petrine argument in 1 Pet 1:22–25 bears this out. The Isaianic passage contributes to the main argument not simply by supporting the concept of new birth, but also by contributing to the command to "love one another earnestly." While all flesh perishes like grass, "the word of the Lord remains (μένει) forever." This statement undercuts any claims to privileged status based on the prominence of family heritage or wealth (1:18). Isaiah 40:6–8 places all people on the same level.

As an introduction to Isaiah 40–55, Isaiah 40 has been analyzed with regard to the four parts that make up Isa 40:1–11.[69] The message of comfort (40:1–2) leads into a proclamation of restoration (40:3–5) for those who are returning from exile. The theme of comfort to those in exile parallels the rhetorical situation of 1 Peter. This leads to the description of frail humanity in contrast to the power of the word of God (40:6–8). The introduction to Isaiah 40–55 concludes (40:9–11) with the call to herald the good news (εὐαγγελίζω translating בשר) on the mountain tops that the Lord comes in might (40:10) but also with tenderness for his people (40:11).[70] The use of εὐαγγελίζω in 1 Pet 1:25 which interprets the word of the Lord points toward Peter's wider reading of the Isaianic context. Isa 40:9 contains the word εὐαγγελίζω twice.

Several themes in 1 Peter show the influence of Isaiah 40. The futility of human means for both the new birth (1:23) and for the holiness of the elect (1:14–15) draws upon the imagery of withering grass in Isa 40:6–7. The power of the word of God as the basis for the new birth and the life of the elect stands over against such futile human efforts. Green astutely sees that "Isaiah 40 is particularly apropos Peter's concerns, since the Isaianic passage addresses Israel in exile, discouraged, with an acclamation of God's faithfulness and the gospel of restoration."[71] Isaiah 40 contributes to the message of comfort to those experiencing social discord in Asia Minor because of belief in Christ Jesus. Moreover, the contrast between frail humanity and the eternal veracity of God's word points to a transcendent scriptural narrative that reveals the restoration of God's presence among his people.

---

69. See e.g., Carr, "Isaiah 40:1–11," 51–65; Marcus, *Way of the Lord*, 18–23; Watts, *Isaiah's New Exodus*, 76–78; Pao, *Acts*, 45–51.

70. Watts (*Isaiah 34–66*, 78–79) structures the passage somewhat differently, but still see this as a prologue for Isaiah 40–55. See also Melugin, *Formation*, 82–86.

71. Green, *1 Peter*, 53.

Nourishment for the Newborn (2:1–3)

The next section begins with a vice list that furthers the exhortation to "love one another earnestly" by indicating conduct that destroys fellowship.[72] The connection of 2:1–3 to the preceding and subsequent passages has been variously argued. While the conjunction οὖν is determinative for Thurén, other factors, such as metaphor, have been used to discern breaks in Peter's discourse from 1:13—2:10.[73] It seems best to connect 2:1–3 with the preceding material rather than making a break in discourse between 1:25 and 2:1.[74] In 2:2, Peter returns to the imagery of infancy by describing the audience as newborn babes, in keeping with the new birth of 1:23.[75] Like infants, they require nourishment, and so Peter exhorts them to desire milk that will help them grow in their salvation. The phrase describing the sustenance (τὸ λογικὸν ἄδολον γάλα) prescribed for believers is peculiar. Elliott argues for a connection between λογικὸν and the word (λόγος) of 1:23.[76] The term literally means "reasonable" or "belonging to reason." However, Peter does not seem to be arguing for rationality as the basis of believers' growth. Instead, the meaning of the term is best understand as "belonging to speech."[77] Elliott translates this awkward phrase, "the guileless milk of the word" which picks up both the connection of λογικὸν to λόγος in 1:23 but also the connection of ἄδολον to δόλον in 2:1. The deceit or guile that can ruin loving relationship is answered by the word that is without guile.

The connection between 2:1–3 and 1:23 carries over the influence from Isaiah 40 into this new context.[78] The eternally abiding word of Isa 40:8 is also the guileless word that nourishes the people of God. The idea of consuming the word as though it were milk nourishing a newborn baby leads Peter to draw a connection with Psalm 33[34]. The word of God in its sustaining power causes the believer to grow in salvation, "if you have tasted that the Lord is good." Because this Psalm recurs again at length in 1 Pet 3:10–12, the context of the Psalm will be developed at a later point.

---

72. Schutter's attempt to correlate the vice list with 1 Pet 1:24–25 is not convincing (*Hermeneutic*, 57–58, 127–28). Cf. the critique by Moyise, *Evoking Scripture*, 84.

73. See Best, *1 Peter*, 96; Dalton, *Christ's Proclamation*, 96–99; Ellul, "Un exemple," 20–21; Martin, *Metaphor*, 174–88; Thurén, *Argument*, 105; Achtemeier, *1 Peter*, 144.

74. So Achtemeier, *1 Peter*, 144; Elliott, *1 Peter*, 394–95; Jobes, *1 Peter*, 130–31; Feldmeier, *First Letter of Peter*, 96–99.

75. So Elliott, *1 Peter*, 395; Richard, *Reading 1 Peter*, 76; Jobes, *1 Peter*, 130–32; Green, *1 Peter*, 48; Feldmeier, *First Letter of Peter*, 97.

76. Elliott, *1 Peter*, 400–401. See also BDAG, 598.

77. McCartney, "Logikos;" Elliott, *1 Peter*, 400; Green, *1 Peter*, 53.

78. See Jobes, *1 Peter*, 132.

However, it is worth looking at the text of the allusion here to consider how the use of the phrase works at this point in the letter.

Table 3.5: **1 Peter 2:3 and Greek Psalm 33:9**

1 Peter 2:3	Psalm 33:9
εἰ <u>ἐγεύσασθε ὅτι χρηστὸς ὁ κύριος</u>	γεύσασθε καὶ ἴδετε <u>ὅτι χρηστὸς ὁ κύριος</u>

Two differences are immediately apparent between the text in 1 Pet 2:3 and the text of Ps 33:9.[79] The verb has changed from the imperative to the indicative to accommodate the conditional conjunction with which Peter leads into the allusion.[80] Such an accommodation, however, alters the sense of the phrase. Instead of commanding God's people to taste or experience the goodness of the Lord, Peter expects that his audience has already experienced that the Lord is good.[81] The second verb of the clause has been omitted.[82] Again, this seems to be due to the author accommodating the allusion to the immediate needs of the context. It is not the sense of sight but the sense of taste that is the best fit for the imagery of nourishing milk for newborn babes.

The later use of material from Ps 33:13–17 in 1 Pet 3:10–12 indicates that Peter has read beyond merely the text quoted in the letter.[83] Psalm 33 has significantly influenced the thought of Peter, as has been argued by Bornemann.[84] However, the extent of this influence is tied up in the relationship between this Psalm and Isaiah. In 1:22—2:3, the pairing of Isa 40:6–8 and Ps 33:9 shows how Peter has read the Psalm together with Isaiah. The intertextual reading of these passages creates for Peter a way of expressing the vital role the narrative of scripture plays in the life of the elect. The scriptural story of God's redemption has been shown to be central to the gospel proclamation received by the audience (1:25) and now as central to their

---

79. Both here and throughout the thesis reference will be to the Greek version of the Psalter unless clarity demands a fuller citation with the numbering of the Hebrew version.

80. Elliott, *1 Peter*, 403.

81. Achtemeier, *1 Peter*, 148; Caulley, "*Chrestos/Christos* Pun," 378–79.

82. Achtemeier, *1 Peter*, 148.

83. Again, the fuller context of Psalm 33 will be developed in chapter 5.

84. Bornemann, *Petrusbrief*; see also Snodgrass, "I Peter II.1–10," 102–3; Schutter, *Hermeneutic*, 44–48.

continuing growth (2:2-3). Peter's reading of Isa 40:6-8 with Ps 33:9 supports the main exhortation of his argument: to love one another earnestly. In order for the elect to love one another, their love must flow from a pure heart, and the imperishable seed of God's word is commended to the audience as the fundamental means of cultivating such an internal countenance.

Conclusion

The study of Peter's use of Isa 40:6-8 and Ps 33:9 allows some general reflections on how Peter approaches scripture. First, both passages exhibit differences between the quoted text and their *Vorlagen*. It was argued that the three differences in the Isaiah passage could be explained in terms of variants in the manuscript. Michaels suggests the role memory might play in Peter's quotation of Isaiah 40.[85] As argued in the first chapter, Peter has likely worked with numerous biblical quotations prior to writing this letter in his preaching work as a missionary. Yet, the context of the letter itself must be the basis of our investigation of how Peter has interpreted the passage. Thus, caution was suggested regarding investing the variant κύριος with theological meaning unintended by the author.[86] The second text contained two differences stemming from the author's accommodation of the text to the needs of his argument.

It was shown that the two texts were read together and that the sections 1 Pet 1:22-25 and 2:1-3 form a unified argument showing the centrality of God's word to spiritual nourishment.[87] Like the previous section, Isaiah is central in the formation of a scriptural narrative of God's redemption. This time, however, it is not the Pentateuch but the Psalter that is read alongside Isaiah.

The two texts differ in their level of explicitness, with Isa 40:6-8 encompassing four clauses of quoted text versus the single clause comprising five words from Ps 33:9. The Isaiah passage is marked by a truncated introductory formula (διότι) whereas the Psalm text is unmarked. These

---

85. Michaels, *1 Peter*, 78.

86. The use of κύριος in 2:3 has likewise been a tempting christological morsel. An interesting parallel occurs in Odes 19:1-2 where the Trinity is depicted as providing nourishing milk:
A cup of milk was offered to me, and I drank it in the sweetness of the Lord's kindness.
The Son is the cup, and the Father is he who was milked; and the Holy Spirit is she who milked him.
(Translation from Cherian, "Moses," 361).

87. See Green, *1 Peter*, 48.

observations establish that Peter is not beholden to carry out his scriptural discourse at a consistently explicit level. In a section devoted to demonstrating the centrality of the narrative of scripture to the life of the elect community, he appears to expect his audience to follow his use of scripture even when he works at more subtle levels.

The argument put forward in 1 Pet 1:22—2:3 employs scripture in support of Peter's conviction that the scriptures of Israel are relevant to the needs of the church.[88] The elect are to live together in loving community transformed by the nourishing word of God. The gospel enacted in the lives of believers grows out of the seedbed of "the living and abiding word of God." Unlike previous studies, which have placed emphasis on the christological import of these passages, the present study highlights the ecclesiological message emanating from the scriptural texts in Peter's discourse. This is not to create a divide between christology and ecclesiology. In fact, the two will be shown to be linked inextricably as the study progresses. However, studies, such as the work of Schutter, have capitalized on idiosyncrasies of the text (e.g., the use of κύριος in 1:25) and "hidden meanings" (e.g., double meanings in κύριος in 1:25 and χρηστός in 2:3).[89] Instead, the surrounding context provides a simpler, more straight-forward insight into the use of Isa 40:6–8 and Ps 33:8: the gospel proclamation and the growth of the elect community is based in the scriptural narrative of God's redemption.

The paraenetic exhortation that controls this section furthers Peter's address to the churches in Asia Minor, which is experiencing suffering due to its discord with the surrounding culture. Here, Peter provides a vision of the church as a community, which has believed the good news of God's redemption. The challenges that reside on a merely human scale have been likened to grass that passes away. Instead, the community can participate in God's overarching redemptive plan, which is living and abiding. In the face of a hostile culture, Peter commends love within the community that is free from vices and emphasizes growth.

---

88. See Pao, *Acts*, 48–49, 147–80. Pao argues that the logos-terminology of Acts draws significantly upon Isa 40:8 and contends that "the function of such evocation of traditions is to establish and justify the identity claim of the early Christian community as the true heirs of the ancient Israelite traditions" (176).

89. Schutter, *Hermeneutic*, 126–28.

Temple Building in Asia Minor: 1 Peter 2:4–10

Although connected to the previous sections of 1 Peter through key phrases,[90] 2:4–10 features a shift in imagery as well as a grammatical shift away from the imperative to the indicative.[91] The familial language and the imagery of infancy give way now to architectonic imagery centered on the term λίθος. The verb οἰκοδομέω in the first place describes the action of constructing some sort of edifice. The sacrificial language employed in this section indicates that this edifice is the temple, but the temple is spiritualized just as the sacrificial offering is.[92] The shift in imagery and grammar make this next section distinct from 1:13—2:3.

The structure of 2:4–10 falls into three sections. The first section (2:4–5) introduces the subject matter and the theological framework by which the scriptural texts of 2:6–10 are interpreted. The second section (2:6–8) contains three scriptural quotations—Isa 28:16; Ps 117[118]:22; Isa 8:14—all containing the key term λίθος. A brief commentary applies these quotations to believers (τοῖς πιστεύουσιν) and unbelievers (ἀπιστοῦσιν).[93] The third section (2:9–10) contains allusions from three scriptural sources—Isa 43:20–22; Exod 19:5–6; Hos 1–2—with all three passages containing the key term λαός.[94] Like the previous section, there is a brief commentary relating the allusions to believers.

The use of key terms drawn from the scriptural material to be used in the subsequent sections makes 2:4–5 important for understanding how those quotations and allusions function. The term λίθος, used twice, anticipates the group of verses in 2:6–8. The living stone (λίθον ζῶντα) is rejected (ἀποδοκιμάζω; Ps 117:22/1 Pet 2:7) by humanity but deemed chosen and honored (ἐκλεκτὸν ἔντιμον; Isa 28:16/1 Pet 2:6) by God. The singular use

---

90. The term ἅγιος centering on the Levitical phrase in 1 Pet 1:15–16 is taken up again in 2:5 and 9. The term ζάω is repeated at key points in participial forms at 1:3 with regard to the believer's hope, at 1:23 with regard to God's living and abiding word and then in 2:4 and 5. The terms καλέω (1:15; 2:9), πιστεύω (1:8; 2:6–7) and τιμή (1:7; 2:9) link 2:4–10 with the previous sections.

91. The verb οἰκοδομεῖσθε is taken as an indicative rather than an imperative, although the forms are identical. So Hort, *First Epistle of St Peter*, 109; Selwyn, *First Epistle of St Peter*, 159; Michaels, *1 Peter*, 100; Achtemeier, *1 Peter*, 155; Elliott, *1 Peter*, 412. But see Bigg, *St. Peter and St. Jude*, 128.

92. The argument of 2:4–10 has similarities with the interpretive practices used by James, according to Acts 15:13–21, at the Jerusalem council. See Bauckham, "James, and the Jerusalem Church," 452–56.

93. Green (*1 Peter*, 57–58) masterfully connects belief and unbelief to the issue of honor and shame vocabulary in 1 Pet 2:4–10.

94. Bauckham, "James, 1 and 2 Peter, Jude," 311.

of λίθον ζῶντα, in contrast to the plural version in 2:5, indicates the christological use of the phrase. These passages are given a christological reading implicitly when they are quoted through the linking term λίθος.[95] This helps explain the lack of christological commentary in 2:7 and 8, since the connection to Christ has already occurred at 2:4.

The phrase λίθον ζῶντα is transformed in 2:5 into the plural phrase λίθοι ζῶντες. Applied directly to the audience, this transformation of the phrase indicates the closest of links between Christ and the community that bears his name. A simultaneous, dual interpretation of the quoted and alluded scriptural passages is indicated by transforming λίθος. So, when the three λίθος passages are quoted, the christological import of each passage is retained, while the commentary develops an ecclesiological argument.[96] The relationship between the singular and the plural establishes a pattern followed in the two following sections. The first set of passages centers on the singular stone whereas the second set of passages focuses exclusively on the audience. The appellatives drawn from Isaiah 43 and Exodus 19 develop the concept of the church's identity and purpose. Two terms from Exod 19:6, ἱεράτευμα and ἅγιον, are drawn into the first section to describe the purpose of the edifice built of living stones in 2:5.[97] The living stones are built into a spiritual house for the purpose carrying out a holy priesthood.

The link between christology and ecclesiology has already been indicated as an important aspect of Peter's use of scripture. Green writes:

> The OT is understood christologically on the way to its ecclesiological appropriation. In other words, Peter's task is not to read the Scriptures christologically but to show how a christological reading of Scripture guides the church in the formation of its identity and pursuit of its mission.[98]

The development of christology in 1 Pet 2:4–10 is rather implicit, amounting to two subtle strands. First, the use of the singular term λίθος coordinates the three quoted passages with the living stone of 2:4.[99] Using

95. Michaels, 1 Peter, 98–99. But see Achtemeier, 1 Peter, 160.

96. Jobes (1 Peter, 146) writes that the living stone is the "dominant image in this passage that has both christological and ecclesiastical significance."

97. The preposition εἰς is particularly problematic in biblical Greek (see BDF §§205–207; Wallace, Greek Grammar, 369–71). The verb οἰκοδομέω usually takes the object being built in the accusative. For this reason, the prepositional phrase is best understood not as the object of the verb but as the purpose for which the οἶκος πνευματικός is built. See also BDAG, 696; Michaels, 1 Peter, 100–101; Achtemeier, 1 Peter, 156; Elliott, Elect, 167; 1 Peter, 412.

98. Green, 1 Peter, 55.

99. Schutter (Hermeneutic, 132–33) correctly identifies the link as λίθος, contra

the language of scripture, Peter demonstrates how Christ is honored by God despite rejection and unbelief on the part of humanity. The three passages of 2:6–8 support this claim and indicate further that the role of Christ is to exacerbate the division of humanity into believers and unbelievers. Christ is "a stone of stumbling and a rock of offence." Elliott points out that the terms σκάνδαλον and πρόσκομμα "denote some person or action causing social offence, violation of the social or moral code, and thereby undermining the cohesion and commitment of the community."[100] A second strand of christological development is carried by the phrase "through Jesus Christ" (διὰ Ἰησοῦ Χριστοῦ) in 2:5. The priestly act of offering spiritual sacrifices (ἀνενέγκαι πνευματικὰς θυσίας) which are pleasing to God is done through Jesus Christ.[101] Beale connects 1 Pet 2:4–9 with Revelation 11 to conclude that both speak about "God's people as a spiritually inviolable temple who spread God's presence and word but whose physical being can be harmed."[102] The plural living stones are being built into an edifice for the purpose of carrying out their spiritual ministry of worship toward God (2:4, 9). The priestly role accorded to the church, however, is dependent upon the priestly role of Jesus Christ.

The mediatorial role of Christ was an emphasis in older commentators and has been picked up recently by Elliott.[103] The spiritual sacrifices are acceptable to God because they are mediated through Jesus Christ (διὰ Ἰησοῦ Χριστοῦ, 1 Pet 2:5). But Elliott also points out that the elect share the attributes of Christ. Selwyn earlier spoke of this as the "union of the Church's sacrifices with His" by the means of faith.[104] It is the unity of Christ and believers that is established through the coordination of the singular (λίθος ζῶν) and the plural (λίθοι ζῶντες), and the prepositional phrase διὰ Ἰησοῦ Χριστοῦ.[105] Green charts the parallels between Christ and Peter's audience thus:[106]

Lindars (*Apologetic*, 169–80) who argues that ἀκρογωνιαῖον (Isa 28:16) and εἰς κεφαλὴν γωνίας (Ps 118:22) form the key link between the passages. See also Bauckham, "James, 1 and 2 Peter, Jude," 10–12.

100. Elliott, *1 Peter*, 432. See also BDAG 882, 926.

101. The language of offering sacrifices harks back to the sacrificial system already alluded to in 1 Pet 1:18–19.

102. Beale, *Temple*, 332.

103. Hort, *First Epistle of St Peter*, 114; Bigg, *St. Peter and St. Jude*, 129; Selwyn, *First Epistle of St Peter*, 162–63; Kelly, *Epistles of Peter and of Jude*, 92; Elliott, *1 Peter*, 423.

104. Selwyn, *First Epistle of St Peter*, 162. Selwyn goes on to point to the Eucharist as the spiritual sacrifice in view here. Against this see Hill, "Spiritual Sacrifices," 60–61.

105. See Jobes, *1 Peter*, 148–49.

106. Green, *1 Peter*, 60.

Jesus	Peter's Audience
a living stone	living stones
rejected by humans	(implicit: rejected by humans)
in God's perspective, elect	in God's perspective, elect
in God's perspective, honored	in God's perspective, honored

The hermeneutical strategy for the following quotations is established here in 2:4–5. The affinities with the Qumran pesharim[107] (a line-by-line commentary on passages of scripture) have led scholars to regard 2:4–5 as a midrash.[108] While there are exegetical techniques which connect the Midrashim with earlier Second Temple writings, Hays is correct in pointing out the flaws of categorizing NT exegesis of scripture as midrash.[109] The similarities to Qumran pesharim occur more at the level of exegetical method rather than sharing the same form or motive.[110] The strategy revealed in 2:4–5 points to Peter's intention to show the connection between Christ and the church.[111]

The three quotations in 1 Pet 2:6–8 are organized around the idea of a unique stone (λίθος) which is highly valued by God and causes a rift in humanity along the fault lines of belief.[112] Belief and unbelief become the salient motif that is developed in 2:6–8. The first passage (Isa 28:16) supplies the subject ὁ πιστεύων, which is drawn out in the brief commentary in 2:7. The second half of the commentary proposes that the other two passages (Ps 117:22; Isa 8:14) be read in accordance with those who do not

---

107. E.g., 1QpHab; 4Q161–165(pIsa^{a-e}); 4Q166–167(pHos^{a-b}); 4Q169(pNah); 4Q170(pZeph); 4Q171, 173 (pPs^{a-b}); 4Q174(Flor); 4Q177(Catena); 11Q13(Melch). A helpful definition of Qumran pesher is provided in Berrin, *Pesher Nahum*, 9–12.

108. So Elliott, *Elect*, 33–49; Selwyn, *First Epistle of St Peter*, 164; Kelly, *Epistles of Peter and of Jude*, 93; Bauckham, "James, 1 and 2 Peter, Jude," 11; Schutter, *Hermeneutic*, 136. Bauckham has more recently articulated an avoidance of the term "midrash" because of the "potential for misunderstanding." Instead, he prefers the terms "exegesis" and "commentary" (*Jude*, 180).

109. Hays, *Echoes*, 10–14; idem., *Conversion*, 164–169.

110. Berrin, *Pesher Nahum*, 10–11. It is important to carefully differentiate between pesher and midrash. See chapter 1.

111. Schutter (*Hermeneutic*, 137) is aware of how "the author's hermeneutic has allowed him to disclose distinctly different meanings from one and the same oracle, Is. 28.16, some associated with a personal Christological application and some associated with a corporate or collective one." Schutter's aim in showing how the passage is typical of pesher-like techniques has not allowed him to develop this important insight further. See Bauckham, "James, 1 and 2 Peter, Jude," 11–12.

112. The text critical issues pertaining to Isa 28:16 and 8:14 and Peter's *Vorlagen* will be dealt with below in comparison with the parallels in Romans 9.

believe. A contrast is made between those who reject the living stone in 2:4 and God's evaluation of the stone as chosen and precious. Likewise, the term stumbling is applied to unbelievers in the commentary in 2:8b. The comment in 2:8 about how unbelievers stumble "because they disobey the word" (λόγος) shows how Peter continues to develop his understanding of the relationship between the church and the narrative of scripture, albeit in this case by way of *exemplum negativum*.

Table 3.6: 1 Peter 2:6–8 and Isaiah 28:16; Psalm 117:22; Isaiah 8:14

1 Peter 2:6–8	Isa 28:16; Ps 117:22; Isa 8:14
διότι περιέχει ἐν γραφῇ· ἰδοὺ τίθημι ἐν Σιὼν λίθον ἀκρογωνιαῖον ἐκλεκτὸν ἔντιμον καὶ ὁ πιστεύων ἐπ' αὐτῷ οὐ μὴ καταισχυνθῇ. ὑμῖν οὖν ἡ τιμὴ τοῖς πιστεύουσιν, ἀπιστοῦσιν δὲ λίθος ὃν ἀπεδοκίμασαν οἱ οἰκοδομοῦντες, οὗτος ἐγενήθη εἰς κεφαλὴν γωνίας καὶ λίθος προσκόμματος καὶ πέτρα σκανδάλου· οἳ προσκόπτουσιν τῷ λόγῳ ἀπειθοῦντες εἰς ὃ καὶ ἐτέθησαν.	ἰδοὺ ἐγὼ ἐμβαλῶ εἰς τὰ θεμέλια Σιων λίθον πολυτελῆ ἐκλεκτὸν ἀκρογωνιαῖον ἔντιμον εἰς τὰ θεμέλια αὐτῆς καὶ ὁ πιστεύων ἐπ' αὐτῷ οὐ μὴ καταισχυνθῇ λίθον ὃν ἀπεδοκίμασαν οἱ οἰκοδομοῦντες οὗτος ἐγενήθη εἰς κεφαλὴν γωνίας καὶ οὐχ ὡς λίθου προσκόμματι συναντήσεσθε αὐτῷ οὐδὲ ὡς πέτρας πτώματι

To understand the role of these passages in this section better, it is necessary to look at the contexts from which they are derived. Isaiah 28 comes after the so-called "Isaianic Apocalypse" of Isaiah 24–27 which depicts final judgment in global terms.[113] The focus of Isaiah then narrows to Ephraim and Jerusalem in chapter 28. It is the judgment on Jerusalem in 28:14–29 that contains the quoted passage. The rulers of Jerusalem are condemned for making a covenant with "death" and "Sheol/Hades"—figurative language used to depict their ill-placed hope in something other than the Lord—to

---

113. Blenkinsopp, *Opening*, 16–18.

protect them from calamity (28:14–15).[114] In contrast to the false shelter the rulers have secured for themselves, the Lord announces that a cornerstone has been placed in Zion (28:16).[115] This is a true shelter to protect the people of God from the calamity set to befall the rulers of Jerusalem (28:18–22).

The stone in Isa 28:16 functions in two ways.[116] First, the stone is laid as the foundation of an edifice in Zion that counters the shelter or refuge the rulers of Jerusalem have erected.[117] Smith points to the theological principle of the section, "If people trust God for security, they will have nothing to fear, but if they refuse to trust God and depend on man's strength . . . God will purposely work against them."[118] The second function focuses on the role of belief relative to the stone. Wildberger writes, "The foundation stone, through which security and salvation is offered, is faith, a faith that takes Yahweh's promises of salvation with utter seriousness."[119] The security of believers is inscribed on the cornerstone.[120] When the verse is brought into 1 Peter, the first function is muted due to the fact that it is drawn out of its immediate context.[121] The second function of the stone is emphasized in the commentary of 2:7a.[122] The reiteration of ὁ πιστεύων directly relates Isa 28:16 to the church so that the remnant who have placed their faith in God's deliverance are equated with the believers in Asia Minor. An additional word-play can be found in the commentary.[123] The stone established in Zion is deemed precious by God. The term used in Isa 28:16 is ἔντιμον. The commentary states that the value of the stone is accounted to the believers and utilizes the cognate term τιμή.[124] The placement of the stone in Zion points to the restoration of divine presence among the people of God through the reestablishment of the temple.

The second passage quoted is Ps 117[118]:22.[125] The text of Ps 117:22 has benefited from stability, largely because the Greek translation agrees

---

114. Watts, *Isaiah 1–33*, 369; Smith, *Isaiah 1–39*, 473–75.

115. Wildberger, *Isaiah 28–39*, 35.

116. On the many possible interpretations of the stone, see Kaiser, *Isaiah 13–39*, 253; Wildberger, *Isaiah 28–39*, 41.

117. Wildberger, *Isaiah 28–39*, 41.

118. Smith, *Isaiah 1–39*, 485.

119. Wildberger, *Isaiah 28–39*, 42.

120. Kaiser, *Isaiah 13–39*, 254.

121. This is similar to the usage in *Barn.* 6:3.

122. So Kaiser, *Isaiah 13–39*, 256.

123. See Wagner, "Psalm 118," 144–45.

124. Elliott, *Elect*, 37.

125. Hereafter referred to by its numeration in the Greek text as Psalm 117.

substantially with the Hebrew.[126] Psalm 117 contains four sections that consider the relationship of the enduring love of the Lord in the context of military conflict.[127] A note of thanksgiving rings out in the first section (vv. 1–4).[128] The conflict with the nations depicted in the second section (vv. 5–18) contains both a personal account of this conflict conjoined with proverbial statements (vv. 8–9). Being surrounded by the nations (vv. 10–11), the psalmist describes a close brush with death (vv. 17–18). The scene changes to the "gates of righteousness" in the third section (vv. 19–22) and with the scene change comes a change to architectural imagery.[129] The fourth section (vv. 23–29) shifts to the first-person plural pronoun.[130] The people praise and thank the Lord as they reflect upon the divine actions this Psalm chronicles.

The passage quoted in 1 Peter is drawn from the third section. The stone of Ps 117:22 is enigmatic and difficult to connect with the surrounding context. The gate of 117:19–20 indicates an edifice to which the "head of the corner" (ראש פנה; κεφαλὴ γωνία) belongs.[131] However, it is reasonable to interpret the stone as a personal reference made by the psalmist reflecting on deliverance from death (117:10–13, 17–18).[132] In line with this personal interpretation of the stone, 1 Peter assumes a christological interpretation of the verse. The shifting singular and plural voice argues that the individual voice of the central portion of the Psalm speaks representatively for the congregation. Mays speaks to this when he notes, "The Lord's salvation has revealed that the rejected are the focus and center of the Lord's way in the world."[133] This supports to some extent the observation made by Woan that the quotation of Ps 117:22 is "to show how the election of Christ leads to the election of those who believe in him as the holy people of God."[134]

126. See Matt 21:42; Mark 12:10–11; Luke 20:17 where, like 1 Pet 2:7, quotations of Ps 117:22(–23) exactly replicate the Greek text. On the use of this Psalm in the NT, see esp. Kraus, *Theology*, 193–94; Wagner, "Psalm 118," 157–61; Moyise and Menken, *Psalms*.

127. Mays, *Hosea*, 374.

128. On thanksgiving Psalms, see Gunkel *Introduction*, 199–220; Allen, *Psalms 101–150*, 122–23; Kraus, *Psalms 60–150*, 51–52.

129. Weiser, *Psalms*, 724.

130. Indicating, perhaps, that the speaker is the king. See Grogan, *Psalms*, 193.

131. See Terrien, *Psalms*, 783. But see Grogan, *Psalms*, 194.

132. Rashi has difficulty determining whether an individual (David) or collective referent (Israel) is in view (Gruber, *Rashi's Commentary*, 672–73). See also Westermann, *Psalms*, 73; Weiser, *Psalms*, 728–29; Terrien, *Psalms*, 786; Grogan, *Psalms*, 193.

133. Mays, "Psalm 118," 306. He goes on to note how this parallels the thought of Isaiah 53.

134. Woan, "Psalms," 219.

The commentary in 1 Pet 2:7–8 draws Ps 117:22 into the sphere of belief and unbelief.[135] Thus, the hermeneutical significance of the verse is not the christologically weighted "stone" but the concept of rejection. The builders have rejected the stone, something that has already been anticipated in the introductory section (2:4) at which point the rejection of the living stone by humanity is contrasted with the divine election and valuation of the stone. By combining Isa 28:16 and Ps 117:22, the stone in each passage is seen to be at the center of a divisive conflict. The conflict in Psalm 117 between the Psalmist and the surrounding nations recedes into the background in the new context of 1 Peter. The terminology chosen by Peter emphasizes a conflict between believers and unbelievers with the living stone factoring as the divisive element.

The thematic correspondence between Psalm 117 and the Isaianic paradigm of the New Exodus is striking.[136] Indeed, such paradigmatic use of the exodus imagery is consistent with the picture of the larger scriptural narrative emerging in our investigation of the use of scripture in 1 Peter. However, the language most beholden to the New Exodus paradigm is not drawn from Psalm 117. The most immediate connection is to an architectural edifice, one that would be created after a return from exile. As Beale shows, this is the culmination of the New Exodus in Isaianic parlance. The eschatological temple becomes a place of divine presence, distinct from "the old, idolatrous world."[137] He shows that Isaiah 57 and 66 greatly informs imagery of the eschatological temple, particularly as a place, which includes "the afflicted and smitten."[138] Psalm 117 further contributes to our understanding of the eschatological temple, inasmuch as the early Church saw Jesus as "the foundation stone of the new temple."[139]

The third passage referred to in 1 Pet 2:6–8 is Isa 8:14. Isaiah 8 extends the message to Ahaz begun in chapter 7. Syria and Ephraim have made an alliance against Judah (7:2–7) but the Lord promises their demise (2:8–9).[140] The sign of Immanuel is given to Ahaz, which portends the rise of Assyria (7:10–17). Four images depict Assyrian aggression against the Syrian/Ephraim alliance (7:18–25). The birth of Maher-shalal-hashbaz (8:1–4) is a prelude to the Assyrian invasion (8:5–10) which extends even to Judah

---

135. Bauckham, "James, 1 and 2 Peter, Jude," 12.

136. In this regard, see esp. Brunson, *Psalm 118*, 81–82, 153–79; Watts, "Psalms," 30–35.

137. Beale, *Temple*, 136.

138. Ibid., 135–37.

139. Ibid., 184.

140. Brueggemann, *Isaiah 1–39*, 74–75; Smith, *Isaiah 1–39*, 219–20.

(8:8).¹⁴¹ Concern over the Assyrian incursion into Judah gives rise to the message of 8:11-15. The Lord tells the prophet not to "walk in the way of this people" (8:11). It is in this context that the architectonic language centering on the building materials is taken up. The Lord himself is described as "a sanctuary and a stone of stumbling and a rock of stumbling." Once again, the imagery of the stone is situated in the midst of conflict, this time involving Judah as part of the collateral damage of Assyria's aggression against Syria and Ephraim. The following passage (8:16-18) provides further interpretation of 8:11-15. The prophet proclaims his hope in the Lord and announces that he and "the children whom the Lord has given me" are protected by God in the midst of this destructive judgment.¹⁴² The disciples of the prophets do not follow in the way of their kinsmen (8:19-22) and are marked by faithfulness to Torah (8:16, 20).¹⁴³

Isaiah 8:14 is connected to the other two passages cited in 1 Pet 2:6-8 by the linking term λίθος. The role of the stone in this passage is similar to the role depicted in Isa 28:16 and Ps 117[118]:22, functioning as a divisive artifact separating the faithful from those who walk apart from the Lord. The role of the stone as sanctuary to the faithful is muted in the Petrine context where a focus on unbelievers draws from Isa 8:14 only the retributive role of the stone.¹⁴⁴ The commentary in 1 Pet 2:8 expands upon Isa 8:16-22 where faithfulness to the Torah is emphasized. The unbelievers stumble because they disobey the word (τῷ λόγῳ ἀπειθοῦντες). The verb ἀπειθέω occurs in Isa 8:11 to describe the disobedience of "this people." The use of this term indicates a contextual reading of the passage has informed Peter of factors bearing upon the role of the stone relative to belief and unbelief. Later in the letter, Peter will return to this passage when Isa 8:12-13 is employed in 1 Pet 3:14-15.

The two Isaianic passages in 1 Pet 2:6-8 are tied together by means of a wordplay that concludes the commentary in 2:8. The verb τίθημι is used to indicate the divine appointment of unbelievers stumbling through unbelief.¹⁴⁵ By combining Isa 28:16 and 8:14 in the commentary, Peter shows how the living stone has been intentionally placed to exacerbate the divisive issue of belief.¹⁴⁶

---

141. Sweeney, *Isaiah 1-39*, 170.

142. Oswalt, *Isaiah*, 1:233-35; Childs, *Isaiah*, 74-75.

143. Wagner ("Faithfulness," 79-81) provides further comments on Isa 8:11-18 as it relates to its appropriation in Romans, 1 Peter and Hebrews.

144. Michaels, *1 Peter*, 106-7; Elliott, *1 Peter*, 430-31.

145. Schutter, *Hermeneutic*, 135; Achtemeier, *1 Peter*, 162.

146. Green, *1 Peter*, 57-58.

The similarities between 1 Peter and Romans regarding the use of the stone collocation has attracted the attention of scholarship perennially. Apart from the simple fact that both authors have paired Isa 28:16 with 8:14, there are several features that are textually unique to the use of these passages in each epistle.[147] First, both quotations of Isa 28:16 are missing the phrase ἐγὼ ἐμβαλῶ εἰς τὰ θεμέλια and have instead the verb τίθημι and the preposition ἐν before Σιων.[148] Second, both quotations of Isa 8:14 have the noun πρόσκομμα in the genitive, feature the noun σκάνδαλον instead of πτῶμα, and coordinate the two truncated phrases with the conjunction καί. These similarities have led scholars to posit either a theory of dependence or a common source.[149]

The text as it stands in each epistle shows clear dependence on a Septuagintal text as is evidenced by the appearance of the prepositional phrase ἐπ αὐτῷ which does not exist in the Hebrew version of Isa 28:16. For Isa 8:14, the genitive προσκόμματος is found in a few manuscripts (301, 538 and the Coptic and Syro-Palestinian versions) as well as in the revisions of Aquila, Symmachus and Theodotion which also use the conjunction καί. The term σκάνδαλον was also used in Aquila's revision of Isa 8:14. These factors indicate that a text form existed at least for Isa 8:14 that was drawn upon by both Paul and Peter. How they came across this text and the means by which it was appropriated is unknown to us. What is clear is that the linking term λίθος was instrumental in the coordinating of these two passages for both authors.

Stanley argues convincingly that for both authors to use common wording makes it likely that there is dependence on an earlier source.[150] Dodd suggested the use of a common *testimonium*,[151] but de Waard cautions against postulating a collection of *testimonia*.[152] The hypothesis that a collection of *testimonia* stands behind the common use of Isa 28:16 and 8:14 does not account for the actual usage of these verses in their epistolary contexts. If Snodgrass is correct that *testimonia* were most commonly used for christological

---

147. See Moyise, *Evoking Scripture*, 86–88; Jobes, *1 Peter*, 147–48.

148. Also missing from the Petrine quotation is the second instance of εἰς τὰ θεμέλια αὐτῆς.

149. Some points of difference between the two quotations are the composite nature of Paul's quotation. Isa 8:14 is spliced into 28:16, eliding the two with a single occurrence of λίθος. Paul's version also omits the phrase ἀκρογωνιαῖον ἐκλεκτὸν ἔντιμον from 28:16. The final verb is rendered as future indicative (καταισχυνθήσεται) in Rom 9:33 whereas 1 Pet 2:6 agrees with Isa 28:16 using the aorist subjunctive (καταισχυνθῇ).

150. Stanley, *Paul*, 121–22.

151. Dodd, *According to the Scriptures*, 43.

152. De Waard, *Comparative Study*, 57–58.

and apologetic purposes, the incorporation of the material in 1 Peter achieves different ends.[153] Apart from the use of these verses along with material from Hosea 1-2 in 1 Pet 2:10, the arguments of Romans and 1 Peter are quite different, and each author draws on a wider array of scriptural quotations and allusions that point away from dependence on a pre-selected set of texts. The *testimonia* hypothesis, then, can only go so far in explaining the scriptural sources in 1 Peter and Romans. Instead, it is suggested that a more direct appropriation of scripture better accounts for the variance between the corresponding texts in Romans and 1 Peter as well as for how these texts are incorporated into the arguments of the respective epistles.

The third unit of this section (1 Pet 2:9-10) contains allusions to three passages: Isa 43:20-21; Exod 19:5-6; Hos 1-2. Unlike the previous section with longer quotations, the allusions amount to short phrases of two words. In 1 Pet 2:9, allusions to Isa 43:20-21 and Exod 19:5-6 are woven together in a series of appellatives describing the church. Like the previous section, there is a commentary that draws the allusions together.

Table 3.7: **1 Peter 2:9 and Exodus 19:5–6; Isaiah 43:20–21**

Exod 19:5–6	1 Peter 2:9	Isa 43:20–21
ἔσεσθέ μοι λαὸς περιούσιος ἀπὸ πάντων τῶν ἐθνῶν ἐμὴ γάρ ἐστιν πᾶσα ἡ γῆ ὑμεῖς δὲ ἔσεσθέ μοι βασίλειον ἱεράτευμα καὶ ἔθνος ἅγιον	ὑμεῖς δὲ γένος ἐκλεκτόν βασίλειον ἱεράτευμα ἔθνος ἅγιον λαὸς εἰς περιποίησιν, ὅπως τὰς ἀρετὰς ἐξαγγείλητε τοῦ ἐκ σκότους ὑμᾶς καλέσαντος εἰς τὸ θαυμαστὸν αὐτοῦ φῶς	ἔδωκα ἐν τῇ ἐρήμῳ ὕδωρ καὶ ποταμοὺς ἐν τῇ ἀνύδρῳ ποτίσαι τὸ γένος μοῦ τὸ ἐκλεκτόν λαόν μου ὃν περιεποιησάμην τὰς ἀρετάς μου διηγεῖσθαι

---

153. Snodgrass, "Use," 422-23. See also Fitzmyer, "4QTestimonia," 513-37; Snodgrass, "I Peter II. 1-10," 101-3.

Short phrases are likewise drawn from the first two chapters of Hosea. The phrase οὐ λαός draws upon Hos 1:9; 2:1 and 25 and the phrase οὐκ ἠλεημένοι draws upon Hos 1:6; 2:25. The positive restatement of the negative phrases also reflects the transformation in Hos 2:1–3.[154] The use of Hosea in concert with the appellatives from Exodus and Isaiah adds a considerable amount of complexity to how these are to be interpreted. For this reason, it is necessary to study the contexts from which these passages are drawn. The commentary at the end of 2:9 also contributes to how these allusions hold together.

The first passage to consider is Exodus 19. This chapter sees the Israelites arrive at Mount Sinai after their exodus from Egypt (Exod 12) and the crossing of the Red Sea (Exod 14). Moses goes up to God on the mountain (19:2–3) and receives a message (19:3–6) about a covenant between God and the people of Israel (19:5). The people accept the terms of the covenant in 19:8.[155] The Lord declares, "You shall be my treasured possession among all people, for all the earth is mine; and you shall be to me a kingdom of priests and a holy nation" (19:5–6). After accepting the terms of the covenant (19:7–9), the people are consecrated to the Lord (19:10–25).[156]

The appellatives drawn from Exod 19:6 describe the people of God with a variety of images. Juxtaposed are images of royalty (ממלכה; βασίλειον) and priesthood (כהנים; ἱεράτευμα).[157] These two roles become institutionalized in the history of Israel with the roles of king and high priest taking on significant spheres of authority. The Hebrew of Exod 19:6 has these terms joined in the construct state—ממלכת כהנים—literally "kingdom of priests."[158] Taken together with the next appellatives, the Israelites are being described as a people set apart from the rest of the world and marked by holiness.[159]

When Exod 19:6 was translated into Greek, the relationship of the two terms was shifted, the first term being translated as an adjective (βασίλειον). Elliott puts forth the two possible understandings of this new grammatical arrangement, βασίλειον ἱεράτευμα "can be understood as either two substantives or as an adjective and a substantive."[160] Taking the two terms as substantives, Elliott proceeds to mount an interpretation in which the

---

154. Note that the English version numbers 2:1–2 as 1:10–11 and 2:3 as 2:1.

155. Childs, *Exodus*, 366–67; Fretheim, *Exodus*, 211–12; Gowan, *Theology*, 173–78.

156. Clements, *Exodus*, 116; Stuart, *Exodus*, 425–26, among others.

157. We can agree with Ska ("Exode 19,3b–6," 298) that the sense of ממלכת כהנים "est difficile à déterminer."

158. Or "priestly kings." So Childs, *Exodus*, 342.

159. Clements, *Exodus*, 115.

160. Elliott, *Elect*, 63.

term βασίλειον becomes a royal residence and ἱεράτευμα becomes a priestly community.[161] The two terms, for Elliott, are understood independent of one another. However, it is worth considering how the new grammatical arrangement opens new possibilities for appropriating this phrase.

One possibility understands that the term βασίλειον modifies ἱεράτευμα. Instead of describing the people of God as a kingdom of priests, they are now royal priests. The priesthood depicted in Exod 19:6 takes on a kingly aspect in the Greek version. Another possibility sees the term βασίλειον as a substantival adjective, but not necessarily with the meaning Elliott derives from it. Having begun with a substantival understanding of βασίλειον, he transforms the term into a royal residence.[162] As a substantival adjective, however, the term could be taken in a personal manner since the phrase is governed by the subject ὑμεῖς (both in Exod 19:6 and in 1 Pet 2:9). In this case, the term would mean "royal people."[163] It is noteworthy that Targums Ps.-Jonathan and Neofiti separate the terms but retain a personal reference: "kings" (מלכין).

Yet another possibility is that the substantival adjective retains the meaning of the Hebrew term it translated: "kingdom" or "realm."[164] It is also possible that the two terms need not be taken independently. The two substantives can be understood in apposition to one another.[165] In this grammatical arrangement, ἱεράτευμα modifies βασίλειον. The meaning here would be something like, "a kingdom which is a priesthood." Thus, it is altogether possible that the Greek, despite the awkwardness it introduces grammatically, retains the meaning of the Hebrew version with the key exception being the change from plural priests (כהנים) to singular priesthood (ἱεράτευμα). The point here is not necessarily to settle on one meaning but to recognize how the Greek version enables new readings.[166] In fact—and

---

161. Best ("I Peter II 4–10," 288–91) largely agrees with Elliott that the two should be read as substantives. However, he sees them both as corporate personal attributes, thus translating βασίλειον as "body of kings."

162. This is suggested in Elliott, *Elect*, 73–75 but he settles on "royal residence" in his later work (*Home*, 169). He argues that the term οἶκος is the "conceptual link for the combination of different traditions and images" (*Home*, 168). Elliott has placed too much weight on the term οἶκος and in so doing has missed other more likely meanings for βασίλειον.

163. Best, "I Peter II 4–10," 291.

164. Ibid., 290. His resistence to this meaning is based on the lack of adjectival qualifier. But he admits this would be the literal sense.

165. As observed in Selwyn, *First Epistle of St Peter*, 165.

166. Elliott and Best set out to prove a particular reading without recognizing that the potential readings created through the awkwardness of the phrase makes absolute precision impossible. There is no way of knowing precisely how Peter read this

this is brought out in Schutter's work—it is the generative potential of such ambiguous passages that makes them ripe for the interpretive picking.

A second image is that of a holy nation (גוי קדוש; ἔθνος ἅγιον). This phrase stands in parallelism with the previous phrase from Exod 19:6.[167] The people of God are formed into a sanctified community set apart from the nations of the world.[168] Israel has been delivered out of Egypt and given a special covenant with the Lord. This is a unique appellative given to Israel, with the phrase "holy people" (עמ קדוש; λαὸς ἅγιος) being the more prominent phrase in scripture.[169]

Drawn into 1 Pet 2:9, the two appellatives from Exod 19:6 are applied to the church.[170] Phrases originally used within the covenant between the Lord and the people of Israel are now employed to describe the nature of the church. Then in the commentary of 2:9b, the church's vocation of proclamation defines the priestly role taken up by the church. Coordinated with 1 Pet 2:5, a picture emerges of the church which carries out a spiritual ritual of sacrifice to God in the form of proclaiming his excellencies.[171] Thus, phrases originally part of the constitution of a new people of God after the Exodus are drawn into a context in which the people of God are reconstituted around the figure of Christ Jesus as the living stone and are given a priestly vocation.[172]

Before leaving Exodus 19, it is worthwhile observing how the phrase "holy nation" is taken up in Isaiah.[173] Two passages subvert the covenantal phrase and together indicate a transformation for the people of God. In Isa 1:4, Israel is called a "sinful nation" (גוי חטא; ἔθνος ἁμαρτωλόν) and "a people full of sin(s)" (עמ כבד עון; λαὸς πλήρης ἁμαρτιῶν). The appellatives describing Israel in Isa 1:4 accuse the people of God with language evoking the covenantal language of Exodus 19. Yet, by the end of Isaiah new appella-

---

collocation of words. Cf. Ulrich, "Light from 1QIsaᵃ," 195–97.

167. Similarly Best, "I Peter II 4–10," 287. See also Achtemeier, *1 Peter*, 164–65. But see Elliott, *Elect*, 123–24; *1 Peter*, 437.

168. Jobes, *1 Peter*, 161.

169. The phrase גוי קדוש occurs only in Exod 19:6 while עמ קדוש occurs in Deut 7:6; 14:2, 21; 26:19; 28:9; Dan 8:24; Hos 12:1; Zech 14:5.

170. Horrell, *1 Peter*, 70–71. Feldmeier (*First Letter of Peter*, 140) notes that the term ἐκκλησία does not occur in 1 Peter but rather utilizes "salvation-historical terminology."

171. Davids, *First Epistle of Peter*, 93.

172. See Green, *1 Peter*, 62.

173. Childs (*Exodus*, 233) finds it "characteristic of the New Testament to shift the emphasis away from the first exodus to the 'second.' That is to say, the Old Testament exodus tradition has been heard primarily through its eschatological appropriation in Ezekiel and II Isaiah."

tives are applied to God's people. In Isa 62:12, they are called "holy people" (עַם־הַקֹּדֶשׁ; λαὸς ἅγιον) in light of the redemption of the Lord. Then in Isaiah 66, the glory of the Lord is extended to the nations (66:12) and declared among the nations (66:19). In both cases, the terms "glory" (כבוד; δόξα) and "nations" (גוים; ἔθνη) demonstrate the reversal of fortunes announced in Isa 1:4 both for Israel and the nations. The inclusion of the nations with Israel is important for understanding how Exod 19:6 becomes situated in the scriptural tapestry of 1 Pet 2:4–10. Prior to Peter's engagement with Exodus 19, Isaiah has already taken up the language of these covenantal phrases. It is therefore not surprising to find Exodus and Isaiah juxtaposed in 1 Pet 2:9.

The second passage to consider in relation to 1 Pet 2:9 is Isaiah 43:20–21. The introduction of the servant of the Lord, Israel, (Isa 41:8; 42:1–4) comes shortly after Isaiah 40, already shown to be important for 1 Peter. The failure of the servant Israel in Isa 42:19–25 is depicted in terms reminiscent of Isaiah's commission in chapter 6 where he is called to preach to a blind and unhearing audience.[174] There are numerous reprisals of the promise to redeem Israel, and alongside this, the servant of the Lord undergoes development in the remainder of Isaiah 40–48.[175] The salvation of Israel is then depicted as a reversal of their fallen condition (43:1–13).[176] Memories of the exodus are recalled in Isa 43:16–17, but the Lord tells his people not to remember them because he will do something new (Isa 43:18–19).[177] Seitz comments on the contrast between "the old exodus-wilderness tradition" and the wilderness way depicted in Isaiah. The old tradition is transformed so that "we are no longer talking about the wondrous production of water at Marah but about full-fledged rivers in the desert (vv. 19–20). Instead of a tradition of murmuring, now we have a tradition of praise (v. 21)."[178] The Lord promises to care for and protect his people during their return to Jerusalem (Isa 43:19–20).[179] In this context, covenantal language reminiscent of Exodus 19 is used to designate the returning exiles as "my chosen people" (עַמִּי בְחִירִי; τὸ γένος μου τὸ ἐκλεκτόν; 43:20) and "the people whom I formed for myself" (עַם־זוּ יָצַרְתִּי לִי; λαόν μου ὃν περιεποιησάμην; 43:21). The Lord returns his people from exile that they might declare his praises (תְּהִלָּה; ἡ ἀρετή).

---

174. Childs, *Isaiah*, 331–32; Goldingay, *Message of Isaiah 40–55*, 177–78, 181.
175. See Blenkinsopp, "Servant and the Servants," 157.
176. Smith, *Isaiah 40–66*, 192.
177. Goldingay and Paine, *Isaiah 40–55*, 292–93.
178. Seitz, "Isaiah 40–66," 378.
179. Goldingay, *Message of Isaiah 40–55*, 211.

The allusions from Isa 43:20–21 surround the allusions from Exod 19:6. There are a few textual differences evident in the Petrine allusion.[180] The first appellative is transformed from the articular adjectival construction of Isa 43:20 to an anarthrous adjectival construction and the pronoun μου is omitted.[181] The second appellative from Isa 43:21 features a change of λαόν to λαός and the pronoun μου is omitted.[182] These differences are attested in the manuscript tradition.[183] Finally, the alteration of the relative clause ὃν περιεποιησάμην into the prepositional phrase εἰς περιποίησιν is similar to the adaptation seen with Ps 33:9 in 1 Pet 2:3. It is possible that the prepositional phrase simultaneously alludes to Isa 40:21 and Exod 19:5 where the Greek reads λαὸς περιούσιος ("a special people"). This explanation is all the more likely given the use of λαός as the word linking Isa 43:20–21; Exod 19:5–6 and the material from Hosea.[184]

The allusion to Isa 43:21 continues in 1 Pet 2:9 with the use of ἡ ἀρετή. The audience of 1 Peter, addressed with the appellatives of Exod 19:6 and Isa 43:20–21, is called to proclaim the excellencies of God based on their "being called out of darkness and into his glorious light." The allusion likely extends to the verb (ἐξαγγείλητε) even though the term is different than the OG equivalent (διηγεῖσθαι).[185] The Lucianic recension of Isaiah reads ἐξηγεῖσθαι, lending support to the Isaianic background to the term rather than Ps 9:15 as some scholars suggest stands behind the Petrine term.[186] The term ἀρετή

---

180. See Achtemeier, *1 Peter*, 163; Moyise, *Evoking Scripture*, 88–89.

181. The Latin version in Irenaeus, *Adv. Haer.* IV.33.14 reads *genus electus* rather than the Vulgate's *populo meo electo meo*.

182. On Isa 43:21 as the text behind the allusion, see Best, "I Peter II 4–10," 277; Michaels, *1 Peter*, 109; Schutter, *Hermeneutic*, 39–40; Davids, *First Epistle of Peter*, 91; Achtemeier, *1 Peter*, 165–66; Elliott, *1 Peter*, 439; Moyise, *Evoking Scripture*, 88. On Exod 19:5 as the background text, see Selwyn, *First Epistle of St Peter*, 166–67. Green (*1 Peter*, 62) calls them "analogs" of both texts without actually replicating the OT text. See also Jobes, *1 Peter*, 162.

183. MSS 239 and 449 have λαός and MS 26 along with the second Hexaplaric group omit μου.

184. Bauckham ("James, 1 and 2 Peter, Jude," 311) indicates that it was the word λαός in both Isa 43:21 and Ex 19:5 "which suggested and made possible the conflation of these two texts in v. 9."

185. Michaels, *1 Peter*, 110; Schutter, *Hermeneutic*, 40. See also Schniewind, "ἐξαγγέλλω," *TDNT* 1:69.

186. The terms διηγέομαι, ἐξηγέομαι and ἐξαγγείλω are synonymous and would sufficiently translate the Piel of ספר of Isa 43:21. For the role of Ps 9:15 in 1 Pet 2:9, see Michaels, *1 Peter*, 110; Elliott, *1 Peter*, 439; Moyise, *Evoking Scripture*, 89. Beale (*Temple*, 331) suggests Ps 92:12–15 as a possible background, but this is not evident textually. Even so, his insights about the development of the eschatological temple in the early church is largely convincing.

combined with the imagery of darkness and light draws upon the preceding context of Isa 42:10–17, since the term ἀρετή occurs in Isa 42:12 with the verb ἀναγγέλλω.[187] Just as Isaiah 43 declares a new event in the history of Israel, Isaiah 42 is the recitation of a new song universally sung throughout the world (42:9–10).[188] The declaration of the Lord's praise (ἀρετή) links these two contexts. The blindness first indicated in Isaiah 6 reverberates in this section of Isaiah since the Lord will guide the blind "in a way they do not know" (42:16). The Lord then transforms their blindness, using language reminiscent of Isa 9:2. Darkness will be turned into light, and rough places will become level. This wider context speaks of divine redemption in which blindness and darkness are overturned so that the people of God may be guided by the Lord.[189]

The new condition of the people of God segues to the use of Hosea 1–2 in 1 Pet 1:10.[190] The first two chapters of Hosea use children's names to evoke images of judgment and salvation.[191] Three children are born and named in Hos 1:3–9. The first, named Jezreel, signifies judgment on the house of Jehu (1:4–5).[192] The second child, named "No Mercy" (לֹא־רֻחָמָה; οὐκ ἠλεημένη), signifies the removal of divine mercy as judgment on the houses of Israel and Judah (1:6–7).[193] The third child, named "Not my people" (לֹא־עַמִּי; οὐ λαός μου; 1:9), recalls and reverses the covenantal language of Exod 6:2–8.[194] Then, in Hos 2:1 an echo of the blessing given to Abraham (Gen 22:17) begins a new section of Hosea in which the negatives of the second and third named children are removed.[195] In Hos 2:3 the people of Israel are to address one another as "You are my people" (עַמִּי; λαός μου) and "You have received mercy" (רֻחָמָה; ἠλεημένη).[196]

First Peter 2:10 succinctly summarizes the reversal of fortunes found in the first two chapters of Hosea. The depiction of the church in 2:9 as being called out of darkness into light is drawn from an Isaianic motif in which the fortunes of Israel are reversed through successive salvation songs.

---

187. Michaels, *1 Peter*, 111; Bauernfeind, "ἀρετή," *TDNT* 1:461.

188. Oswalt, *Book of Isaiah*, 2:332.

189. Brueggemann, *Isaiah 40–66*, 57.

190. An overview on the history of scholarship on Hosea 1–2 is provided in Dearman, *Book of Hosea*, 80–88 which updates Rowley, "Marriage of Hosea," 66–97.

191. A similar device is used in Isaiah 7–8.

192. Ben Zvi, *Hosea*, 46.

193. Dearman, *Book of Hosea*, 96.

194. Mays, *Hosea*, 29; Dearman, *Book of Hosea*, 99.

195. Dearman, *Book of Hosea*, 104.

196. Ibid., 106.

This motif is extended by drawing upon the prophetic naming of Hosea's children and adds another set of appellatives defining the church as God's people and as those receiving mercy.

The use of Hosea in 1 Peter and Romans supplies several contrasts. The abbreviated form in 1 Pet 2:10 is far shorted than Rom 9:25–26 where Paul quotes the entirety of Hos 2:1 after selectively drawing upon Hos 2:25. In Rom 9:25 the phrase "No Mercy" has been changed to "Not Loved."[197] Absent from Peter's use of Hosea 1–2 is any reflection on the inclusion of the Gentiles that features so prominently in Paul's argument at Rom 9:24 and 30. The text form and the rhetorical use of the passages from Hosea are used differently by the two authors. In addition, Paul cites by name the author of his quotation, "Hosea said these things." This form of introduction is absent in all of 1 Peter. Instead, Peter more generally references "scripture" (γραφή).

Space does not permit an engagement with the complex issues surrounding the relationship of the Jews and Gentiles in the early church. As Horrell notes, "The silence of the text about the status of Israel makes it possible to appropriate the text within a wider theology which constructs a positive place both for the Church and for Israel."[198] Only partially helpful is the statement by Achtemeier that "the language and hence the reality of Israel pass without remainder into the language and hence the reality of the new people of God."[199] While this is true, it does not adequately deal with the silence in the text, as per Horrell, about the relationship between Jews and Gentiles, nor does it address the ethnic composition of the far flung congregations of Asia Minor; argued in the first chapter to be ethnically mixed and therefore more complex than accounted for by most Petrine scholars.[200] It cannot be asserted that Peter has engaged in supersessionism—the replacement of Israel with the church—any more than the writers at Qumran themselves took up the language and reality of Israel as the new or true people of God. Green convincingly posits, "Peter's agenda is not so much to work out the relationship between Israel and the Church as to clarify, according to God's perspective, the honorable status of the Christian community in the world."[201]

---

197. Wagner ("Psalm 118," 81–82) argues that the change from ἐλεέω to ἀγαπάω originates with Paul, whereas Stanley (*Paul*, 112) locates the change at Paul's *Vorlage*. I am inclined to agree with Stanley for the simple fact that Paul has used ἐλεέω prominently in the surrounding context (Rom 9:15–twice; 9:18) making it difficult to account for an alteration to the passage.

198. Horrell, *1 Peter*, 105.

199. Achtemeier, *1 Peter*, 69.

200. See chapter 1.

201. Green, *1 Peter*, 255.

Along these lines, Peter builds a case for the participation of the church in a scriptural narrative of restored divine presence. The repetition of the word λόγος in 2:8 recalls the use of λόγος in 1:23 as well as the use of λογικός in 2:2. The people of God are simultaneously defined by their belief in Christ as the living stone (2:4) and by their obedience to the living and abiding λόγος of God (1:23; 2:8).[202] The patterning of restoration from exile upon the exodus is brought out by Peter through the juxtaposition of phrases from the books of Exodus, Isaiah and Hosea. The restoration of the worship of God within a spiritual temple begins with the important qualification of Jesus as the precious, elect stone upon which the stones of the eschatological temple are built. Thus, participation in the scriptural narrative of the restoration of divine presence is predicated upon participation in Christ.

Conclusion

Three observations can be made regarding 1 Pet 2:4–10. The first observation takes as its point of departure the recent work of Koch and Stanley. Both authors analyze the use of scripture in Paul from the standpoint of a reader-centered approach or the so-called minimalist approach.[203] They propose criteria to identify unambiguous quotations of scripture based foremost on the ability of the audience to perceive that an external source has been employed.[204] Allusions, due to the fact that they are more fully integrated into the context of the letter, are excluded from consideration in their study of scripture in Paul. This moves in a different direction than the work of Hays and Wagner who include allusions and echoes of scripture in their study of Pauline hermeneutics. The key issue, as summarized by Moyise, is whether to "locate the meaning of a text in the reconstruction of the author's intentions, in the dynamics of the text itself, or in its reception in a community of readers."[205]

The use of scripture in 1 Pet 2:4–10 imposes itself on this methodological discussion centered exclusively on the Pauline corpus. The markedness of scripture shifts in the course of this passage. The introductory formula, "for it stands in scripture" (διότι περιέχει ἐν γραφῇ) governs the passages that follow in 2:6–10. From this introductory formula, there is a decreasing markedness. The size of subsequent quotations decreases in 2:6–8 and the allusions in 2:9–10 consist of brief phrases of no more than two words.

202. See Michaels, *1 Peter*, 107; Elliott, *1 Peter*, 433.
203. Moyise, *Evoking Scripture*, 44–48.
204. Koch, *Die Schrift*, 21–23; Stanley, *Paul*, 37.
205. Moyise, *Evoking Scripture*, 48; see also Hays, *Echoes*, 28.

The criteria developed by Koch and Stanley has not made allowances for more subtle uses of scripture. However, 1 Pet 2:4–10 suggests that an author can place greater expectations on an audience to perceive less explicit uses of scripture. At what level of explicitness can one expect an audience member to follow the scriptural discourse an author uses? Does Peter needlessly confuse his audience by infusing scriptural quotations and allusions with his own commentary? Is the audience member helpless in selecting what is scripture and what is Petrine in this mixed bag?

Here Stanley's further work on audience competence is helpful to a point. He suggests that the original audience contained people of varied abilities. Once it is accepted that there are people with the ability to perceive the scriptural text that is employed by the author at subtle levels, then it becomes necessary to account for these subtle uses of scripture in the author's hermeneutic. Subtle uses of scripture have their role in the rhetorical product and impose an expectation that the audience be attentive to these subtleties. How members of an audience appropriate these subtle uses of scripture deserves further work, but it cannot be assumed *a priori* that an audience had no ability to perceive these less explicit allusions. Furthermore, it is not possible, having limited the data to only the most explicit quotations of scripture, to arrive at an accurate picture of an author's hermeneutic or exegetical practices. These subtle uses of scripture work in concert with the more explicit uses of scripture to inform us about how authors read scripture and use it in their writings. This observation is important going forward in 1 Peter where the markedness of quotations and allusions diminishes. There are exceptions to this, for instance the use of Psalm 33[34] in 1 Peter 3. More often in the remainder of the letter, passages of scripture are less marked. The use of Isaiah 53 in 1 Pet 2:22–25 is an important case in point. However, without the more subtle uses of scripture factored in, the full picture of the scriptural narrative employed in 1 Peter cannot be ascertained.

The second observation has to do with the theological hermeneutic employed in Peter's use of scripture. Schutter has demonstrated the Jewish hermeneutical background that is evidenced by several of the exegetical techniques. Clearly, the use of linking terms (*gĕzērâ šāwâ*) is an important part of the author's compositional technique, and for Schutter this betrays a correspondence with midrashic prodecures.[206] The method Schutter has pursued depends upon correlations with the suffering/glory motif. For him, the motif organizes scriptures in such a way that the pesher explains Peter's quotation "to be disclosures of eschatological truths often with a reference

---

206. Schutter, *Hermeneutic*, 98.

to Christ or to the upheavels that are the mark of the End."[207] He sees a correspondence with the motif particularly with Ps 117[118]:22, and asserts that Isa 28:16 and Hosea 1–2 are consistent with the motif.[208]

However, this procedure has not been satisfying for all readers of 1 Peter. This stems partially from the lack of detailed exposition regarding how the motif is directly related to each text. Tellingly, he writes, "It therefore seems to be the case that the author's hermeneutic has allowed him to disclose distinctly different meanings from one and the same oracle."[209] This is not altogether problematic, and his inclination to show how the same text can inform christology and corporate realities is sound. But the demonstration of how each text is related to both parts of the suffering/glory motif is absent. Moyise, for instance, has questioned Schutter's approach with regard to 1 Pet 2:4–10. He writes:

> It is not entirely clear that the author of 1 Peter understood Isa. 28.16 and 8.14 as predicting the "sufferings" and "glories" of Christ (or his people). Certainly he equates "believing in the stone" with "believing in Christ" but he does not elaborate that this means believing in Christ's death and resurrection. That is only present if it is imposed in order to conform to the "prophecy theory."[210]

By "theory of prophecy," Moyise is exploring how consciously the authors of the NT have reflected on the meaning of the scripture they quote and the meaning they derive from those scriptures.[211] In terms of his critique of Schutter, his concerns are well founded that scholars erroneously impose a method upon the data. Yet, Moyise certainly agrees that 1 Pet 1:10–12 provides insights into how scripture is used in the letter. Unfortunately, he does not go so far as to suggest an alternative. The argument of this thesis suggests such an alternative, namely that the uses of scripture cohere in a scriptural narrative, often expressed in 1 Peter through the suffering/glory motif.

The understanding of 1 Pet 1:10–12 provided in chapter 2 can be positively applied here. What was shown there is that the central claim was not a development of Peter's Jewish hermeneutical strategies, but his theological reading of scripture.[212] Therefore, it is important now to show how the scrip-

207. Ibid., 123.
208. Ibid., 136–37.
209. Ibid., 137.
210. Moyise, *Evoking Scripture*, 88.
211. Ibid., 79–80.
212. These, of course, are not mutually exclusive. The contention is not that Peter does not employ hermeneutical strategies shared with Jewish communities. Instead, his emphasis is on the new directions his theology allows him to explore as he reads scripture.

tural complex in 2:4–10 works both along christological and ecclesiological lines. There is a clear christological underpinning to the use of λίθος in 2:4 which carries over to the quotations of 2:6–8. The relationship the believer has with God is expressed in 2:5 as occurring through Christ. Built upon this christology, ecclesiology is emphasized in the scriptural argument of 2:6–10. The final section (2:9–10) contains no christological development whatsoever. It is important to note, then, how the movement from singular λίθος to plural λίθοι prepares the audience for how christology and ecclesiology are related in the use of scriptural texts in 2:6–10. While the three texts of 2:6–8 are christologically linked to the key term λίθος, the exegetical payoff for Peter is the ability of these verses to contribute to his ecclesiological reflections.[213]

Having led in with a christological framing of the term λίθος, it is surprising to find little christological development in 2:6–10. This fact contributes to our understanding of Peter's hermeneutic. The christological element is a presupposition of his reading of scripture and not something he is setting out to prove. Instead, he is interested in reading scripture ecclesiologically. The expectation created through the introductory section (2:4–5) and the quotation of the λίθος texts in 2:6–8 is a statement regarding the vital necessity of belief in Jesus as the Christ. Yet, the climax of Peter's argument is an accusation that unbelievers stumble because they disobey the λόγος.[214] After establishing the centrality of the word for belief, Peter pours a steady stream of scriptural appellatives for Israel upon the church. This further contributes to our understanding of Peter's hermeneutic by highlighting the ecclesiocentricity of his reading of scripture.

The third and final observation to be made here has to do with a variety of details pertaining to how scripture is utilized. Previous scholarship has identified that the quotations in 2:6–8 revolve around the key term λίθος and the allusions in 2:9–10 revolve around the key term λαός.[215] However, the link terms recede into the background when these passages are drawn into their Petrine context. This does not mean they are unimportant, but Peter's theological and rhetorical purposes are derived from other terms. For instance, πιστεύω in Isa 28:16 is used to differentiate the elect from those who reject Christ. The term τιμή is likewise drawn from Isa 28:16 to communicate the honor believers have in their unity with Christ even in the face of apparent shame by those who have rejected Christ.[216] Then in 1 Pet

213. Wagner, "Faithfulness," 94.

214. The temptation to interpret this along the lines of the Johannine *logos* must be resisted since the argument of 1 Peter has worked with λόγος and ῥῆμα as the word of God (1:23, 25) which has now been preached in the good news to the church.

215. Bauckham, "James, 1 and 2 Peter, Jude," Schutter, *Hermeneutic*, among others.

216. Jobes, *1 Peter*, 152.

2:9, the use of ἀρετή from Isa 43:21 explains the nature of the ministry the church partakes in, thus informing the purpose of the building implied by the building metaphor in 2:4-5. The importance of the linking terminology lies in how they inform us of Peter's exegetical practices. He clearly views connections between texts that share matching terminology.

In addition, the shape of 1 Pet 2:6-10 reveals the importance of Isaiah within the scriptural narrative of restoration. Of the six scriptural sources in the section, three are drawn from Isaiah. The quotations from Isaiah range widely throughout the book. Different sections of Isaiah are cross interpretive, as is seen in the use of the stone passages from Isa 28:16 and 8:14.[217] The key text which initiates the following series of scriptural texts, is Isa 28:16.[218] At the same time, Isaiah is read together with the Psalter, Exodus and Hosea. The passages that are brought together resonate with one another. In this way, the inauguration of a new people of God in Exodus 19 is combined with the promise to re-inaugurate a people of God in Isaiah 43. These are then combined with the reversal of fortunes depicted for the people of God who were once not a people in Hosea 1-2. By extension, Peter is able to announce to his audience their own constitution as the people of God. It appears, then, that Isaiah provides a narrative of God's work of restoration for his people who are suffering outside the land of promise. This use of scripture is all the more striking when we consider that the audience is situated in the northern and western regions of Asia Minor. Peter designates believers in this region as stones being built into an edifice designed for the worship of God and for proclaiming his excellencies. The chorus of scriptures collated by Peter assist him in building this spiritual temple in Asia Minor.[219] Thus, the narrative of the restoration of divine presence is no longer bound by geographic constraints, in Peter's reading, but is available to those who respond to the good news in faith.

---

217. Such cross-interpretation seems to have already been present in the Greek translation. See Ziegler, *Isaias*, 95; Wagner, "Psalm 118," 145-51.

218. Schutter, *Hermeneutic*, 133; Moyise, "Isaiah in 1 Peter," 181.

219. Beale (*Temple*, 331-32) correctly reads 2:4-9 as defining the church as the new temple, inaugurating the eschatological work of God much like Revelation 11. Elliott (*Elect*, 156; 1 *Peter*, 412) contends there is no temple imagery here, but see Best, "I Peter II 4-10," 280; Achtemeier, 1 *Peter*, 159.

4

The Use of Scripture in 1 Peter 2:11–25

Introduction

THE BODY MIDDLE OF 1 Peter begins with a brief introduction (2:11–12) drawing on language employed in the prescript. In 1:1, the "elect exiles" are portrayed as part of the diaspora. Now in 2:11, the designation of the audience as exiles is combined with the term "sojourners," thus placing the audience within the same frame of reference as at the beginning of the letter.[1] Between these two points has intervened a blessing section (1:3–12) and the body opening of the letter (1:13—2:10). In the body opening, Peter indicated the importance of proper conduct in light of the audience's frame of reference as exiles in 1:17—"conduct yourselves with fear throughout the time of your exile." The introduction to the body middle (2:11) picks up on this frame of reference in order to establish themes that will carry through the following arguments. Because of their status as exiles and sojourners, Peter exhorts his audience to maintain proper conduct, abiding by the ethic he finds in scripture.[2] In particular, the concept of good versus evil is carried from 2:12 through the end of chapter four. A concern for proper conduct gives rise to formal elements in this section such as the use of household codes (2:18—3:7), a vice list (4:3), a virtue list (4:7–9) and a gifts section (4:10–11).

The language of belief and unbelief established in 2:6–8 is transformed in 2:11—4:11 within the exilic frame of reference. The audience is depicted

---

1. Elliott, *1 Peter*, 457–62.

2. Goppelt, *Commentary on I Peter*, 157–62. The connection between ethics and scripture is one of the expressed implications of Schutter's study (*Hermeneutic*, 177) that were beyond the scope of his work.

as living among "Gentiles" (2:12; 4:3). The use of this term draws upon a scriptural antecedent of depicting Israel as living among the Gentiles. This does not necessarily imply that the audience is ethnically Jewish. Instead, this figuration of the audience as living in the midst of the Gentiles is part of the metaphorical depiction of exile and diaspora as the sphere in which the audience experiences the work of God.[3] In the close of the body opening, Peter drew upon scripture to depict divine presence in the restored spiritual temple equated with believers in Christ Jesus. By placing this temple in the sphere of diaspora, Peter reconfigured the understanding of the locus of God's work among his people.[4] Having done so, he now addresses the ongoing problem of suffering despite the recognition that God has made his presence known among his people in the diaspora.

There are several social interactions between the believer and the surrounding world in the body middle. The relationship of believers with the emperor is developed in 2:13–17. Relationships within the household are covered beginning with servants in 2:18–25, then wives and husbands are addressed in 3:1–7. The servant section of the household code establishes a number of concepts that are used to develop Peter's fuller argument about suffering for the entire church community in 3:13—4:6. The body middle concludes (4:7–11) with a return to the exhortation to love one another earnestly (4:8; cf. 1:22).

Each section of the body middle contains scriptural quotations and allusions. As was the case for the body opening, Isaiah plays a prominent role within Peter's continuing development of a scriptural narrative.

"The Day of Visitation": 1 Peter 2:11–12

It is not surprising, then, that the introduction itself should draw upon a scriptural allusion derived from Isaiah, with the final three words of 1 Pet 2:12 containing an allusion to Isa 10:3.[5] The prepositional phrase ἐν ἡμέρᾳ ἐπισκοπῆς is found only here in scripture. The more common phrase found in the prophets to speak of the imminence of divine judgment is "the day of the Lord" (ἡμέρα κυρίου; יוֹם יהוה).[6] Closer to the phrase in Isa 10:3 are

3. Green, *1 Peter*, 67.

4. The (re-)creation of a symbolic universe was a foundational aspect of the NT writings. See, among others, Adams, *Constructing the World*, 245–47; McDonough and Pennington, *Cosmology*, esp. Dennis, "Cosmology," 157–77 on the relationship of cosmology to 1 Peter. As recognized in the literature, the symbols and senses provided by the NT authors for their audiences depended greatly on scripture.

5. Schutter, *Hermeneutic*, 37, 46; *contra* Danker, "1 Peter 1:24—2:17," 98.

6. Isa 13:6, 9; 58:13; Jer 46:10; Ezek 13:5; 30:3; Joel 1:15; 2:1, 11, 31; 3:14; Amos

the occurrences of ἐν καιρῷ ἐπισκοπῆς in Jer 6:15; 10:15[7] and of ἐν ὥρᾳ ἐπισκοπῆς in Sir 18:20.[8]

Table 4.1: 1 Peter 2:12 and Isaiah 10:3

1 Peter 2:12	OG Isaiah 10:3
δοξάσωσιν τὸν θεὸν <u>ἐν ἡμέρᾳ ἐπισκοπῆς</u>.	καὶ τί ποιήσουσιν <u>ἐν τῇ ἡμέρᾳ τῆς ἐπισκοπῆς</u>;

The text of the allusion in 1 Pet 2:12 differs from OG Isa 10:3 through the omission of the two articles. This may suggest a Hebrew *Vorlage* rather than a Septuagintal version. However, the textual tradition of OG Isaiah contains manuscripts with omitted articles.[9] The paucity of text provides slender evidence concerning whether Peter has altered the text. It is as likely that Peter is here relying on memory as it is to suppose that a written source was used and altered.

The allusion supplies several motifs that are important for the body middle of 1 Peter. After looking briefly at the context of this allusion, Isa 10:3 will be situated within the rhetorical setting of 1 Peter. The allusion is transformed in significant ways, as will be spelled out below.

Isaiah 9:8—10:4 comprises four judgment addresses.[10] The first three (9:8–12, 13–17, 18–21) show God intervening in history to judge the people of God.[11] The final address predicts a future visitation in which God intervenes again (10:1–4).[12] Each of these addresses concludes with a repeated refrain—"For all this his anger is not turned back, but still his hand is lifted."[13] The final address advocates for the poor, widows and orphans against injustice, and the unjust gains of the wealthy will be surrendered when judgment

---

5:18, 20; Obad 1:15; Zeph 1:7, 14; Mal 4:5.

7. Jer 6:15 is a pronouncement of judgment on Jerusalem, and 10:15 is a pronouncement of judgment on idols.

8. Sir 18:20 calls the individual to self-examination prior to the hour of judgment in order to find forgiveness. See also 16:18.

9. Ziegler, *Isaias*, 151. *Untergruppe cII*, containing mss 49 and 764, omits the article before ἡμέρα and Alexandrinus (A) omits the article before ἐπισκοπή.

10. Childs, *Isaiah*, 85; Gray, *Rhetoric*, 131–34.

11. There are slight differences between the MT and LXX in this section. For instance, in Isa 9:12 Greece replaces Philistia as opponents of Israel. None of the differences between the versions alters the interpretation of these passages.

12. Childs, *Isaiah*, 86–87.

13. Gray, *Rhetoric*, 131.

comes (10:1-2).¹⁴ This injustice sanctions the divine judgment on "the day of visitation." The question "what will you do" (ומה־תעשו) in 10:3 critiques the unjust actions listed in 10:1-2.¹⁵ Having taken part in acts of injustice, those under judgment will not be prepared to act properly when the Lord visits his people.¹⁶

In the Greek translation, the phrase "what will they do" (τί ποιήσουσιν) connects well with the ethical argument of 1 Peter. The concept of right and wrong action is key to the body middle of 1 Peter in which the terms ἀγαθοποιῶν and κακοποιῶν along with their cognates pervade.¹⁷ Doing what is good joins with statements of divine imminence throughout (2:15, 19; 3:4, 10-12, 17; 4:2, 7).¹⁸ The themes inaugurated in 1 Pet 2:11-12 initiate a discourse employing scriptural texts whereby the Isaianic voice sounds throughout, and the presence of this key verb in Isa 10:3 may have suggested to Peter the connection of Isa 10:3 to his ethical argument.¹⁹

Isaiah 10:3 is transformed in the Petrine context through its application. The elect are depicted in 2:12 as living among "the Gentiles" who "speak against you as evildoers." Peter exhorts his audience to conduct themselves with honor in their current setting. The purpose for this command is that their good deeds will contradict the accusations raised against them.²⁰ While their good conduct could lead to the conversion of unbelievers, it is not clear that conversion stands behind the phrase "glorify God" in 2:12. Campbell suggests that the honor contest is important for understanding 2:11-12. The elect have had their honor challenged by "outsiders" who

---

14. Smith, *Isaiah 1-39*, 258.

15. Note that whereas the MT has the 2nd plural form תאשו, the OG renders the verb as the 3rd plural ποιήσουσιν.

16. Brueggemann, *Isaiah 1-39*, 90.

17. There are numerous ποιέω cognates in the body middle (2:12, 14, 15, 20, 22, 25; 3:6, 11, 12, 17, 18; 4:10). Though not quoted, Isa 10:3 contains this verb connecting it to this important theme in 1 Peter.

18. Schutter (*Hermeneutics*, 62-63) is very much aware of the principle role ἀγαθοποιῶν and κακοποιῶν play in the body middle. However, he does not pursue adequately the connection of Isa 10:3 in 1 Pet 2:12 to this key motif.

19. The same kind of key work link occurred in 1 Pet 2:9-10 around the term λαός. All three quoted texts (Exod 19:5-6; Isa 43:20-21; Hos 1:9; 2:23) contain the term λαός, but the term in 1 Pet 2:9 is probably drawn from Isa 43:21. See Bauckham, "James, 1 and 2 Peter, Jude," 311.

20. Williams (*Persecution*, 267-69) moves discussion of this passage away from the concept of civic benefaction and in the direction of a Second Temple Jewish background. Cf. Winter, "Public Honouring," 87-103; idem., *Seek*, 12-40.

slander their conduct. Rather than taking revenge against this challenge, they are to silently conduct themselves honorably.[21]

> The praise of God by the pagans constitutes not only their verdict on the God of the Christian community, but an honorable public verdict of the believers themselves and their honorable behavior (καλὰ ἔργα, v. 12c). Thus the believers will receive honor at the conclusion of the exchange of challenge and response.[22]

While the context here suggests an honor challenge, it seems that the public verdict is viewed not as an expected present outcome but is rather projected into future reality.[23] This is consistent with the trajectory of suffering followed by glory.[24] This passage suggests that present slander will ultimately be vindicated in the eschaton. Although a possible conversion of the unbeliever could be in view,[25] the phrase from Isa 10:3 seems to indicates final judgment.[26] Difficulties arise when this passage is reconciled with 1 Pet 4:17–18, where the outcome for those who disobey the gospel is bleak. At the very least, the good conduct of believers can quell the slanderous language of unbelievers.[27] Good conduct may also lead those who are hostile to the elect to belief in the gospel.[28] Ultimately, the concept of "the day of visitation" applies to the slanderer in such a way as to comfort the elect with the ultimate justice God brings on their behalf.[29]

The application of Isa 10:3 to "outsiders" for slandering the people of God differs from the original Isaianic context. Rather than leveling complaints against Israel for its injustice against the poor, widow and orphan, Peter reconfigures the statement to encompass those who slander the people of God. This reading of Isa 10:3 eschews the original context slightly. In Isa 10:1–4, the acts of injustice are listed so that the interrogative of 10:3 communicates the hopeless situation of the final judgment. In 1 Pet 2:11–12, the phrase lifted out of the interrogative clause is now infused with hope for the elect in the justice of God. This theme returns in 3:13–17 where the believer must prepare a defense of their hope in the face of suffering and

21. Campbell, *Honor*, 102–5.
22. Ibid., 105.
23. Horrell, *1 Peter*, 81.
24. This is noted by Schutter (*Hermeneutics*, 152 n. 161) but is not developed according to his stated method.
25. Michaels, *1 Peter*, 118–20; Elliott, *1 Peter*, 470.
26. Davids, *First Epistle of Peter*, 97; Achtemeier, *1 Peter*, 178; Elliott, *1 Peter*, 470–71.
27. Horrell, *1 Peter*, 81.
28. Jobes, *1 Peter*, 172.
29. Liebengood, *Eschatology*, 193.

slander. The people of God are to perform good works "in Christ," and the slanderers will be put to shame (there the passive verb καταισχυνθῶσιν in 3:16 expresses that it is God who puts them to shame).

Doing Good as Servants of God: 1 Peter 2:13–17

The main hortatory convention employed by Peter in the body middle of the letter is the household code or station code, which extends from 2:13 to 3:12.[30] Schutter has downplayed the role of scripture in the body middle—in comparison with the body opening—unnecessarily so.[31] To be sure, the introductory formulae have all but disappeared, and the level of explicitness has diminished. However, there are numerous uses that are overlooked by Schutter in his assessment of this section of 1 Peter.

In 1 Pet 2:13–17, scholars have generally identified Prov 24:21 as an allusion that concludes this passage.[32] It will be argued, though, that anticipatory iterations of scripture in this passage establish the interpretive trajectory of quotations to be used in the subsequent sections of the household code. In particular, the use of κακοποιός and ἀγαθοποιός/ἀγαθοποιέω in 2:14–15 anticipates the quotation of Psalm 34 at the end of the household code. Also, the phrase "servants of God" (θεοῦ δοῦλοι) in 2:16 anticipates the use of the Isaianic servant song in the servant's section of the household code.

Anticipatory uses of scripture were shown to be integral to Peter's compositional technique.[33] This was the case with the first quotation of scripture in the letter. Before quoting Lev 19:2 in 1 Pet 1:16, the passage is presented in summary form in 1:15. Then, prior to the quotation of Isa 40:6–8 in 1 Pet 1:24–25, Peter speaks of being "born again of imperishable seed through the living and abiding word of God" (1:23). In anticipation of the many quotations and allusions in 2:6–10, Peter introduces the section

---

30. Elliott, *Elect*, 484–85; cf *1 Peter*, 36 where he clarifies that such codes include, but are not limited to the domestic code. Thus, civil duty (2:13–17) and communal duty (3:8–12; 5:1–5) are to be considered alongside the more formal subordination pairs (wife/husband, servant/master, child/parent). See further Schrage, "Zur Ethik," 1–21; Balch, *Wives*, 1–20; "Hellenization/Acculturation," 79–101; idem., "Household Codes," 25–50; Schutter, *Hermeneutic*, 60–66; Elliott, "1 Peter, Its Situation and Strategy," 61–78; *Home*, 208–20; *1 Peter*, 503–11; Goppelt, *1 Peter*, 162–79; Carter, "Going All the Way?," 14–33; Horrell, "Between Conformity and Resistance," 111–43; *1 Peter*, 78–95; Feldmeier, *First Letter of Peter*, 151–57.

31. Schutter, *Hermeneutic*, 66.

32. Ibid., 62. See also Michaels, *1 Peter*, 131; Achtemeier, *1 Peter*, 188; Elliott, *1 Peter*, 500.

33. See chapter 3 above.

by using key terms from the scriptural texts employed in the section.[34] With such a pattern repeated several times, it is not unreasonable to expect further anticipatory uses of scripture. These anticipatory uses of scripture have established Peter's interpretive trajectory in each instance. Here at the beginning of Peter's household code—one which draws so significantly upon scripture—one would not be off base to consider other possible anticipatory uses that might suggest further Petrine interpretive trajectories.

The first passage to consider briefly is Ps 33:13–17. Because this passage is quoted more explicitly in 1 Pet 3:10–12, a fuller treatment of the text and context will be undertaken in due course. The explicit quotation later provides ample justification for identifying the Psalm as a contributing factor in the present context, albeit at a more subtle level. Like the anticipatory allusions listed in 1:15, 23 and 2:4–5, the use of terminology in the present section functions in similar ways. Despite the greater distance between the anticipatory allusion and the fuller quotation, it is to be recalled that a brief allusion to Ps 33:9 has already occurred in 1 Pet 2:3. This both indicates the importance of the Psalm for Peter, and prepares the audience for the subtler uses of the Psalm that occur between the more explicit uses.[35]

The ethical argument in the body middle of 1 Peter is dominated with the dualism of good and evil works (ἀγαθοποιέω and κακοποιέω), and Psalm 33 contains similar language.[36] Goppelt argues that Ps 33:13–17 underscores "the basic point of reference for the whole parenesis that precedes, namely the antithesis of κακοποιεῖν (2:16; 3:9) and ἀγαθοποιεῖν (2:14f., 20; 3:6; cf. v. 11a: ποιησάτω ἀγαθόν)."[37] Two key phrases stand out from Ps 33:15. The psalmist calls the audience to "turn away from evil" (רע; κακός) and "do what is good" (עשׂה־טוב; ποίησον ἀγαθός) in 33:15.[38] Michaels correctly discerns that the Psalm is "a storehouse of terms and ideas central to 1 Peter's

---

34. Schutter, *Hermeneutic*, 40. With regard specifically to 1 Pet 2:4–10, see Elliott, *Elect*, 48–49; Michaels, *1 Peter*, 94–95; Bauckham, "James, 1 and 2 Peter, Jude," 310; Horrell, *1 Peter*, 68.

35. Although Bornemann ("Der erste Petrusbrief," 143–65) overreached in his assessment of the influence of Psalm 33[34] on 1 Peter, the Psalm still plays an important role. Schutter (*Hermeneutics*, 44–49, 58, 66) has not given it the attention it deserves in his evaluation of Petrine hermeneutics. For more balanced treatments, see Snodgrass, "1 Peter II. 1–10," 102–3; Green, "Use of the Old Testament," 280–83, 287; Jobes, *1 Peter*, 220–24.

36. On ethics in Psalm 33[34], see Ceresko, "ABCs of Wisdom," 99–104; Mays, *Psalms*, 152; Creach, *Psalms*, 18–19; Weiser, *Psalms*, 298–99; Grogan, *Psalms*, 87–88; VanGemeren, *Psalms*, 325–28.

37. Goppelt, *1 Peter*, 236.

38. On key words in Psalm 33[34]—esp. טוב—see Liebreich, "Psalms 34 and 145," 182–86.

message."[39] Because of this, he observes that the use of the phrase "doing good"—though compatible with Hellenistic ethical thought[40]—has "roots in the LXX (cf. Ps 33[34]:15–17)."[41] The centrality of this language to Peter's ethics and their indebtedness to Psalm 33 have been observed by others as well.[42] Elliott sees in these two phrases derivatives that issue a number of verbal echoes in the language of Peter. The directives against wrongdoing (2:11, 16, 19–20; 3:3, 17; 4:2–3, 15; 5:2–3) correspond to the first phrase, and "the relatively rare terms *agathopoieō* (2:15, 20; 3:6, 17), *agathopoios* (2:12), and *agathopoiia* (4:19)" correspond to the second phrase.[43] The emphasis on these words and the placement of the Psalm quotation lead him to surmise that this ethical dualism (doing what is right versus doing what is wrong) is the theme of 2:13–3:9, rather than subordination.[44]

So, the concepts of doing good and evil in 1 Pet 2:13–17 point to the corresponding language in Psalm 33 quoted in 1 Pet 3:10–12.[45] At the same time, the use of these key terms in 2:13–17 recalls the use of κακοποιέω in 2:12, and thus a block of material is made evident.[46] The suggestion was made above that the verb ποιέω in Isa 10:3 furnishes a ready link between the allusion and Peter's ethical argument in the body middle. If this is the case, the verb ποιέω links Ps 33:13–17 in 1 Pet 3:10–12 with the allusion to Isa 10:3 in 1 Pet 2:12. By doing so, Peter constructs an ethical argument commending godly conduct in the midst of a social context that impugns the elect of misdeeds. In the face of slander (2:12), Peter appeals to scripture to encourage correct conduct in correspondence with the divine will (2:15). In 2:13–17, an ordered society is argued to be consistent with the divine will and the elect are to submit to the ruling authorities since they "punish evildoers (κακοποιῶν) and praise those who do good (ἀγαθοποιῶν)" (2:14).[47]

---

39. Michaels, *1 Peter*, 175.

40. See Van Unnik, "Teaching of Good Works," 98.

41. Michaels, *1 Peter*, 126.

42. Elliott, *Elect*, 181; Green, "Use of the Old Testament," 287; Jobes, *1 Peter*, 220; Feldmeier, *First Letter of Peter*, 187.

43. Elliott, *1 Peter*, 613.

44. Ibid., 617.

45. Woan, "Psalms in 1 Peter," 222–26.

46. Further connections between 2:13–17 and 2:12 are explored in Elliott, *1 Peter*, 485.

47. Williams (*Persecution*, 267–68) explores this passage to discuss the kind of conflict Anatolian Christians were suffering. Liebengood (*Eschatology*, 186–87) emphasizes the eschatological significance of 2:11–12, but does not explore the significance of Isa 10:3 in constructing this eschatology.

Turning now to 2:16, the phrase "servants of God" (θεοῦ δοῦλοι) is emphasized through its placement as the concluding element of the clause along with the use of the strong adversative ἀλλά.[48] Many have recognized how this phrase evokes a scriptural background.[49] Such a phrase is consistent with the Isaianic conceptual framework unfolding in 1 Peter. Feldmeier helpfully connects the term δοῦλος with Paul's employment of the term; both as a self designation and as a description of the Christian life.[50] A connection with the עבד of Isaiah 40–55 is readily available, as Feldmeier notes.[51] However, scholars, by misreading the plural δοῦλοι in 2:16, have thereby overlooked an Isaianic connection holding great potential for understanding Peter's reading of Isaiah.[52]

Earlier, I explored the transition from singular servant to plural servants at Isaiah 54.[53] Recent scholarship—assuming a more unified Isaianic corpus than previous generations—has suggested that this transition has bearing on how to understand the message of Isaiah.[54] For Peter, the use of the phrase θεοῦ δοῦλοι points to an ancient reading of Isaiah that is consistent with these more recent findings. When this phrase is coordinated with the use of Isaiah 53 in 1 Pet 2:22–25, a conceptual framework comes into view that has a high correspondence with the message of Isaiah.

In terms of the ethics developed within the body middle, the household code—as a formal element—brings the concept of subordination into Peter's argument. However, Peter informs this concept with scriptural insight. As he addresses his audience, Peter explains how subordination in a variety of roles is actually nothing else than service to God. As Green writes:

> Subordination is thus an expression of freedom, not of coercion. What is more, any potential claims of human institutions to wield ultimate authority are mitigated, even denied, at the

---

48. Michaels, *1 Peter*, 128–29; Achtemeier, *1 Peter*, 186.

49. Goppelt, *Commentary on I Peter*, 188; Davids, *1 Peter*, 102; Schlosser, "'Aimez la fraternité,'" 529; Elliott, *1 Peter*, 497; Green, *1 Peter*, 74; Feldmeier, *First Letter of Peter*, 163.

50. Feldmeier (*First Letter of Peter*, 163) lists Rom 1:1; Phil 1:1; 1 Cor 7:22; Gal 1:10.

51. Ibid., 163 n. 43.

52. In this regard, perhaps Paul's use of the plural δοῦλοι in 2 Cor 4:5 is an instructive parallel. In this passage, Paul considers the ministry he shares with his cohort (e.g., Timothy, Titus) as a service (ἑαυτοὺς δούλους) to the church for the sake of Jesus (διὰ Ἰησοῦν). Following upon this self-designation, Paul alludes to Isaiah 9—"out of darkness a light will shine."

53. See chapter 3.

54. E.g., Blenkinsopp, "Servant and the Servants," 172; Oswalt, *Book of Isaiah*, 2:431–32; Childs, *Isaiah*, 430; Uhlig, *Theme of Hardening*, 82–83.

outset by Peter's locating his directives under the umbrella of obedience to God.⁵⁵

Thus, the phrase θεοῦ δοῦλοι establishes for the entire household code a frame of reference for the concept of subordination. It is therefore consistent with this frame for Peter to allude to Isaiah 53 in such a way as to depict Christ's own suffering at the hands of human institutions, but also to draw Isaiah 53 into the wider sphere of household servants and the entire Christian community.

The final allusion in 1 Pet 2:17 is drawn from Prov 24:21. The last two lines of the quatrain parallel the injunction of the proverb. As in the proverb, both God and the king are placed in the accusative (τὸν θεόν and βασιλέα), whereas the verb φοβέω when used in 1 Peter is only related to God, with the verb τιμάω provided as the attitude directed toward the emperor. The differences between the two passages are that the article is given for τὸν βασιλέα in 1 Pet 2:17 and the verb is presented as a 2nd person plural imperative rather than the 2nd person singular imperative of Prov 24:21. The principle of retribution is reinforced through scriptural support loaned by Prov 24:21-22. Instructions are given to fear the Lord and the king, who together constitute the basis of a retributive system of justice. The Greek version of the Proverb enjoins the listener to "not disobey either of them," that is, either the Lord or the king.⁵⁶ The reason to fear the Lord and the king is that punishment will be repaid by both upon the ungodly.⁵⁷

Retribution in this passage of Proverbs entails a recognition of the Lord's anointing of the king of Israel.⁵⁸ Invested with divine authority, those subject to the king must submit to his just rule as though they were submitting to the Lord. As the representative of the Lord, the king has authority to exact punishment on his subjects.⁵⁹ Peter alters the meaning of the Prov-

55. Green, *1 Peter*, 75.

56. The Hebrew version is difficult here. The phrase עִם־שׁוֹנִים אַל־תִּתְעָרָב is best rendered, "Do not associate with those who do otherwise." Several commentators understand the participial form of שׁנה as indicating a rebellious or seditious contingent who are embroiled in some sort of political intrigue (See McKane, *Proverbs*, 406; Waltke, *Proverbs*, 286, among others).

57. The Greek version reads: ἐξαίφνης γὰρ τείσονται τοὺς ἀσεβεῖς, τὰς δὲ τιμωρίας ἀμφοτέρων τίς γνώσεται;

58. Waltke, *Proverbs*, 287.

59. Garrett, *Proverbs, Ecclesiastes, Song of Songs*, 200. On the relationship between 1 Pet 2:13-17 and Rom 13:1-7, see Teichert, "1 Petrus 2,13," 303-4; Van Unnik, "Teaching of Good Works," 99; Selwyn, *First Epistle of St Peter*, 172; Reicke, *James, Peter, and Jude*, 95-96; Goldstein, "Die politischen Paraenesen," 88-104; Goppelt, *Commentary on I Peter*, 180-82; Lamau, *Des Chrétiens*, 234-42; Légasse, "La soumission," 390-93; Winter, "Public Honouring," 87-103; Gielen, *Tradition und Theologie*, 435-74;

erb by replacing the king of Israel with the Roman emperor. As Feldmeier points out, "While according to that instructive sentence of Proverbs, fear is to be shown equally toward God and the king, in 1 Peter this fear is explicitly limited to the relationship to God alone."[60] Yet, the concept that the king or emperor exists as the divinely appointed representative carries over from one context to the other. By indicating that the emperor serves as the divine representative upholding the principle of retribution, Peter has developed an argument full of tension. While Peter exhorts the elect to live in subordination to the Roman civil authorities, there is already a hint that the devotion they hold for God may put them in conflict with the authorities.[61]

The use of linking terminology was shown to be an important aspect of Peter's use of scripture in the previous chapter, particularly as it related to the collocation of verses in 1 Pet 2:6–10. There, six passages were unified around key terms, with three connected by the term λίθος and another three by the term λαός. Exploring the wider context of the three allusive elements in this passage reveals a potential link drawing on the concept of fear (φόβος/φοβέω). The linking terms have receded into the background in such a way that it only appears in the allusion to Prov 24:21 in 1 Pet 2:17. Now that they are situated in the context of Peter's epistolary argument, each passage contributes to the passage subtly. However, when it is considered that Ps 33:12 features the Psalmist teaching the fear of the Lord (φόβος κυρίου), the material used by Peter remains colored by this concept even if it is not made explicit. The concept of fear is also relevant in the Isaianic material. In Isa 63:17, the servants make supplication, asking the Lord not to harden his heart "that we might not fear you" (τοῦ μὴ φοβεῖσθαί σε; מיראתך). The verse goes on to entreat the Lord to return (ἐπιστρέφω; שוב) for the sake of "your servants" (διὰ τοὺς δούλους σου; למען עבדיך).

The concept of fear is interesting in light of the two passages that open the body middle of 1 Peter. It is likely that Peter has turned to scripture with this concept in mind, forming a strategy to address the concerns of his audience through a scriptural narrative. The strategy aims to move the audience from a sense of fear of their circumstances by transferring their attention to the fear of the Lord. By situating society within a theological paradigm, Peter draws upon scripture to teach that there is no need to fear society if they are striving after good conduct, since ultimate retribution rests in the final judgment (2:11–12) and the present world order is ordained by God to

---

Shimada, "Is 1 Peter Dependent," 119–21; Achtemeier, *1 Peter*, 180–82; Elliott, *1 Peter*, 493–94.

60. Feldmeier, *First Letter of Peter*, 165.
61. Michaels, *1 Peter*, 132; Green, *1 Peter*, 76.

reward good conduct and punish bad conduct (2:13-17). This is consistent with the proposal that the narrative of restored divine presence is integral to the ecclesiology of the letter, since fear of the Lord is predicated upon his direct presence among the elect. With these elements of his argument in place, Peter will now begin to address the issue of suffering that remains alongside these appeals to final judgment and divine world order. Later, in 3:13-17, Peter will further develop the concept of fear with an allusion to Isa 8:12-13.

Servant and Servants: 1 Peter 2:18-25

The next passage to examine is the servant section of 1 Peter's household code (2:18-25). The admonition to submission carries over from the previous section, although the domestic domain now comes into view. The use of scripture in 2:22-25 is less explicit than the uses of scripture in 1:24-25 and 2:6-8. Even so, the consistent use of material from Isaiah 53 marks this passage out as one of the most important for the study of the Petrine use of scripture.

Ostensibly an address to household servants (οἰκέται), this section of the household code admonishes a portion of the general audience to live in submission to their masters without regard to the severity of their masters (2:18). Servants are not merely to submit to good and gentle masters, but also to those that are "crooked." The language of good and evil used in the previous sections is repeated here, maintaining the anticipatory allusion to Ps 33:13-17 to be quoted in 1 Pet 3:10-12.

The address to servants involves a complex argument composed of three statements. First, a general statement (2:19) informs servants that favor (χάρις) is merited in cases where one endures grievances while suffering unjustly (πάσχων ἀδίκως). The rendering "favor" is better here that the more theologically loaded term "grace" for χάρις.[62] While certainly pertaining to servants, the general character of this first statement is sufficiently broad to encompass the entire audience. The second and third statements (2:20) expound the general statement using negative and positive amplification. There is no credit (κλέος) when one endures beatings resulting from wrongdoing (ἁμαρτάνοντες).[63] The positive restatement finds that an individual merits favor with God in cases where one does good (ἀγαθοποιοῦντες) and endures suffering (πάσχοντες). This clarification reiterates the moral lan-

---

62. BDAG 1079; see also Achtemeier, *1 Peter*, 196; Elliott, *1 Peter*, 518.

63. Van Unnik ("Teaching of Good Works," 100) correctly renders ἁμαρτάνω here as "make a mistake"—or better "failure" or "error"—since the term deals with a servant's failure to carry out the commands of a master.

guage of doing good that Peter has been developing in the body middle of the letter. These three statements depict a servant who has two relationships: one to an earthly master and one to God. Peter recognizes that servants suffer unjustly at the hand of masters. Yet, Peter wants to ensure that his audience is suffering while morally upright and not merely suffering the consequences a servant incurs by wrongdoing.

In the midst of this complex argument are three key terms that anticipate passages of scripture central to this section of the letter. The use of the term ἀγαθοποιέω in the third statement maintains the language of doing good which appeared in the previous two sections and anticipates the quotation of Ps 33:13–17 in 1 Pet 3:10–12. Such consistent use of language with close affinity to the Psalm text indicates the extent to which the ethics of 1 Peter are informed by scripture. The second key term is πάσχω. Though the term does not appear in the suffering servant song of Isaiah 53, the term is closely associated with Isaiah 53 in 1 Pet 2:22–25, showing the correspondence between the term and the servant song for Peter. The repetition of πάσχω in 2:21–25 connects the suffering of Christ to Isaiah 53. The third term is ἁμαρτία, which connects the address to servants to the material drawn from Isaiah 53. Although the use of the verb ἁμαρτάνω was shown to be non-theological in 1 Pet 2:20, this does not diminish its role in anticipating the Isaianic focus on the sinless nature of Christ as suffering servant.

With these three key terms, the address to servants anticipates the scriptural material to be used both in 2:21–25 and 3:10–12. This is similar to the anticipatory use of scripture observed in 2:4–5. Although the key terms function at a very subtle level in the discourse to servants, the pattern of anticipatory terms followed by fuller scriptural quotations is a significant feature of Petrine use of scripture.

Numerous passages from Isaiah 53 occur in 1 Peter 2:22–25. Among the many issues raised by their use are the order of their appearance, the textual differences between OG Isaiah and the text of 1 Peter, the question of their prior existence within hymnic material, and whether these uses should be termed quotations or allusions. Before considering what Isaiah 53 contributes to the Petrine context or the theological use Peter makes of this magisterial passage, it is necessary to attend to these issues.

The starting point for this study is the textual character of the Isaianic material in this passage. Each of the four verses draws upon Isaiah 53 to some extent. With the exception of 1 Pet 2:23, there is sufficient text to consider the textual character of each quoted passage. In the first reference, the text of Isa 53:9 is quoted almost without change in 1 Peter 2:22.

Table 4.2: 1 Peter 2:22 and Isaiah 53:9

1 Peter 2:22	Isaiah 53:9
ὅς ἁμαρτίαν <u>οὐκ ἐποίησεν</u> <u>οὐδὲ εὑρέθη δόλος ἐν τῷ στόματι αὐτοῦ</u>	ὅτι ἀνομίαν <u>οὐκ ἐποίησεν</u> <u>οὐδὲ εὑρέθη δόλος ἐν τῷ στόματι αὐτοῦ</u>

The key question here concerns the term ἁμαρτία since OG Isaiah has the term ἀνομία. With no instability in the manuscript tradition to inform the use of ἁμαρτία in 1 Peter 2:22, several possibilities may be offered for the source of the term ἁμαρτία. First, there are numerous occurrences of ἁμαρτία in Isaiah 53—seven in total—compared to the less prominent ἀνομία—amounting to three. The term could have been exchanged since they are synonymous and similar in form.[64] Second, a Hebrew *Vorlage* may be the source of the change. The term חמס is used only once in Isaiah 53, and it is possible that, upon consulting the Hebrew text, Peter revised the term. The translation of חמס as ἁμαρτία is unlikely, however, since ἀδικία and ἀσέβεια are used more frequently.[65] More likely is the possibility of a Greek version that has revised in the direction of the Hebrew text.[66] Finally, it is possible that Peter has altered the text in order to draw out a theological concept prominent in this section.

Evidence exists from two later authors who quoted extensively from Isaiah 53. Both Clement of Rome and Justin Martyr exchange ἁμαρτία for ἀνομία and vice versa. Their use of Isa 53:5 serves as a striking example. In *1 Clem.* 16.5 and *Dial* 13.5 the terms ἁμαρτία and ἀνομία are reversed. Another example occurs in Justin's *First Apology* where Isa 53:12 is repeated within the span of two chapters. Where OG Isaiah has ἁμαρτία, he cites Isa 53:12 using ἄνομος in *1 Apol.* 50.2 and ἀνομία in *1 Apol.* 51.5 (see also *Dial.* 13.7). These examples suggest that the exchange of terms may occur without recourse to the Hebrew text. Peter shows such consistent dependence upon the Greek version that it would be difficult to maintain an argument based on recourse to the Hebrew text.[67]

---

64. Achtemeier, *1 Peter*, 200.

65. See Ps 7:17; 10[11]:5; 26[27]:12; 57[58]:3; 71[72]:14; 72[73]:6; Isa 60:18, inter alia.

66. See Kreuzer, "Translation and Recensions," 48–49.

67. The role of memory, however, cannot be entirely ruled out.

So, does the term ἁμαρτία belong to Peter's source or to his reshaping of the source?[68] Two factors bear upon this question. The noun ἁμαρτία and the verb form ἁμαρτάνω appear with some frequency in the body middle of 1 Peter (2:20, 22, 24; 3:18; 4:1, 8). It is possible that this term has been inserted into the text to bring it into conformity with the theme Peter wants to develop in this section. A parallel case occurs in 1 Pet 4:8 where the allusion to Prov 10:12 includes the term ἁμαρτιῶν which differs from the LXX. At the same time, it is equally possible that Peter has landed upon a version of Isaiah where this term appears. If this is the case, Peter has enjoyed some amount of serendipity by locating a text form that contributes to the very theme he is developing. The exchange of ἁμαρτία and ἀνομία in Clement and Justin is suggestive even if it is not decisive. Without clearer textual evidence one way or the other, this question must be left open.

An avenue that remains open for further exploration is the role of memory. Isaiah 53 was certainly a text that played a significant role in the early church. It is just as likely that Peter quotes sections from Isaiah 53 from memory as from textual sources.[69] This does not mitigate the comparison with known textual sources, since the text must stand behind Peter's memory in some way. But if Peter has quoted Isa 53:9 from memory, then the appearance of ἁμαρτία here is likely due to the transposition of this noun with ἀνομία. This is not difficult to imagine since these synonyms (each pertaining to immoral qualities) are repeated throughout Isaiah 53.

Finally, the suggestion that theological shaping has occurred at the hands of Peter deserves attention. It is commonly suggested that the use of ἁμαρτία reflects a christological understanding of Isaiah 53.[70] But many note that the christological point of the passage does not emphasize the sinlessness of Christ, but that his suffering was unjustified.[71] Schutter finds that the use of ἁμαρτία is likely meant to link the units of Isaiah 53 worked into 1 Pet 2:22–25. He considers how ἁμαρτία might be more appropriate from the vantage point of the slaves being addressed than ἀνομία.[72] Here, Schutter's move away from a purely christological reading can be brought alongside Green's comments about how Peter has not developed mere christology:

---

68. Even if Peter is the source of the term ἁμαρτία, it is clearly meant to be considered as part of the Isaianic quotation.

69. So Beare, *First Epistle of Peter*, 149.

70. Best, *I Peter*, 120–21; Goppelt, *Commentary on I Peter*, 210; Michaels, *1 Peter*, 145; Achtemeier, *1 Peter*, 200; Feldmeier, *First Letter of Peter*, 174.

71. Beare, *First Epistle of Peter*, 149; Michaels, *1 Peter*, 145; Davids, *First Epistle of Peter*, 110–11.

72. Schutter, *Hermeneutic*, 140. See also Elliott, *1 Peter*, 528.

The upshot of these points is that we see how fully Peter's christological remarks are embedded in his instructions to Christians ... Said differently, if it is true that the suffering of Jesus informs how we read the Scriptures of Israel, particularly Isaiah 53, it is also true that the ensuing narrative of Jesus ought to inform how we read the church.[73]

So, if Peter's theological goals were not christologically oriented but ecclesiologically oriented, the motive for altering the text along the lines of the sinlessness of Christ are allayed. This is not to say that christology is not present or even important in Peter's reading of Isaiah 53, but that there are other ends he has in view.

In 1 Pet 2:23, there is a possible echo of Isa 53:7. For hymnic theorists, 2:23 has posed something of a problem. Bultmann considered this to be a secondary interpolation in the hymn text inspired by the author's consideration of the situation surrounding the servants addressed in this section of the household code.[74] Deichgräber counters that the hymn text was likely cited because it addressed the suffering of the servants effectively.[75] To further his point, he contends against scholars who suggest there are no citations of Isaiah in this verse, that the concept of silent suffering is derived from Isa 53:7, even if it is not a literal rendering.[76] Michaels dismisses the hymn theory outright but likewise perceives the influence of Isa 53:7 behind 1 Pet 2:23.[77] In Isa 53:7, the servant does not open his mouth even when led to the slaughter. This speechless response to suffering is drawn into 1 Pet 2:23 as a lack of response when insulted. Again, Peter has in mind the Christ-like example, which his audience is to follow.

Another verbal association with Isaiah 53 found in 2:23 is the verb παραδίδωμι occurring in both Isa 53:6 and 12.[78] In both places the servant is given up for the sins of others.[79] The concept is altered from the Lord giving

---

73. Green, *1 Peter*, 88.

74. Bultmann, "Bekenntnis- und Liedfragmente," 13.

75. Deichgräber, *Gotteshymnus*, 141 (following Lohse, "Paränese und Kerygma," 88).

76. Ibid., 141 n. 6. "An Bultmann schließt sich Hamman 238 an, ferner Descamps 278, der noch betont, daß in V. 23 kein Jesajazitat enthalten ist. Aber der Vers ist—wenn auch nicht wörtlich—auf Js 53,7 bezogen."

77. Michaels, *1 Peter*, 145.

78. Ibid., 147. Michaels too easily dismisses any relation to an Isaianic background for this term. Cf. Schutter, *Hermeneutic*, 139.

79. In Isa 53:6, the Lord actively gives up the servant for sins (κύριος παρέδωκεν αὐτὸν ταῖς ἁμαρτίαις ἡμῶν) whereas in 53:12 the servant is passively given up (παρεδόθη εἰς θάνατον ἡ ψυχὴ αὐτοῦ ... διὰ τὰς ἁμαρτίας αὐτῶν παρεδόθη).

up the servant to the servant's own self giving to the righteous judge. These concepts are not mutually exclusive, but Peter finds the servant's self-giving to be more exemplary for his audience.

The next verse contains a set of the references from Isa 53:4, 5 and 12. This conflation of verses from Isaiah 53 harmonizes the vicarious language in 53:4 and 12 with the benefits spelled out in 53:5.[80] The bearing of sins by the servant (53:4, 12) is shown to be the work of Christ by use of the relative pronoun, simultaneously imitating the use of pronouns in the Isaianic text,[81] and pointing back to its referent in 1 Pet 2:21. The healing work of Isa 53:5 is then coordinated with the work of Christ as the benefit that believers enjoy.

Table 4.3: **1 Peter 2:24 and Isaiah 53:4; 53:12 and 53:5**

1 Peter 2:24	Isaiah 53:4a; 53:12e; 53:5d
ὅς τὰς ἁμαρτίας ἡμῶν[82] αὐτὸς ἀνήνεγκεν	οὗτος τὰς ἁμαρτίας ἡμῶν φέρει καὶ αὐτὸς ἁμαρτίας πολλῶν ἀνήνεγκεν
ἐν τῷ σώματι αὐτοῦ ἐπὶ τὸ ξύλον, ἵνα ταῖς ἁμαρτίαις ἀπογενόμενοι τῇ δικαιοσύνῃ ζήσωμεν, οὗ τῷ μώλωπι ἰάθητε	τῷ μώλωπι αὐτοῦ ἡμεῖς ἰάθημεν

It is not altogether clear why there is a shift from first person plural to second person plural.[83] Elliott suggests that this shift imitates Isaiah 53. He notes that "the underlying Isaian text also varies between 'you' (52:14; 53:10b) and 'we,' 'our' (53:1–2a, c, 4–6; cf. also 'my people' [53:8]; 'I' [53:9]; 'their' [53:11, 12])."[84] This variation, however, has no correspondence with the variation seen in 1 Pet 2:22–25. The passages used do not contain such variation; the second plural does not occur in 53:4–6 nor in 53:12. Instead, the locus of variation may reside in the tension between the Septuagint and

80. The combination of the noun ἁμαρτία with the φέρω verbs makes these two passages particularly ripe for conflation.

81. The first hexaplaric group (88 and the margin of codex Syrohexaplaris) read αὐτός rather than οὗτος at the beginning of 53:4. If such a reading were available to Peter, it would lend itself all the more to the combination of 53:4 and 12.

82. The reading ὑμῶν is found in P[72] and B among others.

83. Numerous manuscripts for 1 Peter read ἰάθημεν here. It is likely that these have sought to harmonize this term with the Greek version of Isaiah 53, a passage, which would become more and more prominent in the early church and beyond.

84. Elliott, *1 Peter*, 533.

the Hebrew text. In the case of 53:10, the Hebrew tradition reads in the third singular, "if his soul makes a guilt offering, he shall see his offspring" (ערז אם־תשים אשם נפשו יראה). In contrast, the Greek tradition has the second plural, "if you give a sin (offering), your soul will see a prolonged seed" (ἐὰν δῶτε περὶ ἁμαρτίας ἡ ψυχὴ ὑμῶν ὄψεται σπέρμα μαρκόβιον).[85] This consideration raises the possibility of a variant Greek text that served as Peter's *Vorlage*.

Michaels maintains that the change to second person plural at the end of 1 Pet 2:24 is due to authorial alteration. He writes, "By changing Isaiah's ἰάθημεν to ἰάθητε, he reverts to the second person plural address which dominates his epistle but from which he had momentarily departed at the beginning of the verse." Two points, however, make this assertion less than satisfactory. First, the momentary departure from the second person plural was entirely arbitrary. If Peter has been so bent on maintaining a second person address, he could have easily altered the previous quotation. Furthermore, the verb ζήσωμεν could likewise have been written as ζήσητε. Such steps would have averted a shift away from the second person plural altogether. Second, a return to the second plural could have been delayed until 2:25. This would have caused no alteration to the text, nor any substantial difference in the flow of the epistle. In short, there is no good explanation for the alteration of the verb ἰάομαι on rhetorical grounds. It is difficult to suggest that Peter envisioned himself in Christ's work of bearing sins, death for sin and life for righteousness and yet excluded himself from the healing work of Christ's wounds.[86] Furthermore, Goppelt and Achtemeier have soundly refuted the notion that the shift occurs due to some application to slaves.[87]

The hymnic theorists account for the shifting of person in the verbs of 2:21–25 differently. Bultmann counts the change in person as the first of four characteristics marking 2:21–24 as a hymn about the suffering of Christ.[88] Goppelt quibbles with some of the points put forward by Bultmann, but concludes that the shift from second person plural to first person plural is

---

85. Ziegler (*Isaias*, 322) notes that the second plural ὄψεσθε creeps into usage as well.

86. See Jobes, *1 Peter*, 198. Her exegesis makes explicit what Michaels implies as a Jew/Gentile divide here. However, there is nothing in this section to indicate an effort to demonstrate the inclusion of Gentiles in the suffering of the servant.

87. Goppelt, *Commentary on I Peter*, 214; Achtemeier, *1 Peter*, 203. See also Selwyn, *First Epistle of St Peter*, 181; Beare, *First Epistle of Peter*, 150; Kelly, *Epistles of Peter and of Jude*, 124.

88. Bultmann, "Bekenntnis- und Liedfragmente," 12. He also includes a disjunction between v. 25 and v. 21, a lack of correspondence between the suffering of Christ and the address to slaves, and the use of relative pronouns (ibid., 12–13).

characteristic of the hymnic origin for 2:22–25.[89] Both Bultmann and Goppelt suggest that the original hymn read entirely in the first person plural. It is one of the ironies of scholarship that in constructing a hypothetical hymn, Bultmann and Goppelt should produce a verbal parallel to the Greek version of Isaiah 53. Osborne and Best suggest that direct use of Isaiah 53 sufficiently accounts for the language in 1 Pet 2:22–25 but are unable to divest themselves completely of the hymnic theory.[90] Michaels, Achtemeier and Elliott have more recently argued against the hymnic theory, showing that the Isaianic text itself is more likely the *Vorlage* behind 1 Pet 2:22–25 than a hymnic source.[91]

It becomes clear that dogmatic statements about the origin of the shift from first person plural to second person plural are impossible. The fact remains, however, that 1 Pet 2:24 contains a text at variance with OG Isa 53:5. In keeping with the observations above concerning Isa 53:9 in 1 Pet 2:22, the role of memory cannot be ruled out. Given the prominence of Isaiah 53 within early Christianity, the likelihood that Peter has memorized the passage provides an explanation for the shifting of the verbs as he incorporates the message of Isaiah into his argument.

In the final reference, Isa 53:6 occurs in 1 Peter 2:25. Reflecting on the differences between the Greek text and 1 Peter, commentators consider the first line of 1 Pet 2:25 to be periphrastic. This assumption, paired with a thoroughgoing hypothesis that the audience of 1 Peter consists of former pagan Gentiles, has led to many speculations about the intention of this construction. For instance, Achtemeier indicates that the periphrastic construction is "intended to describe the life of those addressed prior to their conversion."[92] Similarly, Davids suggests that "the use of past tenses . . . indicates that the thought is of their pagan past."[93] It was argued in the introduction, however, that there is not enough information in 1 Peter to make dogmatic statements about the ethnic identity of the audience of 1 Peter. This being the case, it would be impossible to surmise the intention of a peculiar grammatical construction with regard to how it impacted the previous experience of the audience. The immediate context (2:21–25) shows no regard for the ethnic identity of the audience.

---

89. Goppelt, *Commentary on I Peter*, 207.

90. Osborne, "Guide Lines," 388–89; Best, *I Peter*, 120.

91. Michaels, *1 Peter*, 134–37; Achtemeier, *1 Peter*, 192–93; Elliott, *1 Peter*, 548–50. See also Patsch, "Zum alttestamentlichen Hintergrund," 278–79.

92. Achtemeier, *1 Peter*, 203.

93. Davids, *First Epistle of Peter*, 113.

Table 4.4: 1 **Peter 2:25 and Isaiah 53:6**

1 Peter 2:25	Isaiah 53:6
ἦτε γὰρ ὡς πρόβατα πλανώμενοι	πάντες ὡς πρόβατα ἐπλανήθημεν

A question of greater significance is whether this grammatical construction may even be called periphrastic. The gap between the copula and the participle is great enough to raise doubts about this categorization. Porter contemplates the periphrastic construction in his comprehensive study on linguistics in biblical Greek. Among several points he makes in defining periphrasis, he states, "The Participle not only must be grammatically in suitable agreement with the auxiliary but must be adjacent to it, either before or after." He goes on to clarify that elements modifying the participle may not occur between the auxiliary and participle, "otherwise the Participle is considered not to form a periphrastic construction."[94] This presents difficulties with regard to the Petrine text since the phrase ὡς πρόβατα interrupts the potential connection between ἦτε and πλανώμενοι.[95]

With this grammatical consideration in mind, the text critical work on this passage must next be addressed. Many of the highly regarded manuscripts for 1 Peter support the reading of the critical edition (01, 02, 03, 5, *passim*). While several quality manuscripts have πλανώμενα here (P[72], 04, 33, 81, 307, 1739), so that the participle agrees with the term πρόβατα, this appears to be an effort on the part of scribes to read this as a periphrastic construction, but few regard this reading as preferable. This alteration of the text indicates how the reading πλανώμενοι was not sufficiently periphrastic for these scribes. These considerations bear upon the present study because it impacts the extent to which the text of 1 Peter differs from the Greek version of Isa 53:6. Previous scholarship, assuming that 1 Pet 2:25 contained a periphrastic construction, deemed that the text of Isaiah has been changed from a first person plural aorist verb to a second person plural periphrastic imperfect. However, I contend that the difference between 1 Pet 2:25 and Isa 53:6 centers solely on the participle. This difference may be the result of a variant in the *Vorlage* or the result of allusive license.

Summarizing the textual issues covered so far, 1 Pet 2:22–25 directly appropriated the Septuagint. However, there are a few instances where

---

94. Porter, *Verbal Aspect*, 453; idem., *Idioms*, 45–46. See also BDF §§ 352–56; Boyer, "Classification of Participles," 172–73; Wallace, *Greek Grammar*, 647.

95. Because ὡς πρόβατα is part of the quotation with the participle, the phrase is best understood as modifying the participle and not the copula.

differences occur in comparison with OG Isaiah 53. The points of difference with the Septuagint are probably due to two factors. First, there are indications that the Isaianic text form exhibited some elements of instability. This may be due to either variations within the Greek text at the time or to subtle variants in the Hebrew from which the Greek was translated. To illustrate this last point, the use of the term φῶς in Isa 53:11 sheds light on how the Greek text draws upon variants in the Hebrew tradition. While the MT reads יראה, several scrolls from Qumran read יראה אור.[96] Another example analogous to the textual differences in 1 Peter is the deviation in person and number between the MT and 1QIsaᵃ in 53:8–9. The pronominal shift from the first person singular of עמי in the MT to the third person singular of עמו in 53:8 and the verbal shift from the third person singular of ויתן in the MT to the third plural of ויתנו in 53:9 are important variants in the Hebrew tradition that are comparable to the shift from first person plural to second person plural in 1 Pet 2:24, or the use of a participle in exchange for a first person plural verb in 2:25.

Similar examples abound within the Greek tradition. Among the most prominent difficulties in the Greek text of Isaiah 53 is the first verb of 53:2. Ziegler confesses that certainty can never be reached concerning the confusion between ἀναγγέλειν and ἀνατέλλειν not only in 53:2 but also in 42:9; 43:19; 45:8 and 47:13.[97] Compounding this verbal confusion stands the difficulty of determining whether μεν or δέ appears in the text, with μεν additionally being either a conjunction or verbal ending. Thus, it is not clear whether 53:2 should read ἀνέτειλε μεν or ἀνηγγείλαμεν. Such confusion introduces grammatically diverse elements so that one version has the third singular verb form and the other the first plural verb form. Several pronominal variants occur in the text history of Isaiah 53 which are rather minor yet do provide a basis for considering whether changes in person and number have occurred in Peter's *Vorlage* rather than through his own intentional alteration of the text.

A further consideration has to do with the categorization of quotations and allusions. The suggestion made in the introduction regarding a spectrum of explicitness becomes important here. There are very few formal features that would lead scholars to consider this a strict quotation. However, there is a high level of explicitness, allowing comparison between the Petrine text and the Isaianic *Vorlage*. The location of the Isaianic material within the discourse of the servant section of the household code makes it

---

96. 1QIsaᵃ, 1QIsaᵇ, 4QIsaᵈ. See *DSSSMM* I, pl. XLIV; *DSSHU*, pl. 10; P. W. Skehan and E. Ulrich, *DJD XV*, 83, pl. XIV.

97. Ziegler, *Isaias*, 99.

difficult to fully differentiate the quoted material from the Petrine context. This means our efforts to compare the text of Isaiah with the quoted material in 1 Peter is obscured by the transitions into and out of quotation. In other words, the places where there are textual difficulties are the seams between distinctively Isaianic and Petrine units.

These factors raise important uncertainties regarding assessments of text-types and the role of the author's hand in accommodating the text. This places us in a situation where former bases of knowledge can no longer be held. Furthermore, it becomes less clear what to make of the textual phenomena and undermines some lines of enquiry and analysis. That said, there are several points that can be made concerning the textual character here.

First, there is ample text from a relatively small section of scripture, so that there is a high enough level of explicitness that the reader/hearer could be expected to make the association with Isaiah. There is likewise sufficient text with a high level of correspondence with OG Isaiah that it is reasonable to assert that at some point the written text of Isaiah was consulted. This written text served as the basis not only for the quote but also the line of thought (including exegetical insights and theological extrapolations) that appear in 1 Peter.

Second, the pluriformity of the textual tradition before and during early Christianity provides a textual reason for the variants that occur. For instance, the use of the term ἁμαρτία in Isa 53:9 is later found in Eusebius, *Demonstratio evangelica* I.10, 16 and Cyril of Alexandria, *Commentarius in Isaiam Prophetam* V.I.749C.[98] Neither of these works demonstrates any dependence upon 1 Peter as their textual basis, thus eliminating the idea that 1 Peter has generated the use of ἁμαρτία in the later occurrences. This being the case, there is ample reason to suspect that there existed a textual tradition using this term rather than ἀνομία. It is either the case that Peter has selected a text form to suit his theological purposes or that the text form with the repeated use of the term ἁμαρτία has prompted Peter's hamartiological reflections. The latter seems more likely since one cannot expect that Peter went hunting around the ancient world looking for a variant text to support his theological agenda.

The role of memory has been explored in the course of the textual analysis. It cannot be expected that Peter's encounter with scriptural texts has occurred in close proximity to his use of these texts in his writing. It is more likely that these scriptural texts have repeatedly been used in his missionary preaching and now are reused in this epistolary address. Just as textual pluriformity provides a possible reason for variants in the text, memory gives

---

98. Heikel, *Eusebius Werke*, 6:45; Migne, *PG* 70:1181; see also Ziegler, *Isaias*, 322.

another reason such variants might occur. It is highly likely that Isaiah 53 would have been committed to memory in the early Christian context. Yet, despite the probable role of memory, textual comparison is still necessary, since the text in some form stands behind Peter's memory of the text.[99]

Finally, the use of Isaiah 53 in this section differs from other explicit quotations in 1 Peter in that it is not set apart as quoted material. Instead, scripture is embedded within the Petrine discourse. Thus, the use of scripture here feels more like an allusion even though it achieves a high level of explicitness. Assessments of the textual character of Isaiah here, then, must cautiously account for the role of the Petrine hand alongside the Isaianic material. It is less than clear whether such occurrences as the second plural verbal ending in 2:24 is due to Peter's *Vorlage* or Peter's hand. One of the nuisances of this caution is the realization that far less can be said positively about the textual differences here than has heretofore been asserted by scholarship.

Isaianic Context in Petrine Context

Moving beyond the text of Isaiah 53 in this section, it is important to consider what the Isaianic material contributes to the argument of the letter. Recent scholarship has tended to recognize the importance of context for texts such as Isaiah 53.[100] The four servant songs (42:1–4; 49:1–6; 50:4–9; 52:13—53:12) were extracted from their context by Duhm over a century ago, based on the perception that the style, language and poetry of the songs differed from that of Isaiah 40–66.[101] It is only recently that a contextual reading of these servant songs has reemerged. This has allowed exegesis to forge new directions in Isaian studies as well as recover pre-critical understandings. What is important for Petrine studies is that scholarship has arrived at a place where the final form of Isaiah is able to take center stage, a place it possessed when 1 Peter was written.

A contextual reading of Isaiah on the part of 1 Peter has not received overt challenges in recent scholarship. However, studies have assumed, in the wake of Duhm's work, that the four servant songs ought to be considered together and in distinction from their situation within Isaiah 40–66. For example, Pearson states, "The Servant Songs can be studied independently

---

99. On the problems of "memory error," see Stanley, "Social Environment," 20.

100. Clements, "Unity," 117–29; "Beyond Tradition-History," 95–113; Laato, "Composition," 207–28; Childs, "Retrospective Reading," 362–77, among others.

101. Duhm, *Das Buch Jesaja*, 284. Cf. Childs, *Isaiah*, 291.

from the text of Deutero-Isaiah."[102] The result is that significant aspects of Isaiah 53 are neglected.

A contextual reading of Isaiah 53 in 1 Peter has important implications. The pattern "servant-servants" in Isaiah 40–66 has bearing on how Isaiah 53 is to be understood in 1 Peter. Blenkinsopp has contributed greatly to our understanding of the role of the servant and servants in Isaiah. He finds the servant theme as the key to understanding the formation of the book of Isaiah.[103] While there are few occurrences of עֶבֶד in Isaiah 1–39, it features prominently in Isaiah 40–66. Dividing this latter portion into three sections (40–48; 49–55; 56–66), he summarizes the significance of עֶבֶד in the first two sections, "In 40–48 the term alludes almost exclusively, perhaps exclusively, to a collectivity, while in 49–54(55) the collective reference is the exception rather than the rule."[104] This distinction then opens into the final section where the plural עֲבָדִים occurs ten times.[105] This group, "cherishing eschatological beliefs and alienated from the official leadership," is related to the singular servant of Isaiah 49–55.[106] He writes:

> The texts do, however, permit and even encourage us to think of the relationship between the prophetic Servant who is spoken of and who himself speaks in chaps. 49–54 and the "servants of Yhwh" of the last two chapters in terms of discipleship.[107]

Seitz presents this matter in his commentary on Isaiah 40–66 and considers how the servant-servants relationship explains some of the interpretive difficulties in Isaiah 53. The identity and mission of the servant are of central importance in chapters 40–52.[108] The servants of chapters 54–66 are seen to be disciples of that singular servant. Isaiah 53, then, stands at the seam between these two prominent depictions.[109] Seitz states, "The greatest challenge of this profound tribute to the suffering servant—decisive for exegesis—involves a correct appraisal of who is speaking," and he finds that the servants who follow the servant are "the 'voices' responsible for

---

102. Pearson, *Christological and Rhetorical Properties*, 248.
103. Blenkinsopp, "Servant and the Servants," 157.
104. Ibid., 161–62.
105. Ibid., 166.
106. Ibid., 170.
107. Ibid., 171.
108. Seitz ("Isaiah 40–66," 317) writes, "For all the centrality of the word "servant" in chapter 40–52, there is also some difficulty in knowing how to identify and interpret the servant's role and mission."
109. Ibid., 317–18.

this poem."[110] These servants attest to the death of the individual servant as "expiatory for themselves."[111]

Though seen as a singular servant, the ambiguity within the text complicates matters. The servant also represents corporate Israel. Seitz writes, "The identification of the servant with Israel sets up a different, though affiliated, conception. The servant's death is reckoned as representative of Israel's death and suffering *at the hands of the nations*."[112] Childs identifies "a great variety of tensions" regarding the identity of the servant. He writes:

> The polarity remains between the servant as a corporate reality and as an individual, between the typical features and the historical, between a promised new Israel of the future and a suffering and atoning figure of the past.[113]

With a view to the canonical shape of Isaiah, Childs and Seitz have explored the elements that bear on an interpretation of the servant when understood within its Isaianic context. The result is a greater appreciation for the complexity of the servant songs than was available in the studies of those attempting to identify the servant within an overly atomistic reading.

The convergence of these elements flavors Isaiah 53. The servant interpreted individually retains a significant corporate identity through representation of Israel. In light of this, the death of the servant has two spheres of significance. As an individual, the death benefits a group defined as the "servants"—the disciples of the servant. As a corporate representative, the death stands for Israel's death at the hands of the nations and carries benefits both for Israel and the nations. Seitz summarizes, "The servant's suffering and death are his own, on behalf of the servants. At the same time, the servant's suffering and death are Israel's, on behalf of the nations. These two distinctive theses are here woven together so tightly as to refuse disentanglement."[114]

The contribution Isaiah 53 makes in 1 Pet 2:21–25 can now be better understood in light of these two theses. The servant, interpreted christologically, is not depicted in isolation from either his disciples nor the nations. Already in 2:16 the language of the plural servants of God is employed in an apparent paradox, considering that Peter addresses his audience as people who are free. Peter likewise situates the people of God among the nations (2:12), admonishing the elect to maintain honorable conduct. Thus, when

110. Ibid., 460.
111. Ibid., 462.
112. Ibid., 461. Emphasis original.
113. Childs, *Introduction*, 335.
114. Seitz, "Isaiah 40–66," 462.

Peter arrives at his development of the suffering servant in Isaiah 53, he already has established important interpretive categories. The servant's death for his servants entails the active work of these disciples to carry out their mission to the nations.

With these categories in mind, the language of 1 Pet 2:21 can be seen as the interpretive lens by which Isaiah 53 is viewed. The calling of the disciple servants has its basis in the suffering of Christ for his people. The example of Christ, in turn, establishes a pattern by which the disciple servants comport themselves. Taken by itself, 1 Pet 2:22–25 encompasses only the first of the two theses: that Christ suffered on behalf of his people. However, the broader context within which this passage is situated (2:11—4:11) thoroughly develops the second thesis. First Peter 2:21 ties 2:22–25 into this broadly developed second thesis showing that Isaiah 53 does not merely depict Christ as the suffering servant, but also propels the church to understand its own suffering as part of the mission to the nations. This will be seen in the next chapter where the wives section of the household code is analyzed.

From here, the task shall be to discern how these Isaianic texts have been employed in their Petrine context. Conspicuously situated in the midst of the Isaianic material in 1 Pet 2:22–25 stands a phrase scholars have long considered as deriving from the Pentateuch. An analysis of this phrase in 1 Pet 2:24 leads naturally into an assessment of how Isaiah is used within the Petrine context. Recall that in 1:19, a phrase from Isa 53:7 was combined with sacrificial language in the Mosaic tradition. It is possible that a similar connection is made here with the phrase ἐπὶ τὸ ξύλον. The occurrence of ἐπὶ ξύλου in Gal 3:13 where Paul alludes to Deut 21:23 has drawn attention away from another possible link.[115] The more common phrase has ἐπί with ξύλον in the genitive.[116] However, a less common phrase, ἐπί with ξύλον in the accusative, occurs several time in Leviticus 1.[117] In each occurrence of the phrase ἐπὶ τὰ ξύλα, the context indicates the placement of the burnt offering on the wood of the altar. The first occurrence (Lev 1:8) concerns the burnt offering of a male ox to make atonement for the person bringing the gift (1:2–9). The second occurrence (1:12) concerns the use of either sheep or lambs in the burnt offering (1:10–13). The final occurrence (1:17) concerns the use of birds—either a dove or pigeon—for the burnt offering (1:14–17).

The significance of this potential connection is that the cross is understood as a place of sacrifice in keeping with the wood on the altar in

---

115. Several manuscripts render this phrase in the genitive, probably due to the influence of Gal 3:13. The evidence is overwhelmingly in favor of the phrase in the accusative. See *ECM*, 145.

116. Deut 21:23; Josh 8:29; 10:26; Judg 9:9, 11, 13; 1 Kgs 18:23; Esth 5:14; 7:10.

117. Lev 1:8, 12, 17; 3:5.

Leviticus.[118] This indicates that 1:18–21 should be viewed as an anticipation of this later development of Isaiah 53 in the letter. That both of these passages should read Isaiah 53 together with phrases from the sacrificial code of the Pentateuch suggests that Peter is exploring the interconnectedness of the suffering servant and aspects of the sacrificial code. Lacking in Isaiah 53 is a sense that the servant bears the role of sacrifice. Elliott, for one, correctly finds "the action of the Isaian servant" as "vicarious in nature" but denies that in Isaiah 53 and 1 Peter there is a depiction of either the servant or Christ as a sacrifice.[119] Yet, by drawing on the sacrificial language especially from Leviticus, Peter incorporates sacrificial language into the vicarious activity of the servant/Christ.

The use of the terms sin (ἁμαρτία) and righteousness (δικαιοσύνη) are important here and contribute to an understanding of Christ—as suffering servant—assuming a role as sacrifice for his people. Achtemeier raises the point in his discussion about the shift from first person plural back to second person plural, "So long as the phrase 'our sin' was thematic (v. 24a, b), he used the first person, reverting immediately to the second person (24c) as soon as the discussion centering on that phrase was concluded."[120] Thus, according to Achtemeier, sinfulness and forgiveness of sin creates solidarity between the author and the recipients. As indicated earlier, it is difficult to maintain an argument whereby Peter envisioned himself receiving the benefit of forgiveness of sins without also including himself in the healing by Christ's wounds, and in so doing appears to have overstepped in his exegesis of the passage. Achtemeier, however, has highlighted an important concept developed by Peter in light of his reading of Isaiah 53. The concept creeps into the first quotation of Isa 53:9 in 1 Pet 2:22 and is repeated in the quotation of Isa 53:4/12 in 1 Pet 2:24. This focus on sin reflects a recurring motif in Isaiah 53, demonstrating an engagement with scripture that was formative for Peter's understanding of Christ.[121] The term ἁμαρτία frames Isa 40–55, forming a central part of the initial proclamation (Isa 40:2) as well as the later call to repentance (Isa 55:7).[122] Within this framework, the

---

118. Michaels (*1 Peter*, 148) shies away from seeing Deut 21:23 (cf. Acts 5:30; 10:39; Gal 3:13) as the background for the phrase ἐπὶ τὸ ξύλον in 1 Pet 2:24. He, however, does not take into consideration the phrase as found in Leviticus. He translates the clause, "He himself carried our sins in his body to the cross." Yet, if the cross is being compared to the sacrificial wood on the altar, we may translate the phrase, "on the cross."

119. Elliott, *1 Peter*, 532.

120. Achtemeier, *1 Peter*, 203.

121. This point has been made by Wagner, "Faithfulness and Fear," 104–6, particularly with regard to Isa 8:11–18 in the NT, on which see chapter 3 above.

122. Other instances of ἁμαρτία within Isaiah 40–55, apart from several occurrences

term ἁμαρτία forms a basis of accusation against Israel (Isa 42:24; 43:24; 50:1). Yet, the Lord promises redemption from sin (40:2; 44:22). Therefore, it is not surprising to find in 53:9 an indication that the servant who bore the sins of many (53:12) was himself sinless. In Isa 53:4–6 and 11–12, the bearing of the sins of many is the role depicted for the suffering servant. Through quotation (1 Pet 2:24a) and imitation (2:24c), this theme is carried over into Peter's epistle.[123]

The concept of righteousness stands in contrast to the concept of sinfulness. In 2:24, this contrast is set forth as the result of the sacrifice of Christ. Christ bore sins, "that we might die to sin and live to righteousness (δικαιοσύνη)." In Isa 53:11, the role of the righteous suffering servant is to make the many righteous. The cognates of δικαιοσύνη in Isa 53:11 (δικαιόω and δίκαιος) stand behind Peter's use of the term in 2:24. Later in 1 Pet 3:18, the phrase "righteous for the unrighteous" (δίκαιος ὑπὲρ ἀδίκων) likewise echoes Isa 53:11. There, the use of πάσχω (3:18) works in concert with the phrase to evoke the Isaianic discourse of 1 Pet 2:22–24. The δίκαιος word group is not particularly prominent in the style of 1 Peter. Only the use of δικαιοσύνη in 1 Pet 3:14 appears to be employed apart from any scriptural discourse. Compared with the writing of Paul, James and the author of Hebrews, this suggests strongly that the use of δικαιοσύνη in 1 Pet 2:24 and δίκαιος in 3:18 echo Isa 53:11.[124]

The exchange of sin for righteousness is at the heart of Peter's use of Isaiah and deeply informs his conception of ethics and the constitution of the church. By combining the language of Isaiah 53 with the sacrificial language of the Pentateuch, both here and in 1:19, Christ is depicted as a sacrifice for sin. This sacrifice provides healing to the elect so that they may live according to righteousness. Peter has already established in 2:6–10 that the church is constituted of believers who partake in a ministry patterned on the categories of kingship and priesthood drawn from scripture. Here Peter probes further by identifying Christ as the sacrifice for sins. Because of the exchange of sin for righteousness, the exhortation to maintain honorable conduct (2:12) has its basis in the work of Christ. Furthermore, 2:21–25 adds to Peter's ecclesiology by indicating that Christ's role as suffering servant is the pattern the elect are to follow. This theme will be carried forth throughout the remainder of the epistle's body middle.

---

in Isaiah 53, are Isa 43:24; 44:22; 50:1.

123. See Gignilliat, *Paul and Isaiah's Servants*, 104–6.

124. This is not to say that the δικαιο- word group is not informed by scripture in these other epistles. However, there are clear examples where the language has been employed apart from cases of scriptural discourse.

Reading Isaiah 53 Ecclesiologically

Over the course of the last century, 1 Peter has been analyzed predominantly for its christological statements.[125] Many studies capitalized on the hymnic theories that dominated scholarly discussions of 1 Peter. For instance, Pearson's study analyzes this section from the vantage point of the hymnic theory and assesses the hermeneutic of this section without sufficiently developing the ecclesiological aspects.[126] Even scholars who are not committed to analyzing 1 Peter from a form-critical perspective miss important ecclesiological aspects to Peter's use of Isaiah. Dubis, analyzing the exile/restoration themes drawn from Isaiah in 1 Peter, comments, "First Peter's repeated citation of Isaiah 40–55 indicates extensive reflection upon these chapters and a belief that these Isaianic texts find their realization in Christ."[127]

Scholars who have considered more closely the hermeneutical issues in 1 Peter have tended to regard this section as more nuanced. Schutter understands that a christological apologetic is presupposed in 1 Pet 2:22–25, but that "collective and corporate references" also pertain.[128] Jobes identifies the corporate collectivity that surrounds the Christ figure of Isaiah 53 here in 1 Peter.[129] She, however, locates the corporate identity not in Isaiah 53 but in Isaiah 41. Yet, Peter seems to move more directly from Isaiah 53 to a corporate understanding of this text.[130]

While there are important points to be made about the christology of Peter's use of Isaiah 53 here, Peter develops important ecclesiological points.[131] The concepts of moral speech, lack of retaliation, suffering unjustly

---

125. See Selwyn, *First Epistle of St Peter*, 248–50; Beare, *First Epistle of Peter*, 52–54; Schlosser, "Ancien Testament," 65–96; Best, *I Peter*, 119–20; Osborne, "Guide Lines," 406–8; Richard, "Functional Christology," 133–39; Achtemeier, "Christology," 147; Pearson, *Christological and Rhetorical Properties*, 1–11.

126. Pearson, *Christological and Rhetorical Properties*, 4–11.

127. Dubis, *Messianic Woes*, 49.

128. Schutter, *Hermeneutic*, 170, 174.

129. Jobes, *1 Peter*, 200.

130. Isaiah 41 is not cited in 1 Peter.

131. It is important to recognize that, while 1 Pet 2:21–25 resides within the servants' section of a household code, there are many ways in which the entire community continues to be addressed. First, the language used in this section is repeated elsewhere in the letter for the general audience (Achtemeier, *1 Peter*, 192; Elliott, *1 Peter*, 523). This occurs most prominently in 3:9–10 and 3:13–18, where the vocabulary and phraseology has a high level of correspondence. Second, the concept of "servant" serves as a paradigm for all believers in 1 Peter (Michaels, *1 Peter*, 135; Elliott, *Home*, 206; Jobes, *1 Peter*, 188). Peter has already addressed the entire audience as "slaves of God" in 2:16 (Green, *1 Peter*, 77). Finally, the construction of the address to household slaves betrays a more general address. Michaels and Green locate the general nature of the address

and giving oneself to a just judge are points directly applied to the audience even if they are at first centered upon the figure of Christ. Although scholars have made attempts to spell out the hermeneutical issues in 1 Pet 2:22–25, a satisfying synthesis has not yet been made. The following is an attempt to address this need.

There are three theses to explore here. First, ecclesiology and christology are inextricably linked in the hermeneutic of 1 Peter. In support of this first thesis, the concept of participation in Christ must be contemplated. The participation is indicated numerous times in the phrases ἐν χριστῷ (3:16; 5:10, 14) and διά χριστοῦ (1:3, 21; 2:5; 3:21; 4:11). These prepositional phrases describe an existential relationship between the believer and Christ both "in" and "through" the resurrection. To this may be added the future hope of participation in the revelation of Christ (1:7, 13; 4:13). Taken together, the elect's participation in Christ is both a present reality and a future expectation.

While the main contours of Peter's participatory concepts are developed later in the letter, it is worthwhile to briefly look at these passages now. In 1 Pet 3:13–18, there are two ideas presented regarding the relationship of the elect to Christ. The first idea (3:15) exhorts Christians to "sanctify" (ἁγιάσατε) Christ as the Lord in their hearts (ἐν ταῖς καρδίαις ὑμῶν). Honoring Christ in the heart—using the preposition ἐν—contributes to the concept of participation. The second idea (3:16) views the Christian's good conduct as performed in Christ (ἐν Χριστῷ). These two ideas view the relationship as bi-directional: Christ is in the believer, and the believer is also in Christ. In 3:18–22, participation in Christ is evoked through two activities Christ does on behalf of the elect. The first activity (3:18) sees Christ bringing the Christian to God. This activity is predicated upon a baptism (3:21), which saves "through the resurrection of Christ" (δι' ἀναστάσεως Ἰησοῦ Χριστοῦ). These imply a course of ancillary activities such as going into heaven, arriving at the right hand of God and subjugation of angels, authorities and powers (3:22). The body closing of the epistle begins in 4:12–14 with participatory language. The elect are exhorted to rejoice to the degree that they participate (κοινωνέω) with the sufferings of Christ (4:13). The Christian is likewise blessed if insulted in the name of Christ (ἐν ὀνόματι Χριστοῦ) because "the spirit of glory and of God rests upon" the elect (4:14).

The concept of participation in Christ shows the extent to which the church is linked to Christ in a vital way. Inasmuch as Peter makes statements about Christ, he links these to statements about the church. And statements

---

already in 2:19 (Michaels, *1 Peter*, 135; Green, *1 Peter*, 78). This is somewhat doubtful, given the reference to beating in 2:20. However, 2:21–25 "betrays no hint that the example of Jesus applies to slaves alone" (Green, *1 Peter*, 78).

about the conduct of the church are likewise coordinated with the precedent set by Christ. The intertwining of Christ and the church stands as the first major thesis contributing to how Isaiah 53 is interpreted in 1 Pet 2:18–25.

Second, the depictions of Christ in 1 Peter are generally developed as depicting the church as well. This was seen, for example, in the depiction of Christ as λίθος and the church as λίθοι in 1 Pet 2:4–10. In the present section, the idea and language of "servant" is the dominating concept that links Christ and his followers when it comes to the appropriation of Isaiah 53. The suffering servant of Isaiah 53 is identified as Christ, but Peter emphatically includes believers in the depiction of Christ as suffering servant. This began in 2:16 with the phrase "servants of God" (θεοῦ δοῦλοι) where a dominant Isaianic theme was raised in anticipation of further development throughout the ensuing section. The heading of the servants' section likewise sets the stage for the inclusion of believers within the concepts of Isaiah 53. Finally, the phrases leading up to the use of Isaiah 53 contains concepts such as the calling of the elect, and of the elect following in the footsteps of Christ's example.

These efforts to surround Isaiah 53 with links to the church are significant for appraising the Petrine hermeneutic here. Were these links not present, there would be no question that Isaiah 53 was interpreted christologically. Instead, the main concern of the context is to exhort the church to good conduct and not to supply a theological apologetic for Christ. As part of this exhortation, Peter identifies how Christ has set an example for the church to follow in terms provided by Isaiah 53. In terms of the scriptural narrative utilized in 1 Peter, it is clear that the suffering experienced by Jesus corresponds to the suffering experienced by the servant in the narrative of Isaiah. But this suffering is likewise borne by the plural servants in Isaiah. Thus, it is not unexpected that the theme of suffering would encompass both singular and plural—or christological and ecclesiological—aspects of Peter's depiction of the scriptural narrative.

Following upon this, it must be recognized that the movement toward Isaiah 53 has occurred in response to questions raised regarding the church. The church is Peter's central concern, and he turns to Isaiah 53 in order to provide a basis for exhorting the church to a high moral standard. The connection to christology is more or less assumed rather than argued to be true. Instead, Peter is attentive to the ways in which Isaiah 53 supports his exhortation to the church. He is able to do this because of his developed sense of the participation concept explained above. Not only has Jesus suffered, but he has upheld righteous conduct. Thus, for the elect to participate in the narrative of divine redemption, they must remain righteous even in the face of suffering, since their participation is predicated upon their identity in Christ.

Finally, the redemptive nature of the sacrifice in Isaiah 53, while having unique aspects attached solely to Christ, extends also to the disciple servants, namely, the church. Several commentators have shown how the moral conduct and speech of Christ as the suffering servant provides the example to the elect for their own pattern of conduct and speech.[132] However, there need be no hesitation to consider how the church in its participation in Christ carries a redemptive role. Green goes a long way toward identifying the participatory nature of Christ and the church pointing out "how fully Peter's christological remarks are embedded in his instructions to Christians" and suggests that "the ensuing narrative of Jesus [in 1 Pet 2:22–25] ought to inform how we read the church."[133]

It is in keeping with the pattern established in 1 Pet 2:21 for the church in some way to bear the sins of others.[134] As disciple servants, the church serves as a means for healing through the wounds it bears when it suffers unjustly. This missional role of the church in the world on behalf of Christ is such that it attracts unbelievers, likened to sheep in terms of Isaiah 53, who are returned to the Shepherd. Like the narrative of the restoration of divine presence in Isaiah, Peter is aware that the elect live among the "Gentiles." The Isaianic program depicts the servant not only restoring Zion, but being a light to the nations (Isa 49:6). So, too, the offspring of the righteous servant "shall be known among the nations" (61:9) even as they shall be called "the Zion of the Holy One of Israel" (60:14).

In the next chapter where 1 Pet 3:1–6 is examined, it will be shown how the believing wife provides an example of the disciple servant who carries a redemptive role in the home in terms consistent with this third thesis. It is not that the church is said to be a sacrifice in the same way as Christ. However, the pattern the elect are shown to follow suggests that the church functions in the world in such a way as to suffer sacrificially. This pattern

---

132. Elliott, *1 Peter*, 543; Schreiner, *1, 2 Peter, Jude*, 135, among others.

133. Green, *1 Peter*, 88.

134. Rembaum ("Development," 292–95) explains how the collective interpretation of Isaiah 53 among medieval Jewish exegetes responds to the christological interpretation of Isaiah 53 by Justin Martyr, among others (290 n. 4). Focusing prominently on Rashi (295–99) and later Jewish commentators (304–10), Rembaum highlights how interpreters saw in Isaiah 53 a picture of Israel as vicariously bearing the sins of the nations (297). Two points inform our study of 1 Peter. First, it is illegitimate to impose later christological readings of Isaiah 53 on 1 Pet 2:22–25. Second, even though 1 Peter does not develop the collective interpretation of Isaiah 53 with any of the sophistication of later Jewish interpreters—nor does it share the concerns of the later interpreters—there is evidence that suffering for the sins of others is within the purview of Peter.

is integral to the narrative Peter draws from scripture. The promise of redemption entails present suffering. Inasmuch as this was true for Christ, it is shown to be true for the followers of Christ.

5

The Use of Scripture in 1 Peter 3:1—4:11

Introduction

CONTINUING WITH THE BODY middle of 1 Peter (2:11—4:11), there are five remaining sections containing some amount of scriptural texts. In this chapter, these sections will be covered as follows: 3:1–7 which draws upon several passages of scripture; 3:8–12 which quotes Ps 33[34]:13–17; 3:13–17 which alludes to Isa 8:12–13; and 3:18–22 which draws upon the biblical figure of Noah. A brief allusion to Prov 10:12 in 1 Pet 4:8 closes out the central portion of the letter.

Wives and Husbands as Disciples of Christ: 1 Peter 3:1–7

The household code continues into the third chapter of 1 Peter and features an address to believing wives married to unbelieving husbands with several themes already seen in previous sections reintroduced here.[1] The argument of the address to wives falls into two parts. The first part (3:1–4) proposes that wives maintain respectful and pure conduct—ἀναστροφή is repeated

---

1. The household code in 1 Peter differs from Ephesians and Colossians where three pairs progress from wives/husbands, children/parents, servants/masters. One reason for the structure servants–wives–husbands is to cover all households in the audience. Beginning with audience members who would come under ostracism because the male leader of the home is not a believer, Peter first communicates to servants and then to wives. This stair-stepped approach concludes with the believing male head of the household. In what follows, the structure of the household code will be shown to mirror the progression from Isaiah 53 to 54.

in 3:1 and 2—with the intent to win unbelieving husbands to obedience to the word. A dichotomy is set up in 3:3–4 between external adornment and internal beauty. As was the case with the servants' section of the household code, the addressees are to view their situation from a divine perspective (see 2:19, 20; 3:4). The second part (3:5–6) supports the first part by looking upon the heritage of the patriarchal wives, focusing on Sarah in particular. The addressees are the progeny of Sarah if they maintain the ethic Peter has reiterated throughout this section (2:12, 14, 15, 18, 20 and 3:6 where ἀγαθοποιέω is repeated). Both parts of the address to wives draw upon Isaiah in subtle ways. The first part alludes to terms found in Isaiah 3, and the second part alludes to Isaiah 54 in conjunction with Gen 18:12. The household code concludes with an address to believing husbands in 3:7 and echoes Isaiah 54, linking this address to the previous address.

The address to wives begins with an appeal for believing wives to submit to their husbands, even those who do not obey the word (ἀπειθοῦσιν τῷ λόγῳ, 3:1). This repeats the important phrase from 2:8 which occurs in the midst of Peter's discourse centered on the term λίθος. By doing so, Peter draws the previous discourse concerning the Christian appropriation of scripture into the current section. Peter then tropes the term λόγος in this new context by telling wives they can win their unbelieving husbands without a word (ἄνευ λόγου). This play on words is less an admonition to silence but rather communicates the ineffectiveness of words in the missionary enterprise focused on the unbelieving husband.[2] Peter recommends a different strategy based not on words but on conduct (ἀναστροπή, 3:2; cf. 2:12). Building on this, Peter presents negative (3:3) and positive (3:4) supporting arguments. Pure conduct is not measured by external qualities but is hidden in the heart. Embedded within this argument is an allusion to Isa 3:18.[3]

---

2. Davids, *First Epistle of Peter*, 116; Green, *1 Peter*, 96.

3. Others who have observed connections with Isaiah 3 here are Selwyn, *First Epistle of St Peter*, 183; Kelly, *Epistles of Peter and of Jude*, 129; Best, *I Peter*, 125; Michaels, *1 Peter*, 159; Schutter, *Hermeneutic*, 42; Davids, *First Epistle of Peter*, 117; Achtemeier, *1 Peter*, 211; Elliott, *1 Peter*, 561–62; Gréaux, "Elect Exiles," 205–6.

Table 5.1: 1 Peter 3:3 and Isaiah 3:18

1 Peter 3:3	Isaiah 3:18
ὧν ἔστω οὐχ ὁ ἔξωθεν <u>ἐμπλοκῆς</u> τριχῶν καὶ περιθέσεως χρυσίων ἢ ἐνδύσεως <u>ἱματίων κόσμος</u>	ἐν τῇ ἡμέρᾳ ἐκείνῃ καὶ ἀφελεῖ κύριος τὴν δόξαν τοῦ <u>ἱματισμοῦ</u> αὐτῶν καὶ τοὺς <u>κόσμους</u> αὐτῶν καὶ τὰ <u>ἐμπλόκια</u>

It is necessary first to substantiate the Isaianic allusion. Several terms exemplify external adornment (κόσμος) in 1 Pet 3:3—"braided hair" (ἐμπλοκῆς τριχῶν), "wearing jewelry" (περιθέσεως χρυσίων), and "wearing (fine) garments" (ἐνδύσεως ἱματίων). In Isa 3:18–26, there is a corresponding list, albeit longer, enumerating the adornments taken away from the daughters of Zion in the Lord's judgment on their haughtiness. Three of the terms (ἐμπλοκή, ἱμάτιον and κόσμος) that appear in the list of 1 Pet 3:3 echo terms (ἐμπλόκιον, ἱματίσμος and κόσμος) that appear in Isa 3:18, making this a conspicuous correlation.

The first term—ἐμπλόκιον—is either a hair clasp or braiding and appears in a variety of lists.[4] Exodus 35:22 sees the Israelites contributing to the construction of the Tabernacle with various items including ἐμπλόκια. In Exodus 36[39] ἐμπλόκια are part of the vestments for the priesthood. Numbers 31:50 itemizes ἐμπλόκια among the plunder offered to the Lord after the defeat of the Midianites. These items are variously braided gold-work or hair bands of some kind. The second term is ἱμάτιον which corresponds to ἱματισμός in Isa 3:18. The difference between ἱμάτιον and ἱματισμός is negligible and both are frequent in scripture although there is a preference for ἱμάτιον in the NT.[5] The third term, κόσμος, here means "adornment."[6] This sense of κόσμος is rare in scripture, with 1 Pet 3:3 being the only place in the NT to use this meaning.[7] The use of it with this sense five times in Isa 3:18–26 supports the connection to 1 Pet 3:3.[8] Two dominant images predominate the use of "adornment" in scripture. One has to do with

---

4. LEH 1:147; LSJ 546; Le Boulluec and Sandevoir, *L'Exode*, 349–50; cf. BDAG 324.

5. BDAG 475; LEH 1:214; LSJ 829; Lee, *Lexical Study*, 101.

6. Sasse, "κόσμος, κόσμιος, κοσμικός," *TDNT* 3:869, 880–81, 883; see also BDAG 561; LEH 2:265; LSJ 985.

7. Ibid., 3:883.

8. Ibid., 3:880–81. Apart from Isa 3:18–26, the other passages listed by Sasse are Exod 33:5–6; 2 Sam 1:24; Prov 20:29; 29:17; Isa 61:10; Jer 2:32; 4:30; Ezek 7:20; 16:11; 23:40; Nah 2:10 (LXX).

judgment, such as the bridal adornment being forsaken (see Jer 2:32; Ezek 23:40). The other has to do with the hope of deliverance in which the Lord promises to adorn his people as a bride (see Isa 49:18; 61:10). Isaiah 3:18–26 employs the first image since it forebodes the removal of precious adornments in the Lord's judgment.

The identification of Isa 3:18 in 1 Pet 3:3 is justified by two considerations. First, there are no other passages, which contain all three terms together. While each term has parallels in other parts of scripture, no other two passages contain all three. A second consideration stems from the prominent use of Isaiah throughout 1 Peter. Particularly telling is the use of Isaiah 53 in the servants' section of the household code. The restoration of divine presence among the people of God comes through the sacrificial work of the servant. The church participates in this narrative by participating in the role of disciple servants. In the case of the wives' section, Peter draws upon a unique section in Isaiah. The phrase "daughter of Zion" occurs not only in Isaiah, but elsewhere in scripture.[9] However, the plural "daughters of Zion" occurs only in Isaiah 3–4.[10] The dramatic reversal of fortunes depicted in Isa 3:16–26 is striking because it singles out aristocratic women as the focus of judgment.[11]

Situated in a judgment oracle, Isa 3:18 stands at the beginning of a catalog of items offensive to the Lord because of their opulence which resulted from the oppression of the poor (3:14–15).[12] The book of Isaiah opens in the first section (Isaiah 1–4) with a series of oracles focused on the future day of the Lord in which judgment against Judah and Jerusalem is carried out.[13] Those in leadership who have ruled oppressively will find their fortunes reversed. Within the series of judgment oracles in 2–3, focus turns to the "daughters of Zion" (3:16–17). These women of luxury and opulence have benefited from the oppression of the poor and, through their haughtiness, are complicit in the regime the Lord opposes. Because the catalog of items in 3:18–23 comes on the heels of the address to the daughters of Zion, most scholars have assumed these items belong to them.

---

9. Isa 1:8; 3:16, 17; 4:4; 10:32; 37:22; 52:2; 62:11. Cf. 2 Kgs 19:21; Pss 9:15; 72:28; Mic 1:13; 4:8, 10, 13; Zeph 3:14; Zech 2:14; 9:9; Jer 4:31; 6:2, 23; Lam 1:6; 2:1, 4, 8, 10, 13; 4:22.

10. Oswalt, *Book of Isaiah*, 1:140.

11. Clements, *Isaiah 1–39*, 52; Oswalt, *Book of Isaiah*, 1:140–41; Sweeney, *Isaiah 1–4*, 153–55; Stansell, "Isaiah 28–33," 81; Schmitt, "City as Woman," 99; Childs, *Isaiah*, 34; Smith, *Isaiah 1–39*, 151.

12. See Childs, *Isaiah*, 34; Seitz, *Isaiah 1–39*, 41; Oswalt, *Book of Isaiah*, 1:140; Sweeney, *Isaiah 1–39*, 108.

13. Kaiser, *Isaiah 13–39*, 79; Stansell, "Isaiah 28–33," 81; Smith, *Isaiah 1–39*, 151.

Platt has suggested, based to her archeological work, that the catalog has less to do with the feminine wardrobe and pertains to items found "as signs of high office."[14] Therefore, the items belong to both men and women, and the section is not so narrowly connected with 3:16–17 but to the whole of Isaiah 2–3. Few recent commentators have taken on board her careful study. It is interesting, in light of Platt's thesis, that 1 Peter would tie the catalog into his address to wives. This does not overturn Platt's work, but does show an early interpreter of Isaiah making this connection explicit.

For Peter, the Isaianic context provides several meaningful insights. The catalog of items ties in with the negative argument Peter develops in support of his thesis that wives' conduct may win unbelieving husbands. The daughters of Zion in Isa 3:16 who are complicit in oppression contrast with the conduct called for in 1 Pet 3:2–6. The items themselves are viewed as an extension of their inward depravity. Peter erects an external/internal dichotomy and steers wives away from external adornment and toward cultivating internal beauty.[15] The catalog also ties in with an eschatological perspective last evident in 1 Pet 2:12. There, Isa 10:3 evoked the imminence of divine judgment through the phrase "the day of visitation" (ἐν ἡμέρᾳ ἐπισκοπῆς). At the head of the catalog of items in Isa 3:18 stands the phrase "in that day" (ἐν τῇ ἡμέρᾳ ἐκείνῃ). The word association may indicate the means by which these passages were identified, even though the eschatological perspective recedes into the background in 1 Pet 3:3. Eschatology is further developed later, where conduct and eschaton are again closely connected. In the interval between 2:12 and 4:7, Peter focuses predominantly on the conduct of believers.[16] Yet, eschatology was not far from his mind throughout this section. These insights from Isaiah play into the argument in the Petrine context, especially in light of the allusion to Isaiah 54 in 1 Pet 3:6.

Davids observes how Peter's address to wives about their adornment *vis-a-vis* their conduct benefits the church community.[17] A simplified wardrobe by women belonging to the upper class would allow for solidarity across the classes within the church.[18] If illicit wealth-mongering by the rich to the detriment of the poor, orphans and widows was the sign of apostasy

14. Platt, "Jewelry," 200.
15. Michaels, *1 Peter*, 159–60.
16. Schutter, *Hermeneutic*, 64.
17. Davids, *First Epistle of Peter*, 117–18.

18. Elliott supposes this passage says "little about the actual social status of the wives addressed" since it is part of the negative argument (*1 Peter*, 564). But see Beare, *First Epistle of Peter*, 155; Jobes, *1 Peter*, 205; Horrell, "Aliens," 194–96. Bird (*Abuse*, 94–96) interprets adornment with the context women as commodities, but gives little consideration to the possibility of class struggle.

in the Isaianic narrative, then Peter's advice affords the opportunity for the divestiture of wealth in support of the wider church community.

The second allusion to Isaiah occurs in 1 Pet 3:6. At first, it is not altogether clear why Peter bases his exhortation in the narrative on Sarah's internal dialogue of Gen 18:12 where she calls her husband "my lord" (אֲדֹנִי; ὁ κύριός μου). Difficulties have been noted in the connection between Genesis 18 and 1 Pet 3:6, particularly since the episode in Genesis 18 does not seem to pertain to Peter's argument. Kiley, for instance, seeks to resolve the tension by looking elsewhere in Genesis. He suggests that Genesis 12 and 20, where Sarah submits to Abraham's plot to speak of her as his sister, provides the requisite background to 1 Pet 3:6.[19] Bird takes the three stories of Genesis 12, 20 and 21 as a tapestry of traditions that provide Peter with "a model of obedience."[20] Sly, unconvinced by this, proposes that the retelling of Sarah's story in Philo and Josephus points to discomfort with elements in her story in the Jewish interpretive tradition and accounts for "the same ambiguity of feeling toward Sarah" in 1 Peter.[21] Martin also looks to the Jewish interpretive tradition, finding the *Testament of Abraham* to be the appropriate background to 1 Pet 3:6.[22]

Many commentators, while less disagreeable toward the Gen 18:12 background, have looked elsewhere for the connection between the Genesis text and Peter's argument. Most commonly, Isa 51:2 is suggested as providing the link.[23] Selwyn even goes so far as to venture this is "perhaps our author's immediate source."[24] Heretofore unexplored in connection with Sarah in 1 Pet 3:6 is another Isaianic text; a subtle allusion to the barren woman in Isa 54:1 provides an explanation, I shall argue, for Peter's reference of Sarah in his address to wives.

---

19. Kiley, "Like Sara," 690–92. See also Balch, *Wives*, 103–5; Beare, *First Epistle of Peter*, 156.

20. Bird, *Abuse*, 117–21.

21. Sly, "1 Peter 3:6b," 129.

22. Martin, "TestAbr," 139–46. Fatal to his argument is the late date and possible Christian provenance of *T. Ab.* See also Allison, *Testament of Abraham*, 28–31; Davila, *Provenance*, 205–6.

23. Kelly, *Epistles of Peter and of Jude*, 131; Best, *I Peter*, 127; Michaels, *1 Peter*, 166; McCartney, "Use," 146; Goppelt, *Commentary on I Peter*, 224; Elliott, *1 Peter*, 572; Richard, *Reading 1 Peter, Jude, and 2 Peter*, 134; Gréaux, "Elect Exiles," 208.

24. Selwyn, *First Epistle of St Peter*, 185.

Table 5.2: 1 Peter 3:6 and Isaiah 54:1, 4

1 Peter 3:6	Isaiah 54:1, 4
ὡς Σάρρα ὑπήκουσεν τῷ Ἀβραὰμ κύριον αὐτὸν καλοῦσα, ἧς ἐγενήθητε <u>τέκνα</u> ἀγαθοποιοῦσαι καὶ <u>μὴ φοβούμεναι</u> μηδεμίαν πτόησιν.	εὐφράνθητι στεῖρα ἡ οὐ τίκτουσα ῥῆξον καὶ βόησον ἡ οὐκ ὠδίνουσα ὅτι πολλὰ τὰ <u>τέκνα</u> τῆς ἐρήμου μᾶλλον ἢ τῆς ἐχούσης τὸν ἄνδρα εἶπεν γὰρ κύριος <u>μὴ φοβοῦ</u> ὅτι κατῃσχύνθης μηδὲ ἐντραπῇς ὅτι ὠνειδίσθης

Like the previous allusion, only three terms embedded within the text of 1 Peter provide any hint to an Isaianic allusion. The first term—τέκνα—connects to Sarah, a barren woman who has been promised a child by the elderly Abraham. However, the term τέκνα does not appear in the Genesis account.[25] The term τέκνα occurs in connection with the barren woman in Isa 54:1 where it is promised that the children of the desolate one will exceed the children of the married one. The connection between τέκνα and Sarah is insufficient in itself to suggest Isaiah 54 behind 1 Peter 3, especially since Sarah is not named in Isaiah 54 and occurrences of the term τέκνον are quite numerous.[26] Yet, the parallel in Gal 4:27–28 is instructive. After quoting Isa 54:1, the term highlighted by Paul in his application is τέκνα. Paul's use of Isaiah 54 in connection with Sarah is fraught with difficulties, which shall be addressed further below.

A second set of terms are correlated with τέκνα in 1 Pet 3:6. The phrase "do not fear" (μὴ φοβούμεναι) corresponds with the phrase at the beginning of 54:4 (μὴ φοβοῦ). Scholarship has identified here an allusion to Prov 3:25 due to the collocation of the verb φοβέω and πτόησις.[27] The imperatival force of the participle in 1 Pet 3:6 matches the imperative in Isa 54:4 better than the future tense of φοβέω in Prov 3:25.[28] This is not to deny an allu-

---

25. The term "son" (בן; υἱός) is used in Gen 18:10 and 14. Only in 17:16 does τέκνον translate בן in connection with the promise to Sarah.

26. In this argument, I am following Beuken, "Isaiah LIV," 29–70; see also Brueggemann, *Isaiah 40–66*, 151; Childs, *Isaiah*, 427–28.

27. See Elliott, *1 Peter*, 574; Davids, *First Epistle of Peter*, 121.

28. Both verses have Qal imperfect forms that are Jussive in meaning, making the Hebrew versions of Prov 3:25 and Isa 54:4 identical in meaning.

sion to Prov 3:25 here; to be sure, the use of Prov 3:34 in 1 Pet 5:5 indicates that Peter has consulted this section of Proverbs. Yet, focus on this allusion and the background of Gen 18:12 has obscured the Isaianic voice here. The admonition not to fear is important in Isa 54:1–8 where the barren woman is told that she will not need to fear shame or disgrace since the Lord has called her like a husband calls to a wife. This aspect, absent in Prov 3:25 and Gen 18:12, makes key connections between scripture and Peter's argument in his address to wives. Isaiah 54 provides the link to Sarah, the barren woman who, along with her offspring, needs not fear shame or disgrace, for it is through Sarah's offspring that the Lord's work is carried out.

The connection between the barren woman of Isa 54:1 and Sarah presupposes another Isaianic text. Sarah is mentioned in Isa 51:2 and the similarities between the narratives surrounding her and the language of Isa 54:1–8 have led scholars to identify her as the barren woman of this episode.[29] Central to the connection between these passages is the verb ὠδίνω. In Isa 51:2, the righteous are called upon to "look to Abraham your father and to Sarah who bore you (Σαρραν τὴν ὠδίνουσαν)." Thus, in Isa 54:1 when a nameless barren woman is identified as the one who has not born (ἡ οὐκ ὠδίνουσα) yet bears many children, the connection to Sarah comes full circle.[30] In the midst of her suffering through the shame and disgrace of barrenness, the Lord promises an abundance of children (54:1). The children will expand throughout the earth and the nations will be their inheritance (54:3).

Isaiah 54 features several *topoi* that are picked up in 1 Peter 3. The first centers on the offspring promised to the patriarchal prototypes. Both the barren woman and afflicted Noah are promised progeny (Isa 54:1–3, 13). Stemming from this is the *topos* of inheritance (κληρονομέω and cognate noun). The promise of abundant children to the barren woman entails an inheritance of the nations (ἔθνη κληρονομήσει; 54:3). The servants of the Lord likewise receive an inheritance (κληρονομία; 54:17). Similarly, the *topos* of negated fear draws together the sections pertaining to the barren woman (54:1–8) and the servants of the Lord (54:14–17). The barren woman is exhorted, "Fear not" (54:3; μὴ φοβοῦ) and the servants are encouraged that they shall not fear (54:14; καὶ οὐ φοβηθήσῃ). These *topoi* establish a

---

29. See esp. Beuken, "Isaiah LIV," 37–38 but also McKenzie, *Second Isaiah*, 139; Sawyer, "Daughter of Zion," 98; Brueggemann, *Isaiah 40–66*, 151–53; Baltzer, *Deutero-Isaiah*, 434; Goldingay and Payne, *Isaiah 40–55*, 341. Blenkinsopp (*Isaiah 40–55*, 361–63) and Oswalt (*Book of Isaiah*, 2:416) consider this to be more generally about the patriarchal wives, including Hannah (1 Sam 1–2). Against this reading, see Childs, *Isaiah*, 427–28.

30. See Hays, *Echoes*, 119–20.

relationship between the patriarchal forebears and the plural servants of the Lord. The relationship between these sections suggests an avenue of interpretation in which the patriarchal forebears idealize features that characterize not only the suffering servant of Isaiah 53 but also the disciple servants of Isaiah 54–66. Both the barren woman (=Sarah) and Noah are depicted as sufferers in terms synonymous with the suffering servant of Isaiah 53. And, like the servant, they shall see offspring (Isa 53:10). In the midst of their suffering, there is no need to fear because the Lord will carry out his promises; both for vindication and to produce a heritage.[31]

In 1 Pet 3:6, these *topoi* are used to address wives with unbelieving husbands. Before spelling this out further, it is necessary to situate 1 Peter within an interpretive tradition that has dealt with Isaiah 54 in telling ways. The Isaiah Targum reads, "Sing, Jerusalem, who was like a barren woman who did not bear" (שַׁבְּחִי יְרוּשְׁלֵם דַהֲוֵת כְּאִתָּא עֲקָרָא דְלָא יָלְדַת).[32] The connection to Jerusalem does not appear, at first, to develop Sarah's story. But in the hands of Paul, Sarah and Jerusalem offer interesting possibilities. Paul shows awareness of this interpretive tradition in his own use of Isa 54:1 in Gal 4:27.[33] Paul's allegory in 4:21–31 depends on a correspondence between the barren woman and the "free Jerusalem above" (4:26). Interestingly, whereas Hagar is named as the slave woman who "corresponds to the present Jerusalem, for she is in slavery with her children" (4:25), Sarah remains unnamed.[34] She is referred to as "the free woman" (4:22, 23, 30). Yet, Paul assumes that his readers know enough of the story of Abraham that he may make the shift from the anonymous Sarah to Jerusalem. This shift is likely dependent upon the interpretive tradition evident in the Isaiah Targum.

The context of Galatians 4 is different than 1 Peter 3. However, a few concepts show a high level of correspondence between the letters simply in their employment of this interpretation of Sarah. The first is the use of Sarah as an exemplary character, although in Galatians she remains unnamed. For Paul, she represents some of the key lines of argument he presents, including inheritance (Gal 3:29) and freedom (5:1). The connection

---

31. Note the connection between the repeated κληρονομέω/κληρονομία of Isaiah 54 and its use in Isa 53:12.

32. Chilton, *Isaiah Targum*, 105; Sperber, *Bible in Aramaic*, 109; Stenning, *Targum of Isaiah*, 182–83.

33. Hays, *Echoes*, 118–21; Jobes, "Jerusalem Our Mother," 299–320; Wagner, "Isaiah," 129–30; Wilson, *Curse of the Law*, 42–43. Forman ("Politics of Promise," 306, 308–9, 316) argues for another echo of Isa 54:1–3 behind the mention of Sarah in Rom 4:19–21.

34. Esler (*Galatians*, 213) sets out with clarity the problems of Paul's use of Isaiah 54 in conjunction with his allegory of Sarah and Hagar. See Barrett, "Allegory," 166–67.

between Sarah and the wives of 1 Peter 3 who have unbelieving husbands is not as immediately clear and will require some attention in due course. A second shared concept has to do with a contrast between an exemplary set and a polemical set. The Galatian contrast features Sarah versus Hagar upon whom Paul foists all his polemical vituperation. In 1 Peter, Sarah is representative of "the holy women" (αἱ ἅγιαι γυναῖκες; 3:5) and stands in contrast to women whose adornment is merely external (3:3). A final shared concept is a focus on the children of Sarah in both Galatians and 1 Peter. In Gal 4:28, the audience is told that they "are children (τέκνα) of promise" and this point is reiterated again in 4:31. Likewise, the wives of 1 Peter are called Sarah's children (τέκνα; 3:6).

These shared concepts do not suggest dependence of one letter upon the other. What they do suggest is that both Paul and Peter found Sarah to be a key figure in establishing the point for which they argue in their respective contexts. This turn to Sarah centers in part on the prominent role she plays in the Genesis narrative, to be sure. However, Galatians 4 shows the vital role Isaiah 54 plays in connection with Sarah, particularly regarding barrenness, reproach, shame and vindication.

The two passages underlying 1 Pet 3:1–6 create a dynamic interplay. For Isaiah, the wealthy women of privilege are typecast as candidates to experience the effects of God's wrath. The creature comforts of their status are removed leaving them in a state of forced humiliation. The barren woman of Isaiah 54 contrasts the women of privilege in Isaiah 3. The experience of humiliation in life entails an inverse exaltation. Isaiah suggests two depictions of women; those who are under judgment and those whose consolation is tied up with the Lord's vindication of his servants. This interplay is represented through the subtle use of Isa 3:18 and Isa 54:1–4.[35] The external adornment Peter admonishes believing wives to neglect is drawn from the store of the privileged women's accouterment. The internal qualities that adorn women who carry out good conduct show believing wives to be in the lineage of the barren patriarch Sarah, whose children of promise are shown to be the believing wives.

What Isaiah dichotomizes as two female types, Peter reconfigures along the lines of an internal/external dichotomy. The external adornment draws upon the language used in the catalog of Isaiah 3, but the manner of his usage mutes the punitive tone. It is not clear whether or not believing spouses are permitted to adorn themselves with these things. This passage certainly can be read as preferring internal adornment over external adornment without the divestiture indicated in Isaiah 3. The reasons behind Peter's interpretive

---

35. See Sawyer, "Daughter of Zion," 90.

strategy here remain opaque. Perhaps a greater understanding of the social situation of Peter's audience would shed light on this issue. Unfortunately, the text provides little in terms of the believing wives' situation, apart from the indication that some are wedded to unbelieving husbands.[36]

The second Isaianic text also undergoes transformation. At once, the identification of the barren woman of Isa 54:1 as Sarah leads not to an identification of believing wives as sharing in her suffering barrenness but instead identifies believing wives as her promised children. This identification draws upon an intertextual reading of Isa 54:1 with Gen 18:12 where Sarah refers to Abraham as "lord" (אדני; κύριος). What draws these two passages together is likely the narrative surrounding the promise of a child. Apparently, Peter found in Sarah's appellation of Abraham as lord an example that supported his admonition to believing wives. Through like-minded obedience, believing wives may trace their lineage back to Sarah.

Furthermore, as children in the heritage of Sarah, they need not fear intimidation. Again, an intertextual reading has occurred in which Isa 54:4 has been linked to Prov 3:25. The use of other verses from Proverbs later in the letter, and particularly Prov 3:34, demonstrates that Peter draws texts together through key terms. Here the admonition to "fear not" seems to have caught Peter's attention. To that end, his use of Isa 8:12–13 later in 1 Pet 3:14–15 may have emanated from exegetical work on this linking terminology. Scholars have often read the admonition here as addressing the intimidation believing wives suffer from their unbelieving husbands.[37] However, the Petrine context offers no indication of any malice from harsh husbands. Perhaps interpreters have borrowed from the previous address to servants where it was indicated that some masters were "crooked" and that beatings occurred. If the scriptural contexts be a sufficient guide, it is likely that there is a more general source of intimidation: unbelievers who would question a wife who became a Christian in opposition to their husband. In the Genesis narrative, Sarah and Hagar were at odds with one another and this opposition is picked up in Isaiah 54.[38] In Prov 3:25, the terror or intimidation not to be feared is paralleled with the ruin of the wicked. Drawn into 1 Peter, the intimidation not to be feared concerns the precarious position

---

36. Horrell (*1 Peter*, 105–12) offers a thoughtful analysis of recent scholarly assessments of this text. Feminist readings, in particular, challenge the role this text plays in perpetuating the victimization of women. Horrell suggests that a correct understanding of the historical setting of the text must occur in distinction from the history of interpretation that follows upon it.

37. See Elliott, *1 Peter*, 574; Schreiner, *1, 2 Peter, Jude*, 158; among others.

38. Paul's use of the Sarah typology in conjunction with Isaiah 54 in Gal 4:21–31 is set within an allegory depicting Paul's opponents.

believing wives face when they are surrounded by many voices questioning their newfound religious convictions. This does not in any way imply that unbelieving husbands were not part of this opposition, but recognizes that others within and outside the immediate family contributed to the believing wife's discomfort. When Peter returns to the idea of "fearing not" in 3:14–15, it is tied to preparing a defense in the face of slander.

Peter's reading of scripture provides dramatic images that are metaleptically incorporated into an otherwise straightforward paraenetic address. This reveals that Peter has a grasp of scripture that is far reaching, incorporating imagery from Isaiah, Genesis and Proverbs. The specific contexts of each book appear to be unrelated to one another. Yet, each contributes to a larger narrative of God's redeeming work carried through humble vessels. Sarah becomes the focal point of this narrative. Through her, the wives Peter addresses are invited to participate in this scriptural story as Sarah's children. The brazenly appareled women of Isaiah 3 provide a counter-example to Sarah, who are incapable of seeing God's redeeming work because of their lack of humble conduct. The scriptural imagery developed in the address to wives supports Peter's thesis that unbelieving husbands can be won through proper conduct.

The appeal to Isaiah 54 is not restricted to the address to wives, but also reverberates in the address to husbands in 1 Pet 3:7. The terms κληρονομέω and κληρονομία in Isa 54:3 and 17 indicate the unity of the chapter. When Peter uses the term συγκληρονόμος in 1 Pet 3:7, he shows an awareness of this key term within Isaiah 54 and is reemphasized two verses later with the use of κληρονομέω.[39]

---

39. The noun κληρονομία appeared at the outset of the epistle in 1 Pet 1:4. It likely that Isa 54:17 has influenced Peter's usage here as well. The adjectives ἄφθαρτος, ἀμίαντος and ἀμάραντος that modify κληρονομία have drawn attention because of conspicuous use of alliteration. The use of φθαρτός in Isa 54:17 provides a clue to how Peter's thoughts have been influenced by this passage.

Table 5.3: 1 **Peter 3:7 and Isaiah 54:3, 17**

1 Peter 3:7	Isaiah 54:3, 17
Οἱ ἄνδρες ὁμοίως, συνοικοῦντες κατὰ γνῶσιν ὡς ἀσθενεστέρῳ σκεύει τῷ γυναικείῳ, ἀπονέμοντες τιμὴν ὡς καὶ συγ<u>κληρονόμ</u>οις χάριτος ζωῆς εἰς τὸ μὴ ἐγκόπτεσθαι τὰς προσευχὰς ὑμῶν.	καὶ τὸ σπέρμα σου ἔθνη <u>κληρονομ</u>ήσει καὶ πόλεις ἠρημωμένας κατοικιεῖς. ἔστιν <u>κληρονομ</u>ία τοῖς θεραπεύουσιν κύριον καὶ ὑμεῖς ἔσεσθέ μοι δίκαιοι λέγει κύριος

This term features a strikingly egalitarian usage in light of the direction just given to wives to submit to their own husbands. The term συγκληρονόμος occurs only four times in the NT.[40] In Rom 8:17, believers are fellow heirs with Christ so that if they suffer with him they will also be glorified with him.[41] Ephesians 3:6 features an articulation of the inclusion of Gentiles as fellow heirs with those "from the commonwealth of Israel" (Eph 2:12).[42] And in Heb 11:9, Abraham is called a fellow heir with Isaac and Jacob even when they were foreigners. In each of these uses, there is no explicit indication of the inclusion of women as fellow heirs, even though Paul elsewhere includes women in close proximity to the issue of inheritance (see Gal 3:28-29). Only in 1 Pet 3:7 is there an explicit inclusion of women in the language of the promised inheritance.[43] And it seems that Peter's thoughts on this matter reflect his reading of Isaiah 54 where the barren woman is promised an inheritance on par with the disciple servants of Isaiah 54-66.

The study of 1 Pet 3:1-7 here has suggested that Isaianic passages (particularly Isaiah 54) play an important role in the addresses to believing wives and husbands, even if such passages work at a subtle level. The identification of allusions and echoes stems from two elements that occur previously in 1 Peter. The phrase "servants of God" (θεοῦ δοῦλοι) in 1 Pet 2:16 was shown to initiate Peter's engagement with the latter part of Isaiah where a shift

40. W. Foerster, "κληρονόμος, κτλ." *TDNT* 3:767-85; BDAG 952.

41. The string of συν- prefixed terms (συγκληρονόμος, συμπάσχω, συνδοξάζω) in this verse highlight a participatory theology that matches Peter's own ideas about participation in Christ.

42. Paul again uses here a string of συν- prefixed terms (συγκληρονόμος, σύσσωμος, συμμέτοχος) in this verse.

43. Mbuvi, *Temple*, 110.

occurs from the singular servant of Isaiah 40–53 to the plural servants of Isaiah 54–66. Peter's explanation of discipleship to Christ depends in large part on the pattern of discipleship he observes in Isaiah through the servant-servants motif. This pattern, then, extends into the rest of the household code through the recognition of the barren woman of Isa 54:1–8 as exemplifying key characteristics of the plural servants of the Lord. So, when Peter addresses believing wives, he identifies them through a dynamic interplay of Isaianic relationships—daughters of Zion, barren woman, servants of the Lord. In the final formulation of his address to wives, he has read Isaiah 54 alongside other passages, which expand upon this reading. His reading of Isa 3:18 enables him to establish a contrast between women under divine judgment and women who exemplify the principles of discipleship within Isaiah; although he reconfigures the contrast within his address to wives. The role of Gen 18:12 and Prov 3:25 likewise expound aspects of Isaiah which are present within the passage. Together, these passages draw the household sphere into the scriptural narrative depicted throughout the letter.

The address to husbands in 3:7 contains another extension of Peter's use of Isaiah 54. Husbands are fellow heirs (συγκληρονόμος) with their wives, and as such they must live with them in an understanding way. The husbands section deals less with the idea of discipleship and draws instead upon the idea of inheritance. However, it does so in such a way that the inheritance is not promised to a male head, but to a mutually cooperating pair—one of whom has been addressed in terms of the principles of discipleship.

In keeping with the narrative of the restoration of divine presence among the people of God, the domestic elements of the narrative are present within the Isaianic development of the story. For instance, marriage and offspring are focused on both as an image of the restoration (Isa 62:4–5) as well as a result of the restoration (61:9; 65:23). It is not surprising, then, that Peter should attend to the domestic effects of the scriptural narrative of restoration.

The Ethics of Good and Evil: 1 Peter 3:8–12

The household code ends with the address to husbands (3:7) after which point Peter transitions to the second half of the body middle in 3:8–12.[44] This transition features a move away from the categorical structure of the household code to a more general address. This transition features an ex-

---

44. Achtemeier, *1 Peter*, 221; Elliott, *1 Peter*, 600–601; Feldmeier, *First Letter of Peter*, 185.

tensive quotation of Psalm 33[34]:12-16. Allusions to Psalm 33 have already been noted, particularly in connection to the ethical admonitions of 2:11—3:7, and such admonitions continue into the second half of the body middle. Thus, the placement of the quotation is situated in the transition in such a way as to be relatively proximate to all of the admonitions the Psalm undergirds.[45] The present task focuses on a more comprehensive study of the context of Psalm 33, the Psalm's connection with the ethical admonitions in 1 Peter and the intertextual use of Psalm 33 with Isaiah.

Table 5.4: **1 Peter 3:10–12 and Psalm 33:13–17**

1 Peter 3:10–12	Psalm 33:13–17
ὁ γὰρ θέλων ζωὴν ἀγαπᾶν καὶ ἰδεῖν ἡμέρας ἀγαθὰς παυσάτω τὴν γλῶσσαν ἀπὸ κακοῦ καὶ χείλη τοῦ μὴ λαλῆσαι δόλον, ἐκκλινάτω δὲ ἀπὸ κακοῦ καὶ ποιησάτω ἀγαθόν, ζητησάτω εἰρήνην καὶ διωξάτω αὐτήν· ὅτι ὀφθαλμοὶ κυρίου ἐπὶ δικαίους καὶ ὦτα αὐτοῦ εἰς δέησιν αὐτῶν, πρόσωπον δὲ κυρίου ἐπὶ ποιοῦντας κακά.	Τίς ἐστιν ἄνθρωπος ὁ θέλων ζωὴν ἀγαπῶν ἡμέρας ἰδεῖν ἀγαθάς; παῦσον τὴν γλῶσσάν σου ἀπὸ κακοῦ καὶ χείλη σου τοῦ μὴ λαλῆσαι δόλον. ἔκκλινον ἀπὸ κακοῦ καὶ ποίησον ἀγαθόν, ζήτησον εἰρήνην καὶ δίωξον αὐτήν. ὀφθαλμοὶ κυρίου ἐπὶ δικαίους, καὶ ὦτα αὐτοῦ εἰς δέησιν αὐτῶν. πρόσωπον δὲ κυρίου ἐπὶ ποιοῦντας κακά

As a transition, 1 Pet 3:8-12 reiterates several salient points important for the remainder of the body middle. Two phrases draw upon the servants section of the household code. The calling of believers to suffering is first articulated with the phrase, "For to this you were called" (εἰς τοῦτο γὰρ ἐκλήθητε) in 2:21.[46] Believers are reminded of this calling with the same phrase, "For to this you were called" (ὅτι εἰς τοῦτο ἐκλήθητε) in 3:9. Another phrase drawn from the servants section communicates the silent suffering of Christ in terms reminiscent of the Isaianic suffering servant. In 2:23, Christ is depicted as one who "when he was reviled, he did not revile in return" (ὃς λοιδορούμενος οὐκ ἀντελοιδόρει). In 3:9, this phrase is repeated within a prohibition against retaliation by believers against those who would revile them

---

45. Woan, "Psalms in 1 Peter," 223.
46. Michaels, *1 Peter*, 178–79; Elliott, *1 Peter*, 610.

(μὴ ἀποδιδόντες . . . λοιδορίαν ἀντὶ λοιδορίας).⁴⁷ Beyond the connection with 2:21–25, the use of the term κακός in 3:9 both draws upon prior uses of κακοποιέω (2:12, 14) as well as anticipates the use of κακός in the quotations of Psalm 33.⁴⁸ The use of κακός here and in the Psalm quotation looks ahead to the second half of the body middle in which the term κακοποιέω recurs (3:17).⁴⁹ This interconnectedness points to a unified ethical teaching that is significantly informed by Psalm 33.⁵⁰

The quotation of Psalm 33 encompasses only a portion of the entire Psalm. The text in 1 Peter differs from the Greek Psalter at several points.⁵¹ Many issues must be analyzed in order to make a judgment on the source of the differences found in 1 Peter. The most significant issue is the lack of available information about the text of the Psalter. It is not possible to enter into all the particulars that bear on the text as it appears in 1 Peter or to engage in a comparison with the earliest manuscripts of Psalm 33. A few points, though, are worth reviewing. First, there are nine differences that occur in 1 Pet 3:8–12 in comparison with the text of Ps 33:13–17 as found in Rahlfs.⁵² These are:

1. omission of τίς ἐστιν ἄνθρωπος (3:10a)

2. insertion of γάρ (3:10a)

3. ἀγαπῶν changed to ἀγαπᾶν (3:10a)

4. insertion of καί (3:10b)

5. transposition of ἰδεῖν ἡμέρας (3:10b)⁵³

6. 2nd Sg. Imperatives changed to 3rd Sg. Imperatives (3:10c–11b)

---

47. Selwyn, *First Epistle of St Peter*, 189; Michaels, *1 Peter*, 177; Elliott, *1 Peter*, 607; Green, *1 Peter*, 105–6.

48. Michaels, *1 Peter*, 180; Elliott, *1 Peter*, 606.

49. Schutter, *Hermeneutic*, 148; Goppelt, *Commentary on I Peter*, 234.

50. See Van Unnik, "Teaching of Good Works," 92–110. Unfortunately, he does not explore adequately the role of Psalm 33 in Peter's ethics.

51. Michaels, *1 Peter*, 179–80; Schutter, *Hermeneutic*, 144–45; Woan, "Psalms in 1 Peter," 219–20, Jobes, "Septuagint Textual Tradition," 326–27.

52. See Egan, "Did Peter Change Scripture?," 505–28 for a more in-depth discussion of text-critical issues surrounding this passage. The collation of 2400 manuscripts has not yet been completed. Rahlfs critical edition is unfortunately outdated, but provides at the very least a starting point for comparing texts. It is necessary, though, for scholars to diligently assess manuscripts for themselves. Consultation of Fraenkel, *Verzeichnis der griechischen Handschriften des Alten Testaments* serves as a starting point for this endeavor. My thanks go to Kristen De Troyer for her helpful instruction in the current state of scholarship on the Greek Psalter.

53. Two quality manuscripts do not have these transposed: 04 (Ephraemi) and 81.

7. omission of σου (3:10c, d)
8. insertion of δέ (3:11a)[54]
9. insertion of ὅτι (3:12a)

These differences may be grouped into three grammatical categories: conjunctions, pronouns and verbs.[55] Each of these categories may then be analyzed throughout the manuscript tradition for Psalm 33 in which case variants abound in each grammatical category. Some examples of variants in the manuscript tradition match the differences observed in 1 Peter, but others are less exact and serve instead as analogies. An analysis of the earliest Greek manuscripts[56] for Psalm 33 is such that scholars cannot dismiss the possibility that the differences found in 1 Peter are due to a variant manuscript. For the purposes of the present thesis with its focus on Isaianic quotations and allusions, these findings with regard to the Psalter cannot be spelled out here. However, they are consistent with what has been argued elsewhere concerning the text of Isaiah.

Greek Psalm 33 begins with exaltation in the first three verses but moves to a song of deliverance thereafter.[57] The central section (vv. 12-18) calls upon the people to learn the fear of the Lord.[58] The Psalmist, who has chronicled his own deliverance in v. 5, promises that the Lord delivers the righteous when they cry for help (v. 18), and that the face of the Lord is against the evil (v. 17).[59] The heart of the Psalm admonishes the righteous to good speech and conduct (vv. 14-15).[60] It is this admonition that appears in the quotation in 1 Peter 3.

Peter draws upon the ethical admonition of Psalm 33 through two key terms. These terms occur together in Ps 33:15. The righteous are exhorted to "turn from evil and do good" (ἔκκλινον ἀπὸ κακοῦ καὶ ποίησον ἀγαθόν translating סור מרע ועשה־טוב). The change of the verbs in 1 Pet 3:11 from second singular to third singular does nothing to diminish the key role κακός and ἀγαθός play both in the Psalm text but also in the rhetoric of the body middle

---

54. Several quality manuscripts do not have this insertion: 01 (Sinaiticus), 04^C2, 5, 307, 1739, *passim*.

55. Compare with Osborne, "L'utilisation," 70-71.

56. *Bodmer Papyrus IX, Bodmer Papyrus XXIV* and *Leipzig Papyrus 39* all are dated in IV c.e.

57. Mays, *Psalms*, 152.

58. Terrien, *Psalms*, 303.

59. Limburg, *Psalms*, 111.

60. Weiser, *Psalms*, 298-99.

of 1 Peter.[61] These terms are combined with the verb ποιέω at key points in this section (1 Pet 2:12, 14, 15, 20; 3:6, 17; cf. 2:16, 18; 3:9, 13, 16, 21).[62] The occurrence of κακός and ἀγαθός in combination with ποιέω particularly highlights how Petrine style incorporates the language of Psalm 33.[63]

The quotation of the ethical admonition in Ps 33:13–17 in 1 Pet 3:10–12 indicates the importance the Psalm had upon Peter's argument.[64] Yet, it correlates with several items from Isaiah as well as the character of Christ. Already it has been argued that Isa 10:3 in 1 Pet 2:12 contributes to the ethical content of 1 Peter through an appeal to the day of the Lord. A possible link between these two passages is the prominent use of the verb ποιέω (both translating עשׂה) in conjunction with appeals to conduct. Taken up into Peter's parlance, ποιέω is conjoined with either κακός or ἀγαθός (2:12, 14, 15, 20; 3:6, 16, 17; 4:19) as the building blocks of Peter's ethical address.[65]

An intriguing connection centers on the concept of fear. Four passages converge within the span of a few verses that each addresses various aspects of fear. It was suggested in the previous section that Isa 54:4 elides with Prov 3:25 in 1 Pet 3:6 to encourage wives with unbelieving husbands. Later in 1 Pet 3:14–15, the concept of fear is drawn from Isa 8:12–13. Believers are encouraged to have no fear of those who might cause suffering through slander (1 Pet 3:16). The transfer of human fear to divine fear, though left out of the quotation in 1 Peter, remains an important concept in Isa 8:13. The Greek version emphasizes this transfer through the repetition of φοβέω and φόβος. Including the portion of 8:12 quoted in 1 Pet 3:14, the passage reads, "But do not fear the fear of them (τὸν δὲ φόβον αὐτοῦ οὐ μὴ φοβηθῆτε) nor be troubled, but sanctify the Lord himself and he shall be your fear (καὶ αὐτὸς ἔσται σου φόβος)." It is this transference of human fear to divine fear, or rather divine reverence, that ties in most naturally with the concept of φοβέω/φόβος as used in Psalm 33. The section of the Psalm just prior to the quoted portion admonishes the elect to fear the Lord because those who fear him do not experience lack (33:10). The Psalmist then invites the elect

---

61. Michaels, *1 Peter*, 180; Green, "Use," 287; Elliott, *1 Peter*, 611.

62. Elliott, *1 Peter*, 613–14.

63. Green, "Use," 280–82; Jobes, *1 Peter*, 220.

64. Schutter (*Hermeneutic*, 44–49) and Elliott (*Elect*, 184–208) are overly dismissive of Bornemann ("Der erste Petrusbrief," 143–65), perhaps overcompensating for Bornemann's exaggeration of the evidence. Scholars following Bornemann are Schwank, "Lecture chrétienne," 16–32 and Snodgrass, "I Peter II. 1–10," 97–106. More balanced assessments of the role of Psalm 33[34] in 1 Peter have been provided by Bauckham, "James, 1 and 2 Peter, Jude," 313; Green, "Use," 278–83; Elliott, *1 Peter*, 611; Woan, "Psalms in 1 Peter," 221–26, 228; Jobes, *1 Peter*, 220.

65. Michaels, *1 Peter*, 180; Green, "Use," 288; Elliott, *1 Peter*, 613–14; Woan, "Psalms in 1 Peter," 222; Dryden, *Theology and Ethics*, 161–62.

to listen to his teaching on the fear of the Lord (33:12). The content of this teaching consists largely of the material quoted in 1 Pet 3:10-12. By way of linking terms, φοβέω/φόβος draw together texts from Isaiah in concert with Psalm 33 to present believers in Asia Minor with the proper conduct entailed upon their reverence for God as revealed in Christ. This transference of human fear to divine fear or reverence is seen particularly in 1 Pet 2:17 with regard to fearing God while honoring the emperor, in 2:19 with regard to servants being mindful of God while respecting (ἐν παντὶ φόβῳ) their masters, and in 3:2 where believing wives maintain respectful conduct (ἐν φόβῳ) even while their husbands disobey the word. Thus, the restored presence of the Lord among his people carries the two ideas regarding fear. One, the presence of the Lord is a source of comfort which dispels fear (e.g., Ps 33:17-18; Isa 40:9; 43:5). Two, fear is the appropriate response to the presence of the Lord (e.g., Ps 33:10, 12; Isa 8:13; 51:12-13).

One final connection between Psalm 33 and other passages of Isaiah in 1 Peter deserves attention. The transition from the singular servant of Isaiah 40-53 to the plural servants of Isaiah 54-66 has already been developed in this thesis.[66] Easily coordinated with this is Ps 33:23 where it is promised, "The Lord will redeem the souls of his servants" (λυτρώσεται κύριος ψυχὰς δούλων αὐτοῦ).[67] The servants of the Lord here enjoy the same sort of vindication promised to the servants in Isaiah 54-66. As in the latter part of Isaiah, the righteous servants experience affliction (Ps 33:17-19).[68] This connection between the servants of Isaiah and the servants of Psalm 33 provides a means of intertextual reading.

There is no need to settle on a single link between passages. It is sufficient for the purposes of this study to identify that ample links exist between Psalm 33 and Isaiah to warrant the claim that the Psalm is read in concert with Isaiah. The recurrence of terminology relating to fear in 1 Peter and particularly in quoted material suggests that this was the primary link. At the same time, and supporting the point made earlier with regard to catchwords, the term or terms that linked passages at the exegetical level need not be employed at the compositional level of the epistle. Identifying a linking term does not necessarily provide the key insight a quoted passage provides to its new context.[69] Even if Peter went to Psalm 33 looking for scriptural insights into fear, his quotation does more to support his argument concerning the conduct of believers. Peter's argument concerning fear matches

66. See chapter 3 above, as well as the end of chapter 4.
67. Jobes, *1 Peter*, 223.
68. Green, *1 Peter*, 107.
69. Hays, *Echoes*, 13.

that of Psalm 33, but when it comes to quoting the text, he emphasizes the ethical section and forsakes the tie-in with the concept of fear. Moreover, Psalm 33 and Isaiah together attest to the narrative of restored divine presence which is both a comfort and vindication to God's faithful servants who are experiencing suffering in the world.

Finally, in comparison with the christological use of this Psalm in John 19:36, the employment of Psalm 33 in 1 Peter is considerably ecclesiological in nature. The quotation of Ps 33:21 in John features differences with the Greek version. Psalm 33:21 reads, "He keeps all their bones (πάντα τὰ ὀστᾶ αὐτῶν), not one of them shall be broken (οὐ συντριβήσεται)." The version in John 19:36 reads, "His bone shall not be broken (ὀστοῦν οὐ συντριβήσεται αὐτοῦ)." The quotation in John is marked with an introductory formula, "For these things took place that the scripture might be fulfilled." The textual issues this quotation presents are beyond the scope of the present work, but highlight once again instabilities in the transmission of this particular Psalm. More in keeping with this thesis, though, is the observation that John has read this Psalm christologically as being fulfilled in the crucifixion of Christ. In contrast, Peter has offered no christological reading of this Psalm, finding instead an admonition for the church to follow.

Following Christ through Suffering: 1 Peter 3:13–22

The passage now under consideration is comprised of two sections, the first spanning 3:13–17 and the second section consisting of 3:18–22. Both sections further the argument of the body middle of 1 Peter even while there is a marked move away from the formal structure of the household code. The quotation of Psalm 33 at the transition in 3:8–12 both marks this move and establishes a scriptural basis for the ethical conduct Peter challenges the elect to follow. The first section centers upon the conduct of believers as an answer to hostile accusations while the second section emphasizes the role of Christ as the exemplary sufferer.

The End of Fear in the Sanctity of Christ: 1 Peter 3:13–17

Beginning a new section, Peter queries, "Who is there to harm you if you are zealous for doing good?" Both the question and the answer draw upon Isaianic texts. The question itself draws upon Isa 50:9, from a speech by the Isaianic servant.[70] A series of interrogatives in Isa 50:8–10 question whether

---

70. Kelly, *Epistles of Peter and of Jude*, 140; Best, *1 Peter*, 132; Schutter, *Hermeneutic*,

Israel will follow the servant. The servant's confident assertion is that, even in the midst of adversaries, the Lord will vindicate his servant (Isa 50:8).[71] The Hebrew of 50:9 asks, "Who is there to condemn me?" (מִי־הוּא יַרְשִׁיעֵנִי), but the Greek reads, "Who will harm me?" (τίς κακώσει με). It is the Greek version that has influenced Peter here.

Table 5.5: 1 Peter 3:13 and Isaiah 50:9

1 Peter 3:13	Isaiah 50:9
καὶ <u>τίς ὁ κακώσων</u> ὑμᾶς ἐὰν τοῦ ἀγαθοῦ ζηλωταὶ γένησθε;	ἰδοὺ κύριος βοηθεῖ μοι· <u>τίς κακώσει με</u>;

It has already become apparent that Peter is sensitive to the discipleship motif in Isaiah surrounding the servant and servants of Isaiah 40–66. Isaiah 50 contains statements from the servant requesting that Israel follow him,[72] fitting well into Peter's reading of Isaiah and supporting his ongoing argument. However, Peter alters the voice of the question by shifting the pronoun from first person singular to second plural. In so doing, he shifts the allusion away from the singular servant and uses it to address the disciple servants. The believers Peter addresses are now assumed to be followers of Christ—the singular servant—and may now take up the voice of the plural servants who can withstand threats of harm because of God's vindication of his people. The rhetorical question draws upon the voice of the Isaianic servant, and in 1 Pet 3:13 it becomes connected with the discipleship motif developed most prominently in the servant section of the household code through quotations of Isaiah 53.

Peter further draws Isa 50:9 into his argument by connecting the question to the idea of being zealous for being good (ἐὰν τοῦ ἀγαθοῦ ζηλωταὶ γένησθε). This is important given the very prominent use of Psalm 33 at the transition.[73] As was argued for the previous section, Isaiah was never far from sight even when quoting Psalm 33. The exegetical use of the terminology of fear (φοβέω and φόβος) that links together several Isaianic texts with Psalm 33 appears in the context of Isa 50:9. The third interrogative of

---

38; Davids, *First Epistle of Peter*, 129; Goppelt, *Commentary on I Peter*, 241; Elliott, *1 Peter*, 619; Jobes, *1 Peter*, 226.

71. Wilcox and Paton-Williams, "Servant Songs," 93; Watts, *Isaiah 34–66*, 204; Brueggemann, *Isaiah 40–66*, 123; Seitz, "Isaiah 40–66," 436–37.

72. On this, see Oswalt, *Book of Isaiah*, 2:324.

73. Schutter, *Hermeneutic*, 44, 151.

50:8–10 asks, "Who among you fears the Lord (τίς ἐν ὑμῖν ὁ φοβούμενος τὸν κύριον) and obeys the voice of his servant?" These interlocking terms (fear, servant, good) demonstrate an intertextual reading of scripture drawing Isaiah into contact with other scriptural texts. Yet, the language of scripture is employed as though it were Peter's words. This use of scripture in the midst of epistolary argumentation is also seen in the answer to the rhetorical question where another Isaianic quotation occurs.

Admitting that suffering is a distinct possibility, Peter suggests that such suffering for the sake of righteousness is a blessing. This idea is grounded in his next scriptural quotation from Isa 8:12–13. Isaiah 8 has made a brief cameo earlier in 1 Pet 2:8.[74] In Isaiah 8, the Lord speaks through his prophet that his people are not to fear the threat of attack. Instead, they are to consecrate (8:13; ἁγιάζω translating קדש) the Lord and fear him alone.[75] This image of the people of God comforted and exhorted to fear the Lord in the midst of imminent calamity has captured the attention of Peter so much so that he returns to it twice in his letter.[76]

Drawn into the Petrine context, the quotation is transformed in two significant ways. For one, the context of Assyrian aggression gives way to a Hellenistic setting in which suffering takes on new parameters.[77] The nature of the conflict depicted in 1 Peter focuses on ostracism and verbal confrontation.[78] There are possible legal ramifications to this conflict, as indicated by the ready defense Peter advises in 3:15.[79] The geographical connotations assumed in Isaiah, however, are not assumed by Peter for his audience in Asia Minor. His depiction of them as a diaspora people (1:1; 2:11; 5:13) indicates a reconfiguration of the idea of the promised land and the location of divine presence. The spiritualization of the temple in 2:9 is tied up with this geographical shift. The transformation of Isa 8:12–13 in this way has no overt expression in 1 Pet 3:14–15, but depends upon broader contextual considerations throughout the letter.

---

74. See chapter 4 above.
75. Oswalt, *Book of Isaiah*, 1:233–34; Childs, *Isaiah*, 74–75.
76. See also Wagner, "Faithfulness and Fear," 94–96.
77. Rensburg and Moyise, "Isaiah," 282.
78. Bechtler, *Following in His Steps*, 19.
79. Horrell (*1 Peter*, 53–59) is correct in his rejoinder to the consensus position that Anatolian Christians experienced verbal hostility and ridicule. The legal implications he espouses are clear from the text, but criminal execution cannot be determined from the text. The frequency of these more egregious conflicts with the Christian community needs further exploration, something this thesis cannot provide. It does not appear that this nuance of the consensus position would alter the course of the present thesis.

Table 5.6: 1 Peter 3:14–15 and Isaiah 8:12–13

1 Peter 3:14–15	Isaiah 8:12–13
τὸν δὲ φόβον αὐτῶν μὴ φοβηθῆτε μηδὲ ταραχθῆτε, κύριον δὲ τὸν Χριστὸν ἁγιάσατε ἐν ταῖς καρδίαις ὑμῶν,	τὸν δὲ φόβον αὐτοῦ οὐ μὴ φοβηθῆτε οὐδὲ μὴ ταραχθῆτε, κύριον αὐτὸν ἁγιάσατε καὶ αὐτὸς ἔσται σου φόβος

More explicit is a second transformation. The christological reading of Isa 8:12-13 is apparent through the insertion of τὸν Χριστόν in the midst of the quotation. In order to more fully understand this transformation, it is necessary to briefly consider the text critical issues bearing upon this quotation.

The text of 1 Pet 3:14-15 differs at several points when compared with OG Isaiah. These may be listed in several points:[80]

1. αὐτῶν instead of αὐτοῦ
2. μή instead of οὐ μή
3. μηδὲ instead of οὐδὲ μή
4. Insertion of δὲ after κύριον
5. Insertion of τὸν Χριστόν before ἁγιάσατε.

The first two of these points may be dealt with rather easily while the others require further explanation. The use of the plural pronoun αὐτῶν is not surprising when compared with several manuscripts categorized as Hexaplaric (88, 109, 736) and Lucianic (147, 90, 130, 311, 96, 46) along with numerous others (377, 564, 565, 403, 534, 538 and Coptic versions).[81] In this case, there is ample evidence supporting the manuscript tradition as the source of the difference rather than authorial alteration. The next two differences are difficult to place since the manuscript tradition and revisors (Aquinas, Symmachus and Theodotion) consistently use the double negative in both instances. It is likely that the Hebrew version has exerted influence here. Yet, there has been no evidence in the letter up to this point to suggest that Peter has consulted the Hebrew text himself.[82] If the use of the negative pronoun that appears in 1 Peter is the result of a revision based on

---

80. Compare with Rensburg and Moyise, "Isaiah," 282.
81. Ziegler, *Isaias*, 151–52.
82. Michaels, *1 Peter*, 186–87.

the Hebrew text, then it most likely happened at a stage prior to when Peter consulted the revised text.[83]

The conjunction δέ is an interesting case. There is no evidence that it appeared in the manuscript tradition nor in the revisions, and the Hebrew text offers no support. It seems probable that Peter has inserted the conjunction here to link the two verses. What makes this a peculiar insertion is the fact that the verses occur in sequence making the conjunction superfluous. The peculiarity of the insertion raises the question whether the conjunction serves an interpretive purpose. Many modern English translations insert an adversative conjunction at the beginning of Isa 8:13 and in so doing strengthen the contrast between the fear described in 8:12 and the fear of the Lord in 8:13. As such, Peter's addition to the text amplifies the contrast he wants to point out in the alluded text.[84]

The final difference would appear to be a simple case of inserting ὁ Χριστός for theological purposes.[85] However, before jumping to this conclusion, it must first be recognized that OG Isaiah omits the Hebrew צבעות in Isa 8:13. This omission has an impact on the textual transmission. For instance, codex Venetus inserts τῶν δυνάμεων after κύριον and is reflected in the first hexaplaric group. Similarly, Symmachus and Theodotion add τῶν δυνάμεων in their revisions. One striking example is ms 534, which inserts τὸν θεὸν rather than τῶν δυνάμεων. There is some temptation to correlate this with the substitution of θεὸν for Χριστὸν in 1 Pet 3:15.[86] However, there is overwhelming support for Χριστὸν as the earlier reading in the Petrine text.[87] With these textual differences in mind, it is necessary to consider whether Peter has incited a theological incursion into the text. Has Peter perhaps stumbled across a text ripe for christological use because someone else has filled in the omitted צבעות with τὸν Χριστὸν, albeit erroneously? This hypothesis certainly has no textual support, but given the textual history, the possibility is not as off base as might first appear. If it is maintained that Peter did not consult the Hebrew text or provide his own translation

---

83. Ibid., 187.

84. One option Elliott (1 Peter, 625) sees as the purpose for the additional δὲ is "to explicate the contrast between vv 14c and 15a," but he thinks it more likely serves "to mark 'the Christ' (ton Christon) as appositive to and explanatory of kyrion." While this is not an unreasonable conclusion, the ordinary sense of the conjunction makes most sense (BDF §447, BDAG 213), especially since the apposition does not depend upon the conjunction.

85. Jobes, 1 Peter, 229–30.

86. The reading θεὸν is supported by the Majority text.

87. The reading τὸν Χριστὸν is found in P[72], 01, 02, 03, 04, 044, 33 inter alia.

(which seems to be the overall picture up to this point in the letter), then it is not altogether clear why he would find warrant for this insertion.

For the purposes of this study, it is considered that ὁ Χριστός is inserted by the author in a radical reading of scripture which equates the Christ with the Lord. Davids states, "This way of expressing his high Christology is typical for Peter."[88] However, it is only at this point in the letter that this high christology snaps into focus. Prior use of κύριος may point in this direction. For instance, the use of κύριος in the quotation of Isaiah 40 in 1 Pet 1:25 rather than θεός can only be interpreted as a christological move after this statement is made in 3:15. The same holds true for the use of κύριος in the allusion to Ps 33:9 in 1 Pet 2:3. Yet, none of these is used to express a high christology. It is only with the use of κύριος and Χριστός in apposition in 3:15 that one may begin to work back through the letter and ascertain a high christological meaning in 1:25 and 2:3.[89]

The two texts from Isaiah that appear in close proximity to one another in 1 Pet 3:13–15 allow consideration of their cross-interpretive potential. Read intertextually, they betray an underlying logic that may likewise be related back to Psalm 33 in 1 Pet 3:10–12. These textual links provide insight into the rhetorical thrust of the body middle of 1 Peter, even though within the narrower section (3:13–17) the underlying logic resides at a more subtle level. In 1 Pet 3:13, the allusion to Isa 50:9 contributes the question concerning who might harm the elect. The use of Isa 8:12–13 in 1 Pet 3:14–15 provides the idea of a contrast between fear (φοβέω) that occurs on a horizontal plane and reverence (ἁγιάζω) that occurs on a vertical plane. These ideas contribute to Peter's argument that believers ought to prepare a defense of their faith in the face of slander and reviling (3:15–16). These passages are linked by key terminology. The use of φόβος/φοβέω in Isa 50:9–10 and Isa 8:12–13 provides a link by which the two passages build a common theology. In this theology, it is highlighted that the fear of God usurps fear of earthly persecution. The two passages create antitheses between fear of persecution and godly fear or reverence. Isaiah 8:12–13 compels the people of God to renounce worldly fear, which can be construed either as fear of others or the fear that other people experience (presumably at the judgment). Instead, the people of God are to fear the Lord. The repetition of φόβος/φοβέω in 8:12–13 serves as a foil between earthly and divine understandings of fear. In Isa 50:9, the potential for persecution establishes the rhetorical question,

---

88. Davids, *First Epistle of Peter*, 131.

89. Elliott (*1 Peter*, 625) considers 1:25 and 2:3 to be "instances where Jesus is identified as *Lord*" and therefore "display a similar modification of their sources"—Isa 40:8 and Ps 33:9 respectively. However, neither context supports this identification. Each text remains ambiguous regarding how κύριος ought to be construed.

"Who will harm me?" The fear of harm is implicitly expressed here. Then in 50:10, the next rhetorical question ponders, "Who will fear the Lord?" Thus, like 8:12–13 the progression of 50:9–10 moves from fear that occurs on the earthly sphere to fear that occurs in relation to God.[90] As mentioned earlier,[91] the restored presence of the Lord carries with it two points regarding fear, 1) that the Lord's presence provides comfort against the fearful elements of the world, and 2) that fear is the appropriate response to divine presence.

In 1 Peter, the emphasis from these passages is on the first element: human or earthly fear. The human sphere—the fear that is oriented to harm that derives from persecution—is drawn from these texts into 1 Pet 3:13–15. The second element is transformed in the Petrine context through the insertion of τὸν Χριστόν. Peter highlights Christ as sanctified in the hearts of believers, here, as the antithesis to the fear of others. The antitheses are drawn from a scriptural framework but are modified in a christological direction. This antithesis of human-level fear and Christ propels Peter's argument into the application that believers confidently defend their faith in Christ while facing slander and ridicule (1 Pet 3:15–16).[92] Christ's presence in the heart of believers is put forward decisively as the deposit of divine presence, certifying the veracity of the narrative of restored divine presence in which the church participates.

It was argued in the previous section that the terminology of fear links a number of passages in the body middle of 1 Peter. The prominence of the terminology here in 1 Pet 3:13–15 suggests once again that Isaiah stands as one of the major voices in the scriptural narrative. The key-word links are significant for tracing how Peter sees the interconnectedness of scripture. For instance, an important reiteration of Psalm 33 occurs in 3:17 where the antitheses of doing good (ἀγαθοποιέω) and doing evil (κακοποιέω) transition to the next section about the suffering of Christ. The ethical admonition of the body middle functions alongside the repeated terminology of fear. From this, it may be seen that Peter finds in scripture an address to the church. Yet, more often than not, the voice he brings forward is distinctly Isaianic.

---

90. Rensburg and Moyise ("Isaiah," 283–84) identify an intertextual link with Isa 51:12–13 standing behind Peter's use of Isa 8:12–13. However, because of the terminology already supplied in the immediate context, the link to Isa 50:9–10 is more compelling.

91. See the appropriate sections in chapters 3 and 4 above.

92. Green, *1 Peter*, 117–18.

The Victory of Christ and the Drama of the Eschaton: 1 Peter 3:18–22

The following section (1 Pet 3:18-22) begins with creedal statements focused on the work of Christ leading to the participation of the believer in the work of Christ through baptism. Incorporated into this progression from creed to baptism is a brief section pertaining to the time of Noah (3:19-20). Certain elements of 3:18 are reminiscent of 2:21 so that the previous section with its many references to Isaiah 53 carries over into the new section. The christological statements articulate how Christ suffered for sins, the righteous in exchange for the unrighteous, thereby bringing the elect to God. The creedal section concludes with the antithetical parallel, "put to death in the flesh, but made alive in the spirit." The term πνεῦμα at the conclusion of 3:18 serves as a segue to the spiritual world.

This departure elicits a passage (3:19) that is enigmatic and obscure.[93] Dalton has produced the definitive work on 3:19, and a brief rehearsal of his argument is required particularly as it bears upon the use of scripture in 1 Peter. Dissatisfied with the prevailing interpretations, Dalton turned to *1 Enoch* and found parallels to the turns of phrase in 3:19.[94] The course of his argument thoroughly retraces the interpretive schools for each phrase, and provides detailed exegetical examinations of the principal terms and phrases in 3:19. His main contention is that Christ's proclamation to the imprisoned spirits occurs after the resurrection and during his ascension.[95] Prior schools of interpretation thought that this event occurred after the death but before the resurrection of Christ in his spirit and that the location of the imprisoned spirits was in the underworld. The content of Christ's proclamation and the constituents referred to as imprisoned spirits has likewise been variously understood.[96]

The substance of Dalton's thesis consists of a comparison of 3:19 with salient portions of *1 Enoch*.[97] The comparison isolates six elements paralleled in 1 Pet 3:19-20 and *1 Enoch*, as Dalton explains:

---

93. Luther (*Luther's Works*, 113) considers this "a strange text and certainly a more obscure passage than any other passage in the New Testament."

94. Dalton (*Christ's Proclamation*, 20) names the works of Gschwind (*Die Niederfahrt Christi in die Unterwelt*) and Reicke (*The Disobedient Spirits*) as previous scholars who have connected *1 Enoch* to 3:19.

95. Ibid., 19

96. See Elliott, *1 Peter*, 648-50 for a succinct explanation of the various schools of interpretation.

97. Dalton (*Christ's Proclamation*, 167-70) deals with *1 En.* 6-19, 64-69, 106-8.

A survey of *1 Enoch* reveals a striking and obvious parallel to 1 Pet 3:19–20. In this latter text we have 1. a journey of Christ (πορευθείς), 2. a proclamation (ἐκήρυξεν), 3. to the spirits (τοῖς πνεύμασιν), 4. in prison (ἐν φυλακῇ), 5. who rebelled, or disobeyed (ἀπειθήσασιν), 6. in the setting of the flood (ἐν ἡμέραις Νῶε).[98]

Basing his comparison on the Greek version of *1 Enoch*,[99] linguistic evidence is put forward highlighting the correspondence between the two bodies of literature. While Dalton finds *1 Enoch* to have been influential on the New Testament, he also finds traditions about the antediluvian sin of fallen angels and wicked humans in other Second Temple literature.[100]

The results of Dalton's study are convincing, even though he overstates (perhaps unintentionally) the level of dependence Peter has on *1 Enoch*. It seems best to see Peter drawing upon the interpretive tradition surrounding the "watchers" of Gen 6:1–8, particularly since no single source text can be identified.

What is striking—and unfortunately little explored—about the findings of Dalton's work are the ramifications this has on our understanding of Petrine hermeneutics. Peter has not simply drawn upon Genesis 6 here, since the concepts of proclamation and imprisonment are absent there. Instead, Peter shows himself to be at home in the world of Second Temple Jewish interpretation of this episode. His take on the episode further reveals a christological understanding of how the narrative surrounding the watchers works. Peter draws upon what Nickelsburg calls the "double mythic core" of apocalyptic retellings of Israel's formative stories. He writes that "the story of the flood is transformed into an eschatological myth that accounts for the origin of violence in the author's world and promises its resolution in a final judgment that is the counterpart of the flood."[101] But Peter employs this "double mythic core" by drawing past (the imprisoned spirits in the time of Noah), present (see νῦν in 1 Pet 1:12) and future (see 1:5; 2:12; 4:5, 7, 13, 17; 5:4, 10) into a grand statement of Christ's victory over the supernatural powers of the world (see 3:22).

---

98. Ibid., 167.

99. On which see Nickelsburg, *1 Enoch 1*, 18. He finds "the extant Greek is inferior to the Greek *Vorlage* of the Ethiopic." Cf. Dalton, *Christ's Proclamation*, 153.

100. Dalton (*Christ's Proclamation*, 170–72) highlights *Jubilees* 5; *T.Naph* 3:5; *2 En.* 7:1–3; 18:3; and several passages from the Dead Sea Scrolls: CD 2:18–20; 1QapGen; 1QH; 1QMyst; 1QM. See more recently, however, Campbell, *Honor*, 67–68; Crawford, *Rewriting Scripture*, 105–27; Hughes, *Scriptural Allusions*; Atkinson, "Use of Scripture," 106–23, among others on the use of scripture in specific scrolls.

101. Nickelsburg, *1 Enoch 1*, 57.

The picture of Petrine hermeneutics is rounded out further in 3:20 with the identification of events surrounding Noah. The connection of Noah to the imprisoned spirits is treated succinctly by Dalton as a continuing eschatological theme on the backdrop of apocalyptic writings.[102] So, although Genesis 6–7 is central to the story of antediluvian sin and judgment in the flood, it is the literature of the Second Temple era that provides the necessary categories for Peter's reading of Noahic traditions. For instance, Sir 44:17–18 contemplates the unique role Noah plays in preserving a remnant of humanity on the earth during the flood.[103] A striking parallel is found in Wis 14:5–6 where the author reflects upon the hope people place in a small raft that passes safely through (διασῴζω) the waves and relates this to the hope of the world placed in a raft when the arrogant giants were destroyed.[104] Several elements found in 1 Pet 3:20 are paralleled in *1 En.* 65—68: 1) the preservation of Noah (65:12), 2) the wooden vessel (67:2), 3) those who dwell with Noah (67:3), and 4) the passage through water (67:4-11). These parallels do not indicate sources Peter depended upon, but show how Peter's reflection on Noah is consistent with the Second Temple *milieu*.[105]

An overlooked influence, though, is the role Noah plays in Isaiah 54.[106] Already in 1 Peter, the appearance of the servants of God (θεοῦ δοῦλοι; 2:16), the suffering servant of Isaiah 53 (2:22-25) and Sarah—who exhibits traits that characterize disciples of the suffering servant— (3:6) have pointed to an engagement with the latter portion of Isaiah in a subtle but meaningful way. These appearances suggest that when Noah comes on the scene in 3:20, the scriptural discourse framed by the servant-servants motif of Isaiah remains in play. Contextual markers that support this continued scriptural discourse are the phrases drawing upon Isaiah 53 in 3:18[107] and the repetition of the verb ἀπειθέω in 3:20, which has been used previously to identify unbelievers in connection with scriptural discourse (see esp. 2:8). In Isa 54:9-11, Noah

---

102. Dalton, *Christ's Proclamation*, 191–94.

103. See 4 Macc 15:31.

104. In all likelihood, Wisdom of Solomon was written in the latter half of the 1st century. First quoted in *1 Clem.* 3:4 and 12:12, Davila (*Provenance*, 200, 223–25) argues for Christian authorship. Because of uncertainties surrounding the date and provenance of Wisdom, one cannot insist on Petrine dependence here.

105. See Ezek 14:14, 20; Heb 11:7; 2 Pet 2:5; *2 Bar.* 77:23; *1 En.* 10:2; 65:1; 67:1; 106–7; *Jub.* 5–10; *Sib. Or.* 1:154–343; Philo, *Leg.* 2:60; 3:77; *Det.* 105, 121–22; *Gig.* 1–5; *Deus* 70–140; *Agr.* 1–2, 20, 125, 181; *Plant.* 1, 140; *Mos.* 2:59–65; *QG* 1:87–97; 2:16–17, 25–79; Josephus, *A.J.*, 1.3–4; 1Q19; 4Q186; 4Q435–436; 4Q534–536; 6Q8, *inter alia*.

106. To be fair, Dalton cites Isa 54:9 in a footnote (*Christ's Proclamation*, 192 n. 13).

107. The first clause of 3:18 exactly replicates four terms from 2:21, including the verb πάσχω which was argued to summarize the suffering of the servant in Isaiah 53. The second clause (δίκαιος ὑπὲρ ἀκίδων) further echoes Isa 53:11–12.

represents a second patriarchal character in the chapter whose distinguishing features (affliction, storm-tossed; 54:11) are used to define the characteristics of the disciple servants (54:17).[108]

Unlike the hermeneutic revealed in 1 Pet 3:19, the Noahic material in 3:20 is not interpreted christologically, even though the idea of Noah as saving the world might lend itself to such ends.[109] Instead, Peter employs an ecclesiological interpretation based on a typological comparison of the flood water and baptism (3:21).[110] Like Noah and his family were saved (διασῴζω) through water (δι᾽ ὕδατος), believers are saved (σῴζω) at baptism through the resurrection (δι᾽ ἀναστάσεως) of Jesus Christ. In the narrative of Noah, Peter found a picture of the church saved through the cataclysmic eschatological judgment. This strategy mirrors the strategy of Isaiah 54 in which Noah prefigures characteristics of the servants of the Lord who share in the sufferings of the singular servant of Isaiah 53 but also share in the consolation and vindication of final judgment (Isa 54:10, 17). The use of this strategy in Second Temple apocalyptic appropriations of the Noahic story should not diminish the important role Isaiah 54 plays in the interpretive tradition. Ultimately, Peter's use of the Noah story, tangled though it might be in interpretive traditions, marks an important development in the ecclesiological hermeneutic employed thus far. A hint of this direction was provided in the use of Isa 10:3 in 1 Pet 2:12, but the vision of the church as an eschatological community flowers here and in 4:5–7. In the midst of present sufferings, the church stands in the center of God's plan of eschatological restoration, just as Noah once stood in the center of God's plan, while surrounded by the apathy of those who tried God's patience.

Loving One Another within the Gifted Community: 1 Peter 4:7–11

The section 4:7–11 draws upon themes initiated earlier in the letter, particularly the exhortation to "love one another earnestly" (τὴν εἰς ἑαυτοὺς ἀγάπην ἐκτενῆ ἔχοντες) which mirrors 1:22 (ἀλλήλους ἀγαπήσατε ἐκτενῶς).[111] This

108. Westermann (*Isaiah 40–66*, 275) considers that the inclusion of the flood in Isaiah 54 "represents a bold advance." Gunn ("Deutero-Isaiah," 495–503) traces flood imagery in Isa 44:27; 50:2; 51:10 as one of several allusive elements surrounding the phrase "drying up the waters" and, more convincingly, in Isa 55:10–13 (503–8) based on links with 54:9–10.

109. Such as in Matt 24:37–38 || Luke 17:26–27.

110. Mbuvi's exploration (*Temple*, 112–14) of a Noahic temple is less than convincing.

111. Elliott, *1 Peter*, 750; Green, *1 Peter*, 144.

repeated exhortation is developed with a brief delineation of gifts of service and speech (4:10-11) intended to build up the community and glorify God through Christ.[112] The use of Prov 10:12 in 1 Pet 4:8 is the final allusion and lends support to the final exhortation of the body middle of 1 Peter.[113]

Table 5.7: 1 **Peter 4:8 and Proverbs 10:12**

1 Peter 4:8	Proverbs 10:12
πρὸ πάντων τὴν εἰς ἑατοὺς ἀγάπην ἐκτενῆ ἔχοντες, ὅτι ἀγάπη <u>καλύπτει</u> πλῆθος ἁμαρτιῶν.	μῖσος ἐγείρει νεῖκος πάντας δὲ τοὺς μὴ φιλονεικοῦντας <u>καλύπτει</u> φιλία

For such a small scriptural allusion, the text quoted in 1 Pet 4:8 presents several issues. The allusion and the source text can be identified through the verb καλύπτει with a noun meaning "love" as the subject. However, the quotation differs from Prov 10:12 by employing ἀγάπη rather than φιλία as the subject noun. The object of the verb also differs with Prov 10:12 reading "all who do not enjoy strife" as opposed to 1 Pet 4:8 which has "a multitude of sins." The compound form in Prov 10:12 shows the translator has played with language by combining the prefix φιλός with the verb νεικέω.[114] Thus, the contrasting parallelism is amplified. Hate raises up strife (νεῖκος) but love (φιλία) covers all lovers of strife (οἱ φιλιονεικοῦντες).[115] The Petrine version is closer to the Hebrew than the Septuagint in this case, raising the possibility of a revised text or consultation of a Hebrew text.[116] Another possibility is that Peter has quoted the Proverb from memory. However, the concluding words of the letter of James points to a shared tradition that stands behind both epistolary versions.[117]

The appearance of ἁμαρτιῶν in the allusion connects to the use of ἁμαρτία in the material drawn from Isaiah 53 in 1 Pet 2:22 and 24.[118] The

---

112. Green, *1 Peter*, 145-46.
113. Schutter, *Hermeneutic*, 72-73; Jobes, *1 Peter*, 278-79.
114. Van der Louw, *Transformations*, 313.
115. See Clifford, *Proverbs*, 114; Waltke, *Book of Proverbs: Chapters 1-15*, 461.
116. Schutter, *Hermeneutic*, 125; Green, *1 Peter*, 144 n. 190.
117. Achtemeier, *1 Peter*, 295; Elliott, *1 Peter*, 751. Cf. *1 Clem.* 49:5; *2 Clem.* 16:4.
118. The term ἁμαρτία in 1 Pet 4:8 replaces φιλονεικοῦντας and is likely a revision in light of the Hebrew text (פשע; "transgression"). This does not imply that Peter had recourse to the Hebrew text or made his own translation or revision. The Greek tradition shows a strong tendency to revise this but does so in different ways. Aquila and

repetition of ἁμαρτία in 3:18 and 4:1 furthers Peter's reflection on the role of Christ who suffered once for sins in language reminiscent of Isaiah 53.[119] Just as Christ suffered in the flesh, the elect may also suffer in the flesh to cease from sin (4:1). These reflections go far to connect the use of Prov 10:12 to Peter's use of Isaiah 53. As such, the combined result establishes the exhortation to love one another. Even though Christ died for sins, the problem of sin remains a destructive force for the community of believers. Thus, the allusion to Prov 10:12 complements Isaiah 53 by drawing the christological truths Peter finds there into the ecclesiological argument that governs the body middle.[120]

The connection between the two exhortations to love in 1:22 and 4:8 is matched by a further connection utilizing the λόγος word group. In 1:22—2:3, Peter argued for the vital role the word of God plays in the nurturing of spiritual growth in the community of believers. Tying together Isa 40:6–8 and Ps 33:9 were the words λόγος in 1:23 and λογικός in 2:2 which drew the Isaianic use of ῥῆμα into Peter's argument. Two further uses of λόγος maintain the importance of the scriptural narrative for believers, albeit from the perspective of a negative argument. In the midst of the scriptural discourse of 2:6–10, Peter links the builders who reject the cornerstone to unbelievers who "disobey the word." Later, in the wives' section of the household code, unbelieving husbands are said to "not obey the word." Thus, Peter has constructed an insider/outsider dichotomy based on submission to the word of God, in keeping with his reading of Isa 40:8.

With this buildup around the term λόγος and the cognate λογικός, Peter's use of λογία in his two-item gifts list evokes the previous argument concerning the vital role of scripture for the community of believers. The phrase "λογία θεοῦ"—as what those with speaking gifts ought to communicate—has often been translated as "oracles of God." Bigg previously contended that the phrase should be understood as denoting scripture.[121] Few have followed him in this, since the balanced pair of gifts and their supporting clauses indicate the divine origin of service and speech.[122] Rather

---

Theodotion use ἀθεσία ("faithlessness") whereas the term ἀδικία ("unjust, wicked") is used in Symmachus and Quinta. The Latin translation in Origen along with the Vulgate use *delictum* ("transgression"). Clearly, ἁμαρτία stands among a number of options potentially available to Peter.

119. Michaels, *1 Peter*, 247.

120. Further supporting the link between 4:7–11 and 2:18–25 is the use of οἰκονόμοι as a designation for believers, which echoes the address to servants (οἰκέται).

121. Bigg, *Epistles of St. Peter and St. Jude*, 174.

122. So Elliott, *1 Peter*, 759; Feldmeier, *First Letter of Peter*, 221.

than strictly denoting scripture, λογία θεοῦ means here proclamation that includes, explains and builds upon scripture.[123]

The division between speaking and serving gifts is instructive in light of the continued dialogue this thesis maintains with the reader-centered approach. This bi-partite gift list indicates a speaking role in the congregations that does not necessarily correspond with a designated church office (although eldership is developed later in 5:1-4). It is possible that Peter is establishing through this bi-partite gifts list the means by which the community is to gather around scripture, particularly the parts of scripture highlighted in his letter.

Conclusions for the Body Middle of 1 Peter (2:11—4:11)

The vast array of scriptural passages in the body middle of 1 Peter has required two chapters to do justice to each section. The following conclusions here cover both chapters.

Text and Intertextuality

The use of Isaiah is clear in several cases, but comparisons with the OG *Vorlage* are not decisive in each case. The allusion to Isa 10:3 in 1 Pet 2:12, differing from OG Isaiah through the omission of two articles, provides a striking example. The brevity of the allusion limits conclusions about the text form Peter used. Has this been cited from memory? Or has the language of scripture been subsumed in Petrine style? These questions assume at the outset that a difference exists, though, between the text read and the text used. So an additional question must also be raised: has Peter consulted a text without articles? The absence of articles in the Hebrew version substantiates this possibility. In the end, to champion one source (authorial alteration) over the other (manuscript tradition) without sufficient textual evidence one way or the other is methodologically unsound. Must this allusion, then, be omitted from an investigation of Petrine hermeneutics because of these uncertainties? The answer, this study suggests, is that part of the picture of Petrine hermeneutics is a move toward more subtle employment of scripture at each stage of the letter, and thus to omit this passage would be a disservice.

The address to servants features quotations from Isaiah 53 in 1 Pet 2:22-25. Unlike the block quotes of Isa 40:6-8 in 1 Pet 1:24-25 or Ps

---

123. Michaels, *1 Peter*, 250-51.

33:13–17 in 1 Pet 3:10–12, the use of Isaiah 53 is comprised of several smaller segments woven into the wider rhetorical unit. This example offers ample material for textual study but raises problems similar to the ones explored in connection with Isa 10:3. The salient differences between OG Isaiah and 1 Peter—apart from numerous truncations of the Isaianic text—are the use of ἁμαρτίαν in 1 Pet 2:22 instead of ἀνομίαν in Isa 53:9 and the verb forms in 1 Pet 2:24–25 (ἰάθητε instead of ἰάθημεν in Isa 53:5 and πλανώμενοι instead of ἐπλανήθημεν in Isa 53:6). Although there is ample text, the diminished explicitness throughout the rhetorical unit complicates an assessment of the text. Interestingly, the unit demonstrates in microcosm the general trajectory of the letter. The most explicit passage in 1 Pet 2:22 uses two full clauses from Isa 53:9 and is therefore largely recognizable. From here, the allusions are much shorter and at times spliced together. Beginning with this fuller quotation, the differences between the quotation and the *Vorlage* are minimal, with the inclusion of ἁμαρτίαν being the only variant. With diminishing explicitness comes diminishing correspondence between the alluded text and its *Vorlage*.

The same holds true for the remaining sections of the body middle; the exception being the quotation of Ps 33:13–17 in 1 Pet 3:10–12, which stands out as the most explicit use of scripture in the body middle. There are several differences between the Greek Psalm and 1 Peter that are not easily reconciled. Stanley's observation concerning "two basic patterns of revision" are certainly relevant to any account of these differences.[124] However, it is quite another question as to whether the revision occurs in the manuscript tradition or is due to the hand of the author.

One of the features observed in the body opening of 1 Peter was the use of catchwords (*gĕzērâ šāwâ*). This was particularly prominent in 1 Pet 2:6–10 where the terms λίθος and λαός served as organizing terms for the section. The same device occurs within the body middle and deserves further consideration. Among the results of recent scholarship on Isaiah is the recognition that there is a thematic unity to the book.[125] But what this thematic unity looks like has been variously conceived. In general terms, the themes of judgment and restoration serve to frame the book of Isaiah on a large scale.[126] Rendtorff probes further and suggests that some of the dominant themes of Isaiah consist in comfort, glory, guilt and sin,

---

124. Stanley, *Paul*, 50. The two patterns being: "(1) to bring a manuscript into closer conformity with a particular Hebrew *Vorlage*, or (2) to clarify or improve upon a rendering perceived to be especially awkward by later readers."

125. Clements, *Isaiah 1–39*, 21; Sweeney, *Isaiah 1–4*, 24.

126. Sweeney, *Isaiah 1–39*, 41.

a remnant people, the Holy One of Israel, righteousness and justice.[127] He writes, "The deliberate recapitulation of a certain word or a certain phrase can be a 'signal' indicating that there is a connection between the texts in question—a connection to which the reader's attention is to be drawn."[128] With the somewhat recent exploration of the redactional unity of Isaiah, the exploration of thematic links within Isaiah has exploded.[129] Sommer has correctly cautioned against anachronistically assuming that our modern endeavor to find thematic links in Isaiah corresponds with how ancient readers approached Isaiah.[130] However, the linkages in the text and between texts were certainly recognized by ancient readers, as evinced by the practice of *gĕzērâ šāwâ* and the compilation of *florilegia* or *testimonia*. Among the important themes to highlight as they relate to the present project are the themes of fear,[131] suffering,[132] and the ethics of good and evil.[133]

The relevance of these thematic connections in Isaiah has been noticed by scholars working on the use of Isaiah in the New Testament. Watts, for instance, suggests an Isaianic "narrative thread" that runs throughout the NT use of Isaiah.[134] Such a coherent narrative leads him away from the view that Isaianic quotations were "the product of isolated and near-sighted proof-texting."[135] Wagner's work on the use of Isaiah in Romans is another example of how this has been worked out.[136]

Similarly, Peter shows an awareness of both the thematic message of Isaiah and the contributing factor key terms play. The most prominent key term is the φόβος/φοβέω set. In 2:17, the allusion to Prov 24:21 contains the phrase "fear the Lord" (τὸν θεὸν φοβεῖσθε). The quotation of Isa 8:12-13 in 1 Pet 3:14-15 has both noun and verb forms: τὸν δὲ φόβον αὐτῶν μὴ φοβηθῆτε. Beyond these instances, the body middle has a high concentration of the key term set (2:17, 18; 3:2, 6, 14, 16).[137] One peculiar use occurs

127. Rendtorff, *Old Testament*, 198–200; "Isaiah 56:1," 150–64.

128. Rendtorff, "Isaiah 56:1," 149.

129. See, for instance, Sweeney, *Isaiah 1-39* on the use of torah in Isaiah, or Williamson, *Variations on a Theme* on kingship in Isaiah.

130. Sommer, "Allusions and Illusions," 156–86.

131. Barton, "Ethics," 72; Sheppard, "'Scope' of Isaiah," 271–74.

132. Harrington, *Why Do We Suffer?*, 57; Hägglund, *Isaiah 53*, 4. Also on the suffering servant: Sawyer, *Fifth Gospel*, 33; Childs, *Isaiah*, 422–23, *inter alia*.

133. Davies, *Double Standards*, 34–38.

134. Watts, "Isaiah," 231–33.

135. Ibid., 232.

136. See the summaries in Wagner, "Isaiah," 129; "Moses and Isaiah," 88–89.

137. Goppelt, *Commentary on I Peter*, 113, 242–43. See also H. Balz "φοβέω, φοβέομαι, φόβος, κτλ." *TDNT* 9:213–17.

in 3:6 where the term draws upon two scriptural texts: Isa 54:4 and Prov 3:25. Other scriptural texts utilized in the body middle have been shown to contain the key term set in close proximity to the quoted text although the key term is not employed. These passages include Ps 33:13–17 in 1 Pet 3:10–12 where v. 12 contains the noun φόβος in the Psalmist's promise to teach the fear of the Lord, Isa 50:9 in 1 Pet 3:13 which is followed by the question, "Who among you fears (ὁ φοβούμενος) the Lord?" and the Noahic section of Isa 54:9–14—which stands behind the reference to Noah in 1 Pet 3:20—promises that his children shall not be afraid. Thus, the narrative of the restoration of divine presence dispels fear on a human level, but also insists upon fear as the proper response to the presence of God.

Another set of catchwords that deserves attention are those revolving around the verb ποιέω. It was shown how Ps 33:13–17 provides the language for the moral dualism at the basis of Peter's ethics in the body middle. The terms κακοποιέω and ἀγαθοποιέω repeated in 2:11, 15, 20; 3:6, 17 are drawn from Ps 33:15 quoted in 1 Pet 3:11. The use of ποιέω in the quotation of Isa 53:9 in 1 Pet 2:22 significantly ties together the two passages, particularly regarding the way they both contribute to the ethical argument constructed around Christ's example. Related to these is Isa 10:3 alluded to in 1 Pet 2:12 even though verb itself is not quoted. These three passages show how Peter's ethics derive from his reading of scripture.[138] Indeed, a constituent part of the scriptural narrative is that in the midst of suffering, the servants of the Lord would remain righteous.

This use of key terms is significant for showing how Peter read scripture. A picture emerges concerning these catchwords. In some cases, linking terms bring together passages from Isaiah that are far flung (e.g., Isa 8:14 is linked with Isa 28:16 through the use of λίθος and Isa 10:3 is linked to Isa 53:9 through the use of ποιέω). The Psalter appears twice in the body opening and middle with Ps 117:22 linked with the stone passages of Isaiah in 1 Pet 2:6–8 and with Psalm 33 used twice (1 Pet 2:3 and 3:10–12). The book of Proverbs is also drawn upon through the use of allusion (1 Pet 3:6; 4:7). Apart from the quotation of the Levitical holiness formula (1 Pet 1:16), an allusion to Exo 19:6, and the appearance of Sarah in 3:6 and Noah in 3:20, very little from the Pentateuch is utilized. This limited number of scriptural books is perhaps due to limited availability. But what we can observe is that Isaiah is read both as self-interpretive and as interpreted alongside other texts. As will be explored further below, Peter draws these terms and themes into his argument about what the church is and how it is to act.

---

138. Van Unnik, "Teaching of Good Works," 99–106; Green, "Use," 278–89.

Explicitness without Markedness

The findings of the body middle permit a consideration of questions arising from the reader-centered approach. To what extent would the audience be able to perceive the scriptural discourse present throughout the section? In the body opening, 1 Pet 2:6–10 shifts away from the markedness observed in 1 Pet 1:16, 24 and 2:6. This shift continues in the body middle where sizeable portions of Isaiah are utilized without clear markers. This trajectory away from markedness challenges the criteria of scholars championing the reader-centered approach. The flaw of this approach occurs not in its desire to understand the use of scripture in epistolary literature from the vantage point of the reader *vis-a-vis* the author but from an overly simplified view of the audience. The trajectory in 1 Peter points to an expectation that the audience will continue to comprehend the use of scripture without the aid of rhetorical markers. The dynamic between author and reader is more complex than the reader-centered approach has allowed to date.

However, the upshot of diminishing explicitness is a corresponding decline in comprehensibility. If the audience is composed of readers/hearers of various levels of expertise, then with diminishing explicitness comes a loss of some portion of the audience's ability to fully comprehend Peter's use of scripture in every instance. This does not mean that less skilled hearers are sidelined or that the letter is intended for the more skilled section of the audience. Interestingly, at the same time that Peter decides to utilize a more subtle scriptural discourse, he also employs largely architectonic rhetorical devices such as the household code (2:18—3:9), creed (3:18) and vice list (4:3). So, the whole audience benefits from a rhetorically marked argument while skilled members of the audience benefit from the continued use of scriptural texts.

What I am arguing here is that the act of using scripture without markedness is as intentional as using scripture in otherwise explicit modes (e.g., introductory formulae). The quotations that are more marked occur at the outset of the letter. As the letter progresses, Peter adopts an approach that incorporates scripture more subtly than at the beginning. Peter is no obscurantist. Instead, having established the scriptural basis for his address to the churches of Asia Minor early in his letter, the scripturally informed argument proceeds not so much on the force of quotation, but through the evocation of a large-scale scriptural narrative to which the discrete scriptural texts refer.

These observations reinforce the two points expressed at the conclusion to chapter 3. Subtlety in the use of scripture requires scholars not to limit arbitrarily the field of study to only the most explicit instances of scriptural quotation—to do so unnecessarily decreases an already small sample. The decision to limit our study of epistolary use of scripture to the most explicit examples is based on the assumption that the most unskilled reader must be the arbiter of reader competence. The alternative is not to assume the audience contains monolithically proficient readers. Instead, one must account for varying abilities among the audience. Additionally, the presence of illiterate yet highly competent *hearers* means that assessments of competence cannot assume literacy as the only factor in our study of the audience. Limiting the data based on an inaccurate picture of the original audience leads to an inaccurate picture of the author's hermeneutics and exegetical practices. In the case of the body middle, the picture of Peter's use of scripture would be severely stunted without the insights gained from his subtle use of scripture. In fact, the move to subtlety itself reveals much about his use of scripture and the assumptions he has about his audience.

Christology and Ecclessiology

The body middle of 1 Peter develops the connection between christology and ecclesiology already present in the body opening. The household code provides structure to this in significant ways. The suffering servant of Isaiah 53 applies to the suffering of Christ and provides a theological framework for understanding the death of Christ. However, the foray into christology in 1 Pet 2:21–25 was not for christology's sake. The framing rhetoric is cast in the language of example (ὑπογραμμός; 2:21) and placed within the servants' section of the household code (2:18–25). Peter's use of Isaiah 53 was sensitive to the servant-servants motif whereby the term "servant" in the singular runs throughout Isaiah 40–53 and shifts to the plural use of "servants" in Isaiah 54–66. The use of the phrase "servants of God" (θεοῦ δοῦλοι) in 2:16 demonstrates this sensitivity. This observation has important implications for understanding Peter's use of scripture and the contents of 1 Peter.

The complementary relationship between christology and ecclesiology derives from Peter's reading of scripture.[139] Isaiah provides a narrative that accounts for both the suffering of Christ and the suffering of Christ's followers. The body opening uses a similar device by employing a singular and plural reiteration of λίθος and λίθοι. The divine election of the stone interpreted as Christ and the vocation of the people of God portrays the relationship between Christ and believers in structural terms. The connection of christology and ecclesiology progresses into the body middle. Here, Peter accounts for suffering by employing the language of Isaiah 53–66

---

139. Hays, *Echoes*, 121.

through the use of the servant-servants motif. Just as the suffering servant has suffering disciple servants in Isaiah 54–66, so the suffering Christ now has disciples who suffer. Isaiah 54 establishes the plural servants motif (Isa 54:17) by drawing upon two patriarchal figures: the barren woman (Isa 54:1–8) and Noah (Isa 54:9–14). These two patriarchal figures establish a pattern followed by Peter. The arrangement of the household code is peculiar when compared to the codes in Ephesians and Colossians. However, this peculiarity makes sense when the Isaianic pattern is understood. The suffering servant material from Isaiah 53 is quoted in the servant section of the household code (1 Pet 2:18–25), and the wives section (3:1–6) follows upon this, alluding to the barren woman of Isaiah 54. The patterning of the household code on Isaiah points to the role the servant-servants motif plays in Peter's argument. The pattern extends beyond the household code into the further argument about suffering when Noah enters the scene. The depiction of Noah in Isaiah 54 as an afflicted one (54:11) who has no need to fear (54:14) provides the connection to the Petrine argument that Christ's disciples are suffering servants. Thus, the Noahic baptism in 1 Pet 3:21 serves as a hinge between christology and ecclesiology through participation in both suffering and resurrection.

What this study has thus far revealed is that when Peter turns to scripture, he is not asking questions about christology but about the church. This is not to say that his thoughts on Christ do not undergo development in his reading of scripture. It is simply that his main concern is to address the church. His hermeneutical understanding of the church as the people of God shapes his reading of scripture. At the same time, scripture shapes his understanding of what it means to be the people of God. Isaiah's contribution to this understanding cannot be underestimated, for in Isaiah the depiction of God's suffering servants is set within the larger narrative of the restoration of God's presence among his people.

Christ, Church and Ethics

The body middle of 1 Peter features an extended ethical argument that deserves special attention, particularly as it relates to Petrine use of scripture. The moral dualism provided by Ps 33:13–17 contributes greatly to the ethical admonition to do what is good (ἀγαθοποιέω) even when surrounded by those who do evil (κακοποιέω). There are hints of cosmic and eschatological dualism at points in the body middle that might further inform the ethical dualism presented throughout.[140] In 1 Pet 3:22, the placement of Christ in

---

140. Gammie ("Spatial and Ethical Dualism," 356–85) calls for greater precision in

heaven at the right hand of God might indicate that the material world is the domain of evil. The phrases "on the day of visitation" in 2:12 and "the end of all things is at hand" in 4:7 suggest that the present is the time of evil. However, throughout the body middle, the contest between good and evil occurs spatially and temporally in the present world.

The contest between good and evil places the believer in the crosshairs of injustice. In the face of slander and social ostracism, the elect are called upon to respond with good conduct even if evil or sinful actions were more expedient. This line of reasoning is fundamentally scriptural. With Ps 33:13–17 as the largest block quotation of the body middle, it supplies the language for Peter's moral dualism and thereby demonstrates how it is consistent with scripture. On its own, this argument based on moral dualism is stark and leaves the audience to its own devices to navigate weighty moral issues in the face of suffering. Here, the link to Isaiah 53 and the conduct of Christ rounds out the ethics of 1 Peter. Christ is depicted as a righteous sufferer in terms drawn from Isaiah 53. The quotation of Isa 53:9 in 1 Pet 2:22 uses the key term ποιέω to communicate that he "did not sin" (ἁμαρτίαν οὐκ ἐποίησεν) and connects Christ to the ethical argument of the body middle. The moral duality has been upheld by Christ, validating the categories of good and evil but also leaving an example for Christ's suffering disciples to follow. Despite doing good Christ suffered, a concept repeated several times (1 Pet 2:21, 23; 3:18; 4:1), his response was not retaliation, reviling or threats but to entrust himself to God (2:23).

The christology of 2:22–25 depicts Christ as one who upholds moral virtues. This passage, however, is framed by the language of example (2:21). Christ serves as an example, "that you might follow in his steps." For the ethical contours of 1 Peter, the example of Christ is paradigmatic for the elect. As Dryden describes it, Christ is a moral exemplar.[141] Basing his study of 1 Peter on the identification of the letter as paraenesis, he draws upon the ancient Greco-Roman genre of paraenetic epistle to explain the role of virtue in the moral instruction of 1 Peter.[142] In his section, "*Imitatio Christi* in 1 Peter," he demonstrates convincingly that Christ's work as exemplar and his work as savior are not incompatible.[143] The efforts to either divide the passage into neat categories of example and salvation or to champion one over

---

classifying types of dualism.

141. Dryden, *Theology and Ethics*, 27, 187.

142. Ibid., 15–36 on the genre of paraenetic epistle and 37–54 as it applies to 1 Peter.

143. Ibid., 174–89.

the other does not do justice to the complexity of Peter's argument. Instead, "Christ is at the same moment savior and example."[144]

From here, Dryden's work may be taken in two fruitful directions. First, scripture plays an important role undergirding the salvific and exemplary roles expounded in 1 Pet 2:22-25. Isaiah 53 read in light of what follows in Isaiah 54-66 provides a pattern of based on the virtuous exemplar for disciples who would follow in his footsteps. Thus, the servant-servants motif in the latter part of Isaiah contributes to the ethical instruction by providing the pattern recognized by Dryden as moral exemplar. Isaiah 53 does not stand alone as the wellspring of ethical thought in 1 Peter. Psalm 33:13-17 is read in concert with Isa 10:3 to provide the categories of good and evil.

Second, Christ is not the only individual put forward as an exemplar. If Christ is the exemplar of the servants' section of the household code, then the patriarchal wife Sarah is the exemplar of the wives' section (3:1-6), and in 3:20 Noah is put forward as another exemplar. The argument of the present chapter has proposed that Isaiah 54 stands behind the introduction of these two characters.

A consistent picture emerges regarding the way moral instruction in 1 Peter is based on scripture. Scripture—and primarily Isaiah—provides language that describes the suffering Christ as the virtuous exemplar for a church that is suffering injustice. Scripture, in concert with the narrative of Christ's suffering and exaltation, evokes a narrative in which the believer is to act with high moral conduct. In keeping with the argument of this thesis, the moral conduct of the church is based on the moral conduct of Christ. Participation in the narrative of divine restoration is predicated first upon Christ's participation in righteous suffering leading to the reconciliation of God and humanity. The church thus participates in the narrative of restoration by following Christ's example of moral conduct.

---

144. Ibid., 187.

6

The Use of Scripture in 1 Peter 4:12—5:11

Introduction

THE BODY CLOSING OF 1 Peter (4:12—5:11) is considerably shorter than the previous two parts of the body of the epistle. The trajectory noted in previous chapters about the decreasing explicitness of scriptural discourse means that the amount of material to present in this chapter is likewise smaller than has been the case thus far.

This chapter will deal with the body closing in two sections. The first section covers 4:12–19 in which there are two new passages of scripture introduced into the argument (Isa 11:2 and Prov 11:31). The second section covers 5:1–11 in which three allusions occur (Isa 28:5; Prov 3:34; Ps 22:14). In both sections, the ability to hear echoes of scripture is assisted through the use of key terms and concepts. The two passages that pertain most to such an exercise are Isaiah 40 and 53. Both passages have received special attention in previous sections of 1 Peter, preparing the reader/listener for the subtle use of scripture that continues into this last section of the letter.

Suffering as Christians and Vindication in Final Judgment: 1 Peter 4:12–19

Themes previously employed in 1 Peter are recapitulated throughout 1 Pet 4:12–19. The fiery trial that tests the elect in 4:12 harks back to 1:6–7 where the same language is used.[1] In 4:13, the use of ἀγαλλιάω repeats the verb

---

1. Selwyn, *First Epistle of St Peter*, 221; Michaels, *1 Peter*, 258; Goppelt, *Commentary on I Peter*, 313–14; Achtemeier, *1 Peter*, 306; Elliott, *1 Peter*, 771–72; Dubis, *Messianic*

used in 1:6 and 8,[2] and the suffering of Christ and the glory to be revealed recalls 1:11.[3] The macarism in 4:14 regarding insults for the name of Christ is similar to 3:14 and 16.[4]

1 Peter 4:12–19 offers a summarization of the letter but also has a coherent argument in its own right. Like the body middle of 1 Peter, the body closing continues to address the problem of suffering experienced by the elect.[5] There are two strategies offered to console the audience. First, judgment is brought to bear on all people, both the elect of the "house of God" and those who do not obey the gospel of God (4:17).[6] The idea is put forward that the final judgment will be a time of glory in contrast to the shame of the present slanderous time.[7] Second, the suffering elect are encouraged to entrust themselves to God who is a "faithful creator."[8] Thus, the judge who carries out the judgment becomes a source of consolation as well as the vindicator at the time of judgment.

Scripture plays an important role throughout the course of this argument. In 1 Pet 4:14 there is an allusion to Isa 11:2.[9] The elect are blessed when they are insulted "in the name of Christ" because God's presence is upon them.

Woes, 78–79; Feldmeier, *First Letter of Peter*, 224.

2. Selwyn, *First Epistle of St Peter*, 222; Goppelt, *Commentary on I Peter*, 316–21; Achtemeier, *1 Peter*, 307; Elliott, *1 Peter*, 777; Jobes, *1 Peter*, 286.

3. Michaels, *1 Peter*, 261–62; Schutter, *Hermeneutic*, 74–75; Davids, *First Epistle of Peter*, 165–66; Goppelt, *Commentary on I Peter*, 314–15; Elliott, *1 Peter*, 774–75; Dubis, *Messianic Woes*, 96–117; Green, *1 Peter*, 148.

4. Michaels, *1 Peter*, 263; Goppelt, *Commentary on I Peter*, 322; Elliott, *1 Peter*, 778.

5. Michaels, *1 Peter*, 258–59; Achtemeier, *1 Peter*, 304–5; Elliott, *1 Peter*, 768–70; Green, *1 Peter*, 147–48; Feldmeier, *First Letter of Peter*, 223.

6. Dubis, *Messianic Woes*, 145–62.

7. It is important to note that Peter is not constructing a present/future dualism here. Instead, although suffering continues, the time of judgment has begun (ὁ καιρὸς τοῦ ἄρξασθαι τὸ κρίμα). The inception of judgment provides an imminence that addresses the audience in the present but is not spelled out by Peter in practical terms. Even the quotation of the rhetorical question from Prov 11:31 leaves the judgment upon sinners open to the imagination.

8. Dubis, *Messianic Woes*, 174–76.

9. Schutter (*Hermeneutic*, 37) classifies this as an explicit allusion. See his further discussion on 153–54, 164, 175.

Table 6.1: 1 Peter 4:14 and Isaiah 11:2

1 Peter 4:14	Isaiah 11:2
εἰ ὀνειδίζεσθε ἐν ὀνόματι Χριστοῦ, ὅτι τὸ τῆς δόξης καὶ τὸ <u>τοῦ θεοῦ πνεῦμα ἐφ'</u> ὑμᾶς <u>ἀναπαύεται</u>.	καὶ <u>ἀναπαύσεται ἐπ'</u> αὐτὸν <u>πνεῦμα τοῦ θεοῦ</u>,

The use of this passage is interesting in light of foregoing discussions. A consideration of the context in Isaiah 11 reveals much about Peter's hermeneutic. At the head of the chapter stands a reference to the branch or rod (ῥάβδος; חטר) that emanates from Jesse's root. The image of regrowth in the Davidic line serves as a wellspring of hope for the regathering of remnant Israel (Isa 10:20–21; 11:11, 16).[10] The interpretive history on this passage shows tendencies to interpret the branch either as a corporate or individual entity.[11] Regardless of the identity of the branch, 11:2 indicates the placement of the spirit of the Lord upon the branch bestowing "charismata."[12] The branch takes delight in the fear of the Lord (11:3) and initiates a reversal of the iniquities that led to the punishment meted out in previous chapters of Isaiah.[13]

It would not be surprising, and perhaps would be expected, to find Peter interpreting this passage christologically.[14] However, differences between the Petrine version of the passage and OG Isaiah offer a surprising interpretation. First, the use of the present tense verb ἀναπαύεται differs from the future tense (ἀναπαύσεται) of Isa 11:2. While this may be a variant, several scholars have pointed to Peter's interpretation of this passage as being presently fulfilled in the church.[15] A decisive factor supporting this understanding is the context of Peter's argument, where he indicates the beginning of the time of God's judgment (1 Pet 4:17).

A second difference occurs through the transformation of the prepositional phrase ἐπ' αὐτὸν to ἐφ' ὑμᾶς. Peter indicates that the divine presence promised to rest upon the Isaianic branch rests upon the elect who are in

---

10. Kaiser, *Isaiah 1–12*, 262; Childs, *Isaiah*, 105–6; Smith, *Isaiah 1–39*, 275.
11. See a fuller discussion in Wagner, *Heralds of the Good News*, 318–28.
12. So Childs, *Isaiah*, 102.
13. Oswalt, *Book of Isaiah*, 1:280–81; Brueggemann, *Texts That Linger*, 100.
14. See Michaels, *1 Peter*, 264; Dubis, *Messianic Woes*, 120–21; Green, *1 Peter*, 152.
15. Michaels, *1 Peter*, 265; Achtemeier, *1 Peter*, 308; Dubis, *Messianic Woes*, 122.

Christ.[16] This ecclesiological appropriation of Isaiah 11 is unexpected if the model for the scriptural interpretation of the early church is solely christological.[17] Instead, the use of Isa 11:2 in this way is consistent with the scriptural discourse seen elsewhere in the letter.[18] Peter has consistently returned to Isaiah time and again to find answers not to christological questions but to questions concerning the church. In this particular case, the appropriation of Isa 11:2 for his ecclesiological purposes bypasses a christological move seen in previous sections of 1 Peter (namely 2:6–10 and 2:21–25). Peter contends that the divine presence rests directly on suffering believers. Yet, it is necessary to point out the continuing role of participatory christology.[19] The condition set forth in 1 Pet 4:14 specifies that the believer suffers in the name of Christ (ἐν ὀνόματι Χριστοῦ).[20] The suffering of the believer occurs, then, in fellowship with the suffering of Christ himself (4:13). That said, it still remains the case that Peter does not begin by interpreting Isa 11:2 christologically (e.g., "the spirit of God rests on Christ") and then apply this interpretation to the church. The corporate trajectory of this passage is already present in the interpretive tradition.[21] Schutter demonstrates how the passage "had been read messianically not only in the early Church (Eph. 1.17, Mt. 3:16, Jn. 1.32), but in certain pre-Christian circles also (4QpIsaᵃ, Pss. Sol. 17.39–44)."[22] Wagner notes that the Greek translation itself gives evidence of a messianic interpretation of Isaiah 11.[23] So, there is no reason

---

16. In the textual transmission of Isaiah, the object of the preposition is altered to the dative (αὐτῷ) in only a few cases (Codex Venetus and manuscripts 93 and 301). Compare this with the form of 1QIsaᵃ which has לי instead of עליו. In the textual transmission of 1 Peter, two issues arise. First, εἰς occurs in several manuscripts as a variant of ἐπί. However, there is overwhelming support for the preposition ἐπί. Second, the appearance of ἡμᾶς as a variant of ὑμᾶς is not surprising but occurs in only a few manuscripts. There are no cases where the second person pronoun has been changed to the third person pronoun in the transmission of 1 Peter.

17. Moyise (*Evoking*, 93) arrives at a similar conclusion. See also Jobes, *1 Peter*, 288.

18. Green, *1 Peter*, 152.

19. Schutter (*Hermeneutic*, 75) considers this "the first time in the letter of the idea of 'participation.'" I have argued that participation is initiated much earlier in the letter and is not to be differentiated from the language of imitation in 2:21.

20. Best (*I Peter*, 39) adduces that this is written "not so much from the perspective of the state as from that of the eschatological expectation of the Parousia." This is not to imply that persecution by the state of "Christians" is not in view. As Horrell (*1 Peter*, 90) notes, Peter appears to be transforming a pejorative label (1 Pet 4:16) and claiming it "as a positive one, to be borne with pride."

21. Dubis, *Messianic Woes*, 121–22; Green, *1 Peter*, 152–53.

22. Schutter, *Hermeneutic*, 154. See also the Isaiah Targum at Isa 11:1; 1Q28b 5.20–29; 4Q285 (Wagner, "Psalm 118," 320–21).

23. Wagner, "Psalm 118," 322.

to expect Peter to pursue a corporate reading of Isa 11:2, unless he had already begun with an ecclesiological hermeneutic. The idea of participation in Christ leading up to this use of scripture affords Peter to move directly from Isa 11:2 to the church through the transformed object pronoun.

In light of the use of the φόβος/φοβέω catchword association among texts in the body middle of 1 Peter, it is worth noting how Isa 11:2–3 focuses on the fear of the Lord (φόβος θεοῦ).[24] The previous chapter developed how key terminology represents an important reading strategy on the part of Peter. This particular reading strategy—the φόβος/φοβέω key terminology—is yet another link between 4:12–19 and the previous sections of the epistle.

The phrase "it is time for judgment to begin in the house of God" has received considerable attention as a potential allusion. The question remains, however, to what it is alluding. Many have seen here an allusion to Ezek 9:6,[25] while others have sought other backgrounds.[26] Schutter placed great importance on Ezek 9:6 as the source text. He sees the phrase in 1 Pet 4:17 as moving "beyond the understanding of the Messianic Woes as heralds of the End to one which sees the manifestation of the End itself in at least some of the struggles of his addresses."[27] He then argues that Ezek 9:6 holds interpretive advantages over Jer 25:29 or Mal 3:1 for understanding Peter's argument, with the primary difference being "its graphic scene of carnage within the Temple precincts proper."[28] He admits, however, that all three passages refer to the temple, speak of the beginning of God's judgment and share a concern with the sequence of eschatological events. After identifying parallel usage in Josephus (*A.J.* 10.79; *B.J.* 4.386–388; 5.15–19; 6.109–110) and *Sib. Or.* 6:115–118 concerning the desecration of the Temple,[29] he finds

---

24. The revisions of Aquila, Symmachus and Theodotion have φόβος in 11:2 replacing εὐσεβείας as a better translation of יראה at the end of the verse.

25. McKelvey, *New Temple*, 133; Kelly, *Epistles of Peter and of Jude*, 193; Schutter, "I Peter 4.17," 276–84; idem., *Hermeneutic*, 37–38, 75, 156–63; Michaels, *1 Peter*, 271; Achtemeier, *1 Peter*, 316; Mbuvi, *Temple*, 39, 91.

26. Johnson ("Fire in God's House," 292) argues for the influence of Zech 13:9 and Mal 3:1–3 are more important for 1 Pet 4:17 than Ezek 9:6. Elliott (*1 Peter*, 798–800) finds the link "highly unlikely" and Jobes (*1 Peter*, 292) argues that none of these passages pertains because "when Peter quotes OT passages elsewhere in the letter . . . he consistently preserves the original context." Goppelt (*Commentary on I Peter*, 329) is undecided. Liebengood (*Eschatology*, 22, 143–45) proposes a compelling thesis that "Zechariah 9–14 offers a more satisfying explanation for the modification of Isa 11.2 in 1 Pet 4.14" than either the Jesus tradition (Mark 13:11 par.) or other scriptural texts.

27. Schutter, *Hermeneutic*, 155. See also Schutter, "I Peter 4.17," 276–84, which contains the same argument.

28. Schutter, *Hermeneutic*, 156–57.

29. Ibid., 158–61.

that Peter has likewise seen the church as "the Temple-community" (2:4–10) and, in keeping with the interpretive tradition, views the suffering of the church as "a collective assault on the Temple-community in terms of Ezek 9–11."[30] He concludes that "the collective assault against Christians represents nothing less than the start of the Last Judgment itself."[31] For Schutter, the background of Ezekiel 9–11 explains the pronominal shift in Isa 11:2 in 1 Pet 4:14,[32] and provides a connection to the suffering/glory motif through the "'periodization' of history" he reads into the term καιρός in 4:17.[33]

Considerable doubt has arisen, though, concerning the specific scriptural background to the phrase in 4:17. Dubis largely agrees with Schutter's insistence that Ezek 9:6 provides "the dominant OT background," but suggests that other texts (such as Jer 32:15 and Mal 3:1–5) provide "a subsidiary background."[34] Like Schutter, he explores the interpretive tradition, but arrives at a slightly different conclusion. Peter's use of καιρός does not indicate a periodization of history, but that Peter consistently uses καιρός to indicate "the καιρός that came into being with the arrival of the Messiah (1:11) is of one piece with the καιρός in which judgment begins (4:17) and the καιρός in which salvation will be revealed at the parousia (1:5; 5:6)."[35] Dubis characterizes Peter's use of these traditions as the messianic woes that "function as judgment," but "are not the endpoint of eschatological judgment."[36] Mbuvi also sees Ezekiel 9 in the background and draws upon this to develop the idea that "the Spirit of God rests upon them as the Šhekinah of God rested on the sanctuary" in 4:14.[37] Thus, he sees that God's judgment in 4:17 begins in the temple.[38]

Elliott has raised the most serious critiques to Schutter's view. He begins by listing the few points of verbal correspondence between 1 Pet 4:17 and Ezek 9:6: the verb ἄρχω, and the similar prepositional phrases ἀπὸ τοῦ οἴκου τοῦ θεοῦ and ἀπὸ τῶν ἁγίων μου.[39] The limited nature of the points of connection along with the different messages of each passage lead him to

---

30. Ibid., 161–62.
31. Ibid., 163.
32. Ibid., 162.
33. Ibid., 156.
34. Dubis, *Messianic Woes*, 153.
35. Ibid., 144 n. 9.
36. Ibid., 162.
37. Mbuvi, *Temple*, 116.
38. Ibid., 120–21.
39. Elliott, *1 Peter*, 798–99.

deny Ezek 9:6 as the background.⁴⁰ Instead, he suggests that the primary point of similarity is the idea that "divine judgment begins with God's own people," an idea shared with numerous other writings.⁴¹ Jobes argues in the same direction, noting that "the original context of the passages from Ezekiel, Zechariah, and Malachi do not fit Peter's use, for they are pronouncing God's judgment on his people for violating the covenant. Peter here is saying exactly the opposite."⁴²

Siding with Elliott and Jobes, the difficulties present in making the connection between a specific text and 1 Pet 4:17 seem to me insurmountable. It does seem likely that Peter has evoked a traditional available in early Judaism that understands present suffering within God's unfolding eschatological plan. The universality of God's final judgment not only includes the believer, but has already begun in the suffering of believers. To this point, the participatory language in which the argument is cast allows us to explore further the concept of judgment. The text emphasizes this participation through the phrases "fellowship in Christ's sufferings" (κοινωνεῖτε τοῖς τοῦ Χριστοῦ παθήμασιν, 4:13), "in the name of Christ" (ἐν ὀνόματι Χριστοῦ, 4:14),⁴³ and through the designation "as Christians" (4:16).⁴⁴ As I have argued earlier, this should not be seen as distinct from any other construal of the relationship of the believer to Christ (e.g., 2:4–5; 2:21).⁴⁵ Thus, Peter viewed judgment as falling upon Christ in his suffering, something in which believers now participate through their fellowship in Christ's suffering.⁴⁶

The argument of 4:12–19 is supported by another scriptural passage in 4:18. If Isa 11:2 supplies scriptural support to the idea of divine presence

---

40. Dubis (*Messianic Woes*, 151–52) argues against Elliott, but only on the issue of whether τῶν ἁγίων refers to the temple. He does not answer the main critique.

41. Elliott, *1 Peter*, 800.

42. Jobes, *1 Peter*, 292. She goes on to argue that Peter "consistently preserves the original context." This is an overstatement, particularly in light of the pronoun shift in Isa 11:2.

43. See 4:16 with ἐν τῷ ὀνόματι τούτῳ, which has better manuscript support (P⁷², 01, 02, 03, *passim*). The editors of *ECM* have not provided sufficient warrant to place μέρει in the main text (following the majority text).

44. Dubis, *Messianic Woes*, 103.

45. Selwyn (*First Epistle of St Peter*, 221) agrees that these passages are synonymous, but designates them *imitatio Christi*. Davids (*First Epistle of Peter*, 166) sees "a sense of identification and real unity" in all of the passages of 1 Peter, but subsumes this as a type of *imitatio Christi*. Cf. Dryden, *Theology and Ethics*, 174–91.

46. See Isa 53:10. It is significant that Peter describes Christ as having "given himself to a righteous judge" (παρεδίδου δὲ τῷ κρίνοντι δικαίως) in the midst of his use of Isaiah 53.

upon the elect community, Prov 11:31 supports the idea of the universality of the final judgment.

Table 6.2: **1 Peter 4:18 and Proverbs 11:31**

1 Peter 4:18	Proverbs 11:31
καὶ εἰ ὁ <u>δίκαιος μόλις σῴζεται</u>, <u>ὁ ἀσεβὴς καὶ ἁμαρτωλὸς ποῦ</u> <u>φανεῖται</u>;	εἰ ὁ μὲν <u>δίκαιος μόλις σῴζεται</u>, <u>ὁ ἀσεβὴς καὶ ἁμαρτωλὸς ποῦ</u> <u>φανεῖται</u>;

From a textual standpoint, two observations immediately stand out. First, 1 Pet 4:18 agrees substantially with the Greek version against the Hebrew.[47] As Barr points out, Peter's use of this proverb depends on the word μόλις, which "appears to lack any proper basis in the Hebrew."[48] The word μόλις replaces באדץ in the first clause of the proverb. Second, the omission of the coordinating conjunction μέν is the only difference between Prov 11:31 and the Petrine quotation.[49] The scribe responsible for the inclusion of μέν in the Bodmer papyrus (P[72]) may have been aware of this omission.

From a literary standpoint, there are two key terms, which link this passage to other passages of scripture central to the scriptural discourse of the body middle of 1 Peter. The term δίκαιος is a prominent term in the quotation of Greek Psalm 33.[50] In Ps 33:16 at 1 Pet 3:12, the eyes of the Lord are on the righteous (δίκαιοι) who are distinct from those who do evil (ποιοῦντες κακά). The righteous are those who maintain the ethic of goodness (ἀγαθός). This link brings together texts within the writings (כתובים), which have been an important source for the ethical content of the body middle. The language of good and evil continues to remain prominent in the present body closing, with κακοποιός being used in 4:15 and ἀγαθοποιΐα in 4:19.[51] In the context of the narrative of restored divine presence, the maintenance of conduct marks followers of Christ as righteous sufferers.

---

47. Barr, "באדץ—ΜΟΛΙΣ," 150. See also Osborne, "L'utilisation," 71; Elliott, *1 Peter*, 802.

48. Ibid., 150.

49. Osborne, "L'utilisation," 71.

50. Schutter, *Hermeneutic*, 164.

51. Schutter (*Hermeneutic*, 164–65) insists upon promoting the allusion to Ezek 9:6, which causes him to miss these important ethical considerations. See Liebengood, *Eschatology*, 146–47.

The term ἁμαρτωλός can likewise be linked within the corpus of the writings to Prov 10:12 used in 1 Pet 4:8. This link is particularly conspicuous since the term ἁμαρτία in the Petrine text differs from OG Prov 10:12. The hamartiology of 1 Peter thus far has emphasized the sinlessness of Christ (1 Pet 2:22) and the covering of sins by Christ (2:24; 3:18; 4:1, 8).[52] The use of Prov 11:31 issues the first instance of describing a person as sinful, whereas previous conceptions of those opposed to the elect—at times referred to as "Gentiles" (2:12; 4:3)—have emphasized unbelief (2:7), disobedience (2:8; 4:17), ignorance (2:15) or the abuse they meet out on the elect (3:16).[53]

The key terms together (δίκαιος and the ἁμαρτία word group) form an important link to Isaiah 53. The term ἁμαρτία appears twice in 1 Pet 2:22 and 24 in phrases derived from Isa 53:9 and the merged allusion to 53:4 and 12. These Isaianic passages establish the two main hamartiological ideas of Christ's sinlessness and his bearing of sins.[54] The uses of δικαιοσύνη in 1 Pet 2:24 and δίκαιος in 3:18 echo Isa 53:11 where the righteous (δίκαιος) servant is central in justification (δικαιόω) and the bearing of sins (ἁμαρτίαι).[55]

This intertextual linking to prominent scriptural passages in 1 Peter forms an important basis for contemplating the continuing role of the scriptural narrative of the restoration of divine presence in the current section. Two passages stand out because of interesting word combinations. First, the combination of suffering and glory recalls Isaiah 53. It has been argued earlier that in 1 Pet 2:21–25 the verb πάσχω summarizes the career of the suffering servant who is central in the narrative of the restoration of divine presence among the people of God. The noun form πάθημα reiterates this at key points in the epistle (1:11; 5:1) where the sufferings of the servant are applied to Christ.[56] At such points, the δόξα word group works in tandem with πάθημα, once again drawing on the career of the suffering servant, since at the beginning of the song it is projected that the servant will be exalted (δοξασθήσεται; 52:13). The pairing of πάθημα and δόξα occurs in 1 Pet 4:13 where they are applied to Christ but also to the church which participates (κοινωνέω) in Christ's sufferings.[57] The πάσχω and δόξα word

52. See Goppelt, *Commentary on I Peter*, 298; Elliott, *1 Peter*, 803–4; Green, *1 Peter*, 269–71.

53. Michaels, *1 Peter*, 272.

54. Green, *1 Peter*, 213–14.

55. Elliott, *1 Peter*, 641.

56. Michaels, *1 Peter*, 261.

57. Goppelt, *Commentary on I Peter*, 314–15. The descriptive genitive (τὰ τοῦ Χριστοῦ παθήματα) argued for by Dubis ("First Peter," 90; *Messianic Woes*, 99–103) is unnecessary in this context. The use of κοινωνέω sufficiently draws the church into the

groups are repeated throughout the remainder of the section. In 4:14, the term δόξα is tied into the allusion of Isa 11:2 so that the spirit of God is also the spirit of glory. The manner of suffering remains important in the rhetoric of 1 Pet 4:12–19. It is shameful to suffer (πάσχω) as a murder, thief, evildoer or meddler (4:15) but there is no shame if one suffers as a Christian, in which case the believer glorifies (δοξάζω) God (4:16).[58] The section closes by admonishing believers who suffer (οἱ πάσχοντες) "according to God's will" to entrust their souls to a faithful creator. This mirrors the echo observed in 2:23 where Christ the servant entrusted himself to the one who judges justly. It was argued earlier that this alters the direction of the verb παραδίδωμι since in Isa 53:6 and 12 it is God who "gives up" the servant to pay for the people's iniquities.[59] In 1 Pet 2:23, Christ the servant gives himself up. Now in 4:19, the advice to suffering Christians involves entrusting (παρατίθημι) themselves—in imitation of Christ—to God.[60] This diffusion of key terms throughout the section indicates how Isaiah 53 has continued to inform Peter's reflection on the suffering of the church and draws it into the larger scriptural narrative that informs the ecclesiology of 1 Peter.

Another set of terms can be pointed out, even though their prominence is slighter. The phrase, "the gospel of God" (τὸ τοῦ θεοῦ εὐαγγέλιον) in 4:17 recalls the use of Isaiah 40 in 1 Pet 1:24–25. It was argued above that εὐαγγελίζω in 1:25 accomplishes two things in light of the quotation of Isa 40:6–8.[61] First, it interprets the phrase τὸ ῥῆμα κυρίου from Isa 40:8 as the gospel proclaimed to the audience (see 1 Pet 1:12). Secondly, it points to the wider context of Isaiah 40, since the good news (ὁ εὐαγγελιζόμενος; used twice in parallelism) is proclaimed from the mountains in the verse directly following the quotation used in 1 Peter. Thus, to have the repetition of good news language in genitival relationship to God (i.e., Isa 40:8 in 1 Pet 1:25; cf. 1 Pet 1:23) recalls the earlier discourse at which point the enduring power of God's word was set forth as synonymous with the gospel proclaimed by Peter. In the present context, the good news of God continues to be discussed in connection with the narrative of scripture. This time, though, the good news of God is pivotal in the discussion of final judgment. The question is asked in 4:17, "What will be the end (τέλος) of those who disobey the goods news of God?" The imminent threat is heightened through the further ques-

---

individual sufferings of Christ, and by extension, envisions the church's sufferings as part of his sufferings. See also Achtemeier, *1 Peter*, 306.

58. Horrell, *1 Peter*, 88–89.
59. See chapter 5.
60. Jobes, *1 Peter*, 295.
61. See chapter 3.

tion provided by Prov 11:31, "If the righteous is scarcely saved, what will become of the ungodly and the sinner?" The reuse of the phrase "good news" draws the grace of God's work for humanity into tension with the finality of God's judgment. To Peter's addressees, who are currently experiencing suffering, he points out that despite opposition, the good news is presented also to the unbeliever. Yet, their disobedience (ἀπειθέω) to the good news will result in judgment. Thus, Peter's argument offers consolation to and vindication of the eschatological community. Present suffering, according to Peter's reading of scripture, demonstrates how the church participates in the drama of God's final act of judgment. He articulates an inaugurated view of these eschatological elements (judgment, vindication, comfort and consolation) through God's presence now among his people. This occurs primarily through his ecclesiological reading of Isa 11:2 in 1 Pet 4:14.

The Humble Community and Eschatological Exaltation: 1 Peter 5:1–11

The final section of the body closing of 1 Peter features specific advice to elders (5:1–4) and neophytes (5:5), as well as the entire audience (5:6–11) generally. Various links with previous sections occur here.[62] The concept of Christian suffering which dominated the body middle has remained prominent both in 4:12–19 and in this final section (5:1, 9–10).[63] The structure of the household code (2:18—3:7) is recalled here through the direct address to particular groups within the audience.[64] Similarly, the use of exhortation carries over into this section as a primary mode of instruction used by Peter throughout the body of the letter. The use of scriptural texts also continues into this last section, which shall be explored fully below.

Scholars who have identified Ezek 9:6 in the background of 1 Pet 4:17 have also suggested that the transition to an address to elders is likewise indebted to Ezek 9:6.[65] As argued above, the possible link is so slight that significant doubts attend to the background in 1 Pet 4:17. So, the likelihood of an echo here is even more uncertain.[66]

Other allusions and echoes that have been proposed are more promising in their contribution to Peter's address to the churches of Asia Minor.

---

62. See Elliott, *1 Peter*, 810.

63. Achtemeier, *1 Peter*, 322; Green, *1 Peter*, 162–64.

64. Feldmeier, *First Letter of Peter*, 231.

65. Michaels, *1 Peter*, 277; Grudem, *1 Peter*, 185–86; Schutter, *Hermeneutic*, 165; Schreiner, *1, 2 Peter, Jude*, 230.

66. Elliott, *1 Peter*, 812.

One such allusion occurs in 1 Pet 5:4. Here the elders are encouraged to look forward to the appearance of the chief shepherd, at which point they will receive the "unfading crown of glory" (τὸν ἀμαράντιον τῆς δόξης στέφανον). Schutter recognizes the possible "reminiscence" of Isa 28:5 here, but contests that the differences between the two contexts is too great.[67] Caution is necessary when assessing the correspondence between the original context and the new context. However, the emphasis on future reward makes a rather suggestive link.[68] In Isa 28:5, the text expresses the reward for the remnant in parallelism as "the crown of hope and the diadem of glory" (ὁ στέφανος τῆς ἐλπίδος ὁ πλακεὶς τῆς δόξης). It is possible that the phrase in 1 Pet 5:4 truncates the phrase. Another possibility is that a version existed that more closely approximated the Hebrew text, which reads "crown of glory" (לעטרת צבי).[69] Regardless, the use of the phrase in 1 Peter suggests how the elders who lead faithfully will receive their eschatological reward. Alongside Isa 28:5, a number of other texts also depict the crown of glory as an eschatological reward: Sir 47:6; 1QS 4:6; 1QH 9:25 among others.[70]

The "mighty hand of God" in 1 Pet 5:6 recalls a common scriptural motif.[71] This anthropomorphism evokes most prominently the deliverance of Israel from Egypt (Exod 13:9; Deut 3:24; 4:34; 5:15; 7:19; 9:26; 11:2, passim).[72] The use in 1 Pet 5:6 carries the idea of divine deliverance and evokes a scriptural image of God's direct presence among his people. The suggestion made by Dubis that this scriptural motif evokes God's judgment of his people is only convincing if one reads the fiery trial of 4:17 into this passage.[73] Elliott correctly understands this passage as consolatory, and, therefore, the hand of God is one of protection and deliverance.[74]

Another allusion occurs in 1 Pet 5:7 with the phrase "casting all your (pl.) anxiety upon him" (πᾶσαν τὴν μέριμναν ὑμῶν ἐπιρίψαντες ἐπ' αὐτόν).[75] This phrase apparently borrows from Greek Ps 54:23, "Cast your (sg.) care

---

67. Schutter, *Hermeneutic*, 42.

68. The initial phrase in Isa 28:6 is τῇ ἡμέρᾳ ἐκείνῃ (translating ביום ההוא), which fits well with the coming of the chief shepherd of 1 Pet 5:4.

69. Both possibilities are explored by Schutter (*Hermeneutic*, 42).

70. See Goppelt, *Commentary on I Peter*, 349, n. 32; Elliott, *1 Peter*, 835. Many also include Jer 13:18, but the crown of glory is removed as a symbol of impending exile.

71. Schutter, *Hermeneutic*, 42–43.

72. Selwyn, *First Epistle of St Peter*, 235–36; Michaels, *1 Peter*, 295; Davids, *First Epistle of Peter*, 186; Goppelt, *Commentary on I Peter*, 357; Achtemeier, *1 Peter*, 339; Elliott, *1 Peter*, 850; Jobes, *1 Peter*, 311.

73. Dubis, *Messianic Woes*, 183.

74. Elliott, *1 Peter*, 850.

75. Schutter, *Hermeneutic*, 38, 77.

upon the Lord" (ἐπίρριψον ἐπὶ κύριον τὴν μέριμναν σου). The addition of πᾶσαν and the exchange of the pronoun for κύριον are not as significant as the use of the plural ὑμῶν replacing the singular σου.[76] The psalmist's address to himself becomes an address to the congregations of Asia Minor in the hands of Peter. When combined with the previous echo, God is pictured as one who is able to protect the community of believers and to bring the concerns of the community upon himself.[77] These discrete scriptural allusions contribute to the narrative of God's restored presence among his people. This will be further seen as we now look at another, more explicit use of scripture.

Humility is the concept that unifies 5:1-11. This occurs implicitly in the admonition that elders not be domineering (5:3) and in the subordination of neophytes to elders (5:5). The general principle is expressed to the entire audience in 5:5 where all are to clothe themselves with humility (ταπεινοφροσύνη) toward one another. This is repeated in 5:6 in the imperative, "Humble (ταπεινώθητε) yourselves, therefore, under the mighty hand of God." In the midst of this exhortation is the quotation of Prov 3:34, which deserves special attention because of its more explicit role in the passage.

Table 6.3: 1 Peter 5:5 and Proverbs 3:34

1 Peter 5:5	Proverbs 3:34
ὅτι ὁ θεὸς <u>ὑπερηφάνοις ἀντιτάσσεται, ταπεινοῖς δὲ δίδωσιν χάριν</u>.	κύριος <u>ὑπερηφάνοις ἀντιτάσσεται, ταπεινοῖς δὲ δίδωσιν χάριν</u>,

This quotation features significant changes in the transmission of the subject. The Greek version supplies κύριος for the pronoun הוא in the Hebrew version. This is surprising in light of the parallelism with the previous verse where the Greek translates יהוה with θεός. Perhaps this best accounts for the appearance of θεός in 1 Pet 5:5; the only point at which the Petrine quotation differs with Prov 3:34.[78] The form quoted in 1 Peter does not appear to have been influenced by the Hebrew.[79] The use of θεός is peculiar in light of an apparent predilection for κυρίος in other uses of scripture (i.e., Isa

---

76. Ibid., 38; see also Elliott, *1 Peter*, 851.

77. Green, *1 Peter*, 175-78.

78. The article before θεός does not appear in P[72], the earliest complete manuscript of 1 Peter, along with Vaticanus (03) among a few others.

79. Osborne, "L'utilisation," 71; Actemeier, *1 Peter*, 333.

40:8 in 1 Pet 1:25; Ps 33:9 in 1 Pet 2:3; Gen 18:12 in 1 Pet 3:6; Ps 33:16, 17 in 1 Pet 3:12 and Isa 8:13 in 1 Pet 3:15).[80] It was argued in chapter 3 that the use of κύριος in 1 Pet 1:25—where the quotation differs from the θεός of Isa 40:8—was not due to a theological reshaping of the text by the author.[81] It is equally unlikely that the text has been reshaped by the author here. The fact that James 4:6 quotes the same form of the text confirms the availability of this variant text.[82] Contributing to this assessment of the textual features of the passage is the fact that the interpretive focus of the quoted passage is on the word ταπεινός as it is surrounded by discussion of the humility required of the elect community.

As was the case with the previous quotation from Proverbs in 1 Pet 4:18, the concept of divine judgment is not remote.[83] The quotation from Prov 3:34 stands within a larger unit spanning from 3:32–35.[84] The passage develops the characteristics of two archetypes, the righteous (δίκαιοι, 3:33) and the ungodly (ἀσεβεῖς, 3:33, 35). The righteous are marked by divine blessing (3:33), humility (3:34), wisdom and glory (3:35). Conversely, the ungodly are described as lawless (παράνομος, 3:32), unclean (3:32), cursed (3:33), haughty (3:34), and to be shamed (3:35). Our particular verse highlights God's participation in rewarding the righteous for humility and in giving opposition to the proud.[85]

As advice directed at the community of God's elect, the admonition to humility in mutual relation to one another is clear enough.[86] Situated in its Petrine context, the categories of the righteous and ungodly are no longer

80. Compare with the use of θεός in 2:10 drawn from Hosea 1; 2:16 where it was argued that the language is drawn from Isaiah 54; 2:17 from Prov 24:21; 4:14 from Isa 11:2. By contrast, the use of θεός is more frequent in Peter's language (1:2, 3, 5, 21, 23; 2:4, 5, 12, 15, 19, 20; 3:4, 5, 17, 18, 20, 21, 22; 4:2, 6, 10, 11, 16, 17, 19; 5:2, 6, 10, 12) than κύριος (1:3 and 2:13)

81. It is instructive to compare the reasoning behind Schutter's argument in favor of authorial alteration of the text in 1:24, quoting Isaiah 40, and his argument against any authorial incursion into the text here (*Hermeneutic*, 125–26, 165–66). The contrasting nature of the two textual differences requires that they not be treated in isolation from one another.

82. Selwyn, *First Epistle of St Peter*, 234; Beare, *First Epistle of Peter*, 202; Michaels, *1 Peter*, 290; Schutter, *Hermeneutic*, 166; Goppelt, *Commentary on I Peter*, 354; Achtemeier, *1 Peter*, 333; Elliott, *1 Peter*, 849.

83. Clifford, *Proverbs*, 59.

84. Waltke, *Proverbs: Chapters 1–15*, 270. The beginning of the unit in the Greek translation is marked with γάρ.

85. The Hebrew play on words is lost in the Greek translation: God mocks (לץ) the mockers (לצים).

86. This is in keeping with Perdue (*Proverbs*, 110), who observes that the purpose of Proverbs 1–9 is "for maintaining the well-being of the community."

present. Now the Proverb functions solely at the paraenetic level within the community of the redeemed. In order for the community to function well, they must cultivate humility in their actions toward one another. In light of God's restored presence, the people of God are marked by humility.

Looking beyond 1 Pet 5:5, Peter takes up the concept of humility as the banner for all believers in the face of hostility in the world.[87] Thus, there appears to be a two-fold interpretation of Prov 3:34. Both are directed at the community of believers. But in the first instance, this scriptural text addresses the community in terms of its internal cohesion. In the second instance, the same text admonishes a posture for the community to take in relation to the adversity they find in the world.

Throughout this closing section (5:1–10), Peter continues to depict the church as participating in a narrative that depends in large part on subtle echoes of scripture.[88] The pairing of suffering (πάθημα) and glory (δόξα) has been seen throughout the letter (1 Pet 1:11; 4:13) and in the present section the pair recurs at the beginning (5:1) and end (5:9–10), creating a frame for the section.[89] It was noted earlier in this chapter that this pairing is informed by the career of the suffering servant in Isaiah 53. Here at the end of the letter, Peter works with the same themes. Revolving around Peter's use of Isaiah 53 is the theme of example. This was expressed in 1 Pet 2:21 where an example (ὑπογραμμός) was left for disciple servants to follow in Christ's footsteps. In 5:1, Peter places himself within this theme.[90] He is both a witness to Christ's sufferings (ὁ . . . μάρτυς τῶν τοῦ Χριστοῦ παθημάτων) and a participant in the coming revelation of glory (ὁ καὶ τῆς μελλούσης ἀποκαλύπτεσθαι δόξης κοινωνός). By describing himself this way, he depicts his own role in terms derived from his reading of Isaiah 53.[91] This is a momentary glimpse into Peter's view about his own ministry.[92] Unlike Paul who goes to great lengths to defend his ministry and gospel, Peter appears to assume his authority and gospel are largely unchallenged. Scholars have

---

87. Dubis, *Messianic Woes*, 183.

88. Ibid., 53–56; see also Mbuvi, *Temple*, 122–25.

89. Schutter, *Hermeneutic*, 75–76. It is surprising to find few explorations of how 1 Peter 5 contributes to an understanding of the suffering/glory motif in 1 Peter. A brief note pertaining to the use of terminology occurs in connection with his discussion of 1:10–12 (107). Later, he indicates how 5:1–11 is consistent with the suffering/glory motif, but does not demonstrate how discrete uses of scripture in the passage are specifically connected to the motif. At the same time, Moyise (*Evoking*, 78–95) also does not address 1 Peter 5 in his assessment on Schutter's work.

90. Michaels, *1 Peter*, 282; Goppelt, *Commentary on I Peter*, 342.

91. Elliott, *1 Peter*, 820.

92. Jobes, *1 Peter*, 300–301.

argued about the biographical nature of this brief self-description.[93] However, the Isaianic language interferes with an attempt to link this description with an otherwise straightforward autobiography. Peter has described Christ in terms of the suffering servant of Isaiah 53 in order to develop the idea that Isaiah 53 also applies to the church through the categories of participatory christology. Now that he turns to the leadership of the church, he begins by describing his own leadership role in the language of Isaiah 53: his ministry follows the career of the suffering servant by testifying to the sufferings of Christ and participating in the glory to be revealed.[94] This link between Christ and the leadership of the church is reinforced when Peter refers to himself as συμπρεσβύτερος.[95]

Having addressed elders from the vantage of his own authoritative position, Peter's exhortation to the elders draws upon other themes surrounding the use of Isaiah 53 in 1 Pet 2:25.[96] If the church is composed of people who strayed like sheep (πρόβατα; Isa 53:6), then Christ now leads the church as a shepherd (ὁ ποιμήν) and overseer (ἐπίσκοπος). The exhortation to elders applies the terminology of Christ's leadership. Elders are to shepherd (ποιμάνατε) the flock of God (τὸ ποίμνιον τοῦ θεοῦ) and to provide oversight (ἐπισκοποῦντες).[97] So, despite the expression of his own authority, Peter links the leadership of the elders directly to the ministry of Christ. In light of the example language surrounding Isaiah 53, the exhortation to elders extends Peter's consideration of how the servant-servants motif is drawn into an application to the church. This is seen most clearly through the use of τύπος in 1 Pet 5:3 where elders are to be types or examples to the flock (τὸ ποίμνιον) just as Christ is an example (ὑπογραμμός; 2:21) to the church.[98] The use of pastoral language is extended into the next verse where Christ is now referred to as the chief shepherd (ὁ ἀρχιποίμην). Thus, Christ's paradigmatic role as suffering servant within the larger scriptural narrative

---

93. Brox, *Der erste Petrusbrief*, 228; Beare, *First Epistle of Peter*, 198; Elliott, *1 Peter*, 816–18; Jobes, *1 Peter*, 300–301, *inter alia*.

94. Selwyn (*First Epistle of St Peter*, 228–29) attempts to fit the self-descriptors into claims about Peter's role as a witness to Christ's passion and to Christ's transfiguration, but presses the statements too far.

95. Elliott, *1 Peter*, 821.

96. Green, *1 Peter*, 168.

97. The omission of ἐπισκοποῦντες in Sinaiticus and Vaticanus had been thought important in the previous edition of the Nestle-Aland text. However the agreement between the corrector of Sinaiticus and P[72], Alexandrinus and numerous other manuscripts presents overwhelming support for inclusion of the participle.

98. Michaels, *1 Peter*, 286; Elliott, *1 Peter*, 832.

of the restoration of divine presence serves as the model for leaders in the church, even for Peter himself.

The body of the letter concludes with the word pair πάθημα and δόξα. Set within the admonition to beware of spiritual adversaries, Peter calls his audience to a recognition that suffering is experienced globally by those who identify themselves with Christ. The language of participation seen in the word pair at 1 Pet 4:13 shifts in this final context. Previously, believers participated in the sufferings of Christ, but the final picture in 5:9 is of a brotherhood of sufferers.[99] Glory now takes on a singular focus as the disciple servants are called to eternal glory in Christ (ἐν Χριστῷ; 5:10). With this use of glory (δόξα), Peter makes his grandest statement regarding the hope that belongs to the people of God.[100] Although presently suffering, God is at work within the church to bring it to a glorious resolution when the elect are vindicated in the final judgment (5:6).

Conclusion

The two sections addressed in this chapter advance points made in the previous chapters. In particular, the use of Isaiah remains a prominent voice in the scriptural narrative employed within and throughout the rhetorical units of 1 Peter. The body closing of 1 Peter draws upon terminology from previous sections of the letter, and so it is not surprising to find that prominent passages from Isaiah recur in this final unit, albeit at a less explicit level.

Three passages stand out as more explicit: Isa 11:2 in 1 Pet 4:14; Prov 11:31 in 1 Pet 4:18 and Prov 3:34 in 1 Pet 5:5. Although more explicit than the echoes observed in the body closing, they are hardly as marked as the quotations in the early chapters of 1 Peter. The more formulaic phrases such as διότι γέγραπται (1:16), διότι (1:24) and διότι περιέχει ἐν γραφῇ (2:6) can be contrasted with the use of καί (4:18) and ὅτι (5:5) as ways Peter incorporates quoted scripture into his writing. This basic observation points to one of the contributions of this thesis; namely, that an author may choose to use scripture in more or less explicit ways and may not always follow consistent patterns. For 1 Peter, the trajectory is one of decreasing explicitness. This is not only seen in the introductory formulae, but also in the size and incorporation of quoted material. For instance, the two-clause quotations from Prov 11:31 and 3:34 at the end of 1 Peter are smaller in size than the four clauses quoted from Isa 40:6–8 in 1 Pet 1:24–25 and the nine clauses quoted

---

99. Michaels, *1 Peter*, 301.

100. Goppelt, *Commentary on I Peter*, 365; Elliott, *1 Peter*, 865; Jobes, *1 Peter*, 315–16; Green, *1 Peter*, 175; Feldmeier, *First Letter of Peter*, 251.

from Ps 33:13–17 in 1 Pet 3:10–12, or even the five clauses from Isaiah 53 in 1 Pet 2:22–25. The material from Isaiah 53 serves as an example of how scriptural material can be incorporated in a variety of ways. This mode of incorporation must be attended to carefully since there are other passages that are drawn into the immediate context almost seamlessly. Methodologies that insist on a certain level of markedness or explicitness are apt to overlook these incorporated passages.[101] The use of Isa 11:2 is an example. A reader-centered approach demands that a decision be made about whether the audience would be able to read or hear this as a scriptural quotation.[102] But modern interpreters are simply not able to differentiate between passages of, say, four words and five words or one clause versus two clauses in order to determine how an ancient reader/listener would respond to it. This is why, while retaining a sensitivity to a reader-centered approach, one must also attend to the author-centered approach. For Isa 11:2, the factors that bear upon this are the author's style (incorporation of quoted material) and the pattern of decreasing explicitness.

The example of Isa 11:2 is important in the assessment of Petrine hermeneutics. From the foregoing discussion, justification has been supplied for the inclusion of this passage as one of the data points contributing to a picture of Peter's use of scripture. As noted above, the transformation of the prepositional phrase reveals much about how Peter has read Isaiah. Had he gone to Isaiah to support an apologetic argument in support of his christology, the third person singular would be expected. Instead, an alteration to the second person plural pronoun points to an ecclesiological reading of this passage. This can be coordinated with other instances of ecclesiological appropriations of Isaiah, such as 1 Pet 1:24–25; 2:6–10 and 2:21–25. Peter's reading of Isaiah does not exclude christological interpretations, such as at 3:14–15. However, the participatory christology throughout 1 Peter demonstrates how christology functions largely as a presupposition in Peter's hermeneutic. So, even apparently straightforward christological readings of Isaiah are employed in primarily ecclesiologically oriented interpretive strategies.

Finally, catchwords have received focused attention in this chapter, especially as they relate to the continuing influence of Isaiah 53. Such an enterprise cannot assume that the early audience would have been able to identify such uses as substantially different than Peter's own language. However, because of the prominence of Isaiah 53 earlier in the epistle, its enduring influence remains significant even if this influence is far less

---

101. E.g., Stanley, *Paul*, 37.

102. See the reasonable assessment of both the author-centered and reader-centered approaches by Moyise (*Evoking*, 46–47).

explicit than certain methodologies can tolerate. However, two general observations can be made about how Isaiah 53 plays a continuing role in Peter's discourse. First, the vocabulary employed in the body closing—and in retrospect throughout the letter—plays with imagery of an Isaianic hew. The suffering and glory terminology conveys the career of the suffering servant of Isaiah 53, and Peter uses this image liberally, particularly in the body middle and body closing of the epistle. Secondly, the exhortations of 1 Peter 5:1–6 seem to draw upon Isaianic themes. The leadership of the church is to shepherd the flock of God. This echoes the prominent interaction the book of Isaiah has with the leadership of Israel so that wicked leaders are condemned and humble leadership is praised. The ideas of shepherding and humility, which form the ethical demands set forward by Peter in 5:1–6, are seen in Isaiah 40, but are also exemplified by the suffering servant and the disciple servants of Isaiah 54–66. Thus, as Peter addresses the leadership of the church, he maintains the narrative of restored divine presence to underscore how their role likewise participates in the scriptural narrative through participation in Christ.

In every way, though, the overall effect of the scriptural quotations and allusions in the body closing emphasizes an address to the community of believers who are suffering. Through a variety of scriptural texts, Peter portrays the Christian community as participating in the dramatic events culminating in God's final plan. In this, the concepts of divine judgment and reward provide a context for the continuing suffering of believers in a world of opposition. The promise of retribution, protection and glorification holds out hope for the beleaguered elect. The inauguration of this eschatological plan has been announced (by the use of Isa 11:2 in 1 Pet 4:14 and the use of scriptural themes) as inaugurated through the direct presence of God among his people.

7

Conclusion

Reading the Isaianic Narrative within 1 Peter

HAVING NOW LOOKED CLOSELY at quotations and allusions in the body of 1 Peter, the central task of this final chapter is to piece together the parts into a meaningful whole. In my analysis, I divided the body of the epistle into three sections: body opening (1:13—2:10), body middle (2:11—4:11), and body closing (4:12—5:11). This structure roughly corresponds with the three movements in the scriptural narrative that shapes the argument of the letter. First, the body opening proclaims God's renewed presence among his people, utilizing imagery from scripture, including Isa 8:14; 28:16; 40:6-8; 43:20-21; 52:3; 53:7 along with the Levitical holiness formula, Pss 33:9; 117[118]:22; Exod 19:5-6 and Hosea 1-2. Second, the churches of Asia Minor are called to a high moral standard of conduct based on the pattern of Christ even while suffering. This second movement begins in the body middle and extends into the body closing. Numerous texts point to the general outline of this section: Isa 3:18; 8:12-13; 10:3; Pss 33[34]:13-17 and Prov 10:12. Furthermore, the shift discerned in Isaiah 53-54 whereby the singular servant is followed by plural servants was argued to be a fundamental paradigm within the body middle. Third, the body closing portrays the ultimate vindication of God's people in the final judgment. An important allusion to Isa 11:2 places the churches of Asia Minor in the midst of God's final plan for his people. Other allusions round out this section, including Isa 28:5; Prov 3:34; 11:31; Ps 22:14. With the contours of this three-movement narrative established, it remains to explore how the argument of the letter is rooted in this story.

The proclamation of the gospel, or good news (εὐαγγελίζω/εὐαγγέλιον), provides both an arc to the overall narrative as well as a point of entry into the narrative. The first mention of the good news occurs within 1 Pet 1:10-12, where the key to the letter's hermeneutic was revealed to be centered around theological concepts. Within this hermeneutical proposition, Peter connects the prophetic message of salvation with the gospel that was proclaimed by gospel preachers (διὰ τῶν εὐαγγελισαμένων, 1:12). This indication that scriptural prophecy and gospel proclamation are intertwined is furthered in 1:24–25. The quotation of Isa 40:6–8 connects the living and abiding word of God with the good news preached in Asia Minor (τὸ ῥῆμα τὸ εὐαγγελισθὲν εἰς ὑμᾶς, 1:25). By using Isaiah 40 in this way, Peter evokes the inauguration of God's restored presence among his people in Isaianic terminology. The arc is completed in 1 Pet 4:17. Integral to the final judgment is the disbelief of the good news which is the ground for condemnation (τὸ τέλος τῶν ἀπειθούντων τῷ τοῦ θεοῦ εὐαγγελίῳ). Contributing to the shape of this arc are passages that speak to disbelief, such as 2:8 where those who stumble in the presence of the stone (λίθος) are the very ones who do not believe the word. Similarly, wives are instructed to win their unbelieving husbands in 3:1. In both of these passages, there are clear connections with the underlying scriptural narrative. In the case of 2:8, the stone passages are incorporated into a larger expression (2:4–10) of a renewed, spiritual temple service expressing the direct presence of God among his people. In the case of 3:1, the patterning of the plural servants after the singular suffering servant is based in large part on the servant-servants motif drawn from Isaiah. The focus on belief serves as a point of entry into the Isaianic narrative. Those who believe in the good news are participants in the narrative of restoration, esteeming the stone as elect and precious (2:4, 6) or glorifying God in the midst of eschatological suffering (4:16). By contrast, disbelief in the good news is fundamentally a refusal to participate within the narrative. The resulting distinction between belief and unbelief is furthered by the scripturally informed use of "gentiles," so that the insider group is equated with Israel/the people of God and the outsider group is equated with the gentiles.

The suffering and glories motif is another expression that draws upon the Isaianic narrative and undergirds the argument of the letter. Regarding the general shape of the Isaianic narrative, this serves well as a shorthand summation of a suffering people living faithfully in the present while anticipating a glorious eschatological vindication. Within 1 Pet 1:10–11, the story of Christ also follows this narrative pattern, a pattern foretold in scriptural prophecy to encompass sufferings (παθήματα) followed by glories (δόξας). The Christ story is further explicated in 2:22–24 where the narrative of the Isaianic suffering servant is equivalent to the narrative of Christ. Thus, the story of Christ is clearly based on and an extension of the narrative contained in the scriptures. The story is further extended, though, to the audience. Both elements of the motif are developed in such a way that suffering and glory are shown to be constituent elements in the narrative of the church. Three passages illustrate this development. First, 3:13–18 develop the concept of suffering in the heart of the second movement of the narrative structure. There, believers are encouraged, even though they suffer, to maintain good ethical conduct (3:13–17), because Christ suffered as a righteous person for the unrighteous (3:18). Both the ethical exhortation and the example of Christ are informed by scriptural language, in one case with language drawn from Psalm 33[34] and in the other with imagery from Isaiah 53. Second, the audience is drawn into drama of God's eschatological program in 1 Pet 4:12–19. As in the prior passage, the churches of Asia Minor are called to suffer as morally righteous followers of Christ. They are partakers in the sufferings of Christ and rejoice in the revelation of his glory (4:13). Finally, glory is shown to be the ultimate inheritance of the church in 5:1–10. God calls the church into his eternal glory in Christ (5:10). These are things that are shared both by the author (5:1) and the global church (5:9). In these ways, the shorthand summary of the Isaianic narrative serves to structure the story of Christ and the story of the church in 1 Peter. The Christ story is assumed to be a true extension of the Isaianic narrative. Therefore, the story of the church is really a further extension of the Isaianic narrative through participation in Christ. To be in Christ is to perform within the drama of God's redemptive story.

Rooted in this scriptural narrative, the shape of the argument in 1 Peter follows the contours of this narrative, frequently drawing on scripture through quotations and allusions that point to this underlying story. In microcosm, 1 Pet 1:10–12 spells out an overarching narrative, attested to by the prophets, of suffering that is followed by glory. Green points out:

> What Peter makes clear, actually, is that this theological pattern is resident already in the Scriptures of Israel themselves. The issue is not that we are taught by the advent of Christ to read the Scriptures retrospectively, but that the Christ in whom Christians place their trust and now worship is the same Christ who long ago revealed the ways of God in the Scriptures.[1]

Central to this sequence—suffering followed by glory—is the story of God's use of suffering for redemptive purposes. The suffering servant of Isaiah 53 has tremendous explanatory value to this end. The suffering Christ accomplishes the justification of sinners (1 Pet 1:19; 2:24). By extension, Christian suffering is in keeping with God's redemptive purposes based upon the model of Christ as the suffering servant. The church become servants of God (2:16) as they participate in God's unfolding redemptive purposes.

---

1. Green, *1 Peter*, 251.

As constituents of this redemptive story, Peter indicates that believers in Christ Jesus are unified with the people of God in the scriptures. The good news of the gospel was already attested by Isaiah, inasmuch as the living and abiding word of God present in Isaiah 40 corresponds to the gospel preached to the elect of Asia Minor. Building upon the conception of the church as a spiritual temple, Peter applies the honorary titles scripture bestows upon Israel (Isa 43:20–21 and Exod 19:5–6) to the church (1 Pet 2:9–10). Drawing both from the exodus tradition and the new exodus tradition, the elect of Asia Minor are addressed as constituting God's present act of deliverance and restoration. Thus constituted as a spiritual temple maintaining a spiritual priesthood, Peter goes to great lengths to establish the proper conduct of the people of God during their present sojourn.

This occurs even from the beginning of the body opening through the holiness formula drawn from Leviticus (1 Pet 1:16). As Peter spells out the implications for how believers in Asia Minor participate in God's redemptive narrative, he further draws upon scripture to encourage the proper conduct during the present chapter of the story. Here Psalm 33 is instrumental in supplying the categories of good and evil works. Christ's example of moral conduct, spelled out in the language of Isaiah 53, gives additional support to Peter's ethical admonition in the body middle. Thus, in light of God's restored presence, his people must follow the example of Christ's righteousness even in the midst of suffering.

Peter understands that the present people of God are not without opponents in the world. Here, too, he understands this opposition as part of the larger scriptural narrative. Those who do not believer are equivalent to the builders who rejected the chief cornerstone (Ps 118:22). The "ungodly sinners" (Prov 11:31) who instigate the persecution of believers are promised their just desserts at the final judgment (1 Pet 4:17–18). To this end, present suffering should not be regarded as being outside God's redemptive purposes, but part of it. As Isaiah 53 indicated the suffering of Christ, it also establishes the pattern to which believers are called (1 Pet 2:21). There is therefore no need to fear the present calamities (Isa 8:12–13 in 1 Pet 3:14–15), but instead to uphold reverent fear of the Lord.

But hope is held out—again in the language of scripture—for God's decisive final act of redemption. This is most clearly seen in 1 Pet 4:12—5:11, but is already present in 2:12 through an allusion to "the day of visitation" (Isa 10:3). The people of God are marked by the presence of God's spirit upon them (Isa 11:2 in 1 Pet 4:14). The time of God's judgment begins in the "house of God" and spells the end of opposition to the "gospel of God" (4:17). The use of Prov 11:31 in 1 Pet 4:18 contrasts the fates of the righteous and the ungodly. Thus Peter presents a picture of ultimate deliverance from their present calamities through both divine judgment and final salvation. This picture continues into the final chapter where elements of final reward (5:4-5) and protection from diabolic adversity lead to "eternal glory in Christ" (5:10). At the same time, Isa 11:2 in 1 Pet 4:14 depicts God's spirit as presently restored among his people. Thus, the time of God's judgment, vindication and consolation has already been inaugurated.

This scriptural narrative gives shape to 1 Peter and gives rise to the intermittent quotations and allusions to scripture throughout the letter. The selection of texts has every appearance of being thematically driven, as is seen through the identification of key terms the unite different texts. Isaiah is clearly a major contributor to this narrative, but what Peter finds there he finds to be consistent with the rest of scripture.

In this thesis, I have proposed that the ecclesiology of 1 Peter draws upon a narrative of the restoration of divine presence among the people of God presently experiencing suffering. Themes and images from Isaiah inform this scriptural narrative and contribute to the identification of the church as participants in the narrative of restoration through participation in Christ. There are many places where Isaianic passages directly address ecclesiological concerns in 1 Peter. The use of Isa 40:6-9 in 1 Pet 1:24-25 centers on the relationship of the church to the word of God. Peter claims that the enduring and imperishable word of God has been preached through the gospel to Christians in Asia Minor. By using Isa 40:6-9 to support this claim, Peter has availed himself of the universal condition of mankind ("all flesh is like grass") and the relationship of the word (ῥῆμα) to the Lord. After quoting Isaiah 40, Peter comments, "This is the word (ῥῆμα) that was preached (εὐαγγελισθέν) to you." Thus, as Peter explains it, the gospel message is equivalent with the proclamation of God's renewed presence among his people.

The ecclesiological interpretation of Isa 11:2 in 1 Pet 4:14 is surprising especially since it is drawn from a passage ripe for the christological picking. In 1 Peter, however, the spirit of the Lord rests upon the church. Such direct ecclesiological appropriation of scripture represents one strategy employed by Peter to bring Isaiah into conversation with concerns of the church. And through this allusion, the restored presence of God among his people inaugurates the eschatological judgment, vindication and consolation of his people.

Another strategy grounds an ecclesiological point in a christological point. The christological interpretation of the three quotations in 1 Pet 2:6-8 (Isa 28:16; Ps 118:22; Isa 8:14) occurs by linking Christ with λίθος in 1 Pet 2:4. Having invested the singular stone with christological properties at the outset, the quotations proceed without christological comment. Instead, the three quotations are built into an argument centering on the audience's belief. Peter is able to do this by transforming the linking term into the plural λίθοι. The audience shares the properties of Christ. Therefore, when Peter actually uses his quotations, they are simultaneously invested with christological properties and meaningful for understanding the nature of the church. In like manner, the language of scripture used in 2:9–10 is anticipated in 2:5 where the christological element is drawn in through the phrase διὰ Ἰησοῦ Χριστοῦ, highlighting the participatory christology developed in the letter. Thus, when the passages (Exo 19:5–6; Isa 43:20–21; Hosea 1–2) are worked into the argument in 2:9–10, Peter's interpretation is clearly ecclesiological, dealing with the nature and purpose of the church. The strategy of 2:4–10 involves an expression of christology in the set-up of the passages (2:4–5) which serves as the foundation for the passages drawn into an ecclesiological argument (2:6–10). By doing so, Peter shows how the church participates in the narrative of the restoration of divine presence through its participation in Christ.

The same approach occurs in 1 Pet 2:21–25, albeit in a different way. The quotation of passages from Isaiah 53 occurs (with the exception of the final quotation) with Christ as the subject. Here Peter is making a christological point as a basis for further ecclesiological ramifications. This is done by setting the quotation and its christological interpretation within an ecclesiological argument that begins and ends the unit. Christ is an example (ὑπογραμμός) for the church and the church follows in his footsteps (2:21). Furthermore, the unit is placed within the servants' section of the household code (2:18–25). The address to servants works metaleptically to address the entire church.[2] This trope likens Christ as the suffering servant of Isaiah 53 and the church as the plural servants of Isaiah 54–66, a concept inaugurated in 2:16 where the church was described as "servants of God." The strategy of 1 Pet 2:21–25 involves the christological interpretation of Isaiah 53 as the foundation for an ecclesiological argument employing the language of example.

The same approach is used with the quotation of Isa 8:12–13 in 1 Pet 3:14–15. The insertion of Χριστός into the quotation marks a bold statement of high christology. Yet, the context in which it is set focuses on the suffering experienced by the church. Peter draws upon Isaiah 8 to form the argument that human fear is displaced by the fear of God. In the hands of Peter, though, the passage demonstrates how the church, participating in Christ, need not fear present danger. Furthermore, Peter claims that the restoration of God's presence occurs through the sanctifying work of Christ within believers.

2. See chapter 5.

Peter's approach was argued to be dependent upon a major motif in Isaiah. The movement from singular servant in Isaiah 40–53 to plural servants in Isaiah 54–66 contributes a major motif to the scriptural narrative developed within 1 Peter and provides a background for the relationship between christology and ecclesiology. Peter has drawn this motif into his own language and argument, but the movement from singular to plural remains a significant component of the scriptural narrative in 1 Peter particularly where it pertains to Peter's development of ecclesiology.

Peter's reading of Isaiah, focused as it is on the church, covers three major lines of thought. The first contention, set forth in the body opening, has to do with the appropriation of the scriptural narrative of God's restored presence by and for the followers of Christ. Peter sees continuity between the present people of God and Israel's scriptures, a continuity that is based on the presence of Christ past (1:10) and present (1:21; 2:5). Scripture is meaningful for the proclamation of the gospel (1:25), and those who believe are drawn into a scripturally defined community: a people for his own possession to proclaim his excellencies (2:9). Second, Peter develops the idea that the present people of God are disciples of Christ. This entails that inasmuch as Christ suffered, the church is called to suffering (2:21). Peter finds in Isaiah a strategy to describe this discipleship in terms of the servant-servants motif. The Isaianic disciple servants of the suffering servant share affliction and sorrow, but also vindication at the final judgment. Yet, the example of Christ is that of a righteous sufferer. Therefore, the community of Christ must maintain the highest ethical standards in the midst of suffering as a matter of honor (2:12; 3:16). Finally, Peter pictures the church as the eschatological people of God. Present suffering as a sign of participation in Christ anticipates ultimate vindication at the revelation of Christ (4:13). Peter draws from Isaiah a dramatic story depicting the people of God as awaiting "the end of all things" (4:7). At the same time, he also draws from Isaiah an argument that the final act of God's redemptive plan has already been inaugurated, since God's presence to judge, vindicate and comfort has been placed upon the church (Isa 11:2 in 1 Pet 4:14).

Observations and Implications

Textual Matters

One of the outcomes that has informed the main argument of this thesis is a close examination of textual data for scriptural quotations in 1 Peter. The task here is to draw together briefly the results of these comparisons between the quoted texts and their *Vorlagen*. There was no attempt to establish criteria for inclusion or exclusion of data. However, the more explicit occurrences of scriptural discourse affords a greater basis of comparison and carry more weight in the evaluation of Petrine hermeneutics. There are fifteen passages in 1 Peter that occur with sufficient explicitness to allow some concluding thoughts here.

The use of the Levitical tradition in 1 Pet 1:16 involves two brief clauses of five or six words depending on how the exact phraseology occurs in Leviticus.[3] Because of the variety in the Levitical tradition, one's decision regarding the inclusion of εἰμί does little to inform us about Peter's text. Instead, this passage shows how he identifies summary phrases that draw upon wide contexts rather than honing in on a single phrase from a specific context.

Minor changes have occurred in the use of Isa 40:6–9 in 1 Pet 1:24–25. It was noted that the text in 1:24–25 corresponds with OG Isaiah against the MT, pointing Peter's dependence upon the Greek tradition. The most significant difference is the use of the term κύριος. It was argued that both the rhetorical context and Petrine style point away from the use of κύριος as a reference to Christ. There is no obvious theological motive behind the difference and therefore there is little reason to suspect that Peter has altered the text. These factors point to a text that differs from OG Isaiah in slight ways. This does not mean that Peter has not made theological use of the text (indeed, an ecclesiological point has been made). However, there is no sign of altering the text nor of consulting differing texts on theological grounds.

The three quotations in 1 Pet 2:6–8 are an interesting group. Of the three, the quotation of Psalm 118:22 in 1 Pet 2:7 shows no differences with the Greek Psalm. The first text, Isa 28:16 is substantially the same as OG Isaiah with a few exceptions. The case of the third text, Isa 8:14, is different. Only a few words appear in the Petrine version compared to OG Isaiah. The later revisions by Aquila, Symmachus and Theodotion tend toward placing πρόσκομμα in the genitive rather than the dative of the OG and using σκάνδαλον instead of πτῶμα. Romans 9:33 presents an interesting parallel since all of the differences in 1 Peter, with the exception of the transposition, are found there. It is impossible to identify the source of this text form. This parallelism, though, indicates that Peter is not the source of these differences. He has encountered this text form and, like Paul, has seen fit to insert it into his argument. The Petrine version seems to occur in a more pristine version since Paul has incorporated Isa 8:14 into Isa 28:16.

---

3. The *ECM* has excluded εἰμί, overturning the decision in NA27 to include the verb. There is strong support for both readings (01, 02, 03 omit εἰμί and P[72], the corrector of 02 and 04 include εἰμί).

There are several brief allusions at the beginning of the body middle of 1 Peter. Only two offer enough material to warrant special consideration here. The allusion to Isa 10:3 in 1 Pet 2:12 features only the omission of two articles, matching the Hebrew version of the text, although the meaning of the passage is hardly altered. The allusion to Prov 24:21 at the end of 1 Pet 2:17 amounts to four words. The plural imperative φοβεῖσθε differs from the singular imperative φοβοῦ. The direct object is placed before the verb in 1 Peter and an article is inserted before βασιλέα. These differences draw the allusion from Proverbs into the careful structure of the Petrine construction: article—direct object—plural imperative.

The quotation of Isaiah 53 in 1 Pet 2:22-25 occurs by way of inserting clauses intermittently. This differs from the block quotation style exhibited elsewhere in the epistle. Three verses from this section deserve attention. The fullest quotation occurs first in 1 Pet 2:22 quoting Isa 53:9. There are no differences between 1 Peter and OG Isaiah with one exception, depending on whether the interpreter includes ἁμαρτίαν as part of the quotation, which differs from the OG ἀνομίαν. It was argued that ἁμαρτίαν should be considered as part of the quotation but there was insufficient evidence to determine whether Peter has altered the text or read a text with this different reading. At the beginning of 1 Pet 2:24, Isa 53:4 and 12 are blended together and linked by the term ἁμαρτίας. There are no differences between the text as presented in 1 Peter and OG Isaiah. However, at the end of 1 Pet 2:24, the brief quotation of Isa 53:5 features the alteration of the verb from first person plural to second person plural. It was argued that the evidence for authorial alteration of the verb is inconclusive. In 1 Pet 2:25 there is a small quotation of Isa 53:6. The verb form differs between the OG and 1 Peter here. It was argued that, in the main, most of these differences are likely due to their incorporation into Peter's argument, although difficulties still abound.

Of the several differences between Greek Ps 33:13-17 and the quotation of this Psalm in 1 Pet 3:10-12, the verb forms have garnered the most attention. The four third person singular imperative verbs in 1 Pet 3:10-11 differ from the second person singular imperatives of Ps 33:14-15. For these differences and several other minor omissions or insertions, it was proposed that a variant manuscript could plausibly stand behind the text form in 1 Peter as opposed to the author being the source of alteration.

The use of Isa 8:12-13 in 1 Pet 3:14-15 features several differences with OG Isaiah. The most important difference is where the Petrine hand appears in the insertion of τὸν Χριστόν revealing a christological reading by the author.

Two changes occur in the quotation of Isa 11:2 in 1 Pet 4:14. First, the order occurs backwards in sequence, which is likely done to fit the quoted clause into the syntax of the surrounding sentence. Second, a second person plural pronoun replaces the third person singular pronoun of OG Isaiah. This transforms the quote so that the divine presence is placed upon the community of believers rather than more particularly upon the branch of Jesse's root.

The final two quotations involve passages from Proverbs. The only difference between the quotation of Prov 11:31 in 1 Pet 4:18 and the Greek Proverb is the omission of the conjunction μέν. The quotation of Prov 3:34 in 1 Pet 5:5 differs at only one point, if one accepts the subject of the sentence as part of the quotation.

These observations serve to illustrate, as best as can be discerned, the textual basis for Peter's quotations and allusions. The overwhelming impression is one of high correspondence between a Greek *Vorlage* and the text as represented in 1 Peter. The differences that do exist point less to the author's interference in the transmission of the text, but to the likelihood of variants in the textual tradition. Some are possibly due to revisions to the text that were available during the early Christian era.[4] The role of memory was at times explored as a means of explaining variants, but the explanatory value of "memory lapse" has limited value.[5] As Wagner points out, "Deliberate modifications may be made to memorized texts as well as to written ones."[6] On the whole, considerable doubt must be expressed about the deliberate use of variant text-types on the level that Schutter proposes.[7] Instead, it would appear that the texts used in 1 Peter reflect the fluid textual environment of the early Christian era. Most of the differences do not contribute to the Petrine argument. Where we do find this, the hand of the author becomes most apparent. One case is the addition of τὸν Χριστόν in the quotation of Isa 8:12–13 in 1 Pet 3:14–15. This is an important example of christological interpretation. Another example is the modification of Isa 11:2 in 1 Pet 4:14. Here the difference is clearly in keeping with Peter's address to the church. Instead of the spirit of God resting upon the branch of Jesse's root (ἐπ᾽ αὐτὸν), Peter now sees the spirit resting upon the church (ἐφ᾽ ὑμᾶς).

Diminishing Explicitness

In this thesis the observation was made that the explicitness of scriptural quotations diminishes over the course of the letter. This was first observed

---

4. See Tov, *Greek and Hebrew Bible*, 9; Stanley, *Paul*, 37–51.
5. Ellis, *Paul's Use*, 14.
6. Wagner, "Psalm 118," 23.
7. Schutter, *Hermeneutics*, 170, cf. 141.

Conclusion

in the transition from the body opening to the body middle since the former featured the use of introductory formulae and the latter did away with such formulae. A reason for such a departure from formulaic introductions has not been ventured here. The use and subsequent disuse of formulae have simply been shown to fit within a pattern of decreasing explicitness. The concept of diminishing explicitness is not a central feature of the present thesis, yet it does deserve a place within the broader methodological discussions this thesis assumes. The following represents a modest contribution to a discussion that has focused primarily on the Pauline epistles. It is hoped that a fuller discourse may be achieved that incorporates all of the epistolary literature within the NT in considerations of the use of scripture and hermeneutics within the early church.

The series of quotations and allusions in 1 Pet 2:6–10 exhibit this trend in microcosm. Beginning with an introductory formula (διότι περιέχει ἐν γραφῇ), there are three explicit quotations with clear key-term links. Following these, several allusions occur with far greater subtlety. The absence of introductory formulae throughout the remainder of the letter continues this trend. There remain a number of quotations at more explicit levels, such as the two quotations from Proverbs in 1 Pet 4:18 (Prov 11:31) and 5:5 (Prov 3:34). It would seem that such quotations, especially the large block quotation from Psalm 33 in 1 Pet 3:10–12, argue against the proposed trajectory here. However, the point being made here is not necessarily that Peter has used scripture in increasingly implicit ways at every instance, but that he has allowed himself the liberty to engage in scriptural discourse with less explicitness than was used in the body opening of the epistle.

This liberty carries with it an implicit expectation that the audience will follow the author down a path of diminishing explicitness. The author does not need to indicate his use of scriptural texts with the same kind of markedness in the latter part of the letter as he did in the early part of the letter since the audience has been made aware of the fact that a scriptural narrative is a significant part of his argument. The move toward more implicit modes of scriptural quotation likely forfeits a portion of the audience who will not have the ability to perceive the more subtle textual interplay. But readers with an adequate level of competence will be able to handle the less explicit uses of scripture because they have been prepared by the more explicit scriptural quotations early in the letter. The oral presentation of the letter, with possible repetition and/or explanation by the reader/letter-carrier, has potential ramifications for assisting the audience's perception.

The trajectory of decreasing explicitness proposed here challenges the polarization that has happened in studies centered on Paul's use of scripture.[8] The author-centered approach and the reader-centered approach create a tension in studies of an author's hermeneutics by establishing criteria unable to grapple with the changing nature of an author's style. The present study has benefited from the growing body of literature centered on Paul's use of scripture. However, the study of Peter's use of scripture requires a reconsideration of two important factors. First, an author's use of scripture is not static. An author may choose to deal with scriptural quotation in different ways to meet different rhetorical aims at various points in an argument. Second, an audience is not a monolith. There are individuals with greater or lesser ability to perceive the use of scripture. And this ability is not necessarily determined by literacy.

The scaled approach taken in this study allows for flexibility by not rigidly counting words or delimiting data based on markedness. Instead, by indicating whether a use of scripture is more or less explicit, certain dynamics have been revealed that highlight the interplay between author and audience. The trajectory of decreasing explicitness would not have been apparent had the data been limited from the outset by the criteria proposed in the reader-centered approach.

Implications

This study has examined the uses of scripture from several vantage points—a consideration of textual *Vorlagen*, the immediate scriptural context of each text used, and its contribution to the argument of the letter, all in support of the contention that the ecclesiology of 1 Peter is fundamentally informed by the narrative of the restoration of divine presence. This work allows us to consider how this focus on Peter's use of scripture contributes to our understanding of this letter. Foremost is the recognition that the suffering addressed is cast within a larger scriptural narrative so that it is shown to be consistent with the suffering God's people have faced in every age. Peter's use of scripture in this letter attests to and contributes to a narrative of God's work among and for his people, which can be summarized through the motif of suffering followed by glory. As Peter understood it, this is the path Jesus followed. He provides consolation for those followers of Christ presently experiencing suffering, because he can show that the greater narrative redeems the suffering of God's people and culminates in a glory shared with Christ. I believe this has tremendous exegetical value in many contemporary contexts where the suffering of Christians is a practical

---

8. Ciampa ("Scriptural Language," 57) observes that the more subtle uses of scripture "will pose the greatest challenge" in studies of Paul's use of scripture.

concern. Peter's hermeneutical strategy of locating the church within an overarching scriptural narrative can be commended as an example to be followed by modern exegetes.[9]

Beyond this, several areas deserve recognition as fruitful avenues of further study. First, this study has indicated that Peter's use of scripture has contributed significantly to the shape and content of the argument of the letter. One of the implications, therefore, relates to the purpose of the letter. In other words, how does the scriptural narrative of 1 Peter factor into our understanding of its rhetorical strategy?

Second, it has commonly been articulated that scriptural quotations are used to conclude arguments. Dalton writes that an important factor for determining the structure of 1 Peter "was the use of citations from the Old Testament to round off an argument or development of thought. The more important and massive the scripture citation, the more emphatic is the break between this section and the following."[10] Given the diverse and complex uses of scripture in 1 Peter, the role scripture plays in assessing the structure of the letter is open to further consideration.

Third, many scholars have recognized a relationship with dominical sayings in 1 Peter.[11] To be sure, if there are points of relationship, there certainly is an overlap with the hermeneutical observations made here. A case in point in the macarism of 1 Pet 4:14. The language corresponds closely with Matt 5:11 || Luke 6:22.[12] The reason given for their blessedness when they are reviled is that the spirit of God rests upon them (quoting Isa 11:2). A study devoted to the presence of Jesus teaching in Peter's hermeneutics would take the present work in a fruitful direction. Does Peter's hermeneutical strategy show dependence upon Jesus traditions?

Finally, it has been recognized that Peter's use of scripture is theologically oriented. As such, it is worthwhile to consider how Peter's work might contribute to current questions surrounding theological hermeneutics. Green has provided a *précis* of 1 Peter's potential contribution to questions currently *en vogue* raised by those who want to see a greater intersection of biblical and theological studies.[13] I find that his sense of Peter's reading

---

9. What Hays (*Echoes*, 183-87) spells out concerning Paul's example for modern readers of scripture can largely be said for 1 Peter.

10. Dalton, *Christ's Proclamation*, 95. See also Osborne, "L'utilisation," 74-75; Martin, *Metaphor*, 136.

11. Gundry, "Verba Christi," 336-50; idem., "Further Verba," 211-32; Best, "I Peter and the Gospel Tradition," 95-113; Maier, "Jesustradition," 85-128; Metzner, *Die Rezeption*.

12. Elliott, *1 Peter*, 782.

13. Green, *1 Peter*, 244-58.

of scripture is much the same as my thinking. A large-scale work could certainly build upon this fruitfully

In each of these directions, the scriptural hermeneutics of Peter is vitally important. This makes complete sense, though, given what has been demonstrated here about the vital importance of scripture to 1 Peter.

Bibliography

Achtemeier, Paul J. "The Christology of 1 Peter." In *Who Do You Say That I Am? Essays on Christology*, edited by Mark A. Powell and David R. Bauer, 140-54. Louisville: Westminster John Knox, 1999.
———. *1 Peter: A Commentary on First Peter*. Hermeneia. Minneapolis: Fortress, 1996.
———. "Newborn Babes and Living Stones: Literal and Figurative in 1 Peter." In *To Touch the Text: Biblical and Related Studies*, edited by Maurya P. Horgan and Paul J. Kobelski, 207-36. New York: Crossroad, 1989.
———. "Suffering Servant and Suffering Christ in 1 Peter." In *The Future of Christology*, edited by Abraham J. Malherbe and Wayne A. Meeks, 176-88. Minneapolis: Fortress, 1993.
Adams, Edward. *Constructing the World: A Study in Paul's Cosmological Language*. SNTW. Edinburgh: T. & T. Clark, 2000.
Agnew, Francis H. "1 Peter 1:2—An Alternative Translation." *CBQ* 45 (1983) 68-73.
Aitken, Ellen Bradshaw. *Jesus' Death in Early Christian Memory: The Poetics of the Passion*. NTOA 53. Göttingen: Vandenhoeck and Ruprecht, 2004.
Alexander, P. S. "Midrash and the Gospels." In *Synoptic Studies: The Ampleforth Conferences of 1982 and 1983*, edited by Christopher M. Tuckett, 1-18. JSNTSup 7. Sheffield: JSOT, 1984.
Allegro, John M., ed. *Qumran Cave 4. I (4Q158-4Q186)*. DJD 5. Oxford: Clarendon, 1968.
Allen, Leslie C. *Psalms 101-150*. WBC 21. Waco: Word, 1983.
Allison, Dale C. *Testament of Abraham*. Berlin: De Gruyter, 2003.
Atkinson, Kenneth R. "On the Use of Scripture in the Development of Militant Davidic Messianism at Qumran: New Light from *Psalm of Solomon 17*." In *The Interpretation of Scripture in Early Judaism and Christianity: Studies in Language and Tradition*, edited by C. A. Evans, 106-27. London: T. & T. Clark, 2004.
Bacq, Phillipe. *De l'ancienne à la nouvelle Alliance selon S. Irénée: Unite du Livre IV de l'Adversus Haereses*. Paris: Dessain et Tolra, 1978.
Bal, Mieke. *Narratology: Introduction to the Theory of Narrative*. Toronto: University of Toronto Press, 1985.
Balch, David L. "Hellenization/Acculturation in 1 Peter." In *Perspectives on First Peter*, edited by Charles H. Talbert, 79-101. Macon, GA: Mercer, 1986.
———. "Household Codes." In *Graeco-Roman Literature and the New Testament*, edited by David E. Aune, 25-50. SBLSBS 21. Atlanta: Scholars, 1988.

———. *Let Wives be Submissive: The Domestic Code in 1 Peter*. SBLMS 26. Atlanta: Scholars, 1981.
Balentine, Samuel E. *Leviticus*. Interpretation. Louisville: Westminster John Knox, 2002.
Baltzer, Klaus. *Deutero-Isaiah: A Commentary on Isaiah 40–55*. Minneapolis: Fortress, 2001.
Barclay, John M. G. "Mirror-Reading a Polemical Letter: Galatians as a Test Cast." *JSNT* 31 (1987) 73–93.
Barr, James. "בארץ—ΜΟΛΙΣ: Prov. xi.31, 1 Pet. iv.18." *JSS* 20 (1975) 149–64.
Barrett, C. K. "The Allegory of Abraham, Sarah, and Hagar in the Argument of Galatians." In *Essays on Paul*, 154–70. London: SPCK, 1982.
Barrier, Jeremy W. *The Acts of Paul and Thecla: A Critical Introduction and Commentary*. WUNT 2.270. Tübingen: Mohr Siebeck, 2009.
Barton, John. "Ethics in the Book of Isaiah." In *Writing and Reading the Scroll of Isaiah: Studies of an Interpretive Tradition*, edited by Craig C. Broyles and Craig A. Evans, 67–77. VTSup 70/1. Leiden: Brill, 1997.
Bauckham, Richard J. *God Crucified: Monotheism and Christology in the New Testament*. Carlisle: Paternoster, 1998.
———. "The Great Tribulation in the Shepherd of Hermas." *JTS* 25 (1974) 27–40.
———. "James and the Jerusalem Church." In *The Book of Acts in Its First-Century Setting*, vol. 4: *The Book of Acts in Its Palestinian Setting*. Edited by Richard Bauckham, 415–80. Grand Rapids: Eerdmans, 1995.
———. "James, 1 and 2 Peter, Jude." In *It is Written: Scripture Citing Scripture*, edited by D. A. Carson and H. G. M. Williamson, 303–17. Cambridge: Cambridge University Press, 1988.
———. "James, 1 Peter, Jude and 2 Peter." In *A Vision for the Church: Studies in Early Christianity in Honour of J. P. M Sweet*, edited by Marcus Bockmuehl and Michael B. Thompson, 153–66. Edinburgh: T. & T. Clark, 1997.
———. *Jude and the Relatives of Jesus in the Early Church*. London: T. & T. Clark, 2004.
———. "Pseudo-Apostolic Letters." In *The Jewish World around the New Testament: Collected Essays*, 1:123–49. WUNT 223. Tübingen: Mohr Siebeck, 2008.
Beale, G. K. *The Temple and the Church's Mission: A Biblical Theology of the Dwelling Place of God*. NSBT 17. Downers Grove, IL: InterVarsity, 2004.
Beare, F. W. *The First Epistle of Peter: The Greek Text with Introduction and Notes*. 3rd ed. Oxford: Blackwell, 1970.
Beaton, Richard. *Isaiah's Christ in Matthew's Gospel*. SNTSMS 123. Cambridge: Cambridge University Press, 2004.
Bechtler, Steven Richard. *Following in His Steps: Suffering, Community and Christology in 1 Peter*. SBLDS 162. Atlanta: Scholars, 1998.
Ben Zvi, Ehud. *Hosea*. FOTL 21A/1. Grand Rapids: Eerdmans, 2005.
Berges, Ulrich. "The Literary Construction of the Servant in Isaiah 40–55: A Discussion about Individual and Collective Identities." *SJOT* 24 (2010) 28–38.
Bernstein, Moshe J. "Introductory Formulas for Citation and Re-citation of Biblical Verses in the Qumran Pesharim: Observations on a Pesher Technique." *DSD* 1 (1994) 30–70.
Berrin, Shani L. *The Pesher Nahum Scroll from Qumran: An Exegetical Study of 4Q169*. STDJ 53. Leiden: Brill, 2004.
Best, Ernest. *I Peter*. NCB. Sheffield: Sheffield Academic, 1971.

———. "I Peter and the Gospel Tradition." *NTS* 16 (1970) 95–113.
———. "I Peter II 4–10: A Reconsideration." *NovT* 11 (1969) 270–93.
Beuken, W. A. M. "Isaiah LIV: The Multiple Identity of the Person Addressed." In *Language and Meaning: Studies in Hebrew Language and Biblical Exegesis*, edited by James Barr et al., 29–70. OTS 19. Leiden: Brill, 1974.
———. "The Main Theme of Trito-Isaiah: The Servants of YHWH." *JSOT* 47 (1990) 67–87.
Bigg, Charles. *The Epistles of St. Peter and St. Jude*. ICC. New York: Scribners, 1901.
Bird, Jennifer G. *Abuse, Power and Fearful Obedience: Reconsidering 1 Peter's Commands to Wives*. LNTS 442. London: T. & T. Clark, 2011.
Blenkinsopp, Joseph. *Isaiah 40–55: A New Translation with Introduction and Commentary*. AB 19a. New York: Doubleday, 2000.
———. *Opening the Sealed Book: Interpretations of the Book of Isaiah in Late Antiquity*. Grand Rapids: Eerdmans, 2006.
———. "The Servant and the Servants in Isaiah and the Formation of the Book." In *Writing and Reading the Scroll of Isaiah: Studies of an Interpretive Tradition*, edited by Craig C. Broyles and Craig A. Evans, 155–75. VTSup 70/1. Leiden: Brill, 1997.
Bockmuehl, Marcus. *The Remembered Peter: In Ancient Reception and Modern Debate*. WUNT 262. Tübingen: Mohr Siebeck, 2010.
———. *Simon Peter in Scripture and Memory: The New Testament Apostle in the Early Church*. Grand Rapids: Baker Academic, 2012.
Boismard, M.-É. "Une liturgie baptismale dans las Prima Petri. I. Son influence sur Tit., 1 Jo. Et Col." *RB* 63 (1956) 182–208.
———. "Une liturgie baptismale dans las Prima Petri. II. Son influence sur l'épître de Jacques." *RB* 64 (1957) 161–83.
———. *Quatres hymnes baptismales dans la première épître de Pierre*. LD 30. Paris: Editions du Cerf, 1961.
Bonhoeffer, Dietrich. "König David." In *Illegale Theologenausbildung: Finkenwalde 1935–1937*, edited by O. Dudzus and D. Henkys, 878–904. Gütersloh: Chr. Kaiser, 1996.
Boring, M. Eugene. *1 Peter*. ANTC. Nashville: Abingdon, 1999.
Bornemann, W. "Der erste Petrusbrief—eine Taufrede des Silvanus?" *ZNW* 19 (1919–20) 143–65.
Boyer, James. "A Classification of Participles: A Statistical Study." *Grace Theological Journal* 5 (1984) 163–79.
Brockington, L. H. "The Greek Translator of Isaiah and his Interest in ΔΟΞΑ." *VT* 1 (1951) 23–32.
Brooke, George J. "Biblical Interpretation at Qumran." In *The Bible and the Dead Sea Scrolls*, vol. 1: *Scripture and the Scrolls*, edited by James H. Charlesworth, 287–319. Waco: Baylor University Press, 2006.
———. *The Dead Sea Scrolls and the New Testament*. Minneapolis: Fortress, 2005.
———. *Exegesis at Qumran: 4QFlorilegium in its Jewish Context*. JSOTSup 29. Sheffield: JSOT, 1985.
———. "The Place of Prophecy in Coming Out of Exile: The Case of the Dead Sea Scrolls." In *Scripture in Transition: Essays on Septuagint, Hebrew Bible, and Dead Sea Scrolls in Honour of Raija Sollamo*, edited by Anssi Voitila and Jutta Jokiranta, 535–50. JSJSup 126. Leiden: Brill, 2008.

Brownlee W. H. "Biblical Interpretation Among the Secretaries of the Dead Sea Scrolls." *The Biblical Archaeologist* 14 (1951) 54–76.
Brox, Norbert. *Der erste Petrusbrief.* 2nd ed. EKK 21. Zürich: Benziger, 1986.
———. "'Sara zum Beispiel': Israel im 1. Petrusbrief." In *Kontinuität und Einheit*, edited by Paul-Gerhard Müller and Werner Stegner, 484–93. Freiburg: Herder, 1981.
Brueggemann, Walter. *An Introduction to the Old Testament: The Canon and Christian Imagination.* Louisville: Westminster John Knox, 2003.
———. *Isaiah 1–39.* WBComp. Louisville: Westminster John Knox, 1998.
———. *Isaiah 40–66.* WBComp. Louisville: Westminster John Knox, 1998.
———. *Texts That Linger, Words That Explode: Listening to Prophetic Voices.* Minneapolis: Fortress, 2000.
Brunson, Andrew C. *Psalm 118 in the Gospel of John: An Intertextual Study on the New Exodus Pattern in the Theology of John.* WUNT 2.158. Tübingen: Mohr Siebeck, 2003.
Bultmann, Rudolph. "Bekenntnis- und Liedfragmente im ersten Petrusbrief." In *Coniectanae Neotestamentica XI*, 1–14. Lund: Gleerup, 1947.
Burrows, M., ed. *The Dead Sea Scrolls of St. Mark's Monastery.* New Haven: American Schools of Oriental Research, 1951.
Campbell, Barth L. *Honor, Shame, and the Rhetoric of 1 Peter.* SBLDS 160. Atlanta, GA: Scholars, 1998.
Campbell, Jonathan G. *The Exegetical Texts.* CQS 4. London: T. & T. Clark, 2006.
———. *The Use of Scripture in the Damascus Document 1-8, 19-20.* BZAW 228. Berlin: De Gruyter, 1995.
Caragounis, Chrys C. *The Development of Greek and the New Testament: Morphology, Syntax, Phonology, and Textual Transmission.* WUNT 2.167. Tübingen: Mohr Siebeck, 2004.
Carmignac. "Le document de Qumrân sur Melkisédeq." *RevQ* 7 (1970) 343–78.
Carr, David MacLain. "Isaiah 40:1–11 in the Context of the Macrostructure of Second Isaiah." In *Discourse Analysis of Biblical Literature*, edited by Walter Ray Bodine, 51–65. Atlanta: Scholars, 1994.
Carson, D. A. "1 Peter." In *Commentary on the New Testament Use of the Old Testament*, edited by G. K. Beale and D. A. Carson, 1015–45. Grand Rapids: Baker, 2007.
Carter, Warren. "Going All the Way? Honoring the Emperor and Sacrificing Wives and Slaves in 1 Peter 2.13—3.6." In *A Feminist Companion to the Catholic Epistles*, edited by A.-J. Levine and M. M. Robbins, 14–33. London: T. & T. Clark, 2004.
Caulley, Thomas Scott. "The *Chrestos/Christos* Pun (1 Pet 2:3) in P[72] and P[125]." *NovT* 53 (2011) 376–87.
Ceresko, Anthony R. "The ABCs of Wisdom in Psalm XXXIV." *VT* 35 (1985) 99–104.
Cherian, Jacob. "The Moses at Qumran: The הצדק מורה as the Nursing-Father of the יחד." In *The Bible and the Dead Sea Scrolls*, vol. 2: *The Dead Sea Scrolls and the Qumran Community*, edited by James H. Charlesworth, 351–61. Waco: Baylor University Press, 2006.
Childs, Brevard S. *Exodus.* OTL. Louisville: Westminster John Knox, 1974.
———. *Introduction to the Old Testament as Scripture.* Philadelphia: Fortress, 1979.
———. *Isaiah.* OTL. Louisville: Westminster John Knox, 2001.
———. "Retrospective Reading of the Old Testament Prophets." *ZAW* 108 (1996) 362–77.

———. *The Struggle to Understand Isaiah as Christian Scripture*. Grand Rapids: Eerdmans, 2004.
Chilton, Bruce D. *The Isaiah Targum: Introduction, Translation, Apparatus and Notes*. The Aramaic Bible 11. Wilmington, DE: Glazier, 1987.
Ciampa, Roy E. "Scriptural Language and Ideas." In *As It Is Written: Studying Paul's Use of Scripture*, edited by Stanley E. Porter and Christopher D. Stanley, 41–57. SBLSymS 50. Atlanta: Society of Biblical Literature, 2008.
Clements, Ronald E. "Beyond Tradition-History: Deutero-Isaianic Development of First Isaiah's Themes." *JSOT* 31 (1985) 95–113.
———. *Exodus*. Cambridge Bible Commentaries: Old Testament 32. Cambridge: Cambridge University Press, 1972.
———. *Isaiah 1–39*. NCB. Grand Rapids: Eerdmans, 1980.
———. "The Unity of the Book of Isaiah." *Interpretation* 36 (1982) 117–29.
Clifford, Richard. *Proverbs: A Commentary*. OTL. Louisville: Westminster John Knox, 1999.
Crawford, Sidnie White. *Rewriting Scripture in Second Temple Times*. SDDSRL. Grand Rapids: Eerdmans, 2008.
Creach, Jerome F. D. *Psalms*. Interpretation. Louisville: Westminster John Knox, 1999.
Cross, F. L. *1 Peter: A Paschal Liturgy*. London: Mowbray, 1954.
Cullmann, Oscar. *Peter: Disciple, Apostle, Martyr: A Historical and Theological Study*. Translated by F. V. Filson. London: SCM, 1962.
Cureton, William. *Ancient Syriac Documents Relative to the Earliest Establishment of Christianity in Edessa and the Neighboring Countries*. Edinburgh: Williams and Norgate, 1864.
Dalton, William Joseph. *Christ's Proclamation to the Spirits: A Study of 1 Peter 3:18—4:6*. AnBib 23. Rome: Pontificio Instituto Biblico, 1989.
Danker, F. "1 Peter 1:24–2:17—A Consolatory Pericope." *ZNW* 58 (1967) 93–102.
Davids, Peter H. *The First Epistle of Peter*. NICNT. Grand Rapids: Eerdmans, 1990.
Davies, Andrew. *Double Standards in Isaiah: Re-evaluating Prophetic Ethics and Divine Justice*. BIS 46. Leiden: Brill, 2000.
Davies, Paul E. "Primitive Christology in 1 Peter." In *Festschrift to Honor F. Wilbur Gingrich*, edited by Eugene H. Barth and Ronald E. Cocroft, 115–22. Leiden: Brill, 1972.
Davila, James R. *The Provenance of the Pseudepigrapha: Jewish, Christian, or Other?* JSJSup 105. Leiden: Brill, 2005
Dearman, J. Andrew. *The Book of Hosea*. NICOT. Grand Rapids: Eerdmans, 2010.
Deichgräber, R. *Gotteshymnus und Christushymnus in der frühen Christenheit: Untersuchungen zu Form, Sprache und Stil der frühchristlichen Hymnen*. SUNT 5. Göttingen: Vandenhoeck and Ruprecht, 1967.
Dennis, John. "Cosmology in the Petrine Literature and Jude." In *Cosmology and New Testament Theology*, edited by Sean M. McDonough and Jonathan T. Pennington, 157–77. SNTS 355. London: T. & T. Clark, 2008.
De Waard, Jan. *A Comparative Study of the Old Testament Text in the Dead Sea Scrolls and in the New Testament*. STDJ 4. Leiden: Brill, 1965.
Dodd, C. H. *According to the Scriptures: The Substructure of New Testament Theology*. London: Nisbet, 1952.
Dryden, J. De Waal. *Theology and Ethics in 1 Peter: Paraenetic Strategies for Christian Character Formation*. WUNT 2.209. Tübingen: Mohr Siebeck, 2006.

Dubis, Mark. "First Peter and the 'Sufferings of the Messiah.'" In *Looking into the Future: Evangelical Studies in Eschatology*, edited by David W. Baker, 85-96. Grand Rapids: Baker, 2001.

———. *Messianic Woes in First Peter: Suffering and Eschatology in 1 Peter 4:12-19*. SBL 33. New York: Lang, 2002.

Duhm, Bernhard. *Das Buch Jesaja*. 3rd ed. Göttingen: Vandenhoeck and Ruprecht, 1914.

Dunn, James D. G. *The Theology of Paul the Apostle*. Grand Rapids: Eerdmans, 1998.

———. *Unity and Diversity in the New Testament: An Inquiry into the Character of Earliest Christianity*. 2nd ed. London: SCM, 1990.

Egan, Patrick T. "Did Peter Change Scripture? The Manuscript Tradition of Greek Psalms 33-34 and 1 Peter 3:10-12." In *Die Septuaginta—Entstehung, Sprache, Geschichte: 3. Internationale Fachtagung veranstaltet von Septuagints Deutsch (LXX.D), Wuppertal 22.-25. Juli 2010*, edited by Siegried Kreuzer, Martin Meiser and Marcus Sigismund, 505-28. Tübingen: Mohr Siebeck, 2012.

Elledge, C. D. "A Graphic Index of Citation and Commentary Formulae in the Dead Sea Scrolls." In *The Dead Sea Scrolls: Hebrew, Aramaic, and Greek Texts with English Translations*, vol. 6B: *Pesharim and Related Documents*, edited by James H. Charlesworth, 367-77. PTSDSSP. Tübingen: Mohr Siebeck, 2001.

Elliott, John H. "Disgraced yet Graced: The Gospel according to 1 Peter in the Key of Honor and Shame." *BTB* 25 (1995) 166-78.

———. *The Elect and the Holy: An Exegetical Examination of 1 Peter 2:4-10 and the Phrase* basileion hierateuma. NovTSup 12. Leiden: Brill, 1966.

———. *1 Peter: A New Translation with Introduction and Commentary*. AB 37B. New York: Doubleday, 2000.

———. "1 Peter, Its Situation and Strategy: A Discussion with David Balch." In *Perspectives on First Peter*, edited by Charles H. Talbert, 61-78. Macon: Mercer, 1986.

———. *A Home for the Homeless: A Social-Scientific Criticism of 1 Peter, Its Situation and Strategy*. Minneapolis: Fortress, 1990.

———. "The Rehabilitation of an Exegetical Step-child: 1 Peter in Recent Research." *JBL* 95 (1976) 243-54.

Ellis, E. E. *Paul's Use of the Old Testament*. Edinburgh: Oliver and Boyd, 1957.

———. *Prophecy and Hermeneutic in Early Christianity*. WUNT 2.18. Tübingen: Mohr Siebeck, 1978.

Ellul, Danielle. "Un exemple de cheminement rhétorique: 1 Pierre." *Revue D'Histoire et de Philosophie Religieuses* 70 (1990) 17-34.

Esler, Philip. *Galatians*. New York: Routledge, 1998.

Feldmeier, Reinhard. *Die Christen als Fremde: die Metaphor der Fremde in der antiken Welt, im Urchristentum und im 1. Petrusbrief*. WUNT 2.64. Tübingen: Mohr Siebeck, 1992.

———. *The First Letter of Peter: A Commentary on the Greek Text*. Translated by P. H. Davids. Waco: Baylor University Press, 2008.

Feuillet, André. "Les 'sacrifices spirituels' du sacerdoce royal des baptisés (1 P 2,5) et leur préparation dans l'Ancien Testament." *NRTh* 96 (1974) 704-28.

Fishbane, Michael A. *Biblical Interpretation in Ancient Israel*. Oxford: Oxford University Press, 1988.

———. "Inner-Biblical Exegesis." In *Hebrew Bible/Old Testament: The History of Its Interpretation*, edited by Magne Sæbø, 33–48. Göttingen: Vandenhoeck and Ruprecht, 1996.

Fitzmyer, Joseph A. "4QTestimonia and the New Testament." *TS* 18 (1957) 513–37.

———. "The Use of Explicit Old Testament Quotations in Qumran Literature and in the New Testament." *NTS* 7 (1960) 297–333.

Forman, Mark. "The Politics of Promise: Echoes of Isaiah 54 in Romans 4.19–21." *JSNT* 31 (2009) 301–24

Fraenkel, Detlef, ed. *Verzeichnis der griechischen Handschriften des Alten Testaments*. Vol. 1: *Die Überlieferung bis zum VIII. Jahrhundert*. Göttingen: Vandenhoeck and Ruprecht, 2004.

Fretheim, Terence E. *Exodus*. Interpretation. Louisville: Westminster John Knox, 1991.

Friesen, Ivan D. *Isaiah*. Scottdale, PA: Herald, 2009.

Gammie, John G. "Spatial and Ethical Dualism in Jewish Wisdom and Apocalyptic Literature." *JBL* 93 (1974) 356–85.

Garrett, Duane A. *Proverbs, Ecclesiastes, Song of Songs*. NAC 14. Nashville: Broadman and Holman, 1993.

Gerstenberger, Erhard S. *Leviticus: A Commentary*. Translated by D. W. Stott. OTL. Louisville: Westminster John Knox, 1996.

Gielen, Marlis. *Tradition und Theologie neutestamentlicher Haustafelethik: Ein Beitrag zur Frage einer christlichen Auseinandersetzung mit gesellschaftlichen Normen*. BBB 75. Frankfurt am Main: Hain, 1990.

Gignilliat, Mark. *Paul and Isaiah's Servants: Paul's Theological Reading of Isaiah 40–66 in 2 Corinthians 5:14—6:10*. London: T. & T. Clark, 2007.

———. "Who Is Isaiah's Servant? Narrative Identity and Theological Potentiality." *SJT* 61 (2008) 125–36.

Glenny, Edward W. "The Hermeneutics of the Use of the Old Testament in 1 Peter." PhD diss., Dallas Theological Seminary, 1987.

Goldingay, John. *The Message of Isaiah 40–55: A Literary-Theological Commentary*. London: T. & T. Clark, 2005.

Goldingay, John, and David Payne. *Isaiah 40–55*. Vol 2. ICC. London: T. & T. Clark, 2006.

Goldstein, H. "Die politischen Paraenesen in 1 Petr. 2 und Röm. 13." *BibLeb* 14 (1973) 88–104.

Goppelt, Leonhard. *A Commentary on I Peter*. Edited by Ferdinand Hahn. Translated by John E. Alsup. Grand Rapids: Eerdmans, 1993.

Gowan, Donald E. *Theology in Exodus: Biblical Theology in the Form of a Commentary*. Louisville: Westminster John Knox, 1994.

Gray, Mark. *Rhetoric and Justice in Isaiah*. LHBOTS 432. London: T. & T. Clark, 2006.

Gréaux, Eric J. "The Lord Delivers Us: An Examination of the Function of Psalm 34 in 1 Peter." *RevExp* 106 (2009) 603–13.

———. "'To the Elect Exiles of the Dispersion . . . from Babylon': The Function of the Old Testament in 1 Peter." PhD diss., Duke University, 2003.

Green, Gene L. "The Use of the Old Testament for Christian Ethics in 1 Peter." *TynBul* 41 (1990) 276–89.

Green, Joel B. *1 Peter*. THNTC. Grand Rapids: Eerdmans, 2007.

Greene, Thomas M. *The Light in Troy: Imitation and Discovery in Renaissance Poetry*. New Haven: Yale University Press, 1982.

Grogan, Geoffrey. *Psalms*. THOTC. Grand Rapids: Eerdmans, 2008.
Gruber, Mayer I., ed. *Rashi´s Commentary on Psalms*. Leiden: Brill, 2004.
Grudem, Wayne. *1 Peter*. TNTC. Grand Rapids: Eerdmans, 1988.
Gschwind, Karl. *Die Niederfahrt Christi in die Unterwelt: Ein Beitrag zur Exegese des Neuen Testaments und zur Geschicte des Taufsymbols*. NTAbh 2.3–5. Münster: Aschendorff, 1911.
Gundry, Robert H. "Further Verba on Verba Christi in First Peter." *Bib* 55 (1974) 211–32.
———. "Verba Christi in I Peter: Their Implications concerning the Authorship of I Peter and the Authenticity of the Gospel Tradition." *NTS* 13 (1967) 336–50.
Gunkel, Hermann. *Introduction to Psalms: The Genres of the Religious Lyric of Israel*. Translated by James D. Nogalski. Macon: Mercer University Press, 1998.
Gunn, David M. "Deutero-Isaiah and the Flood." *JBL* 94 (1975) 493–508.
Guthrie, Donald. *New Testament Introduction*. 4th ed. Downers Grove, IL: InterVarsity, 1990.
Hafemann, Scott. "Paul and the Exile of Israel in Galatians 3–4." In *Exile: Old Testament, Jewish, and Christian Conceptions*, edited by J. M. Scott, 329–71. JSJSup 56. Leiden: Brill, 1997.
Hägglund, Fredrik. *Isaiah 53 in the Light of Homecoming after Exile*. FAT 2.31. Tübingen: Mohr Siebeck, 2008.
Hanson, A. T. "The Scriptural Background to the Doctrine of the *Descensus ad Inferos* in the New Testament." In *The New Testament Interpretation of Scripture*, 122–56. London: SPCK, 1980.
———. *Studies in Paul's Technique and Theology*. London: SPCK, 1974.
Harink, Douglas. *1 and 2 Peter*. BTCB. Grand Rapids: Brazos, 2009.
Harrington, Daniel J. *Why Do We Suffer? A Scriptural Approach to the Human Condition*. Franklin: Rowman and Littlefield, 2000.
Harris, William V. *Ancient Literacy*. Cambridge, MA: Harvard University Press, 1989.
Hauck, Friedrich. *Die Briefe des Jakobus, Petrus, Judas, und Johannes*. 8th ed. NTD 10. Göttingen: Vandenhoeck and Ruprecht, 1957.
Hays, Richard B. *The Conversion of the Imagination: Paul as Interpreter of Israel's Scripture*. Grand Rapids: Eerdmans, 2005.
———. *Echoes of Scripture in the Letters of Paul*. New Haven: Yale University Press, 1989.
———. *The Faith of Jesus Christ: An Investigation of the Narrative Substructure of Galatians 3:1—4:11*. SBLDS 56. Chico, CA: Scholars, 1983.
———. *The Moral Vision of the New Testament: A Contemporary Introduction to New Testament*. London: T. & T. Clark, 1997.
Hays, Richard B., and Joel B. Green. "The Use of the Old Testament by New Testament Writers." In *Hearing the New Testament: Strategies for Interpretation*, edited by Joel B. Green, 222–38. Grand Rapids: Eerdmans, 1995.
Head, Peter M. "Named Letter-Carriers among the Oxyrhynchus Papyri." *JSNT* 31 (2009) 279–99.
Heikel, Ivar A., ed. *Eusebius Werke*. Vol. 6: *Die Demonstratio evangelica*. GCS. Leipzig: Hinrichs, 1913.
Hengel, Martin. *The Atonement: The Origins of the Doctrine in the New Testament*. Translated by John Bowden. Philadelphia: Fortress, 1981.

———. *Saint Peter: The Underestimated Apostle*. Translated by Thomas H. Trapp. Grand Rapids: Eerdmans, 2010.

———. *The Septuagint as Christian Scripture: Its Prehistory and the Problem of Its Canon*. Translated by Mark E. Biddle. Grand Rapids: Baker, 2002.

Hermisson, Hans-Jürgen. "The Fourth Servant Song in the Context of Second Isaiah." In *The Suffering Servant: Isaiah 53 in Jewish and Christian Sources*, edited by Bernd Janowski and Peter Stuhlmacher, 16–47. Grand Rapids: Eerdmans, 2004.

Hill, David. "'To Offer Spiritual Sacrifices . . .' (1 Peter 2:5): Liturgical Formulations and Christian Paraenesis in 1 Peter." *JSNT* 16 (1982) 45–63.

Hillyer, Norman. "First Peter and the Feast of Tabernacles." *TynBul* 21 (1970) 39–70.

———. "'Rock-Stone' Imagery in 1 Peter." *TynBul* 22 (1971) 58–81.

———. "Spiritual Milk . . . Spiritual House." *TynBul* 20 (1969) 126.

Hofius, Otfried. "The Fourth Servant Song in the New Testament Letters." In *The Suffering Servant: Isaiah 53 in Jewish and Christian Sources*, edited by Bernd Janowski and Peter Stuhlmacher, 163–88. Grand Rapids: Eerdmans, 2004.

Hollander, John. *The Figure of Echo: A Mode of Allusion in Milton and After*. Berkeley: University of California Press, 1981.

Hooker, Morna D. *Jesus and the Servant: The Influence of the Servant Concept of Deutero-Isaiah in the New Testament*. London: SPCK, 1959.

Horrell, David G. "Aliens and Strangers? The Socioeconomic Location of the Addressees of 1 Peter." In *Engaging Economics: New Testament Scenarios and Early Christian Reception*, edited by Bruce Longenecker and Kelly Liebengood, 176–202. Grand Rapids: Eerdmans, 2009.

———. "Between Conformity and Resistance: Beyond the Balch–Elliott Debate Towards a Postcolonial Reading of First Peter." In *Reading First Peter with New Eyes: Methodological Reassessments of the Letter of First Peter*, edited by Robert L. Webb and Betsy Bauman-Martin, 111–43. LNTS 364. London: T. & T. Clark, 2007.

———. *1 Peter*. NTG. London: T. & T. Clark, 2008.

Hort, F. J. A. *The First Epistle of St Peter I.1—II.17: The Greek Text, with Introductory Lecture, Commentary, and Additional Notes*. London: Macmillan, 1898.

Horton, Fred L. "Formulas of Introduction in the Qumran Literature." *RevQ* 7 (1971) 505–14.

Howe, Frederic R. "Christ, the Building Stone, in Peter's Theology." *BSac* 157 (2000) 35–43.

———. "The Cross of Christ in Peter's Theology." *BSac* 157 (2000) 190–99.

Hughes, Julie A. *Scriptural Allusions and Exegesis in the Hodayot*. STDJ 59. Leiden: Brill, 2006.

Jaffee, Martin S. *Torah in the Mouth: Writing and Oral Tradition in Palestinian Judaism 200 BCE—400 CE*. Oxford: Oxford University Press, 2001.

Janowski, Bernd, and Peter Stuhlmacher, eds. *The Suffering Servant: Isaiah 53 in Jewish and Christian Sources*. Grand Rapids: Eerdmans, 2004.

Jobes, Karen H. *1 Peter*. BECNT. Grand Rapids: Baker, 2005.

———. "Jerusalem Our Mother: Metalepsis and Intertextuality in Galatians 4:21–31." *WTJ* 55 (1993) 299–320.

———. "The Septuagint Textual Tradition in 1 Peter." In *Septuagint Research: Issues and Challenges in the Study of the Greek Jewish Scriptures*, edited by Wolfgang

Kraus and R. Glenn Wooden, 311–33. SBLSCS 53. Atlanta: Society of Biblical Literature, 2006.

Jobes, Karen H., and Moisés Silva. *Invitation to the Septuagint*. Grand Rapids: Baker, 2000.

Johnson, Dennis E. "Fire in God's House: Imagery from Malachi 3 in Peter's Theology of Suffering (1 Pet. 4:12–19)." *JETS* 29 (1986) 285–94.

Joosten, Jan. *People and Land in the Holiness Code: An Exegetical Study of the Ideational Framework of the Law in Leviticus 17–26*. VTSup 67. Leiden: Brill, 1996.

Joseph, Abson Prédestin. *A Narratological Reading of 1 Peter*. LNTS 440. London: T. & T. Clark, 2012.

Kaiser, Otto. *Isaiah 1–12: A Commentary*. Translated by J. Bowden. OTL. Philadelphia: Westminster, 1983.

———. *Isaiah 13–39*. Translated by R. A. Wilson. Philadelphia: Westminster, 1974.

Kaiser, Walter C. "The Eschatological Hermeneutics of Evangelicalism: Promise Theology." *JETS* 13 (1970) 94–96.

———. "The Single Intent of Scripture." In *The Right Doctrine for the Wrong Texts? Essays on the Use of the Old Testament in the New*, edited by G. K. Beale, 55–69. Grand Rapids: Baker, 1994.

Kelly, J. N. D. *The Epistles of Peter and of Jude*. HNTC. New York: Harper and Row, 1969.

Kelsey, David H. *The Uses of Scripture in Modern Theology*. Philadelphia: Fortress, 1975.

Kiley, Mark. "Like Sara: The Tale of Terror behind 1 Peter 3:6." *JBL* 106 (1987) 689–92.

Koch, Dietrich-Alex. *Die Schrift als Zeuge des Evangeliums: Untersuchungen zur Verwendung und zum Verständnis der Schrift bei Paulus*. BHT 69. Tübingen: Mohr Siebeck, 1986.

Köstenberger, Andreas J. "The Use of Scripture in the Pastoral and General Epistles and the Book of Revelation." In *Hearing the Old Testament in the New Testament*, edited by Stanley E. Porter, 230–54. MNTS. Grand Rapids: Eerdmans, 2006.

Kraus, Hans-Joachim. *Psalms 60–150: A Continental Commentary*. Translated by H. C. Oswald. Minneapolis: Fortress, 1993.

———. *Theology of the Psalms: A Continental Commentary*. Translated by K. Crim. Minneapolis: Fortress, 1992.

Kraus, Wolfgang. "Contemporary Translations of the Septuagint: Problems and Perspectives." In *Septuagint Research: Issues and Challenges in the Study of the Greek Jewish Scriptures*, edited by Woflgang Kraus and R. Glenn Wooden, 63–83. SBLSCS 53. Atlanta: Society of Biblical Literature, 2006.

Kreutzer, Siegfried. "Translation and Recensions: Old Greek, Kaige, and Antiochene Text in Samuel and Reigns." *BIOSCS* 42 (2009) 34–51.

Kristeva, Julia. "Word, Dialogue and Novel." In *The Kristeva Reader*, edited by Toril Moi, 34–61. New York: Columbia University Press, 1986.

Laato, Antti. "The Composition of Isaiah 40–55." *JBL* 109 (1990) 207–28.

Lamau, Marie-Louise. *Des Chrétiens dans le monde: Communautés pétriniennes au Ier siecle*. LD 134. Paris: Cerf, 1988.

Langkammer, Hugolinus. "Jes 53 und 1 Petr 2,21–25: Zur christologischen Interpretation der Leidenstheologie von Jes 53." *BL* 60 (1987) 90–98.

Lapham, F. *Peter: The Myth, the Man and the Writings: A Study of Early Petrine Text and Tradition*. JSNTSup 239. Sheffield: Sheffield Academic Press, 2003.

Lattke, Michael. *Hymnus: Materialien zu einer Geschichte der antiken Hymnologie.* NTOA 19. Göttingen: Vandenhoeck and Ruprecht, 1991.
Leaney, A. R. C. "1 Peter and the Passover: An Interpretation." *NTS* 10 (1964) 238–51.
Le Boulluec, Alain, and Pierre Sandevoir. *La Bible d'Alexandrie: L'Exode.* Paris: Cerf, 1989.
Lecomte, Pierre. "Aimer la vie: 1 Pierre 3/10 (Psaume 34/13)." *ETR* 56 (1981) 288–93.
Lee, J. A. L. *A Lexical Study of the Septuagint Version of the Pentateuch.* SCS 14. Chico, CA: Scholars, 1983.
Légasse, S. "La soumission aux authorités d'après 1 Pierre 2.13–17: Version spécifique d'une parénès traditionelle." *NTS* 34 (1988) 378–96.
Liebengood, Kelly D. *The Eschatology of 1 Peter: Considering the Influence of Zechariah 9–14.* SNTSMS 157. Cambridge: Cambridge University Press, 2014.
Liebreich, Leon J. "Psalms 34 and 145 in the Light of Their Key Words." *HUCA* 27 (1956) 181–92.
Lim, Timothy H. *Holy Scripture in the Qumran Commentaries and Pauline Letters.* Oxford: Clarendon, 1997.
———. *Pesharim.* CQS 3. London: Sheffield, 2002.
Limburg, James. *Psalms.* WBC. Louisville: Westminster John Knox, 2000.
Lindars, Barnabas. *New Testament Apologetic: The Doctrinal Significance of the New Testament Quotations.* Philadelphia: Westminster, 1961.
Lohse, Eduard. "Paränese und Kerygma im 1. Petrusbrief." *ZNW* 45 (1954) 68–89.
Longenecker, Bruce W. "Narrative Interest in the Study of Paul: Retrospective and Prospective." In *Narrative Dynamics in Paul: A Critical Assessment*, edited by Bruce W. Longenecker, 3–16. Knoxville: Westminster John Knox, 2002.
———. "Sharing in Their Spiritual Blessings? The Stories of Israel in Galatians and Romans." In *Narrative Dynamics in Paul: A Critical Assessment*, edited by Bruce W. Longenecker, 58–84. Louisvile: Westminster John Knox, 2002.
Luther, Martin. *Luther's Works.* Vol. 30: *The Catholic Epistles.* Edited by Jaroslav Pelikan and Helmut T. Lehmann. St Louis: Concordia, 1967.
Maier, Gerhard. "Jesustradition im 1 Petrusbrief?" In *Gospel Perspectives*, vol 5: *The Jesus Tradition Outside the Gospels*, edited by David Wenham, 85–128. Sheffield: JSOT, 1984.
Manns, Frederic. "Sara, modèle de la femme obéissante: Étude de l'arrière-plan juif de 1 Pierre 3,5–6." *BeO* 26 (1984) 65–73.
Marcus, Joel. *The Way of the Lord: Christological Exegesis of the Old Testament in the Gospel of Mark.* Louisville: Westminster John Knox, 1992.
Marks, Herbert. "Pauline Typology and Revisionary Criticism." *JAAR* 50 (1982) 71–92.
Marshall, I. Howard. "An Assessment of Recent Developments." In *It Is Written: Scripture Citing Scripture*, edited by D. A. Carson and H. G. M. Williamson, 1–21. Cambridge: Cambridge University Press, 1988.
———. *1 Peter.* IVPNTC. Downers Grove, IL: InterVarsity, 1991.
Martin, Ralph P. *A Hymn of Christ: Philippians 2:5–11 in Recent Interpretation and in the Setting of Early Christian Worship.* Downers Grove, IL: InterVarsity, 1997.
Martin, Troy W. *Metaphor and Composition in 1 Peter.* SBLDS 131. Atlanta: Scholars, 1992.
———. "The TestAbr and the Background of 1Pet 3,6." *ZNW* 90 (1999) 139-46.
Mays, James Luther. *Hosea: A Commentary.* OTL. Philadelphia: Westminster, 1969.

———. "Psalm 118 in the Light of Canonical Analysis." In *Canon, Theology, and Old Testament Interpretation*, edited by Gene M. Tucker, David L. Petersen, and Robert R. Wilson, 299–311. Philadelphia: Fortress, 1988.

———. *Psalms*. Interpretation. Louisville: Westminster John Knox, 1994.

Mbuvi, Andrew M. *Temple, Exile and Identity in 1 Peter*. LNTS 345. London: T. & T. Clark, 2007.

McCartney, Dan G. "Logikos in 1 Peter 2,2." *ZNW* 82 (1991) 352–59.

———. "The Use of the Old Testament in the First Epistle of Peter." PhD diss., Westminster Theological Seminary, 1989.

McDonald, Lee M., and James A. Sanders. *The Canon Debate*. Peabody, MA: Hendrickson, 2002.

McDonough, Sean M., and Jonathan T. Pennington, eds. *Cosmology and the New Testament*. LNTS 355. London: T. & T. Clark, 2008.

McKane, William. *Proverbs*. OTL. Philadelphia: Westminster, 1970.

McKelvey, R. J. *The New Temple: The Church in the New Testament*. London: Oxford University Press, 1969.

McKenzie, John L. *Second Isaiah: Introduction, Translation, and Notes*. AB 20. New York: Doubleday, 1968.

McLay, R. Timothy. "Biblical Texts and the Scriptures for the New Testament Church." In *Hearing the Old Testament in the New Testament*, edited by Stanley Porter, 38–58. Grand Rapids: Eerdmans, 2006.

———. *The Use of the Septuagint in New Testament Research*. Grand Rapids: Eerdmans, 2003.

Melugin, Roy F. *The Formation of Isaiah 40-55*. BZAW 141. Berlin: De Gruyter, 1976.

———. "On Reading Isaiah 53 as Christian Scripture." In *Jesus and the Suffering Servant: Isaiah 53 and Christian Origins*, edited by William R. Farmer and W. H. Bellinger, 55–69. Harrisburg: Trinity, 1998.

Mettinger, Tryggve N. D. "Israelite Aniconism: Developments and Origins." In *The Image and the Book: Iconic Cults, Aniconism, and the Rise of Book Religion in Israel and the Ancient Near East*, edited by Karel van der Toorn, 173–203. CBET 21. Leuven: Peeters, 1997.

Metzger, Bruce M. "The Formulas Introducing Quotations of Scripture in the NT and the Mishnah." *JBL* 70 (1951) 297–307.

Metzner, Rainer. *Die Rezeption des Matthäusevangeliums im 1. Petrusbrief: Studien zum traditionsgeschichtlichen Einfluss des 1. Evangeliums auf den 1. Petrusbrief*. WUNT 2.74. Tübingen: Mohr Siebeck, 1995.

Michaels, J. Ramsey. *1 Peter*. WBC 49. Waco: Word, 1988.

Milgrom, Jacob. *Leviticus: A Book of Ritual and Ethics*. Minneapolis: Augsburg Fortress, 2004.

Moyise, Steve. *Evoking Scripture: Seeing the Old Testament in the New*. London: T. & T. Clark, 2008.

———. "Intertextuality and the Study of the Old Testament in the New Testament." In *The Old Testament in the New Testament*, edited by Steve Moyise, 14–41. Sheffield: Sheffield Academic Press, 2000.

———. "Isaiah in 1 Peter." In *Isaiah in the New Testament*, edited by Steve Moyise and M. J. J. Menken, 175–88. London: T. & T. Clark, 2005.

———. *The Old Testament in the New: An Introduction*. London: T. & T. Clark, 2004.

———. "Quotations." In *As It Is Written: Studying Paul's Use of Scripture*, edited by Stanley E. Porter and Christopher D. Stanley, 15–28. SBLSymS 50. Atlanta: Society of Biblical Literature, 2008.

Moyise, Steve and M. J. J. Menken, eds. *Psalms in the New Testament*. London: T. & T. Clark, 2004.

Neusner, Jacob. *What is Midrash? and A Midrash Reader*. Atlanta: Scholars, 1994.

Nickelsburg, George W. E. *1 Enoch 1: A Commentary on the Book of 1 Enoch: Chapters 1–36; 81–108*. Hemeneia. Minneapolis: Fortress, 2001.

North, Christopher R. *Isaiah 40–55: The Suffering Servant of God*. London: SCM, 1956.

Osborne, T. P. "Guide Lines for Christian Suffering: A Source-Critical and Theological Study of I Peter 2,21–25." *Biblica* 64 (1983) 381–408.

———. "L'utilisation des citations de l'Ancien Testament dans la première épître de Pierre." *Revue theologique de Louvain* 12 (1987) 64–77.

Oswalt, John N. *The Book of Isaiah*. Vol. 1: *Chapters 1–39*. Grand Rapids: Eerdmans, 1986.

———. *The Book of Isaiah*. Vol. 2: *Chapters 40–66*. Grand Rapids: Eerdmans, 1998.

Pao, David W. *Acts and the Isaianic New Exodus*. Grand Rapids: Baker, 2002.

Patsch, Hermann. "Zum alttestamentlichen Hintergrund von Röm 4, 25 und I. Petrus 2, 24." *ZNW* 60 (1969) 273–79.

Payne, Philip Barton. "The Fallacy of Equating Meaning with the Human Author's Intention." In *The Right Doctrine for the Wrong Texts? Essays on the Use of the Old Testament in the New*, edited by G. K. Beale, 70–81. Grand Rapids: Baker, 1994.

Pearson, Sharon Clark. *The Christological and Rhetorical Properties of 1 Peter*. SBEC 45. Lampeter, Wales: Mellen, 2001.

Peppard, Micheal. "'Poetry', 'Hymns' and 'Traditional Material' in New Testament Epistles or How to Do Things with Indentations." *JSNT* 30 (2008) 319–42.

Perdelwitz, Richard. *Die Mysterienreligionen und das Problem des I. Petrusbriefes*. RVV 11/3. Giessen: Töpelmann, 1911.

Perdue, Leo G. *Proverbs*. Interpretation. Louisville: Westminster John Knox, 2000.

Perkins, Pheme. *Peter: Apostle for the Whole Church*. Minneapolis: Fortress, 2000.

Pietersma, Albert. "A New Paradigm for Addressing Old Questions: The Relevance of the Interlinear Model for the Study of the Septuagint." In *Bible and Computer*, edited by Johann Cook, 337–64. Leiden: Brill, 2002.

Platt, Elizabeth Ellen. "Jewelry of Bible Times and the Catalog of Isa 3:18–23." *AUSS* 17 (1979) 189–202.

Pleket H. W. Review of *Ancient Literacy*, by W. V. Harris. *Mnemosyne* 45 (1992) 416–23.

Porter, Stanley E. "Allusions and Echoes." In *As It Is Written: Studying Paul's Use of Scripture*, edited by Stanley E. Porter and Christopher D. Stanley, 29–40. SBLSymS 50. Atlanta: Society of Biblical Literature, 2008.

———. "Further Comments on the Use of the Old Testament in the New Testament." In *The Intertextuality of the Epistles: Explorations of Theory and Practice*, edited by Thomas L. Brodie, Dennis R. MacDonald, and Stanley E. Porter, 98–110. NTM 16. Sheffield: Sheffield Phoenix, 2006.

———. *Idioms of the Greek New Testament*. Sheffield: Sheffield Academic Press, 1994.

———. "The Use of the Old Testament in the New Testament: A Brief Comment on Method and Terminology." In *Early Christian Interpretation of the Scriptures of Israel: Investigations and Proposals*, edited by Craig A. Evans and James A. Sander, 79–96. JSNTSup 148; SSEJC 5. Sheffield: Sheffield Academic Press, 1997.

———. *Verbal Aspect in the Greek of the New Testament, with Reference to Tense and Mood*. New York: Lang, 1989.
Porton, Gary. "Midrash: Palestinian Jews and the Hebrew Bible in the Greco-Roman Period." In *ANRW* II.19.2, edited by Hildegard Temporini and Wolfgang Haase, 103–38. Berlin: De Gruyter, 1979.
Quinn, Jerome D. "Notes on the Text of P^{72} 1 Pet 2,3; 5,14; and 5,9." *CBQ* 27 (1965) 241–49.
Rajak, Tessa. "The Jewish Diaspora." In *The Cambridge History of Christianity: Origins to Constantine*, edited by Margaret M. Mitchell and Frances M. Young, 53–68. Cambridge: Cambridge University Press, 2006.
Reicke, Bo. *The Disobedient Spirits and Christian Baptism: A Study of I Pet. III.19 and Its Context*. ASNU 13. Copenhagen: Munksgaard, 1946.
———. *The Epistles of James, Peter, and Jude: Introduction, Translation, and Notes*. New York: Doubleday, 1964.
Rembaum, Joel E. "The Development of a Jewish Exegetical Tradition Regarding Isaiah 53." *HTR* 75 (1982) 289–311.
Rendtorff, Rolf. "Isaiah 56:1 as a Key to the Formation of the Book of Isaiah." In *Canon and Theology: Overtures to an Old Testament Theology*, 181–89. Translated by Margaret Kohl. OBT. Minneapolis: Fortress, 1993.
———. *The Old Testament: An Introduction*. Translated by J. Bowden. Minneapolis: Fortress, 1985.
Rensburg, Fika van, and Steve Moyise. "Isaiah in 1 Peter 3:13–17: Applying Intertextuality to the Study of the Old Testament in the New." *Scriptura* 80 (2002) 275–86.
Reventlow, Henning. "Basic Issues in the Interpretation of Isaiah 53." In *Jesus and the Suffering Servant: Isaiah 53 and Christian Origins*, edited by W. H. Bellinger and William R. Farmer, 23–38. Harrisburg: Trinity, 1998.
Richard, Earl. "The Functional Christology of 1 Peter." In *Perspectives on 1 Peter*, edited by Charles H. Talbert, 121–40. Macon: Mercer, 1986.
———. *Reading 1 Peter, Jude, and 2 Peter: A Literary and Theological Commentary*. Macon: Smyth and Helwys, 2000.
Rowley, H. H. "The Marriage of Hosea." In *Men of God: Studies in Old Testament History and Prophecy*, 66–97. London: Nelson, 1963.
Safrai, Shemuel. "Education and the Study of the Torah." In *The Jewish People in the First Century: Historical Geography, Political History, Social, Cultural and Religious Life and Institutions*, edited by Shmuel Safrai and Menahem Stern, 945–70. Assen: Van Gorcum, 1974.
Sawyer, John F. A. "Daughter of Zion and Servant of the Lord in Isaiah: A Comparison." *JSOT* 44 (1989) 89–107.
———. *The Fifth Gospel: Isaiah in the History of Christianity*. Cambridge: Cambridge University Press, 1996.
Scharlemann, Martin H. "Exodus Ethics: Part One—1 Peter 1:13–16." *Concordia Journal* 2 (1976) 165–70.
———. "Why the 'Kuriou' in 1 P 1:25?" *CTM* 30 (1959) 352–56.
Schlosser, Jacques. "'Aimez la fraternité' (1 P 2,17): a propos de l'ecclésiologie de la première lettre de Pierre." In *Patrimonium fidei: Traditionsgeschichtliches Verstehen am Ende?*, edited by Marinella Perroni and Elmar Salmann, 525–45. Rome: Pont Ateneo S Anselmo, 1997.

———. "Ancien Testament et christologie dans la prima Petri." In *Etudes sur la premiere Lettre de Pierre*, edited by Charles Perrot, 65–96. Paris: Cerf, 1980.
Schmitt, John J. "The City as Woman in Isaiah 1–39." In *Writing and Reading the Scroll of Isaiah: Studies of an Interpretive Tradition*, edited by Craig C. Broyles and Craig A. Evans, 1:95–119. VTSup 70/1. Leiden: Brill, 1997.
Schnabel, Eckhard J. *Early Christian Mission*. Vol. 1: *Jesus and the Twelve*. Downers Grove, IL: InterVarsity, 2004.
———. *Early Christian Mission*. Vol. 2: *Paul and the Early Church*. Downers Grove, IL: InterVarsity, 2004.
Schrage, Wolfgang. "Zur Ethik der neutestamentlichen Haustafeln." *NTS* 21 (1974) 1–22.
Schreiner, Thomas R. *1, 2 Peter, Jude*. NAC 37. Nashville: Broadman and Holman, 2003.
Schutter, William L. "1 Peter 4.17, Ezekiel 9:6, and Apocalyptic Hermeneutics." In *Society of Biblical Literature 1987 Seminar Papers*, edited by Kent H. Richards, 276–84. SBLSP 26. Atlanta: Scholars, 1987.
———. *Hermeneutic and Composition in I Peter*. WUNT 2.30. Tübingen: Mohr Siebeck, 1989.
Schwank, B. "Lecture chrétienne de la Bible (1 Pierre 3:8–15)." *Assemblees du Seigneur* 59 (1966) 16–32.
Seitz, Christopher. "How Is the Prophet Isaiah Present in the Latter Half of the Book? The Logic of Chapters 40–66 within the Book of Isaiah." *JBL* 115 (1996) 219–40.
———. *Isaiah 1–39*. IBC. Louisville: Westminster John Knox, 1993.
———. "Isaiah 40–66." In *The New Interpreter's Bible*, edited by Leander E. Keck, 6:307–551. Nashville: Abingdon, 2001.
———. "'You are my Servant, You are the Israel in whom I will be glorified': The Servant Songs and the Effect of Literary Context in Isaiah." *CTJ* 39 (2004) 117–34.
Selwyn, E. G. *The First Epistle of St Peter*. London: Macmillan, 1958.
Senior, Donald. *1 Peter*. Sacra pagina 15. Collegeville, MN: Liturgical, 2003.
Sevenster, J. N. *Do You Know Greek? How Much Greek Could the First Jewish Christians Have Known?* NovTSup 19. Leiden: Brill, 1968.
Sheppard, Gerald T. "The 'Scope' of Isaiah as a Book of Jewish and Christian Scriptures." In *New Visions of Isaiah*, edited by Roy F. Melugin and Marvin A. Sweeney, 257–81. Sheffield: Sheffield Academic Press, 1996.
Shimada, Kazuhito. "Is 1 Peter Dependent on Romans?" *AJBI* 19 (1993) 87–137.
Ska, J. L. "Exode 19,3b–6 et l'identité de l'Israël post-exilique." In *Studies in the Book of Exodus*, edited by Marc Vervenne, 289–317. Leuven: Peeters, 1996.
Sly, Dorothy I. "1 Peter 3:6b in the Light of Philo and Josephus." *JBL* 110 (1991) 126–29.
Smith, Gary V. *Isaiah 1–39*. NAC 14A. Nashville: Broadman and Holman, 2007.
———. *Isaiah 40–66*. NAC 15B. Nashville: Broadman and Holman, 2009.
Snodgrass, Klyne R. "I Peter II. 1–10: Its Formation and Literary Affinities." *NTS* 24 (1978) 97–106.
———. "The Use of the Old Testament in the New." In *New Testament Criticism and Interpretation*, edited by David A. Black and David S. Dockery, 409–34. Grand Rapids: Zondervan, 1991.
Sommer, Benjamin D. "Allusions and Illusions: The Unity of the Book of Isaiah in Light of Deutero-Isaiah's Use of Prophetic Tradition." *JSOT* 214 (1996) 156–87.
Sperber, Alexander, ed. *The Bible in Aramaic: Based on Old Manuscripts and Printed Texts*. Vol. 3: *The Latter Prophets according to Targum Jonathan*. Leiden: Brill, 1962.

Sperber, Daniel. "Rabbinic Knowledge of Greek." In *The Literature of the Sages*, edited by Shmuel Safrai et al., 2:627–40. Assen: Van Gorcum, 2006.

Stamps, Dennis C. "The Use of the Old Testament in the New Testament as a Rhetorical Device: A Methodological Proposal." In *Hearing the Old Testament in the New Testament*, edited by Stanley E. Porter, 9–37. Grand Rapids: Eerdmans, 2006.

Stanley, Christopher D. *Arguing with Scripture: The Rhetoric of Quotations in the Letters of Paul*. London: T. & T. Clark, 2004.

———. *Paul and the Language of Scripture: Citation Technique in the Pauline Epistles and Contemporary Literature*. SNTSMS 74. Cambridge: Cambridge University Press, 1992.

———. "The Rhetoric of Quotations: An Essay on Method." In *Early Christian Interpretation of the Scriptures of Israel: Investigations and Proposals*, edited by Craig A. Evans and James A. Sander, 44–58. JSNTSup 148; SSEJC 5. Sheffield: Sheffield Academic Press, 1997.

———. "The Social Environment of 'Free' Biblical Quotations in the New Testament." In *Early Christian Interpretation of the Scriptures of Israel: Investigations and Proposals*, edited by Craig A. Evans and James A. Sander, 18–27. JSNTSup 148; SSEJC 5. Sheffield: Sheffield Academic Press, 1997.

Stansell, Gary. "Isaiah 28–33: Blest Be the Tie that Binds (Isaiah Together)." In *New Visions of Isaiah*, edited by Roy F. Melugin and Marvin A. Sweeney, 68–103. JSOTSup 214. Sheffield: Sheffield Academic Press, 1996.

Stauffer, Ethelbert. *New Testament Theology*. Translated by J. Marsh. London: SCM, 1955.

Stenning, J. F., ed. *The Targum of Isaiah*. Oxford: Clarendon, 1949.

Streeter, B. H. *The Primitive Church*. New York: Macmillan, 1929.

Stuart, Douglas K. *Exodus*. NAC 2. Nashville: Broadman and Holman, 2006.

Stuhlmacher, Peter. "Isaiah 53 in the Gospels and Acts." In *The Suffering Servant: Isaiah 53 in Jewish and Christian Sources*, edited by Bernd Janowski and Peter Stuhlmacher, 147–62. Grand Rapids: Eerdmans, 2004.

Sukenik, E. L. *The Dead Sea Scrolls of the Hebrew University*. Jerusalem: Magnes, 1955.

Sundberg, Albert C., Jr. "On Testimonies." *NovT* 3 (1959) 268–81.

Sweeney, Marvin Alan. *Isaiah 1–4 and the Post-exilic Understanding of the Isaianic Tradition*. BZAW 171. Berlin: De Gruyter, 1988.

———. *Isaiah 1–39: With an Introduction to Prophetic Literature*. FOTL 16. Grand Rapids: Eerdmans, 1996.

Tasker, R. V. G. *The Old Testament in the New Testament*. Philadelphia: Westminster, 1947.

Teichert, Horst. "1 Petrus 2,13: Eine crux interpretum?" *TLZ* 74 (1949) 303–4.

Terrien, Samuel L. *The Psalms: Strophic Structure and Theological Commentary*. ECC. Grand Rapids: Eerdmans, 2003.

Teugels, Lieve M. *Bible and Midrash: The Story of "The Wooing of Rebekah" (Gen. 24)*. CBET 35. Leuven: Peeters, 2004.

Thomas, Rosalind. *Literacy and Orality in Ancient Greece*. Cambridge: Cambridge University Press, 1992.

Thraede, Klaus. "Hymnus I." *RAC* 16 (1993) 915–46.

Thurén, Lauri. *Argument and Theology in 1 Peter: The Origins of Christian Paraenesis*. JSNTSup 114. Sheffield: JSOT, 1995.

———. *The Rhetorical Strategy of 1 Peter: With Special Regard to Ambiguous Expressions.* Åbo: Åbo Academy Press, 1990.
Tov, Emanuel. *The Text-Critical Use of the Septuagint in Biblical Research.* JBS 8. Jerusalem: Simor, 1997.
———. *The Greek and Hebrew Bible: Collected Essays on the Septuagint.* VTSup 72. Leiden: Brill, 1999.
Trebilco, Paul R. *Jewish Communities in Asia Minor.* SNTSMS 69. Cambridge: Cambridge University Press, 1991.
Tuñi, Joseph Oriel. "Jesus of Nazareth in the Christology of 1 Peter." *HeyJ* 28 (1987) 292–304.
Uhlig, Torsten. *Theme of Hardening in the Book of Isaiah: An Analysis of Communicative Action.* FAT 2/39. Tübingen: Mohr Siebeck, 2009.
Ulrich, Eugene. "The Canonical Process, Textual Criticism, and Latter Stages in the Composition of the Bible." In *Sha'arei Talmon: Studies in the Bible, Qumran, and the Ancient Near East*, edited by Michael Fishbane, Emanuel Tov, and Weston W. Fields, 267–91. Winona Lake, IN: Eisenbrauns, 1992.
———. "Light from 1QIsa^a on the Translation Technique of the Old Greek Translator of Isaiah." In *Scripture in Transition: Essays on Septuagint, Hebrew Bible, and Dead Sea Scrolls in Honour of Raija Sollamo*, edited by Anssi Voitila and Jutta Jokiranta, 193–204. Leiden: Brill, 2008.
Ulrich, Eugene, Frank Moore Cross, et al., eds. *Qumran Cave 4. X. The Prophets.* DJD 15. Oxford: Clarendon, 1997.
Van der Louw, Theo A. W. *Transformations in the Septuagint: Towards an Interaction of Septuagint Studies and Translation Studies.* CBET 47. Leuven: Peeters, 2007.
VanGemeren, Willem A. *Psalms.* Expositor's Bible Commentary 5. Rev. ed. Grand Rapids: Zondervan, 2008.
Vanhoozer, Kevin J. *First Theology: God, Scripture and Hermeneutics.* Downers Grove, IL: InterVarsity, 2002.
Van Unnik, W. C. "Christianity according to 1 Peter." *ExpT* 68 (1956) 79–83.
———. "The Teaching of Good Works in 1 Peter." *NTS* 1 (1954) 92–110.
Vermes, Geza. *The Complete Dead Sea Scrolls in English.* Harmondsworth: Penguin, 1997.
Vermeylen, Jacques, ed. *The Book of Isaiah—Le livre d'Isaïe: les oracles et leurs relectures unité et complexité de l'ouvrage.* BETL 81. Louvain: Peeters, 1989.
Voorwinde, S. "Old Testament Quotations in Peter's Epistles." *Vox Reformata* 49 (1987) 3–16.
Wagner, J. Ross. "Faithfulness and Fear, Stumbling and Salvation: Receptions of LXX Isaiah 8:11–18 in the New Testament." In *The Word Leaps the Gap: Essays on Scripture and Theology in Honor of Richard B. Hays*, edited by J. Ross Wagner, Christopher Kavin Rowe, and A. Katherine Grieb, 76–106. Grand Rapids: Eerdmans, 2008.
———. *Heralds of the Good News: Isaiah and Paul in Concert in the Letter to the Romans.* Leiden: Brill, 2002.
———. "Isaiah in Romans and Galatians." In *Isaiah in the New Testament*, edited by Steve Moyise and M. J. J. Menken, 117–32. London: T. & T. Clark, 2005.
———. "Moses and Isaiah in Concert: Paul's Reading of Isaiah and Deuteronomy in the Letter to the Romans." In *"As Those Who are Taught": The Interpretation of*

Isaiah from the LXX to the SBL, edited by Claire Matthews McGinnis and Patricia K. Tull, 87–103. SBLSymS 27. Atlanta: SBL, 2006.

———. "Psalm 118 in Luke-Acts: Tracing a Narrative Thread." In *Early Christian Interpretation of the Scriptures of Israel: Investigations and Proposals*, edited by Craig A. Evans and James A. Sanders, 154–78. Sheffield: Sheffield Academic Press, 2003.

Wallace, Daniel B. *Greek Grammar Beyond the Basics: An Exegetical Syntax of the New Testament*. Grand Rapids: Zondervan, 1995.

Waltke, Bruce K. *The Book of Proverbs: Chapters 1–15*. NICOT. Grand Rapids: Eerdmans, 2004.

———. *The Book of Proverbs: Chapters 15–31*. NICOT. Grand Rapids: Eerdmans, 2005.

Watson, Francis. *Paul and the Hermeneutics of Faith*. London: T. & T. Clark, 2004.

Watts, John D. W. *Isaiah 1–33*. WBC. Waco: Word, 1985.

———. *Isaiah 34–66*. WBC. Waco: Word, 1987.

Watts, Rikki E. "Isaiah in the New Testament." In *Interpreting Isaiah: Issues and Approaches*, edited by David G. Firth and H. G. M. Williamson, 213–33. Downers Grove, IL: InterVarsity, 2009.

———. *Isaiah's New Exodus and Mark*. Grand Rapids: Baker, 2000.

———. "The Psalms in Mark's Gospel." In *The Psalms in the New Testament*, edited by Steve Moyise and M. J. J. Menken, 25–46. London: T. & T. Clark, 2004.

Webb, Robert L., and Betsy Bauman-Martin, eds. *Reading First Peter with New Eyes: Methodological Reassessments of the Letter of First Peter*. London: T. & T. Clark, 2007.

Weiser, Artur. *The Psalms: A Commentary*. Translated by H. Hartwell. Louisville: Westminster John Knox, 2000.

Wells, Jo Bailey. *God's Holy People: A Theme in Biblical Theology*. Sheffield: Sheffield Academic Press, 2000.

Wengst, Klaus. *Christologische Formeln und Lieder des Urchristentums*. 2nd ed. SNT 7. Gütersloher: Mohn, 1974.

Wenham, Gordon J. *The Book of Leviticus*. NICOT 3. Grand Rapids: Eerdmans, 1979.

Westermann, Claus. *Isaiah 40–66*. Translated by D. M. G. Stalker. Philadelphia: Westminster, 1969.

———. *The Psalms: Structure, Content and Message*. Minneapolis: Augsburg, 1980.

Wilcox, Peter, and David Paton-Williams. "The Servant Songs in Deutero-Isaiah." *JSOT* 42 (1988) 79-102.

Wildberger, Hans. *Isaiah 28–39: A Continental Commentary*. Translated by Thomas H. Trapp. Minneapolis: Fortress, 2002.

Wilk, Florian. *Die Bedeutung des Jesajabuches für Paulus*. FRLANT 179. Göttingen: Vandenhoeck and Ruprecht, 1998.

Williams, Travis B. *Persecution in 1 Peter: Differentiating and Contextualizing Early Christian Suffering*. NovTSup 145. Leiden: Brill, 2012.

Williamson, H. G. M. *The Book Called Isaiah: Deutero-Isaiah's Role in Composition and Redaction*. Oxford: Clarendon, 1994.

———. "Recent Issues in the Study of Isaiah." In *Interpreting Isaiah: Issues and Approaches*, edited by H. G. M. Williamson and David G. Firth, 21–39. Downers Grove, IL: InterVarsity, 2009.

———. *Variations of a Theme: King, Messiah and Servant in the Book of Isaiah*. Carlisle: Paternoster, 1998.

Wilson, Todd A. *The Curse of the Law and the Crisis in Galatia: Reassessing the Purpose of Galatians*. WUNT 2.225. Tübingen: Mohr Siebeck, 2007.

Windisch, H. *Die katholischen Briefe*. 3rd ed. Revised by H. Preisker. HNT 15. Leipzig: Deichert, 1951.

Winter, Bruce W. "The Public Honouring of Christian Benefactors: Romans 13.3-4 and 1 Peter 2.14-15." *JSNT* 34 (1988) 87-103.

———. *Seek the Welfare of the City: Christians as Benefactors and Citizens*. First-Century Christians and the Graeco-Roman World. Grand Rapids: Eerdmans, 1994.

Witherington, Ben, III. *Letters and Homilies for Hellenized Christians*. Vol. 2: *A Socio-Rhetorical Commentary on 1-2 Peter*. Downers Grove, IL: InterVarsity, 2007.

———. *Paul's Narrative Thought World: The Tapestry of Tragedy and Triumph*. Louisville: Westminster John Knox, 1994.

Woan, Sue. "The Psalms in 1 Peter." In *The Psalms in the New Testament*, edited by Steve Moyise and M. J. J. Menken, 213-29. London: T. & T. Clark, 2004.

Wright, N. T. *The Climax of the Covenant: Christ and the Law in Pauline Theology*. Edinburgh: T. & T. Clark, 1991.

———. *The New Testament and the People of God*. Philadelphia: Fortress, 1992.

Young, Edward J. *The Book of Isaiah*. Vol 1: *Chapters 1-18*. Grand Rapids: Eerdmans, 1965.

Ziegler, Joseph. "Die Vorlage der Isaias-Septuaginta (LXX) und die erste Isaias-rolle von Qumran (1QIsa)." *JBL* 78 (1959) 34-59.

———, ed. *Isaias*. Vetus Testamentum Graecum Auctoritate Academiae Scientiarum Gottingensis 14. 3rd ed. Göttingen: Vandenhoeck and Ruprecht, 1983.

Subject Index

ʾAl tiqrēʾ, 21, 59
Allusions to scripture, 7–9, 27–28, 61–63, 74, 76–77, 82–84, 86, 107–8, 115–16, 125–27, 131–32, 185–88, 204–6, 212–13, 215–17, 221–23
Asia Minor, 2–4, 12, 17–18, 30, 32–34, 36, 38–40, 46–47, 50–51, 55, 74, 79, 84, 87, 92, 96–97, 102, 114, 119, 171, 174, 189, 204, 206, 213–17
Audience, 3–4, 11–13, 15–16, 27–43, 60–63, 76–77, 79–80, 98–100, 115–23, 130–32, 138, 189–90, 223–24

Babylon, 65, 81–82

Christology, 1–2, 16, 23, 51–58, 60–61, 90–91, 96–100, 134–35, 148–51, 190–92, 217–19, 221–22
Citations, 7, 26–27
Community, Christian/eschatological, 9–10, 18–19, 36, 47, 56, 69, 96, 98, 109–10, 129, 157–58, 182–85, 201, 204, 206–8, 212, 219, 222
Conduct, 2, 37, 62, 76–88, 93, 120–31, 148–51, 157–64, 169–172, 192–93, 201, 213–16
Criteria to identify explicit quotations, 25–27, 115–16, 189, 220, 224

Divine presence, 2, 12–13, 43, 62–64, 69, 74, 80, 84, 86, 92, 99, 102, 104, 115, 119, 121, 131, 151, 156, 166, 171–72, 174, 178, 188, 191, 195–97, 200–206, 208, 210, 212–14, 216–19, 222, 224
Dualism, 126–27, 188, 191–92

Ecclesiology, 2, 4, 10, 16–18, 54–61, 70–71, 80, 96, 98, 118, 131, 135, 147–50, 172, 182, 184, 190–91, 197–98, 203–4, 211, 217–20, 224
Echoes, 7–11, 14–17, 84–85, 115, 127, 135, 147, 154–55, 165, 194, 204, 208, 210
Ethics, 92, 127–28, 132, 147, 166–68, 187–88, 191–92
Explicit use of scripture, 1–2, 7–11, 14, 25–27, 31, 76, 79–80, 86, 95–96, 116, 125–26, 131, 140–42, 186, 189–90, 194, 206, 210–12, 220, 222–24

Fear of the Lord, 79, 129–31, 159–64, 169–74, 176–78, 187–88, 191, 196, 198, 216–18

Genre, 13, 20–25, 192
Gentiles, 5, 11, 16–18, 27–30, 32–34, 39, 62, 72–73, 114, 121–23, 138, 151, 165, 202, 214
Gĕzēra šāwa, 18–21, 59, 83, 88, 116, 186–187
Glory. See Suffering/glory motif.

Subject Index

Gospel, 2, 5, 12–19, 25, 41–42, 46–49, 54–58, 70, 74–75, 88, 94, 96, 124, 195, 203, 208, 213–19

Hebrew text, 5–6, 15, 20–22, 42, 89, 103, 106, 108–9, 122, 133, 137, 140, 175–76, 183, 185, 201, 205–6, 221
Hermeneutics, 2–4, 9, 13, 16–19, 22–25, 43, 44–60, 64, 70–71, 75, 100, 104, 116–18, 148–50, 180–82, 185, 190–91, 196–98, 211, 214, 220, 223–26
Holiness, 61, 76–86, 92, 108, 188, 213, 216
Holy Spirit, 52, 56, 95
Household code, 61, 69, 120–21, 125–31, 135, 140, 145, 153–56, 166–67, 172–73, 184, 189–193, 204, 218

Interpretation, 15–16, 21–22, 24–26, 36, 50, 56–59, 64, 73, 103, 179–82, 196, 197, 208, 211, 217–22
Introductory formulae, 7, 26, 79, 86, 95, 115, 125, 172, 189, 210, 223
Isaianic narrative, 2, 12–13, 18–20, 25, 67, 69–74, 80, 104, 119, 121, 150–51, 158, 166, 187, 190–91, 210, 213–15
Israel, 2, 11–12, 16–20, 38, 51, 54, 63–68, 72–74, 80–82, 87, 92, 96, 108, 110–14, 118, 121, 124, 135, 144, 147, 151, 155, 165, 173, 180, 187, 196, 205, 212, 214–16, 219

Jew/Jewish, 6, 10–12, 15–16, 18, 21–22, 27–30, 32–34, 39, 45–49, 57–59, 71, 114–17, 121, 158, 180
Judgment, 11–12, 63–64, 68, 74, 101, 105, 113, 121–24, 130–31, 155–57, 162, 166, 168, 177, 180–82, 186, 194–96, 198–201, 203–7, 210, 212–14, 216–17, 219

Levitical formula, 76–78, 83–86, 88, 188, 213, 216, 220

Markedness, 26, 86, 95, 115–16, 172, 189, 210–11, 223–24
Memory, 29–31, 42, 95, 122, 134, 138, 141–42, 183, 185, 222
Messianic woes, 11, 198–99
Metaphor, 10–12, 19, 63, 93, 119, 121
Midrash, 20–24, 100, 116
Moral example, 61–62, 188, 192–93, 213, 215–16

Narrative substructure, 17–19

Oral culture, 30, 39, 42, 223

Participatory Christology, 2, 12, 38, 43, 56, 60–63, 69–71, 77, 82, 115, 149–51, 156, 178–79, 191–93, 197–98, 200, 202, 208–12, 215, 217–19
Paul, 4–5, 7, 13–22, 25–31, 40–43, 56, 72–75, 106, 114–15, 128, 145, 147, 159–65, 208, 220, 223–24
Pesher, 20–25, 48, 59, 75, 90, 116
Peter, as author of 1 Peter, 40–41
Preexistence of Christ, 52–53
Proclamation of the gospel, 12, 25, 41, 55, 64, 74–75, 81–82, 94, 96, 213–14, 217, 219
Prophecy/prophets, 46–57, 60, 63–65, 70, 87, 105, 114, 117, 121, 174, 214–15

Qumran, 20–22, 24–25, 31, 48–49, 58–59, 71, 100, 114, 140
Quotations, 1, 3, 5–9, 14–15, 17–19, 21–22, 25–28, 38–39, 45, 49, 57, 63, 74–77, 95, 97, 107, 115–16, 118–21, 125, 132, 140–42, 173–74, 189–90, 211–15, 217–25

Reader, 14–15, 25–29, 115–17, 141, 161, 187, 189–90, 194, 211, 223
Reader-centered, 28–29, 31, 115, 185, 189, 211, 224
Redemption, 12–13, 19, 56, 66–67, 82, 94–96, 111–13, 147, 150–52, 216
Restoration, 2, 11–13, 20, 25, 38, 43–44, 56–58, 62–64, 69, 70, 74–75, 80,

Subject Index

84, 92, 102, 115, 119, 148, 151, 156, 166, 182, 186, 188, 191, 193, 202, 210, 214, 216–18, 224

Righteousness, 17, 19–20, 57–58, 61–70, 136–37, 146–47, 150–51, 160, 169, 171, 174, 179, 187–88, 192–93, 200–204, 207, 215–16, 219

Sarah, 86n41, 154, 158, 159, 160, 161, 162, 163, 164, 181, 188, 193

Scriptural narrative, 2–4, 10, 12, 16, 31, 34, 37–38, 43–45, 49, 51, 56, 58, 63, 71, 75, 86, 92, 95–96, 104, 115–17, 119, 121, 130, 150, 166, 178, 184, 188–89, 202–3, 209–10, 212–17, 219, 223–25

Septuagint, 3, 5–6, 27, 106, 122, 136, 139–40, 183

Servant/servants, 9, 15, 19–20, 61–72, 74, 80–86, 111, 121, 125, 128–32, 135–36, 140–48, 150–51, 154, 156, 160–67, 171–74, 181–82, 185, 188, 190–93, 202–3, 208–15, 218–19

Spirit of Christ, 47, 51, 53, 55, 57

Stone/stones, 55, 70, 97–106, 110, 115, 117, 119, 184, 188, 190, 214, 216–17

Subtle use of scripture, 1, 8, 14, 27, 31, 39–40, 86, 96, 116, 126, 130, 154, 158, 162, 165, 181, 185, 189–90, 194, 208, 223–24

Suffering. *See* Suffering/glory motif.

Suffering/glory motif, 9–12, 23, 43, 53–54, 58–63, 70–71, 74, 116–17, 199, 214, 224

Temple, 11–13, 74, 85, 97, 99, 102, 104, 115, 119, 121, 174, 198–200, 214, 216

Theological hermeneutic, 13, 45, 116, 225

Vindication, 9, 12–13, 68–70, 74, 161–62, 171–73, 182, 194, 204, 213–14, 217, 219

Author Index

Aalen, S., 68n110
Achtemeier, Paul J. 35n194, 40n223, 40n224, 48–49, 50n27, 80n14, 80n15, 83n27, 86n42, 89n54, 93n73, 93n74, 97n91, 98n95, 98n97, 105n145, 110n167, 112n180, 112n182, 114, 119n219, 124n26, 125n32, 128n48, 130n59, 131n62, 134n70, 137–38, 146, 148n125, 148n131, 154n3, 194n1, 195n2, 195n5, 196n15, 198n25, 203n57, 205n72, 206n79, 207n82
Adams, Edward, 121n4
Agnew, Francis H., 56n52
Aitken, Ellen Bradshaw, 7n18
Allen, Leslie C., 103n128
Atkinson, Kenneth R., 180n100

Bacq, Phillipe, 9n28
Bailey, Daniel P. 67n102
Bal, Mieke, 12, 73
Balch, David L., 125n30, 158n19
Balentine, Samuel E., 78n4
Baltzer, Klaus, 160n29
Balz, H., 187n137
Barclay, John M. G., 34n190
Barr, James, 201
Barrett, C. K., 161n34
Barrier, Jeremy W., 31n179
Barth, Karl, 64
Barton, John, 187n131
Bauckham, Richard J., 21n109, 23n118, 40n225, 44n1, 64n73, 64n77,
69n119, 83n29, 97n92, 97n94, 99n100, 100n108, 100n111, 104n135, 112n184, 118n215, 123n19, 126n34, 170n64
Bauernfeind, O., 113n187
Beale, G. K., 99, 104, 112n186, 119n219
Beare, F. W., 35n192, 40n223, 41n224, 134n69, 134n71, 137n87, 148n125, 157n18, 158n19, 207n82, 209n93
Beaton, Richard, 6
Bechtler, Stephen Richard, 10n41, 33–38, 54n46, 174n78
Ben Zvi, Ehud, 113n192
Berges, Ulrich, 65–66
Bernstein, Moshe J., 79n8
Berrin, Shani L., 100n107, 100n110
Best, Ernest, 35n194, 40n223, 40n224, 48–49, 93n73, 109n161, 109n163, 109n166, 110n167, 112n182, 119n219, 134n70, 138, 148n125, 154n3, 158n23, 172n70, 197n20, 225n11
Beuken, W. A. M., 68n109, 83n30, 159n26, 160n29
Bigg, Charles, 97n91, 99n103, 184
Bird, Jennifer G., 157n18, 158
Blenkinsopp, Joseph, 69n117, 101n113, 111n175, 128n54, 143, 160n29
Bockmuehl, Marcus, 41n225, 42n232
Bonhoeffer, Dietrich, 53n41
Bornemann, W., 94, 126n35, 170n64
Boyer, James, 139n94
Brockington, L. H., 68n111

Author Index

Brooke, George J., 20n99, 20n101, 21, 22n114, 24n127, 24n132, 31n178, 46n6
Brownlee, W. H., 59n62
Brox, Norbert, 40n223, 40n224, 209n93
Brueggemann, Walter, 64n76, 64n79, 66n95, 66n97, 67n106, 81n20, 85n36, 104n140, 113n189, 123n16, 159n26, 160n29, 173n71, 196n13
Brunson, Andrew C., 104n136
Bultmann, Rudolph, 54n45, 80n13, 135, 137–38

Calvin, John, 64
Campbell, Barth L., 24n129, 87n44, 123, 124n21, 180n100
Caragounis, Chrys C., 91n63
Carmignac, J., 24
Carr, David MacLain, 92n69
Carter, Warren, 125n30
Caulley, Thomas Scott, 91n64, 94n81
Ceresko, Anthony R., 126n36
Cherian, Jacob, 95n86
Childs, Brevard S., 1n1, 6n16, 64n79, 65n84, 65n90, 67n101, 67n107, 69n115, 69n117, 105n142, 108n155, 108n158, 110n173, 111n174, 122n10, 122n12, 128n54, 142n100, 142n101, 144, 156n11, 156n12, 159n26, 160n29, 174n75, 187n132, 196n10, 196n12
Chilton, Bruce D., 161n32
Ciampa, Roy E., 7n22, 224n8
Clements, Ronald E., 65n84, 108n156, 108n159, 142n100, 156n11, 186n125
Clifford, Richard, 183n115, 207n83
Crawford, Sidnie White, 180n100
Creach, Jerome F. D., 126n36
Cullmann, Oscar, 41n225

Dalton, William Joseph, 40n223, 93n73, 179–81, 225
Danker, F., 121n5
Davids, Peter H., 35n194, 40n224, 79n7, 86n42, 89n54, 110n171, 112n182, 124n26, 128n49, 134n71, 138, 154n2, 154n3, 157, 159n27, 173n70, 177, 195n3, 200n45, 205n72
Davies, Paul E., 54n46, 187n133
Davila, James R., 158n22, 181n104
Dearman, J. Andrew, 113n190, 113n193, 113n194, 113n195
Deichgräber, R., 80n13, 135
Dennis, John, 121n4
De Waard, Jan, 106
Dimant, D., 24n133
Dodd, C. H., 106
Dryden, J. De Waal, 22n115, 170n65, 192–93, 200n45
Dubis, Mark, 10–11, 148, 194n1, 195n3, 195n6, 195n8, 196n14, 196n15, 197n21, 199, 200n40, 202n57, 205, 208n87
Duhm, Bernhard, 65, 142
Dunn, James D. G., 25, 72

Egan, Patrick T., 168n52
Elledge, C. D., 79n8
Elliott, John H., 2n3, 4, 5n8, 12, 35–36, 40n223, 40n224, 53n40, 55n49, 77n2, 80n14, 80n15, 81n17, 86n42, 88n49, 88n54, 89n58, 91n64, 93, 94n80, 97n91, 98n97, 99, 100n108, 102n124, 105n144, 108–9, 110n167, 112n182, 112n186, 115n202, 119n219, 120n1, 124n25, 124n26, 125n30, 125n32, 126n34, 127, 128n49, 130n59, 131n62, 134n72, 136, 138, 146, 148n131, 151n132, 154n3, 157n18, 158n23, 159n27, 163n37, 166n44, 167n46, 168n47, 168n48, 170n61, 170n62, 170n64, 170n65, 173n70, 176n84, 176n89, 179n96, 182n111, 183n117, 184n122, 194n1, 195n2, 195n3, 195n4, 195n5, 198n26, 199, 200, 201n47, 202n52, 202n55, 204n62, 204n66, 205, 206n76, 207n82, 208n91, 209n93,

209n95, 209n98, 210n100, 225n12
Ellis, E. E., 20n98, 21n105, 222n5
Ellul, Danielle, 87n44, 93n73
Esler, Philip, 161n34

Feine, Gerlinde, 67n102
Feldmeier, Reinhard, 2n3, 36, 40n223, 40n224, 78n3, 79n5, 79n11, 82n26, 89n54, 91n61, 93n74, 93n75, 110n170, 125n30, 127n42, 128, 130, 134n70, 166n44, 184n122, 195n1, 195n5, 204n64m 210n100
Fishbane, Michael A., 14
Fitzmyer, Joseph A., 79n8, 107n153
Foerster, W., 165n40
Forman, Mark, 161n33
Fraenkel, Detlef, 31, 168n52
Fretheim, Terence E., 108n155
Friesen, Ivan D., 63n71, 66n98

Gammie, John G., 191n140
Garrett, Duane A., 129n59
Gerstenberger, Erhard S., 77n1, 78n4
Gielen, Marlis, 129n59
Gignilliat, Mark, 19, 45n4, 64, 65n88, 66n99, 67, 69n116, 69n118, 70n121, 84n33, 147n123
Glenny, Edward W., 5, 6n11, 8n25, 23
Goldingay, John, 66n98, 66n100, 67n107, 81n19, 111n174, 111n177, 111n179, 160n29
Goldstein, H., 129n59
Goppelt, Leonhard, 17n81, 35n194, 40n223, 40n224, 49, 50n26, 53n40, 80n14, 80n15, 83n27, 86n42, 89n54, 120n2, 125n30, 126, 128n49, 129n59, 134n70, 137–38, 158n23, 168n49, 173n70, 178n92, 187n137, 194n1, 195n2, 195n3, 195n4, 198n26, 202n52, 202n57, 205n70, 205n72, 207n82, 208n90, 210n100
Gowan, Donald E., 108n155
Gray, Mark, 122n10

Gréaux, Eric J., 7n18, 8, 11, 154n3, 158n23
Green, Gene, 127n42, 170n61, 170n63, 170n64, 170n65, 188n138
Green, Joel, 35n193, 35n194, 40n223, 53n38, 57, 79, 81n25, 86n42, 87n45, 89n54, 91n68, 92, 93n75, 93n77, 95n87, 97n93, 98–99, 105n146, 110n172, 112n182, 114, 121n3, 126n35, 128–29, 130n61, 134–35, 148n131, 151, 154n2, 168n47, 171n68, 182n111, 183n112, 183n116, 195n3, 195n5, 197n18, 197n21, 202n52, 202n54, 204n63, 206n77, 209n96, 210n100, 215, 225
Greene, Thomas, 3
Greeven, H., 59n58
Grogan, Geoffrey, 103n130, 103n131, 103n132, 126n36
Gruber, Mayer I., 103n132
Grudem, Wayne, 40n223, 204n65
Gschwind, Karl, 179n94
Gundry, Robert H., 225n11
Gunkel, Hermann, 103n128
Gunn, David M., 182n108
Guthrie, Donald, 40n223

Hafemann, Scott, 11n50
Hägglund, Fredrik, 187n132
Hanson, A. T., 13n55, 21n105
Harrington, Daniel J., 187n132
Harris, William V., 27n151, 38n218
Harris, J. Rendel, 31n176
Hatch, Edwin, 31n176, 41
Hays, Richard B., 7–8, 11, 13n55, 14–19, 21, 31, 56, 58n55, 72–73, 75, 81n18, 100, 115, 160n30, 161n33, 171n69, 190n139, 225n9
Head, Peter M., 39n219
Heikel, Ivar A., 141n98
Hengel, Martin, 6n16, 41n225, 84n32
Hermisson, Hans-Jürgen, 64n79
Hill, David, 99n104
Hofius, Otfried, 67n105, 86n42
Hollander, John, 7, 14

Hooker, Morna D., 84n32
Horrell, David G., 12n51, 36, 40n223, 41n224, 110n170, 114, 124n23, 124n27, 125n30, 126n34, 157n18, 163n36, 174n79, 197n20, 203n58
Hort, F. J. A., 40n223, 48, 80n15, 97n91, 99n103
Horton, Fred L., 79n8
Howe, Frederic R., 54n46
Hughes, Julie A., 180n100
Hüllstrung, Wolfgang, 67n102

Jaffee, Martin S., 24n131
Janowski, Bernd, 67
Jobes, Karen H., 5n9, 6n16, 40n223, 41n224, 78n3, 89n56, 93n74, 93n75, 93n78, 98n96, 99n105, 106n147, 110n168, 112n182, 118n216, 124n28, 126n35, 127n42, 137n86, 148, 157n18, 161n33, 168n51, 170n63, 170n64, 171n67, 173n70, 176n85, 183n113, 195n2, 197n17, 198n26, 200, 203n60, 205n72, 208n92, 209n93, 210n100
Johnson, Dennis E., 198n26
Joosten, Jan, 80n12
Joseph, Abson Prédestin, 72n127, 73–74

Kaiser, Otto, 102n116, 102n120, 102n122, 156n13, 196n10
Kaiser, Walter C., 45n2
Kelly, J. N. D., 35n194, 41n224, 80n15, 99n103, 100n108, 137n87, 154n3, 158n23, 172n70, 198n25
Kelsey, David H., 45n3
Kiley, Mark, 158
Kittel, Gerhard, 68n110
Koch, Dietrich-Alex, 25, 26, 27, 115, 116
Köstenberger, Andreas J., 8n24
Kraus, Hans-Joachim, 103n126, 103n128
Krause, Wolfgang, 6n16
Kreuzer, Siegfried, 133n66
Kristeva, Julia, 8n23

Laato, Antii, 142n100
Lamau, Marie-Louise, 129n59
Lapham, F. Peter, 41n225
Lee, J. A. L., 155n5
Légasse, S., 129n59
Liebengood, Kelly D., 124n29, 127n47, 198n26, 201n51
Liebreich, Leon J., 126n38
Lim, Timothy H., 20–21, 24–25, 41, 43n233
Limburg, James, 169n59
Lindars, Barnabas, 99n99
Lohse, Eduard, 135n75
Longenecker, Bruce W., 72, 73n129
Luther, Martin, 179n93

Maier, Gerhard, 225n11
Marcus, Joel, 92n69
Marks, Herbert, 17n82
Marshall, I. Howard, 13n55, 40n223
Martin, Troy W., 10–11, 87n46, 93n73, 158, 225n10
Mays, James Luther, 103, 113n194, 126n36, 169n57
Mbuvi, Andrew M., 11–13, 85, 165n43, 182n110, 198n25, 199, 208n88
McCartney, Dan G., 5n8, 7n18, 8, 9n31, 22n115, 22n116, 23, 37n209, 40n223, 40n224, 93n77, 158n23
McDonald, Lee M., 22n111
McDonough, Sean M., 121n4
McKane, William, 129n56
McKelvey, R. J., 198n25
McKenzie, John L., 160n29
McLay, R. Timothy, 6n13, 22
Melugin, Roy F., 65n82, 66n100, 68, 82n23, 92n70
Menken, M. J. J., 103n126
Mettinger, Tryggve N. D., 81n19, 81n20
Metzger, Bruce M., 79n8
Metzner, Rainer, 225n11
Michaels, J. Ramsey, 35n194, 40n223, 40n224, 69n115, 79n9, 80n13, 80n14, 80n15, 82n27, 83n29, 95, 97n91, 98n95, 98n97, 105n144, 112n182, 112n185, 112n186, 113n187, 115n202, 124n25, 125n32, 126, 127n39, 127n41, 128n48, 130n61, 134n70,

134n71, 135, 137–38, 146n118,
148n131, 154n3, 157n15,
158n23, 167n46, 168n47,
168n48, 168n51, 170n61,
170n65, 175n82, 184n119,
185n123, 194n1, 195n3, 195n4,
195n5, 196n14, 196n15, 198n25,
202n53, 202n56, 204n65,
205n72, 207n82, 208n90,
209n98, 210n99
Milgrom, Jacob, 78n4, 79
Moyise, Steve, 8n23, 8n24, 8n27,
22n113, 29n165, 59–60, 71,
81n18, 89n54, 89n58, 91n62,
91n67, 93n72, 103n126,
106n147, 112n180, 112n182,
112n186, 115, 117, 119n218,
174n77, 175n80, 178n90,
197n17, 208n89, 211n102

Neusner, Jacob, 24n132
Nickelsburg, George W. E., 180
North, Christopher R., 65n82

Osborne, T. P., 2n2, 5n8, 7n18, 8n25, 9,
138, 148n125, 169n55, 201n47,
201n49, 206n79, 225n10
Oswalt, John N., 64n72, 65n83, 69n117,
81n21, 85n36, 105n142,
113n188, 128n54, 156n10,
156n11, 156n12, 160n29,
173n72, 174n75, 196n13

Paine, David, 111n177
Pao, David W., 92n69, 96n88
Paton-Williams, David, 65, 66, 173n71
Patsch, Hermann, 138n91
Payne, Philip Barton, 45n2, 160n29
Pearson, Sharon Clark, 2n2, 9, 10,
23, 54n46, 142–43, 148n125,
148n126
Pennington, Jonathan T., 121n4
Peppard, Michael, 10n36
Perdue, Leo G., 207n86
Perkins, Pheme, 41n225
Pietersma, Albert, 6n16
Platt, Elizabeth Ellen, 157
Pleket, H. W., 38n218

Porter, Stanley E., 7n17, 7n20, 8n23, 139
Porton, Gary, 24

Quinn, Jerome D., 91n64

Rajak, Tessa, 32n182
Reicke, Bo, 40n223, 129n59, 179n94
Rembaum, Joel E., 151n134
Rendtorff, Rolf, 186–187n127, 187n128
Rensburg, Fika van, 174n77, 175n80,
178n90
Reventlow, Henning, 65n82
Richard, Earl, 2n2, 40n223, 54n46,
82n24, 91n61, 93n75, 148n125,
158n23
Rowley, H. H., 113n190

Safrai, Shemuel, 39n220
Sanders, James A., 22n111
Sandevoir, Pierre, 155n4
Sasse, H., 155n8
Sawyer, John F. A., 160n29, 162n35,
187n132
Schlosser, Jacques, 2n2, 2n3, 128n49,
148n125
Schmitt, John J., 156n11
Schnabel, Eckhard J., 32n181, 32n183
Schniewind, J., 112n185
Schrage, Wolfgang, 125n30
Schreiner, Thomas R., 35n194, 40n223,
41n224, 51, 78n3, 91n65,
151n132, 163n37, 204n65
Schutter, William L., 5, 7–9, 22, 24,
37–38, 41n227, 45, 47–49, 53,
58–60, 63, 75, 78n3, 83n29,
84, 89n58, 90–91, 94n84,
96, 100n108, 100n111, 110,
112n182, 112n185, 116–17,
118n215, 120n2, 124n24, 125,
126n35, 134, 135n78, 148,
154n3, 168n51, 172n70, 195n3,
197–99, 204n65, 205, 207n81,
207n82, 208n89, 222
Schwank, B., 170n64
Seitz, Christopher, 65, 67n106, 111, 143,
144, 156n12, 173n71
Seitz, M., 59n58

Author Index

Selwyn, E. G., 40n223, 41n224, 46–49, 97n91, 99, 100n108, 109n165, 112n182, 129n59, 137n87, 148n125, 154n3, 158
Senior, Donald, 40n224
Sheppard, Gerald T., 187n131
Shimada, Kazuhito, 130n59
Silva, Moisés, 5n9
Ska, J. L., 108n157
Skehan, P. W., 140n96
Sly, Dorothy I., 158
Smith, Gary V., 66n98, 67n106, 102, 104n140, 156n11, 156n13, 196n10
Snodgrass, Klyne R., 21n105, 94n84, 106, 107n153, 126n35, 170n64
Sommer, Benjamin D., 187
Sperber, Alexander, 41n229, 161n32
Stählin, G., 47n12
Stanley, Christopher D., 26–31, 38–39, 41–42, 43n233, 106, 114n197, 115–16, 186, 211n101, 222n4
Stansell, Gary V., 156n11, 156n13
Stauffer, Ethelbert, 10n33
Stenning, J. F., 161n32
Strathmann, H., 53n42
Stuhlmacher, Peter, 67n102
Sundberg, Albert C., Jr., 89n54
Sweeney, Marvin Alan, 63n71, 156n11, 156n12, 186n125, 187n129

Tasker, R. V. G., 13n55
Teichert, Horst, 129n59
Terrien, Samuel L., 103n131, 103n132, 169n58
Teugels, Lieve M., 24
Thomas, Rosalind, 30n172
Thurén, Lauri, 40n224, 87n43, 93
Tov, Emanuel, 6n16, 222n4
Trebilco, Paul R., 32–33
Tuñi, Joseph Oriel, 54n46

Uhlig, Torsten, 64n73, 69n117, 128n54
Ulrich, Eugene, 22n111, 110n166, 140n96

Van der Louw, Theo A. W., 183n114
VanGemeren, Willem A., 126n36
Vanhoozer, Kevin J., 45n3

Van Unnik, W. C., 40n223, 127n40, 129n59, 131n63, 168n50, 188n138
Vermes, Geza, 50n25, 50n28
Vermeylen, Jacques, 65n84
Voorwinde, S., 5, 7n18, 8n24

Wagner, J. Ross, 14n63, 16, 17n78, 18–21, 22n110, 28–30, 31n176, 42, 81n20, 81n22, 102n123, 103n126, 105n143, 114n197, 115, 118n213, 119n217, 146n121, 161n33, 174n76, 187, 196n11, 197, 222
Wallace, Daniel B., 98n97, 139n94
Waltke, Bruce K., 129n56, 129n58, 183n115, 207n84
Watson, Francis, 28n164
Watts, John D., 63n71, 64n74, 66n95, 66n98, 69n120, 81n20, 92n69, 92n70, 102n114, 104n136, 173n71, 187n134
Watts, Rikki E., 187
Weiser, Artur, 103n129, 103n132, 126n36, 169n60
Wells, Jo Bailey, 83n30
Wengst, Klaus, 80n13
Wenham, Gordon J., 78n4
Westermann, Claus, 103n132, 182n108
Wilcox, Peter, 65–66, 173n71
Wildberger, Hans, 102
Wilk, Florian, 6n14, 14n63
Williams, Travis B., 123n20, 127n47
Williamson, H. G. M., 64n75, 65n84, 67n106, 187n129
Willis, Sam K., 84n32
Wilson, Todd A., 161n33
Windisch, H., 35n192
Winter, Bruce W., 123n20, 129n59
Witherington, Ben, III, 72
Woan, Sue, 103, 127n45, 167n45, 168n51, 170n64, 170n65
Wright, N. T., 10n37, 72

Young, Edward J., 65n83

Ziegler, Joseph, 6n16, 119n217, 122n9, 137n85, 140, 141n98, 175n81

Scripture Index

Old Testament

Genesis	31, 86n41, 158–59, 162–64
6–7	181
6	180
6:1–8	180
12	158
17:16	159n25
18	158
18:10	159n25
18:12	154, 158, 160, 163, 166, 207
18:14	159n25
20	158
21	158
22	83n29
22:17	113

Exodus	12, 31, 81n19, 108, 110–11, 115, 119
6:2–8	113
6:6	80n16
12	108
13:9	205
14	108
19	98, 108, 110–11, 119
19:5–6	86n41, 97, 107–8, 112, 123n19, 213, 216, 218
19:5	112
19:6	55, 76, 98, 108–12, 188
29:38	83
33:5–6	155n8
35:22	155
36[39]	155

Leviticus	31, 76–78, 84–86, 146, 216, 220
1	145
1:2–9	145
1:8	145
1:10–13	145
1:12	145
1:14–17	145
1:17	145
3:5	145n117
4:6	84n31
4:17	84n31
5:1	84n31
5:6–7	84
5:9	84n31
5:17	84n31
6:20	84n31

Leviticus (continued)

7:18	84n31
8:11	84n31
8:30	84n31
10:17	84n31
11:44	78
11:45	78
12:6	83
14:7	84n31
14:10	83
14:13	83
14:16	84n31
14:27	84n31
16:14–15	84n31
16:16	84
16:19	84n31
16:21–22	84
16:22	84n31
17–27	78n4
17:16	84n31
19:2	44, 78, 125
19:8	84n31
19:34	78
20:7	78
20:17	84n31
20:19–20	84n31
20:26	78
22:9	84n31
22:16	84n31
23:18	83
23:20	83
24:15	84n31

Numbers

6:14	83
8:7	84n31
19:4	84n31
19:18–19	84n31
19:21	84n31
24:17	55n47
28–29	83
31:50	155

Deuteronomy 31

3:24	205
4:34	205
5:15	205
7:6	110n169
7:8	81n16
7:19	205
9:26	81n16, 205
11:2	205
13:5	81n16
14:2	110n169
14:21	110n169
15:15	81n16
18:15	55n47
21:23	145, 146n118
24:18	81n16
26:19	110n169
28:9	110n169

Joshua

8:29	145n116
10:26	145n116

Judges

9:9	145n116
9:11	145n116
9:31	145n116

1 Samuel

1–2	160n29
10:6	53n39

2 Samuel

1:24	155n8
7:23	81n16
23:2	53n39

1 Kings

18:23	145n116

2 Kings

19:21	156n9

1 Chronicles

17:21	81n16

Scripture Index

Esther

	10n40
5:14	145n116
7:10	145n116

Psalms
1, 5n9, 31, 95, 119, 126, 168–69, 188

7:17	133n65
9:15	112, 156n9
10[11]:5	133n65
22:14	194, 213
26[27]:12	133n65
33[34]	44, 74, 87, 93–94, 116, 125, 127, 167–73, 177–78, 188, 201, 215–16, 223
33:5	169
33:8	91, 96
33:9	94–95, 112, 126, 177, 184, 207, 213
33:10	170–71
33:12–18	169
33:12–16	167
33:12	130, 171
33:13–17	94, 126–27, 131–32, 153, 167–70, 186, 188, 191–93, 211, 213, 221
33:14–15	169, 221
33:15–17	127
33:15	126, 169, 188
33:16	201, 207
33:17–19	171
33:17–18	171
33:17	169, 207
33:18	169
33:21	172
33:23	171
54:23	205
57[58]:3	133n65
71[72]:6	133n65
72[73]:28	156n9
92:12–15	112n186
117[118]	74, 103–4
117:1–4	103
117:5–18	103
117:8–9	103
117:10–13	103
117:10–11	103
117:17–18	103
117:19–22	103
117:19–20	103
117:22	44, 55, 97, 99n99, 100–105, 117, 188, 213, 216–17, 220
117:23–29	103

Proverbs
31, 129, 164, 221–23

3:25	159, 160, 163, 166, 170, 188
3:32–35	207
3:32	207
3:33	207
3:34	160, 163, 194, 206–8, 210, 213, 222–23
3:35	207
10:12	134, 153, 183–84, 202, 213
11:3	44
11:31	194, 201–2, 204, 210, 213, 216, 222–23
20:29	155n8
24:21	125, 129–30, 187, 207n80, 221
24:21–22	129
29:17	155n8

Isaiah
1–3, 8n22, 10–12, 14n63, 15, 17–21, 25, 29, 31, 41–44, 48, 58n55, 62–67, 70–72, 74–77, 80, 85–86, 88–89, 94–95, 101, 104–5, 108, 110–13, 115, 119, 121, 123, 125, 128, 130, 134, 137–40, 142–44, 148, 154, 156–58, 162–67, 169–78, 181, 185–91, 193, 196–97, 210–12, 214, 216–17, 219–22

1–39	64n75, 143

Isaiah (continued)

Reference	Pages
1–4	156
1:4	63, 110
1:8	156
1:16–17	63
1:17	64
1:19	82
2–3	157
2:8–9	104
3–4	156
3	154, 162, 164
3:14–15	64, 156
3:16–26	156
3:16–17	156–57
3:16	156n9, 157
3:17	156n9
3:18–26	155–56
3:18–23	156
3:18	154–57, 162, 166, 213
4:4	156n9
6	64, 111, 113
6:1	64n73
6:3	68, 71
6:10	65
6:11	48, 51
7–8	113n191
7	104
7:2–7	104
7:10–17	104
7:11	85n35
7:18–25	104
8	104, 174, 218
8:1–4	104
8:5–10	104
8:8	105
8:11–18	105n143, 146n121
8:11–15	64, 105
8:11	64, 105
8:12–13	105, 131, 153, 163, 170, 174–75, 177, 178n90, 213, 216, 218, 221–22
8:12	170, 176
8:13	170–71, 174, 176, 207
8:14	5, 55, 70, 97, 100–101, 104–6, 117, 119, 188, 213, 217, 220
8:16–22	105
8:16–18	105
8:16	64, 105–6
8:18	64
8:19–22	105
8:20	105
9	128n52
9:2	113
9:7	64
9:8—10:4	122
9:8–12	122
9:12	122n11
9:13–17	122
9:18–21	122
10:1–4	122–23
10:1–2	123
10:3	121–24, 127, 157, 170, 182, 185–86, 188, 193, 213, 216, 221
10:20–21	196
10:22	64
10:32	156n9
10:33	85n35
11	196–97
11:2–3	198
11:2	62, 70, 74, 194–200, 203–4, 207n80, 210–13, 216–17, 219, 221–22, 225
11:3	196
11:11	196
11:16	196
13:6	121n6
13:9	121n6
24–27	101
28	101
28:5	194, 205, 213
28:6	205n68
28:14–19	101
28:14–15	102
28:16	55, 70, 97, 99n99, 100–102, 104–5, 117–19, 188, 213, 217, 220

Scripture Index

28:18–22	102	42:24	147
37:22	156n9	43	98, 113, 119
40–66	2, 19, 20, 64, 67, 68n108, 70, 142–43, 173	43:1–13	66, 111
		43:5	171
		43:16–17	111
40–55	11, 15, 58n55, 64n75, 92, 128, 146, 148	43:18–19	111
		43:19–20	111
40–53	64, 68n108, 166, 171, 190, 219	43:19	140
		43:20–22	97
40–52	143	43:20–21	70, 86n41, 107, 111–12, 123n19, 213, 216, 218
40–48	65–66, 111, 143		
40	44, 64, 74, 81n22, 87, 92–93, 95, 111, 177, 194, 203, 212, 214, 216–17	43:20	111–12
		43:21	55, 111–12, 119, 123n19
		43:24	147
40:1–11	81, 88, 92	44:1–2	66
40:1–2	92	44:21	66
40:2	146–47	44:22	147
40:3–5	92	44:27	182n108
40:5	68–69, 71	45:4	66
40:6–9	90, 217, 220	45:8	140
40:6–8	62, 70, 88–92, 94–96, 125, 184–85, 203, 210, 213–14	47:13	140
		48:14	81n21
		48:16	65
40:6–7	89n54, 92	48:20	55, 66, 68n108
40:6	89	49–55	69n117, 143
40:8	89, 93, 96n88, 177n89, 184, 203, 207	49–54	143
		49–53	67
		49	65–66, 74
40:9–11	92	49:1–13	65
40:9	171	49:1–7	71
40:10	81	49:1–6	142
40:11	92	49:3	68
40:21	112	49:5	66, 68n108
41	148	49:6	151
41:8–9	64, 66	49:7	68n108
41:8	111	49:18	156
42	113	50	173
42:1–9	65	50:1	147
42:1–4	111, 142	50:2	182n108
42:1	66	50:4–9	65, 142
42:9–10	113	50:8–10	172, 174
42:9	140	50:8	173
42:10–17	113	50:9–10	177, 178n90
42:12	55, 113	50:9	172–73, 177, 188
42:16	113	51:2	158, 160
42:19	66, 68n108	51:9	81n21
42:19–25	111		

Isaiah (continued)

51:10	182n108
51:12–13	171, 178n90
52	80–82, 86
52:1–12	88n50
52:2	81, 156n9
52:3	80–81, 88, 213
52:4	81
52:7	81
52:10	19, 66, 81
52:13—53:12	65, 142
52:13	64n73, 69, 84, 85n35
52:14	136
52:15	84
53–66	190
53–54	213
53	2, 9, 23, 38n217, 44, 55, 56n49, 61, 64, 66–71, 74, 79, 81–84, 86, 116, 128–29, 131–36, 138, 140, 142–48, 150–51, 153n1, 156, 161, 173, 179, 181–86, 189, 191–94, 200n46, 202–3, 208–9, 211–12, 215–16, 218, 221
53:1–2	136
53:1	81
53:2	140
53:3	68
53:4–6	136, 147
53:4	69, 84, 136, 146, 202, 221
53:5	84, 133, 136, 138, 186, 221
53:6	84, 135, 138, 186, 203, 209
53:7	69, 82–84, 135, 145, 213
53:8–9	83, 140
53:8	84, 136, 140
53:9	132–34, 136, 138, 140–41, 146–47, 186, 188, 192, 202, 221
53:10	67, 68n109, 84, 85, 136, 137, 161, 200n46
53:11–12	147, 181n107
53:11	67–68, 84, 136, 140, 147, 202
53:12	67, 84–85, 133, 135–36, 146–47, 161n31, 202–3, 221
54–66	67–69, 143, 161, 165–66, 171, 190–91, 193, 212, 218–19
54	67, 69, 74, 128, 153n1, 154, 157–66, 181–82, 191, 193, 207n80
54:1–8	160, 166, 191
54:1–4	162
54:1–3	160, 161n33
54:1	158–59, 161, 163
54:3	67, 160, 164–65
54:4	159, 163, 170, 188
54:9–14	188, 191
54:9–11	181
54:9–10	182n108
54:9	67, 181n106
54:10	182
54:11–17	71
54:11	68, 182, 191
54:13	160
54:14–17	160
54:14	160, 191
54:17	68, 88n50, 160, 164–65, 182, 191
55:7	146
55:9	85n35
55:10–13	182n108
56–66	143
56	67n106
57	104
57:1	19
57:7	85n35
58:13	121n6
60:14	151
60:18	133n65
61:1	53n39
61:9	151, 166
61:10	155–56

Scripture Index   263

62:4–5	166
62:8	81
62:11	156n9
62:12	111
63	69, 74
63:15–19	68, 71
63:15	68
63:17	130
65:8–9	68
65:13–16	68
65:23	166
66	69, 74, 104
66:11	68, 71
66:12–14	68
66:12	68, 71, 111
66:14	68
66:18–19	69, 71
66:18	68, 71
66:19	68, 71, 111

Jeremiah   10n40

2:32	155–56
4:30	155n8
4:31	156n9
6:2	156n9
6:15	122
6:23	156n9
10:15	122
13:18	205n70
25:29	198
32:15	199
46:10	121n6

Lamentations

1:6	156n9
2:1	156n9
2:4	156n9
2:8	156n9
2:10	156n9
2:13	156n9
4:22	156n9

Ezekiel   10n40, 110n173, 200

7:20	155n8
9	37, 199
9–11	199
9:6	37, 198–200, 201n51, 204
11:5	53n39
13:5	121n6
14:14	181n105
14:20	181n105
23:40	156
30:3	121n6
46:4	83
46:6	83
46:13	83

Daniel   10n40, 22

8:24	110n169

Hosea   108, 112–15, 119

1–2	97, 107, 113–14, 117, 119, 213, 218
1	207n80
1:3–9	113
1:4–5	113
1:6–7	113
1:6	108
1:9	108, 113, 123n19
2:1–3	108
2:1	108, 113–14
2:3	113
2:16	207n80
2:23	123n19
2:25	108, 114
4:16	81n27
12:1	110n169

Joel

1:15	121n6
2:1	121n6
2:11	121n6
2:31	121n6
3:14	121n6

Amos

5:18	122n6
5:20	122n6

Obadiah

1:15	122n6

Micah

1:13	156n9
4:8	156n9
4:10	156n9
4:13	156n9

Nahum

2:10	155n8

Habakkuk

2:1–3	55n47
2:1–2	50
2:3	50

Zephaniah

1:6	50, 59
1:7	122n6
3:14	156n9

Zechariah

	47, 200
2:14	156n9
9–14	198n26
9:9	156n9
13:9	198n26
14:5	110

Malachi

	200
3:1–5	199
3:1–3	198n26
3:1	198
4:5	122

Apocrypha and Pseudepigrapha

1 Maccabees

	10n40

2 Maccabees

	10n40
7:16	88n50
11:19	52n35

3 Maccabees

	10n40
4:7	52n36

4 Maccabees

	10n40
4:4	52n35
11:12	52n35
12:14	52n35
15:31	181n103

Sirach/Ecclesiasticus

18:20	122
44:17–18	181
47:6	205

Wisdom of Solomon

	181n104
9:15	88n50
14:5–6	181
14:8	88n50

Apocalypse of Abraham

	11n42

2 Baruch (Syriac)

	10n40, 11n42
77:23	181n105

1 Enoch

	10n40, 179–80
6–19	179n97
10:2	181n105
64–69	179n97
65–68	181
65:1	181n105
65:12	181

67:1	181n105
67:2	181
67:3	181
67:4–11	181
106-7	181n105
106-8	179n97

2 Enoch

7:1–3	180n100
18:3	180n100

4 Ezra

	10n40

Jubilees

	11n42, 31
5–10	181n105
5	180n100

Odes of Solomon

	31
19:1–2	95n86

Psalms of Solomon

17.39–44	197

Sibylline Oracles

	10n40
1:154–343	181n105
6:115–18	198

Testament of Naphtali

3:5	180n100

Testament of Abraham

	158

New Testament

Matthew

3:16	197
4:4	79n8
4:6	79n8
4:10	79n8
5:11	225
21:42	103n126
24:37–38	182n109
26:31	79n8

Mark

12:10–11	103n126
13:11	198n26
14:27	79n8

Luke

1–2	47
3:4	7
4:10	79n8
6:22	225
17:26–27	182n109

20:17	103n126
24:46	79n8

John

1:32	197
5:39	47
19:36	172

Acts

	33, 40n222, 48n17, 96n88
1:20	79n8
2:9–10	32
4:5	128n52
5:30	146n118
6:9	42
7:22	128n50
10:39	146n118
15:13–21	97n92
15:15	79n8

Scripture Index

Acts (continued)

20:21	52n35
23:5	79n8
24:24	52n36
26:6	52n35

Romans   11, 18, 29, 72, 105–7, 114, 187

1:1	128
1:17	79n8
1:23	88n50
3:4	79n8
4:19–21	161n33
8:9	51n32
8:17	165
9–11	16
9	100n112
9:15	114n197
9:18	114n197
9:24	114
9:25–26	114
9:25	114
9:30	114
9:33	106n149, 220
10:15–16	81n22
10:15	79n8
11:9	7
12:19	79n8
13:1–7	129n59
14:11	79n8
15:4	16n76

1 Corinthians

1:2	40n222
1:19	79n8
3:19	79n8
9:5	40n222
9:25	88n50
10:7	79n8
10:11	16n76
15:5	40n222
15:45	79n8
15:53	88n50
15:54	88n50

2 Corinthians

5:15—6:10	84n33

Galatians   11, 161–62

1:10	128n50
1:18	40n222
2:7–14	40n222
2:11–14	42n232
3:10	79n8
3:13	79n8, 145–46
3:28–29	165
3:29	161
4	161–62
4:21–31	161, 163n38
4:22	161
4:23	161
4:25	161
4:26	161
4:27	79n8, 161
4:27–28	159
4:28	162
4:30	161
4:31	162
5:1	161

Ephesians   153n1, 191

1:17	197
2:12	165
3:5	47n12
3:6	165

Philippians

1:1	128n50

Colossians   153n1, 191

2:25	52n35

Hebrews   105n143

11:7	181n105
11:9	165

Scripture Index 267

James	183	1:12	12, 40–41, 48, 52, 55–57, 87, 180, 203, 213
1:9–11	89n54		
1:18	89n54	1:13—2:10	22, 43, 74, 76–77, 93, 120, 213
4:6	207		
		1:13—2:3	97
1 Peter	1–6, 8–13, 16–25, 27, 29, 31–38, 40–49, 51, 53–60, 63, 69–71, 73–78, 81–82, 85, 88–90, 92, 97, 102–4, 106–7, 112, 114, 116–18, 120–23, 125–26, 128–30, 132, 134, 138–43, 146–51, 153, 156–59, 161–63, 165, 167–72, 174–75, 177–79, 181, 183, 185–86, 189–98, 201–3, 205–6, 210–11, 213, 215, 217, 219–22, 224, 225, 226	1:13–21	77, 86
		1:13	46, 54n43, 77, 80, 86–87, 90, 149
		1:14—2:10	87n46
		1:14–21	87n46
		1:14–19	12
		1:14–15	92
		1:14	34, 87–88
		1:15–16	76, 88, 97n90
		1:15	57, 77, 79, 88, 97n90, 125–26
		1:16	77–79, 82–83, 125, 188–89, 210, 215, 220
		1:17	11–12, 34, 77, 120
		1:18–21	10, 80, 86, 146
		1:18–19	81–82, 99n101
		1:18	34, 77, 80–81, 84, 88, 92
1:1	10–12, 32–34, 82, 120, 174	1:19	81–86, 90, 145, 147, 215
1:2	56, 88, 207n80	1:20	53, 57, 86
1:3–12	10, 59, 120	1:21	82, 84–86, 149, 207n80, 219
1:3	46, 56–57, 88, 90, 97n90, 149, 207n80	1:22—2:3	94, 96, 184
		1:22–25	70, 87–88, 92, 95
1:4	164n39	1:22	88, 121, 182, 184
1:5	54n43, 180, 199, 207n80	1:23	87–90, 92–93, 115, 118n214, 125–26, 184, 203, 207n80
1:6–7	194		
1:6	34, 195	1:24–25	23, 62, 88, 90, 93n72, 125, 131, 185, 203, 210–11, 214, 217, 220
1:7	34, 46, 54n42, 90, 97n90, 149		
1:8	97n90, 195		
1:10–12	2, 9–10, 22–23, 43–45, 50, 54, 57–59, 63, 70–71, 75, 117, 208n89, 213–15	1:24	79, 89, 189, 207n81, 210
		1:25	12, 41, 74, 89–94, 96, 118n214, 177, 203, 207, 214, 219
1:10	46–51, 113, 219		
1:11	9, 23, 35, 47, 53–54, 56, 60, 62, 70–71, 90, 195, 199, 202, 208	2:1–3	87, 93, 95
		2:1	87, 93
		2:2–3	95

Scripture Index

1 Peter *(continued)*

2:2	87, 93, 115, 184
2:3	57, 87n46, 90–91, 94–96, 112, 126, 177, 188
2:4–10	70, 74, 87n46, 97–98, 111, 115–18, 150, 199, 214, 218
2:4–9	99, 119n219
2:4–5	79n5, 88, 97, 100, 118–19, 126, 132, 200, 218
2:4	55, 87n46, 97–99, 101, 104, 115, 118, 207n80, 214, 217
2:5	55, 76, 97–99, 110, 118, 149, 207n80, 218–19
2:6–10	2, 23, 88, 97, 115, 118–19, 125, 130, 147, 184, 186, 189, 196, 211, 218, 222
2:6–8	55, 97, 99–101, 104–5, 115, 118, 120, 131, 188, 217, 220
2:6–7	97n90
2:6	7, 79, 97, 106n149, 189, 210, 214
2:7–8	104
2:7	97–98, 100, 102, 202, 220
2:8	5, 98, 101, 105, 115, 154, 174, 181, 202, 214
2:9–10	97, 107, 115, 118, 123n19, 216, 218
2:9	76, 86n41, 97n90, 99, 107–13, 118–19, 123n19, 174, 219
2:10	107, 113–14, 207n80
2:11—4:11	61n67, 74, 120, 145, 153, 185, 213
2:11—3:7	167
2:11–12	11, 120, 123–24, 130
2:11	10, 12, 34, 82, 120, 127, 174, 188
2:12—4:11	43
2:12—3:16	2
2:12	35n191, 38n214, 54n43, 62, 120–24, 127, 144, 147, 154, 157, 168, 170, 180, 182, 185, 188, 192, 202, 207n80, 216, 219, 221
2:13—3:9	127
2:13–17	37–38, 121, 125, 127, 129n59, 131
2:13	125, 207n80
2:14–15	125
2:14	38n214, 123n17, 126–27, 154, 168, 170
2:15	57, 123, 127, 154, 170, 188, 202, 207n80
2:16	125–28, 144, 150, 165, 170, 181, 190, 207n80, 218
2:17	129, 130, 171, 187, 207n80, 221
2:18—3:9	189
2:18—3:7	120, 204
2:18–25	61, 63, 121, 131, 150, 184n120, 190–91, 218
2:18	38n217, 131, 154, 170, 187
2:19–20	127
2:19	35, 61, 123, 131, 149n131, 154, 171, 207n80
2:20	35, 61, 123n17, 126–27, 131–32, 134, 149n131, 154, 170, 188, 207n80
2:21–25	2, 10, 61, 80, 132, 137–38, 144, 147, 149n131, 168, 190, 196, 202, 211, 218
2:21–24	137
2:21	2, 20, 35, 55–57, 61, 67, 70, 79, 136, 145, 151, 167, 179, 190,

Scripture Index 269

	192, 200, 208, 216, 218–19	3:10	168–69
2:22–25	20, 55, 67, 69, 72, 85, 86, 116, 128, 131–32, 134, 136, 138–39, 145, 148–49, 151, 181, 185, 192–93, 211, 221	3:11	123n17, 126, 169, 188
		3:12	123n17, 125, 169, 188, 207
		3:13—4:1	61
		3:13—4:6	121
		3:13–22	172
2:22–24	147, 214	3:13–18	149, 215
2:22–23	61	3:13–17	37–38, 41, 124, 131, 153, 172, 177, 215
2:22	123n17, 132–34, 138, 146, 183, 186, 188, 192, 202, 221	3:13–15	177–78
		3:13	170, 173, 177, 188
2:23	35, 61, 132, 135, 167, 192, 203	3:14–15	55n48, 105, 164, 170, 174–75, 177, 187, 211, 216, 218, 221–22
2:24–25	186		
2:24	134, 136–38, 140, 142, 145–47, 183, 202, 215, 221	3:14	35, 61, 147, 170, 176n84, 187, 195
		3:15–16	177–78
2:25	123n17, 137–40, 209, 221	3:15	38n214, 57, 90, 149, 174, 176–77, 207
3	79, 86n41, 116, 159–62, 169	3:16	35n191, 54n43, 125, 149, 170, 187, 195, 201–2, 219
3:1–7	121, 153, 165		
3:1–6	151, 162, 191, 193	3:17	35, 55n48, 57, 61, 123, 127, 168, 170, 178, 188, 207n80
3:1–4	153		
3:1	41, 154, 214		
3:2–6	157	3:18–22	10, 149, 153, 172, 179
3:2	154, 171, 187		
3:3–4	154	3:18	35, 57, 61, 123n17, 134, 147, 149, 179, 181, 184, 189, 192, 202, 207n80, 215
3:3	127, 154–57, 162		
3:4	123, 154, 207n80		
3:5–6	154		
3:5	162, 207n80	3:19–20	179–80
3:6	86n41, 123n17, 126–27, 154, 157–59, 161–62, 170, 181, 187–88, 207	3:19	179, 182
		3:20–21	86n41
		3:20	57, 181–82, 188, 193, 207n80
3:7	154, 164–66	3:21	149, 170, 182, 191, 207n80
3:8–12	125n30, 153, 166–68, 172		
		3:22	57, 149, 180, 191, 207n80
3:9	35n191, 126, 167–68, 170	4:1	35, 55n48, 61, 134, 184, 192, 202
3:10–12	93, 94, 123, 126–27, 131–32, 170–71, 177, 186, 188, 211, 221, 223		
		4:2–3	127
		4:2	123, 207n80
3:10–11	168	4:3–5	34

1 Peter (continued)

4:3	120–21, 189, 202
4:4	35n191
4:5–7	182
4:5	180
4:6	57, 207n80
4:7–11	121, 182, 184n120
4:7–9	120
4:7	54n43, 123, 157, 180, 188, 192, 219
4:8	5, 88n48, 121, 134, 153, 183–84, 202
4:9	57
4:10–12	62
4:10–11	120, 183
4:10	123n17, 207n80
4:11	62, 149, 207n80
4:12—5:10	74
4:12—5:11	43, 61n67, 194, 213, 216
4:12–19	11, 62–63, 70, 194–95, 198, 200, 203, 215
4:12–16	41
4:12–14	149
4:12	34, 194
4:13	35, 53–54, 60, 62, 149, 180, 194, 196, 200, 202, 208, 210, 215, 219
4:14	35n191, 37n211, 62–63, 71, 149, 195–96, 199–200, 203–4, 207n80, 210, 212, 216–17, 219, 221–22, 225
4:15–16	62
4:15	35, 37–38, 127, 201, 203
4:16	56, 200, 203, 207n80, 214
4:17–18	124, 216
4:17	12, 180, 195–96, 198–200, 202–5, 207n80, 214, 216
4:18	200, 201, 207, 210, 216, 222–23
4:19	35, 57, 127, 170, 201, 203, 207n80
5	62, 208n89
5:1–11	206
5:1–10	208, 215
5:1–6	212
5:1–5	125n30
5:1–4	185, 204
5:1	17, 20, 35, 60, 62–63, 202, 204, 208, 215
5:2–3	127
5:2	57, 207n80
5:3	206, 209
5:4–5	217
5:4	54n43, 63, 180, 205
5:5	90, 160, 204, 206, 208, 210, 222–23
5:6–11	204
5:6	199, 205–6, 207n80, 210
5:7	205
5:9–10	11, 62, 204, 208
5:9	35, 41, 63, 210, 215
5:10	35, 53–54, 57, 60, 63, 71, 149, 180, 207n80, 210, 215, 217
5:12	207n80
5:13	10–12, 82, 174
5:14	149

2 Peter

2:5	181n105

Revelation

	11n42, 33, 35n193, 47, 48n17
2–3	32
11	99, 119n219

Dead Sea Scrolls

Damascus Document (CD)

2.18–20	180n100
5.1	79n8
9.5	79n8
11.20	79n8

1QIsa^a

11:2	197n16
53:8–9	140
53:11	140n96

1QIsa^b

53:11	140n96

1QpHab 100n107

7.1–8	50

1Q19 181n105

1Q28

5.20–29	197n22

1QapGen 180n100

1QMyst 180n100

1QS

4.6	205
5.11	49, 50, 59

1QM 180n100

1QH 31, 180n100

9.25	205

4QIsa^a

53:11	140n96

4Q161pIsa^a	100n107, 197
4Q162pIsa^b	100n107
4Q163pIsa^c	100n107
4Q164pIsa^d	100n107
4Q165pIsa^e	100n107
4Q166–167(pHos^{a-b})	100n107
4Q169(pNah)	100n107
4Q170(pZeph)	100n107
4Q171, 173 (pPs^{a-b})	100n107
4Q174(Flor)	100n107
4Q177(Catena)	100n107
4Q186	181n105
4Q285	197n22
4Q435–436	181n105
4Q534–536	181n105
6Q8	181n105
11Q13(Melch)	100n107

Early Jewish Writings

Philo 21

Agr.

1–2	181n105
20	181n105
125	181n105
181	181n105

Det.

105	181n105
121–22	181n105

Deus

70–140	181n105

Gig.

1–5	181n105

Leg.

2:60	181n105
3:77	181n105

Mos.

2:59–65	181n105

Plant.

1	181n105
140	181n105

QG

1:87–97	181n105
2:16–17	181n105
2:25–79	181n105

Josephus 158

A.J.

1.3–4	181n105
10.79	198

B.J.

4.386–388	198
5.15–19	198
6.109–110	198

Targum of Isaiah 22, 161

11:1	197n22
54:1	161

Targum Neofiti 109

Targum Pseudo-Jonathan 109

Greco-Roman Writings

Diodorus Siculus

Bib. Hist.

4.8.5	34n188
15.74.5	34n188
17.2.3	34n188
17.4.1	34n188

Dionysius of Halicarnassus

Ant. Rom.

5.48.2	34n188

Early Christian Writings

Barn.
6:3 — 102n121

1 Clem.
3:4 — 181n104
12:12 — 181n104
16:5 — 133
49:5 — 183n117

2 Clem.
16:4 — 183n117

Cyril of Alexandria
Commentarius in Isaiam Prophetam
V.I.749C — 141

Eusebius
Demonstratio evangelica
I.10 — 141
I.16 — 141

Irenaeus — 9n28
Adv. Haer.
IV.33.14 — 112n181

Justin
1 Apol. — 133
50.2 — 133
50.3 — 85n35
51.5 — 133

Dial.
13.5 — 133
13.7 — 133

www.ingramcontent.com/pod-product-compliance
Lightning Source LLC
Chambersburg PA
CBHW071238230426
43668CB00011B/1495